For Military Merit
RECIPIENTS OF THE PURPLE HEART

Fred L. Borch

NAVAL INSTITUTE PRESS
Annapolis, Maryland

Naval Institute Press
291 Wood Road
Annapolis, MD 21402

Library of Congress Cataloging-in-Publication Data

Borch, Frederic L., 1954-
    For military merit / Fred Borch.
        p. cm.
    Includes bibliographical references and index.
    ISBN 978-1-59114-086-3 (alk. paper)
    1. Purple Heart. 2. United States—Armed Forces—Biography.   3. United States—Armed Forces—
Registers. I. Title.
    UB433.B664 2010
    355.1'342—dc22

                                                                                        2010009804

Printed in the United States of America on acid-free paper ∞

14 13 12 11 10   9 8 7 6 5 4 3 2
First printing

Contents

Illustrations

Foreword

It is an honor to have the opportunity to participate in this work, the first devoted entirely to Purple Heart recipients. It is important; the Purple Heart means a lot to the people who wear them and to the people who award them.

In 1990 I was assigned as the flight surgeon for the 2nd Battalion, 229th Aviation Attack Helicopter Regiment, and deployed to Saudi Arabia as part of Operation Desert Storm. Six months later, on February 27, 1991, we were flying a search and rescue mission for a downed F-16 pilot. Our UH-60 Black Hawk helicopter was flying very low and very fast. Unfortunately, we were not successful in rescuing the pilot, and our Black Hawk was shot down by Iraqi ground fire. Five of the eight soldiers on the helicopter were killed. I was very lucky to survive the crash with a gunshot resulting in a fractured right shoulder and a left humeral fracture from the crash. These wounds made it clear to me what "direct result of enemy action" means to a soldier.

The Iraqis held me as a prisoner of war until the end of hostilities. After being released from captivity on March 5, 1991, and returning to the United States for medical treatment, I received a number of medals and decorations. These included a Distinguished Flying Cross, a Bronze Star Medal, and a Purple Heart.

Years later, from July 2003 to July 2005, I had the privilege to command Landstuhl Regional Medical Center, the major stop in the evacuation chain from Europe, Africa, and Southwest Asia. I saw thousands of men and women who had been awarded Purple Hearts for wounds received in action in Afghanistan and Iraq, and I was privileged to personally award some to patients in our intensive care unit.

The point is that I know something about the Purple Heart—and those who receive it. Consequently, I am really pleased to write a few words as the Foreword for this book.

As *For Military Merit: Recipients of the Purple Heart* makes clear, the Purple Heart is not an award for suffering. It is not an award for hardships endured, or pain experienced during battle. On the contrary, as retired Army colonel Fred Borch, the author of this book, explains in the first chapter, the Purple Heart was intended by Gen. Douglas MacArthur to inspire the living by recognizing soldiers who had been wounded as a direct result of enemy action. But while MacArthur believed that those who had been wounded in combat had performed meritorious service, he never intended for every war injury to recognized with a Purple Heart. Rather, only wounds that were serious enough to require treatment by a medical officer were eligible. These are still the requirements today. This explains why the Purple Heart is specifically not awarded for post-traumatic stress disorder, frostbite, or heat stroke, for example. While these conditions frequently develop during combat operations and may be devastating, they are indirect results of combat and depend on the psychological and physiological makeup of the individual soldier, sailor, Marine, airman or Coast Guardsman.

More than a million Purple Hearts have been awarded to military personnel since 1932, and the medal continues to be viewed by Americans—both in and out of uniform—as proof that a soldier was wounded during honorable combat with the enemy.

Rhonda L. Cornum
Washington, D.C.

Brig. Gen. Rhonda L. Cornum, PhD, MD, serves as the director of Comprehensive Soldier Fitness in the Department of the Army. She is the only female general officer in history to be awarded the Purple Heart

Introduction

More than one million men and women have been awarded the Purple Heart since its revival in 1932 and more will receive it in years to come. Given these numbers, it is impossible for any book to list all Purple Heart recipients. Additionally, even a monograph about all World War II or Korean War or Vietnam War recipients could not be all-inclusive because no comprehensive list of men and women awarded the Purple Heart exists.

This is why *For Military Merit: Recipients of the Purple Heart* instead looks at categories of recipients and then profiles men and women in those categories who are well-known or who received the Purple Heart under unusual or heroic circumstances, or both.

The book begins with a brief history of the Purple Heart. Chapter 1 covers the medal's origins as a purple-in-color, heart-shaped cloth badge created by Gen. George Washington during the Revolution and then explains how this old award was revived by the U.S. Army in 1932. The chapter then discusses the Purple Heart's design and the evolution of criteria for awarding the Purple Heart over the last seventy-eight years. This discussion includes an explanation of how and why the Purple Heart was initially an award for fidelity or service but was transformed into a decoration for combat wounds. This opening chapter also shows how award criteria have been expanded so that the Purple Heart may now be awarded not only to military personnel wounded or killed "in action against an enemy of the United States" but also to men and women who are injured or lose their lives in an "international terrorist attack" or while engaging a "hostile foreign force," serving on a "peacekeeping force," or held as prisoners of war.

Chapters 2 through 6 cover Purple Hearts awarded to soldiers, sailors, airmen, Marines, and Coast Guardsmen, respectively. Each of those chapters profiles recipients from each conflict, military operation, or geographic location in which Purple Hearts were awarded. Chapter 2, for example, looks at selected soldier recipients in wars and armed conflicts from the Revolutionary War to Afghanistan and Iraq. But it also examines Purple Hearts awarded to soldiers wounded or killed in the 1970s and 1980s in Belgium, El Salvador, France, Germany, Greece, and Honduras. Similarly, chapter 5 covers Marines who received Purple Hearts in the Spanish–American War, China Relief Expedition/Boxer Rebellion, and Vietnam. But chapter 5 also provides details on Purple Hearts to Marines wounded or killed in international terrorist attacks in the 1980s and 1990s in El Salvador, Kenya, and Lebanon. There also is information on Purple Hearts to Marines wounded while serving in the USS *Pueblo* in 1968 and killed during the rescue of the SS *Mayaguez* in 1975.

Chapter 7 tells the story of civilian Purple Heart recipients. In World War II, the U.S. War Department and the U.S. Navy Department began decorating war correspondents, Red Cross employees, and other civilians who were wounded or killed while accompanying military and naval forces in an official capacity. About one hundred civilians were awarded Purple Hearts between 1942 and 1997, when Congress enacted legislation restricting the medal to military personnel. The civilian recipients deserve to have their own chapter.

Chapter 8 looks at Purple Hearts awarded to brothers, fathers and sons, and husbands and wives. Some of these recipients who shared familial bonds are well-known, like the Sullivan brothers, who received posthumous Purple Hearts after their ship was sunk by the Japanese in 1942. Similarly, many readers will recognize Lewis B. "Chesty" Puller and Lewis B. Puller Jr. as father–son recipients.

The final chapter—one of the longest—describes Purple Hearts awarded to film and television actors, writers, politicians, athletes, and other public figures. Some of these recipients—such as the actors James Arness and James Garner, and the U.S. senators Bob Dole, Daniel Inouye, and Jim Webb— are familiar to almost all Americans. Others are not, but their stories are no less compelling.

For Military Merit illustrates that those who have received America's oldest decoration all have one thing in common: They have sacrificed their blood for our country. Perhaps this explains why the Purple Heart remains a unique decoration, and why it is so prized by all who receive it.

On a final note, I extend a special thanks to Ron Fischer, who is an expert on U.S. medals and decorations, for allowing me to take photographs of Purple Hearts in his collection. I also wish to acknowledge the kindness of FJP Auctions Inc., the nation's premier auction house for military medals, for permitting me to illustrate this book with photographs of Purple Hearts used in the firm's catalogues.

I have checked with experts and checked and rechecked the facts presented here. Nonetheless, there are sure to be errors. Those are my responsibility alone.

CHAPTER 1

A Short History of the Purple Heart: Background, Design, and Award Criteria

The Purple Heart is the oldest American military decoration and was originally established as the Badge of Military Merit by General Washington on August 7, 1782. After the Revolutionary War, however, the badge was forgotten, and 150 years passed before Gen. Douglas MacArthur revived the award as the Purple Heart on February 22, 1932. But, while today's Purple Heart has its roots in the Badge of Military Merit and the medal's design has remained the same since 1932, the criteria for awarding a Purple Heart have undergone major modifications.

This chapter examines the historical background of the Purple Heart, discusses the award's design, and then explores the evolution of the award criteria, including a discussion of World War I and later awards for meritorious service and the transformation of the Purple Heart into a "wound-only" decoration in World War II. This chapter also looks at how the original criteria for receiving a Purple Heart—which specified that an individual must be wounded in action "against an enemy of the United States"—were expanded to permit Purple Heart awards to men and women wounded by a "hostile foreign force," injured while serving on a "peacekeeping force," wounded in "international terrorist attacks," and injured while a prisoner of war. Finally, this chapter includes a brief discussion of what type of combat injury qualifies as a wound for the purposes of receiving a Purple Heart.

BADGE OF MILITARY MERIT

On August 7, 1782, General Washington, announced the following in his Orders of the Day:

> The General ever desirous to cherish a virtuous ambition in his soldiers, as well as to foster and encourage every species of Military Merit, directs that whenever any singularly meritorious action is performed, the author of it shall be permitted to wear on his facings, over his left breast, the figure of a heart in purple cloth, or silk, edged with narrow lace or binding. Not only instances of unusual gallantry, but also of extraordinary fidelity and essential service in any way shall meet with a due reward. Before this favor can be conferred on any man, the particular fact, or facts on which it is to be grounded, must be set forth to the commander in chief, accompanied with certificates from the commanding officers of the regiment and brigade to which the candidate for reward belonged, or other incontestable proofs, and upon granting it the name and regiment of the person with the action so certified are to be enrolled in the Book of Merit which will be kept at the Orderly Office. Men who have merited this last distinction to be suffered to pass all guard and sentinels which officers are permitted to do.
>
> The road to glory in a patriot army and a free country is thus opened to all. This order is also to have retrospect to the earliest days of the war, and to be considered as a permanent one.[1]

Only three recipients of the original purple, heart-shaped Badge of Military Merit announced in this Order of the Day are known today: Sgt. Daniel Bissell, Sgt. William Brown, and Sgt. Elijah Churchill. Details on these three noncommissioned officers are in Chapter 2.

REVIVAL OF THE PURPLE HEART

After the Revolutionary War, Washington's "Book of Merit" was lost, and the cloth Purple Heart badge was all but forgotten for almost 150 years. In early 1925, however, the secretary of war asked the Army's General Staff for their views on whether the Purple Heart should be resurrected or revived as a "new" Army decoration.

A number of comments were received. For example, Col. John W. Wright of the Army War College wrote the following statement:

This should have been our first and highest decoration as it is older than the Constitution and founded by Washington; it should today be the Medal of Honor, but, unfortunately, it was neglected. The army disbanded, the men scattered over an immense territory, and all were tired of war; therefore it died. . . . Other decorations have been created and consecrated by blood. Our mission, clearly, is to revive it and respect the later decorations. However, if this decoration is recreated properly it will be unique and have a value all its own, assured by its history.

Wright believed that the Army needed another decoration to complement the existing Medal of Honor, Distinguished Service Cross, and Distinguished Service Medal. He particularly believed that a medal for distinguished service below that required for a Distinguished Service Medal was needed, particularly, Wright wrote, "where the man is in a position of responsibility; in other words, covering younger officers." He continued: "As the Purple Heart has its own history it will be a decoration that will have high standing. I would not call it a second D.S.M. (Distinguished Service Medal). It should stand alone as the decoration reserved for all officers and men, not being in positions of great responsibility, yet who perform services calling for recognition. It will be the decoration within the grasp of younger officers; afterwards they may also receive the D.S.M. but that could come only with high rank and very responsible duty."[2]

John C. Fitzpatrick, assistant chief of the Manuscript Division of the Library of Congress concurred with Wright and felt the proposed award should be given in peacetime as well. Fitzpatrick wrote that "the design of the medal, if the decoration is revived, would need careful consideration. . . . I imagine that a heart in purple enamel with a green gold edge . . . could be embossed on a circular medal."[3]

Based on input from men like Wright and Fitzpatrick, the Army's General Staff recommended to the secretary of war that the Purple Heart be revived as the "Order of Military Merit" and awarded for exceptionally meritorious service not involving great responsibility. The General Staff also recommended that the new decoration be limited to soldiers, that it be awarded for heroic acts not performed in actual conflict, and that it be available in peacetime as well as during war.

The issue was given additional impetus in November 1925, when a well-known numismatist named Carleton S. Gifford wrote to President Calvin Coolidge recommending (among other things) that the president revive "General Washington's Badge of the Purple Heart which did not survive the Revolutionary War."[4] Gifford's letter was referred to the War Department where, because of the ongoing interest in the subject, the letter was given serious consideration.

As a result of this staff study, the Army adjutant general (G-1)—with the unanimous concurrence of the intelligence chief (G-2), operations officer (G-3), and logistics director (G-4)—recommended to Maj. Gen. John L. Hines, the Army chief of staff, that the Purple Heart be revived. But nothing happened, and a December 3, 1925, memorandum from the Army deputy chief of staff to the G-1 "returned" the staff study with the comment that it was "not the intention of the War Department at the present time to alter the existing status with respect to decorations." But, noted the memorandum, if the United States were to mobilize for war, then the issue of creating "a decoration junior to the D.S.C. (Distinguished Service Cross) and D.S.M." would be revisited.[5]

In December 1930 identical bills were introduced in both houses of Congress (H.R. 14570 and S. 5207) proposing the establishment of a "Military Cross" in lieu of the silver citation star and a "Military Medal." In response to this legislation, Secretary of War Patrick J. Hurley wrote nearly identical letters to the House Committee on Military Affairs and Senate Committee on Military Affairs in early 1931. He informed the committees that the War Department was "considering the continuance of General George Washington's Badge of Military Merit, for much the same purposes as are contemplated by the proposed legislation. This would be done in connection with the celebration in honor of the 200th anniversary of General Washington's birth. In view of these arrangements, which are considered as confidential for the present, the War Department does not recommend enactment (of the proposed legislation) at this time."[6]

MACARTHUR'S ROLE

On November 21, 1930, Douglas MacArthur pinned on four stars and began serving as Army chief of staff. Less than five months later, on April 8, 1931, MacArthur wrote to Charles Moore, the chairman of the U.S. Commission of Fine Arts, and informed Moore that the Army planned to "revive" Washington's old Badge of Military Merit on February 22, 1932, the bicentennial of Washington's birth.

MacArthur went on to note that the project was to be kept confidential and pointed out that the badge was to be awarded for "extraordinary fidelity or essential service" in war or peace. MacArthur further advised Moore that he wanted to retain the characteristics of the original award, which had been designed by Pierre Charles L'Enfant in 1782 in accordance with Washington's personal instructions. At the same time, however, MacArthur wanted "to follow the modern design of decorations."[7]

MacArthur included two proposed designs with his letter to Moore. Both drawings used the form of a heart and included Washington's coat of arms. MacArthur noted that the War Department preferred the design that also included a bust of Washington. MacArthur closed his letter by writing that he would be grateful if "the subject can be given the earliest consideration of the Commission" and again stressing that, in the interim, the revival of the award and its design should be kept confidential.

DESIGNING THE NEW PURPLE HEART

The Commission of Fine Arts turned MacArthur's request over to A. A. Weinman the sculptor member of the commission. Weinman, in turn, recommended the selection of a design with an obverse design featuring Washington's bust and a reverse bearing the inscription "For Military Merit." Weinman made several other suggested changes to the design. The commission adopted Weinman's proposal and passed it on to MacArthur on April 18, 1931, along with a request for $1,500 to secure the services "of a competent medalist to prepare the models."[8]

MacArthur agreed with the commission's recommendations, and the result was that sculptors Gaetano Cecere, Walker Hancock, and John R. Sinnock—the chief engraver at the U.S. Mint in Philadelphia—were asked to submit designs and told that the successful competitor would be paid $1,500 for the final finished model.

After the three sculptors submitted their drawings, Weinman selected the sketch by Sinnock and made some minor suggestions for its improvement. On May 29, 1931, the commission notified MacArthur that Sinnock had won the competition. Sinnock then made some large plaster models from his drawings, and these were sent to MacArthur for approval. MacArthur was pleased with the models, and the result was that the commission gave final approval for Sinnock's design on November 4, 1931.

Sinnock's final design for the new Badge of Military Merit was a purple, heart-shaped 1¹¹⁄₁₆-inch long medal suspended from a purple-and-white ribbon. The obverse of the medal featured a profile head of George Washington in military uniform and the shield of Washington's coat of arms between two sprays of leaves in green enamel. Washington's image on the Purple Heart symbolized the link between the original cloth Badge of Military Merit and the new metal Purple Heart.

The reverse of the medal consisted of a raised bronze heart with the inscription "For Military Merit" in relief and sufficient space to engrave the recipient's name. Like Washington's image on the obverse, the inscribed words provide linkage with the original cloth badge.

As for the ribbon, which was 1⅜ inches in length and 1⅜ inches in width, the colors—purple (pansy) edged in white—were selected because Washington's original badge consisted of purple-colored cloth edged in white.

With an approved design, and concurrence by the secretary of war on December 9, 1931, the next and last step in the resurrection of the Badge of Military Merit was to announce its rebirth in War Department General Orders. Before this happened, however, MacArthur made one final decision in the process: He changed the name of the new decoration from "Badge of Military Merit" to "Purple Heart." The end result was that on February 22, 1932, the War Department announced in General Orders No. 3 that it had revived the Purple Heart "out of respect" to Washington's "memory and military achievements," and that the new decoration was "to be awarded to persons who, while serving in the Army of the United States perform any singular meritorious act of extraordinary fidelity or essential service."[9]

AWARD CRITERIA

Early Years: The Purple Heart as an Army-Only Award

When the Purple Heart was revived in 1932, it was not expressly established as a decoration for wounds. On the contrary, the award criteria for the Purple Heart originally published in paragraph 11(a) of Army Regulation 600-45 state the decoration was for any single "act" of "fidelity" or "essential service." While paragraph 11(b) of the regulation did note that some combat-related wounds might qualify as an act of fidelity or service, the fact that this language appears in paragraph (b)—rather than paragraph (a)—and the fact that paragraph (b) expressly states that not all combat injuries qualified for the Purple Heart, clearly indicated an intent for the new decoration to be awarded principally for fidelity or service. It is worth setting out the original language from the regulation in its entirety:

Purple Heart, to whom awarded.

a. The Purple Heart, established by General George Washington in 1782, is awarded to persons who, while serving in the Army of the United States, perform any singularly meritorious act of extraordinary fidelity or essential service.

b. A wound, which necessitates treatment by a medical officer, and which is received in action with an enemy of the United States, or as a result of an act of such enemy, may, in the judgment of the commander authorized to make the award, be construed as resulting from a singularly meritorious act of essential service.[10]

So while the War Department may have intended to revive the Purple Heart as a decoration for fidelity and service, the language in paragraph 11(b) practically ensured that most of the 77,958 men who applied for the new decoration between 1932 and 1942 were soldiers who had been wounded in combat, if for no other reason than that more than 75,000 soldiers had been injured while fighting the Germans during World War I. Relatively few individuals—less than 1,200 soldiers—had performed an act of fidelity or demonstrated the essential service required to be awarded a Purple Heart under the criteria published in paragraph 11(a). The result was that the Purple Heart was soon considered—at least in the mind of its recipients—to be an award only for combat-related injuries.

Still, because, the Army's regulatory language provided that the Purple Heart could be awarded for fidelity or service, about 1,200 Purple Hearts were awarded on the basis of the Meritorious Service Citation Certificate (MSCC) issued by the American Expeditionary Force. The MSCC was a printed paper certificate signed by Gen. John J. Pershing. It read, in part, "For exceptionally meritorious and conspicuous services as . . . American Expeditionary Forces; in testimony thereof, and as an expression of appreciation of these services, I award him this citation."

Any soldier who had received this MSCC while serving in France during World War I could apply to the Army "to exchange the certificate for the Purple Heart."[11]

While regulations clearly stated that only an individual who had received a combat wound or an MSCC was eligible for the Purple Heart, the Army nonetheless awarded a very small number of Purple Hearts for meritorious service—apparently to individuals who should have received an MSCC but were not issued the certificate due to administrative oversight. Pvt. Leopold Strauss, for example, was awarded the Purple Heart in 1933 "for services in connection with trench fever experiments" during World War I. Similarly, Sgt. Maj. Charles E. Laird was awarded the Purple Heart in 1934 for refusing to be evacuated during the 1918 Meuse–Argonne offensive despite being "sick."[12]

Two final points about initial eligibility rules for the Purple Heart should be made. First, when the War Department revived the Purple Heart, the Navy took the position that it was purely an Army decoration and was not interested in obtaining authority to award it to sailors or Marines. Consequently, the Navy could not award the Purple Heart to sailors or Marines wounded in action during World War I or earlier conflicts in which its personnel had participated. The Navy did, however, permit sea service personnel who had served with the American Expeditionary Force in France to apply to the Army for the Purple Heart for wounds they had received in action in World War I. As a result, small numbers of sailors and Marines did apply and were awarded Army Purple Hearts in the 1930s.

Second, posthumous awards of the Purple Heart initially were prohibited. This was because MacArthur believed that the medal should be reserved for the living and because MacArthur had controlled the manner in which the decoration had been revived, there were no Purple Hearts for the dead. As MacArthur explained in a 1938 radio message, Washington's Badge of Military Merit was "not intended . . . to commemorate the dead, but to animate and inspire the living." Consequently, said MacArthur, the Purple Heart was not to be awarded posthumously. "To make it a symbol of death, with its corollary depressive influences," MacArthur reasoned, "*would be to defeat the primary purpose of its being*" (emphasis added).[13]

World War II: Posthumous, "Wounds-Only," Navy, Marine, and Coast Guard Awards

After the disaster at Pearl Harbor and the deaths of thousands of soldiers in Hawaii and the Philippines, the War Department abandoned the "no posthumous award" policy implemented by MacArthur. Circular No. 125, issued by the War Department on April 28, 1942, provided that "the posthumous award of the Purple Heart is authorized to members of the military service who are killed ... or who die as a result of a wound received in action ... on or after December 7, 1941." Note that posthumous awards of the Purple Heart were not permitted for pre–World War II conflicts; only those killed after the Japanese attack on Hawaii were eligible for the medal.[14]

Some five months later, on September 4, 1942, the Army made another major change in Purple Heart eligibility when it published Change 4 to Army Regulation 600-45. This revision states that the Purple Heart would, henceforth, be awarded exclusively to soldiers who suffered combat wounds. The reason for this change was that the creation of the Legion of Merit in 1942 meant that the War Department had a junior decoration for meritorious service or achievement, making it unnecessary to continue using the Purple Heart to recognize such service or achievement.

The last major event in the Purple Heart's development in 1942 was that the Navy obtained its own legal basis for awarding the decoration. This occurred on December 3, 1942, when President Franklin Roosevelt signed an executive order giving the secretary of the navy the authority to award the decoration "to persons who, while *heretofore* or hereafter serving in any capacity with the Navy, Marine Corps or Coast Guard ... are wounded in action against an enemy of the United States" (emphasis added).[15]

This language gave the Navy the authority to award the Purple Heart to any sailor, Marine, or Coast Guardsman who had been wounded during World War II, and also to make retroactive awards to any naval personnel wounded in earlier conflicts like the Spanish–American War or China Relief Expedition/Boxer Rebellion. Additional language in Roosevelt's executive order also permitted posthumous awards of the Purple Heart to sea service personnel, but only to those who had been killed on or after December 7, 1941.

As a result, the Navy—like the Army—could award the Purple Heart to sailors and Marines who had been wounded in action in pre–Pearl Harbor conflicts and who were still alive to receive it. Posthumous Purple Hearts, however, were limited to sea service personnel killed on or after the outbreak of World War II. As discussed in chapter 3, "Sailors: Spanish–American War to Afghanistan and Iraq," the Navy did, in fact, award a small number of Purple Hearts to sailors and Marines who had been wounded in conflicts occurring prior to December 7, 1941, including the Spanish–American War, Philippine Insurrection, China Relief Expedition/Boxer Rebellion, Veracruz, World War I, and Nicaragua.

Korean War: Pre–World War II Posthumous Sea Service Awards Permitted

The prohibition on pre–World War II posthumous awards of the Purple Heart was lifted in 1952, when President Harry S. Truman signed an executive order making the Purple Heart retroactive to April 5, 1917, for all sea service members. As a result surviving family members of sailors and Marines killed during World War I could apply to receive the medal as next of kin.

Vietnam War: U.S. Advisors Wounded or Killed in Southeast Asia

On April 25, 1962, President John F. Kennedy signed Executive Order 11016, which expanded the Purple Heart's award criteria so that American soldiers, sailors, airmen, and Marines serving as advisors in South Vietnam could receive the decoration.

Under the Roosevelt and Truman executive orders then in effect, these men could not be awarded the Purple Heart because they were serving in an advisory capacity rather than as combatants and because the United States was not formally a participant (as a matter of law) in the ongoing war between the South Vietnamese and the Viet Cong and their North Vietnamese allies.

As a result of Kennedy's order, the Purple Heart could be awarded to those wounded or killed "while serving with friendly foreign forces" or "as a result of action by a hostile foreign force."[16] By 1973, when the last U.S. combat units withdrew from Vietnam, thousands of sailors and Marines wounded or killed in Southeast Asia had received the Purple Heart. Additionally, Kennedy's expansive language permitted the award of Purple Hearts to sea service personnel killed or wounded in lesser known actions, including the Israeli attack on the USS *Liberty* (June 8–9, 1967) and the attack and capture of the USS *Pueblo* (January 23, 1968).

Reagan Era: International Terrorism and Peacekeeping Missions

The next major change in the Purple Heart's award criteria occurred on February 23, 1984, when President Ronald Reagan signed Executive Order 12464. This order permitted the Purple Heart to be awarded to those killed or wounded as a result of an "international terrorist attack against the United States or a foreign nation friendly to the United States," and it was retroactive to March 28, 1973.[17] This date was chosen as a starting point for retroactivity because it was the day after the cessation of hostilities involving U.S. forces in Vietnam.

Reagan's executive order also expanded Purple Heart eligibility so that individuals killed or wounded "outside the territory of the United States" while serving "as part of a peacekeeping mission" could be awarded the decoration. This provision also was retroactive to March 28, 1973.

As a result of Reagan's expanded Purple Heart criteria, a fairly large number of Purple Hearts have been awarded to soldiers, sailors, airmen, and Marines wounded or killed in international terrorist attacks or peacekeeping missions. For example, Navy BMMC Sam Novello was posthumously awarded a Purple Heart after being assassinated by Turkish leftists in Istanbul in 1980, and Navy Lt. Robert E. Nelson received a Purple Heart after he was wounded while serving as a United Nations military observer in Lebanon in 1978.

Other Purple Heart Eligibility Changes: Fratricide, Civilians, Prisoners of War, and Wounds

From 1989 through 2009, modifications to the Purple Heart's eligibility criteria were made in four areas. First, Congress enacted legislation permitting awards to those injured or killed in fratricide incidents. Second, Congress passed a statute prohibiting the award of the Purple Heart to civilians. Third, both Congress and the U.S. Department of Defense revised the criteria for awarding the Purple Heart so that any prisoner of war (POW) who was wounded or died while held captive could be awarded the decoration. Fourth, and finally, the services continued to wrestle with the issue of what type of combat-related injury qualified as a "wound" for Purple Heart eligibility, with heat exhaustion and PTSD being the two most prominent problematic examples.

Fratricide

In 1993 Congress enacted legislation requiring the Army, Navy, Air Force, and Marine Corps to award the Purple Heart to military and naval personnel wounded or killed in a friendly-fire incident. As a general rule, "friendly fire," or fratricide, means death or injury occurring "while actively engaging the enemy" and when the projectile or agent causing the harm was released with full intent of inflicting damage on the enemy or destroying its equipment.[18] While the statute expressly prohibits the award of a Purple Heart for an intentionally self-inflicted wound, a soldier or Marine who, while firing his weapon with the full intent of destroying the enemy accidentally wounds himself or herself is eligible for the Purple Heart.[19]

Historically, all the services had usually awarded the Purple Heart to personnel wounded or killed in friendly-fire incidents, and that led some commentators to insist that this legislation was unnecessary. But Congress was not happy with the lack of uniform Purple Heart eligibility criteria in the Army, Navy, Air Force, and Marine Corps and the possibility of disparate outcomes. Consequently, the legislative fix provided clearly stated and uniform criteria applicable to all the services.

Civilians

Starting in World War II the Army and the Navy began awarding Purple Hearts to civilians who were wounded or killed while accompanying soldiers, sailors, and Marines in combat. Most of the early civilian recipients were war correspondents or Red Cross personnel, but by the 1990s, most civilian awardees were government employees wounded or killed in international terrorist attacks.

While the services were comfortable having civilians eligible for the Purple Heart and only about one hundred civilians had received the Purple Heart between 1941 and 1997, veterans and the Military Order of the Purple Heart increasingly complained that a military award should not be given to civilians—even those "serving with" the armed forces. As a result of these complaints, Congress passed legislation in November 1997 that prohibited any future awards of Purple Heart to civilians.

Prisoners of War

In 1996 Congress modified the award criteria for the Purple Heart when it passed a statute requiring the services to award the Purple Heart to soldiers, sailors, airmen, Marines, and Coast Guardsmen wounded by the enemy while being held as prisoners of war during World War II and in Korea.[20]

Prior to the enactment of this legislation, the services had been consistent only in awarding the Purple Heart to those who had suffered as prisoners during the war in Vietnam. The 1996 law created a uniform rule that all military and naval personnel who were tortured, beaten, or otherwise brutalized by the enemy while in captivity were eligible for the Purple Heart. Today, any service member beaten or wounded by the enemy after being captured is eligible for the Purple Heart; some of the most recent awards went to three U.S. soldiers beaten by Yugoslav forces after being captured in 1999.[21]

In 2008 the Department of Defense further revised the Purple Heart's eligibility criteria so that any U.S. POW who is killed or dies in captivity after December 7, 1941, may be awarded the Purple Heart "provided they qualify for the Prisoner of War Medal." As a practical matter, this means that "unless compelling evidence is presented which shows the member's death was not the result of enemy action," all military and naval personnel who die while prisoners of war will be awarded the Purple Heart. The Defense Department also announced that the next of kin of "a former Service member" who was killed or died in captivity "can apply for posthumous award of the PH."[22]

Wounds

No sooner had the Purple Heart been revived in 1932, than the Army had to wrestle with the question of what type of injury constituted a wound.

During World War I the War Department issued the Purple Heart to soldiers, sailors, and Marines in the American Expeditionary Force who had been cut by barbed wire, struck by bullets, hit by shrapnel, harmed by poison gas, and cut by an enemy bayonet.

Veterans of World War II and Korea received Purple Hearts for wounds caused by bullets, shrapnel, bayonet, smoke inhalation, and blows to the head. The Navy even awarded a Purple Heart to a cook who had sprained his right ankle while serving in the USS *Tucker* on August 4, 1942.

Purple Hearts also were awarded—but only to aircrew members—for frostbite and other similar cold-weather injuries suffered while flying long bombing runs at high altitudes. While cold-weather injuries suffered on the ground did not qualify a service member for a Purple Heart because the Army and Navy took the view that such injuries were preventable, airmen flying in unheated aircraft in bitterly cold temperatures were considered to be at unavoidable risk for frostbite and hypothermia. This "Purple-Heart-for-frostbite" provision was rescinded in the middle of the Korean War, when improvement in aircraft design—and comfort—greatly reduced the risks of cold-weather injuries for airmen.

In 1989 the Army awarded the Purple Heart to Army Pfc. Grant Gipe, a paratrooper in the 82nd Airborne Division, for heat exhaustion suffered on December 20, 1989, during the U.S. invasion of Panama. The public outcry from veterans groups and active duty personnel, however, was so great that the Army immediately amended the eligibility criteria for the Purple Heart to exclude such awards in the future.

In 2008, as increasing numbers of military and naval personnel returning from combat in Afghanistan and Iraq were diagnosed as suffering from PTSD, some commentators proposed awarding the Purple Heart for these psychological wounds. After carefully examining the issue, however, the Defense Department concluded that having PTSD did not qualify a service member or veteran for the Purple Heart because the disorder was "not a wound intentionally caused by the enemy ... but a *secondary effect* caused by witnessing or experiencing a traumatic event"(emphasis added). Consequently, while PTSD is a serious mental disorder and affects "up to 20 percent of returning Iraq war veterans," those who suffer from it are ineligible for the Purple Heart.[23]

Today's Award Criteria

Today, the Purple Heart may be awarded to any member of the Armed Forces of the United States who, while serving under competent authority in any capacity with one of the Armed Forces after April 5, 1917, has been killed or wounded:

1. In action against an enemy of the United States;
2. In action with an opposing armed force of a foreign country in which the Armed Forces of the United States are or have been engaged;
3. While serving with friendly foreign forces engaged in an armed conflict against an opposing armed force in which the United States is not a belligerent party;
4. As the result of an act of any such enemy or opposing armed force;
5. As the result of an act of any hostile foreign force;
6. As the result of friendly weapon fire while actively engaging the enemy;
7. As the indirect result of enemy action (e.g., injuries resulting from parachuting from a plane brought down by enemy or hostile fire);
8. After March 28, 1973, as the result of an international terrorist attack against the United States or a foreign nation friendly to the United States;
9. After March 28, 1973, as a result of military operations outside the United States while serving as part of a peacekeeping force.[24]

CHAPTER 2

Soldiers: Revolutionary War to Afghanistan and Iraq

More than 1 million Purple Hearts have been awarded to soldiers. This is more than all of the Purple Hearts awarded to sailors, airmen, Marines, and Coast Guardsmen combined, and the disparity is not surprising when one remembers that the Army has always had more personnel than any other American fighting organization and that the Purple Heart was an Army-only award from 1932 until 1942.

This chapter profiles soldiers who received Purple Hearts for the following armed conflicts, military operations, and terrorist attacks:

- Revolutionary War (1775–1783)
- Civil War (1861–1865)
- Indian Wars (1867–1891)
- Spanish–American War (1898)
- Philippine Insurrection (1899–1913)
- China Relief Expedition/Boxer Rebellion (1900–1901)
- Punitive Expedition into Mexico (1916–1917)
- World War I (1917–1918)
- Civilian Conservation Corps (1933–1936)
- World War II (1941–1945)
- Korean War (1950–1953)
- Vietnam, Cambodia, and Laos (1958–1975)
- Korea (1976–1984)
- Germany (1976–1986)

- France (1982)
- Lebanon (1982–1984)
- El Salvador (1983 and 1989)
- Grenada (1983)
- Greece (1984–1985)
- Honduras (1984 and 1988)
- Namibia (1984)
- Belgium (1985)
- Sinai (1988)
- United Kingdom (1988)
- Panama (1989–1990)
- Persian Gulf War (1990–1991)
- Western Sahara (1992)
- Somalia (1992–1995)
- Iraq Black Hawk Shoot-Down (1994)
- Haiti (1994–1995)
- Saudi Arabia (1995–1996)
- The Balkans (1995–2001)
- Attack on the Pentagon (2001)
- Afghanistan (2001–)
- Philippines (2002)
- Iraq (2003–)

REVOLUTIONARY WAR (1775–1783)

While the first Purple Heart medals were issued in 1932, any comprehensive history of soldier recipients of the award must include three men who received the original "Purple Heart" during the Revolutionary War. This is because the War Department, in announcing on February 22, 1932, that a new Purple Heart medal was being created, insisted that it was merely "reviving" Gen. George Washington's Badge of Military Merit. In fact, the War Department initially planned to retain the original name of Washington's old badge for its new medal. It was only at the last moment—in December 1931—that Army Chief of Staff Douglas MacArthur directed that the name of the resurrected award would now be "Purple Heart" rather than "Badge of Military Merit." It follows, then, that recipients of Washington's Badge of Military Merit were the first soldier recipients. It should be noted that Washington did not consider his Badge of Military Merit as a decoration to be given for wounds suffered in combat, but rather as a high award for valor. In this regard, the Revolutionary War–era Purple Heart was the forerunner of the modern-day Medal of Honor.

Daniel Bissell: Purple Heart (Badge of Military Merit)— August 1781–August 1782

Daniel Bissell was awarded the Badge of Military Merit for courage and intelligence in "deserting" from the Continental Army, joining the British forces, collecting information, and then returning with this intelligence to American lines.

Born in Windsor, Connecticut, Bissell was five foot eight and had brown hair. After the Revolutionary War, he first settled in Randolph, Vermont, before moving to Richmond, New York, where he died on August 5, 1824, at the age of sixty-nine.

The citation for Bissell's Purple Heart was published in Washington's General Orders, dated June 8, 1783. It reads, "Serg. Bissell of the 2nd Connecticut Regiment having performed some important services within the immediate knowledge of the Commander-in-Chief, in which the fidelity, perseverance and good sense of the said Serg. Bissell were conspicuously manifested, it is, therefore ordered: That he be honored with the badge of merit; he will be called at headquarters on Tuesday next for the insignia and certificate to which he is hereby entitled."[1]

Bissell operated under the personal direction of Washington, having volunteered for "important services" in which he would pretend to desert from Washington's army and then enlist with the British in order to spy. In August 1781 Bissell traveled to New York and joined the very regiment Benedict Arnold had received in return for his "services to the king." Bissell served with Arnold's regimen for longer than a year in New York City and on Staten Island, extending his initial mission from a single month and obtaining all the information he could on the strength of the British forces, fortifications, and plans.

Just before he was to "redesert" from the British forces, Bissell became sick with a fever. He nearly died. While in a delirium brought about by the fever, he made some incriminating admissions, and the British surgeon treating Bissell guessed he was a spy. The doctor, however, did not disclose Bissell's identity and reportedly help him to return to American lines. In any event, when Bissell returned, he provided valuable intelligence to Washington and the Continental Army, and his bravery was recognized with the Purple Heart.

William Brown: Purple Heart (Badge of Military Merit)—October 14, 1781

Sgt. William Brown, 5th Regiment, Connecticut Line, received the Purple Heart on April 24, 1783, for gallantry in action. The citation for his award states that "in the assault of the enemy's left redoubt at Yorktown, in Virginia, on the evening of October 14, 1781, Brown conducted a forlorn hope with great bravery, propriety and deliberate firmness."[2]

Little is known about Brown, but military records show that he was born in Stamford, Connecticut. After the war, he moved to Cincinnati, Ohio, where he died in 1808 at the age of forty-seven.

Elijah Churchill: Purple Heart (Badge of Military Merit)— November 23, 1780, and October 3, 1781

The first-known Badge of Military Merit went to Sgt. Elijah Churchill, 2nd Regiment of Light Dragoons. He received his award for his heroism in two raids inside British lines. The first was on November 23, 1780, and the second was on October 3, 1781.

Born in Enfield, Connecticut, Churchill was five foot nine and dark-complexioned with gray eyes. He was a carpenter before joining the Continental Army, and he soldiered until the end of the war, when he moved to Chester, Massachusetts. Churchill died there on April 11, 1841, at the age of eighty-eight.

The citation for Churchill's Purple Heart reads, "In the several enterprises against Fort St. George and Fort Slongo on Long Island, Sgt. Churchill of the 2nd Regiment of Light Dragoons acted a very conspicuous and singularly meritorious part.... At the head of each body of attack he not only acquitted himself with great gallantry, firmness and address, but that the surprise in one instance and success of the attack in the other, proceeded in a considerable degree from his conduct and management."[3]

Both the St. George and Slongo raids were planned and executed by Maj. Benjamin Tallmadge, 2nd Continental Dragoons, who was the chief of Washington's intelligence service. In the first operation, Tallmadge had learned about a large supply of hay that had been stored for winter forage at Fort St. George at Coram, New York, on the north shore of Long Island. Given the importance of animal transport in the military of that time, this was an important supply and a prize worth great risks.

Tallmadge relayed this intelligence to Washington and proposed that the hay and Fort St. George be attacked and destroyed. The fort consisted of three sturdy blockhouses surrounded by a tall stockade of twelve-foot-high pointed wooden posts. A deep trench surrounded the stockade, and this was guarded by a wall of earth and stones.

Late on the afternoon of November 21, 1780, a detachment of fifty dismounted dragoons of the 2nd Continental embarked in whaleboats at Fairfield, Connecticut, and headed across the sound toward Fort St. George, some twenty miles away. Apparently, bad weather or bad navigation, or both, caused the party to go ashore about twelve miles below their objective.

As the landing had been made too late to attempt a march on the fort, the group pulled their boats out of sight and camped for the night. During daylight the next day, the soldiers hid in the woods. When darkness finally did come, they began their movement, and by about 3 AM, they had arrived, unnoticed, within two miles of St. George.

The Americans then halted, and Tallmadge divided the men into three groups, with each tasked with attacking a specific blockhouse. Churchill was placed in charge of sixteen men and ordered to attack the main (and largest) blockhouse. The assault began at 4 AM, and the raiders got to within fifty feet of the fort before they were discovered by British sentries. Churchill's party stormed the central blockhouse before its defenders could organize their resistance. Additionally, when a British schooner at anchor near the fort began to fire on the raiders, a group of men was sent to capture the ship, which they did. The fort, the schooner, and the winter forage—more than three hundred tons of hay—were set on fire, and by four o'clock in the afternoon, the raiders and their prisoners reached their boats. By 11 PM on November 23, 1780, the raiders and their fifty English prisoners were back in Fairfield.

The second raid mentioned in the Churchill citation occurred about a year later, on October 3, 1781, and was against Fort Slongo, a British-built fortification on the north shore of Long Island. This time, again under the command of Tallmadge, then twenty-six–year-old Churchill led the main attack upon the fort. Fort Slongo fell with no American losses and with the capture of twenty-one prisoners and a large amount of ammunition, powder, food, and clothing.

CIVIL WAR (1861–1865)

As explained in the preceding chapter, the Army regulations governing eligibility for the revived Purple Heart emphasized its dual-purpose nature as an award for "any singularly meritorious act of extraordinary fidelity or essential service" and any serious combat-related wound. These same regulations also explained, however, that the new Purple Heart would only be awarded for nonmortal wounds and only to war veterans who were still alive. No posthumous awards were permitted, and no applications from next of kin would be accepted. Finally, because the Purple Heart was an Army award, only soldiers could receive it. The only exceptions were that sailors and Marines who had been wounded while serving with the American Expeditionary Force during World War I could apply for a Purple Heart because the War Department considered these men to have been "serving in the Army of the United States."[4]

While these restrictions meant, in practical terms, that the new Purple Heart would be awarded only to individuals who had been wounded in action and were alive to apply for the new decoration in 1932, the Army did not limit applicants to veterans of any particular war or conflict. As a result, while most of the men who requested the new decoration did so on the basis of wounds received or meritorious service performed in World War I, the Army Adjutant General received applications from middle-aged and elderly veterans who had been wounded in earlier conflicts. The result was that a handful of Purple Hearts were awarded to applicants who had soldiered—and been wounded in action—during the Civil War, Indian Wars, Spanish–American War, China Relief Expedition/Boxer Rebellion, Philippine Insurrection, and Punitive Expedition into Mexico.

No official list of Civil War veterans awarded the Purple Heart exists, but at least fourteen men applied to the War Department and received the decoration in the 1930s. These men are listed in alphabetical order below.

John E. Andrew: Purple Heart—July 20, 1864

Born in Westboro, Ohio, on June 6, 1848, John E. Andrew's grandparents had moved to Ohio from North Carolina because of their opposition to slavery. Andrew's father died five months before John was born, and he lived with his mother on a farm until enlisting on February 22, 1864, as a private in Company C of the 79th Ohio Volunteer Infantry. Andrew was serving with Maj. Gen. William T. Sherman's forces near Atlanta when he was wounded in the thigh at Peach Tree Creek. Apparently, this wound made "him lame for the rest of his life," although Andrew did rejoin his regiment on November 1, 1864, and was in Sherman's March to the Sea. He participated in the Battle of Averysboro in North Carolina on March 16, 1865, and the Battle of Bentonville in North Carolina, March 19–21, 1865. He was also present at Confederate Gen. Joseph Johnston's surrender on April 26, 1865. Andrew subsequently took part in the

Grand Review of the Union Army in Washington, D.C., on May 24, 1865. He was honorably discharged at Camp Dennison, Ohio, on July 22, 1865.

After the war Andrew had a successful public career in Illinois. In 1882 he was elected sheriff of Platt County, Illinois, and subsequently served three terms as mayor of Monticello, Illinois. In 1913 he was appointed commandant of the Illinois Soldiers' and Sailors' Home in Quincy, Illinois, and held that post for eight years.

He was active in the Grand Army of the Republic and served as the organization's commander in chief in the late 1930s. Andrew died on June 30, 1940, at the age of 91.[5]

David Ballinger: Purple Hearts—July 3, 1863, and May 10, 1864

While serving as a private in Company H of the 12th New Jersey Infantry, David Ballinger was wounded in action at Gettysburg on July 3, 1863, and at the Battle of Spotsylvania Courthouse in Virginia on May 10, 1864. His Purple Heart and oak leaf cluster were awarded on September 13, 1937.[6]

William R. Bell: Purple Heart—July 14, 1864

Born to Thomas Bell in Burlington, New Jersey, on October 19, 1844, William R. Bell enlisted at Davenport, Iowa, on January 2, 1863. He was eighteen years old. On July 14, 1864, then-Private Bell was serving in Company K of the 14th Iowa Volunteer Infantry when he was wounded in action by a bullet or shrapnel in his upper right thigh near Tupelo, Mississippi, during the Battle of Old Town Creek, which was part of the Vicksburg campaign. Bell was discharged on August 1865 and died in Creston, Iowa, in March 1939. His Purple Heart was issued to him on August 26, 1932.[7]

Henry N. Comey: Purple Hearts—May 3, 1863, and July 3, 1863

Henry Newton Comey was born in 1840 in Hopkinton, Massachusetts, and enlisted as a private in Company A of the 2nd Massachusetts Volunteer Infantry on May 25, 1861. He saw action at the Battle of Antietam in September 1862 and was twenty-three years old when he accepted a commission as a second lieutenant on November 1, 1862. Comey was serving in Company C when he was "wounded—very slight" at the Battle of Chancellorsville on May 3, 1863. Three days after his promotion to first lieutenant on June 6, 1863, Comey took part in the Battle of Brandy Station in Virginia. Less than a month later, he was at the Battle of Gettysburg, where he suffered a "gun-shot wound in the left arm" on July 3, 1863. Comey subsequently served in Company E, saw action at the Battle of Cedar Creek in Virginia during October 1864 and participated in the March to the Sea through Georgia in 1865. Comey finished the war as a captain.

After returning to Massachusetts, Comey lived in Lynn and was active in the Grand Army of the Republic. The War Department issued a Purple Heart with oak leaf cluster to him on April 5, 1932. He died on April 15, 1932, ten days after this award was made.[8]

Joseph W. Cotes: Purple Hearts—April 6, 1862, and July 14, 1864

Born in Holland Patent, New York, Joseph Warren Cotes—who also spelled his name Coates—grew up in Iowa and enlisted in 1861. He was wounded at the Battle of Shiloh on April 6, 1862, and at the Battle of Vicksburg near Tupelo, Mississippi, on July 14, 1864. After the war, he settled in Crandall, South Dakota, and attended the 75th Gettysburg Reunion in 1938.[9]

Ludwick D. Davis: Purple Heart—May 16, 1863

Ludwick Davis served as a corporal with Company C of the 56th Ohio Volunteer Infantry and was wounded in combat on May 16, 1863. His Purple Heart was awarded on August 31, 1932.[10]

Andrew C. Gibbs: Purple Heart—June 1, 1864

Andrew Gibbs first enlisted on September 26, 1862, in Company G of the 48th Massachusetts Militia Infantry and was discharged on July 7, 1863. He then reenlisted on March 12, 1864, in the 58th Massachusetts Volunteer Infantry. Gibbs was on guard duty at Cold Harbor on June 1, 1864, when he received a gunshot wound to his leg. His Purple Heart was awarded on April 18, 1933.[11]

John W. Hays: Purple Heart—June 28, 1862

Born on May 26, 1844, John Hays enlisted on May 4, 1861, less than a month after Confederate troops fired on Fort Sumter. Hays served under Union generals John Pope, Joseph Hooker, George McClellan, and Ambrose Burnside. He fought at the Battle of Antietam and was wounded in action on June 28, 1862, at the Battle of Gaines' Mill, Virginia, which is also known as the First Battle of Cold Harbor or the Battle of Chickahominy River. Hays was still living in Brookview, New York, on May 26, 1944, at the age of one hundred.[12]

Charles W. McKibben: Purple Heart—May 2, 1863

Born in 1845 Charles McKibben enlisted as a private in Company I of the 75th Ohio Volunteer Infantry. He was later wounded at the Battle of Chancellorsville on May 2, 1863. McKibben received his Purple Heart from the War Department on March 17, 1933.[13]

Thomas F. Palmer: Purple Heart—September 19, 1864

After enlisting in Company F of the 38th Massachusetts Volunteer Infantry on August 15, 1862, Thomas Palmer fought in the Army of the Potomac. He was wounded in his "side and jaw" at Opequam Creek near Winchester, Virginia, on September 19, 1864. Palmer was honorably discharged as a sergeant on June 30, 1865, and lived in Brockton, Massachusetts, at the time he received his Purple Heart on May 3, 1933.[14]

Oran J. Randlett: Purple Hearts—May 3, 1863, and June 3, 1864

Oran Josiah Randlett enlisted on August 19, 1862, as a private in Company H of the 12th New Hampshire Regiment. He was serving as a corporal in the Army of the Potomac when he was wounded by a bullet or shrapnel to his right wrist at Chancellorsville, Virginia, on May 3, 1863. Slightly more than a year later, on June 3, 1864, Randlett was severely wounded in his right arm and chest in the fighting at Cold Harbor. According to his June 19, 1937, application for a Civil War Campaign Medal, Randlett "attended Ford's Theatre" on April 14, 1865, and "saw President Lincoln's assassination." Randlett was discharged as a corporal on June 3, 1865. His Purple Heart with oak leaf cluster was issued to him on October 22, 1937.[15]

George N. Smith: Purple Heart—May 14, 1864

George N. Smith served as private in Company G of the 1st Battalion, 18th U.S. Infantry, and was wounded in action at May 14, 1864. Since the 18th Infantry was in Georgia with the Army of the Cumberland in May 1864, it is likely that Smith was wounded in the fighting near the town of Resaca. On May 13, 1864, Union forces moved against Confederate troops near Resaca, driving their outposts into their main works. On May 14, 1864, troops of the 18th Regiment advanced again and, "after a sharp contest, drove the enemy into his main works." Smith's Purple Heart was awarded to him on August 30, 1932.[16]

William H. Thomas: Purple Heart—February 22, 1865

The only African American recipient of a Civil War Purple Heart, William H. "Will" Thomas was born a "free black" on a farm in Ohio on May 4, 1843. When war broke out, he joined the 42nd Ohio Volunteer Infantry as a captain's private servant in September 1861. There was no indignity in this job, as then-existing Army regulations permitted an infantry captain to have one servant to wash, clean, cook, and perform other odd jobs for him.

In November 1862 Thomas transferred to the 95th Ohio Volunteer Infantry, again in an official, albeit civilian, capacity as a private servant. Then, on September 23, 1863, Thomas made the transition from civilian to military life when he enlisted in the 127th Ohio Volunteer Infantry. When that unit became the 5th U.S. Colored Troops (USCT) on November 1, 1863, Thomas became part of one of the most highly decorated African American units in the Civil War. Of the sixteen black soldiers awarded the Medal of Honor during the Civil War, four were soldiers from the 5th USCT.

Thomas saw action at Petersburg, Virginia, in July 1864 and New Market Heights outside of Richmond, Virginia, in September 1864, where the 5th USCT suffered heavy losses. Then-Sergeant Thomas suffered his own wound outside of Wilmington, North Carolina, on February 20, 1865. During a frontal assault on Confederate entrenchments, a musket ball hit Thomas' right arm. An infection in the wound caused the surgeon in the regimental field hospital to amputate the lower third of Thomas' right arm. Thomas remained hospitalized for five months, after which he was discharged for medical disability on July 25, 1865.

In the summer of 1932, eighty-nine-year-old Thomas applied for a Purple Heart on the basis of his Civil War wound, and the War Department issued him the decoration on August 31, 1932.[17]

Frank Williams: Purple Heart—December 16, 1864

After enlisting as a private in Company C of the 32nd Iowa Volunteer Infantry on August 6, 1862, Frank Williams served for the remainder of the war until being discharged as a corporal on July 7, 1865. He was wounded on December 16, 1864, near Nashville, Tennessee. Williams received his Purple Heart from the War Department on May 16, 1934.[18]

★ ★ ★

What about Purple Hearts for men who had fought for the Confederate States of America?

In 1950, H.R. 3956 was introduced in the U.S. House of Representatives. The bill would have permitted the next of kin of soldiers who had served the Confederacy to apply for a posthumous Purple Heart. The Defense Department's Personnel Policy Board, speaking for the secretary of defense, objected to the provision. In a letter to the House Armed Services Committee, J. Thomas Schneider, the personnel board's chairman, explained that eligibility for the Purple Heart was restricted to individuals who served as members of the Armed Forces of the United States. Schneider continued: "*This precludes awards in the case of individuals who served as members of the armed forces of the Confederacy. This is proper because those forces were fighting the United States. It seems inadvisable, however, to raise that distinction in connection with this proposal at this time or at any time in the future*" (emphasis added).[19] Schneider's opinion—that the Purple Heart was for Union veterans only—seems to have been tempered by the recognition that this view might be sensitive with some members of Congress.

INDIAN WARS (1867–1891)

Purple Hearts to soldiers wounded in combat with Native Americans are rarer than those to Civil War veterans, probably because the numbers of troopers who fought on the Western frontier were small and because records verifying combat injuries were scant. The Purple Hearts awarded to Indian Wars veteran David L. Brainard and Charles A. Windolph are two of only a handful known to exist.

David L. Brainard: Purple Heart—May 6, 1877
David Legg Brainard was a remarkable man. During forty years of soldiering, he fought Sioux warriors as a private, served in a two-year expedition to the North Pole, and finished his career as a brigadier general.

Born on a farm in Norway, New York, on December 21, 1856, Brainard attended State Normal School in Cortland, New York, and enlisted in the Army when he was nineteen years old. When he was assigned to Company L of the 2nd Cavalry and sent to Fort Ellis, Montana Territory, only three months had passed since Lt. Col. George A. Custer and his men had been annihilated at Little Bighorn.

While serving with Troop L of the Second Cavalry in Montana in May 1877, Sgt. David L. Brainard was injured by a gunshot wound to his right cheek. (Glenn M. Stein, FRGS)

Brainard's officially hand-engraved Purple Heart is one of only two known to have been awarded to soldiers wounded in combat during the Indian Wars. (Glenn M. Stein, FRGS)

In the spring of 1877, Brainard's company and other troopers from the 2nd Cavalry reported to Fort Keogh, near the confluence of the Yellowstone River and Tongue River. Col. Nelson A. Miles had established the fort as a base from which to operate against the Cheyenne and Sioux who had wiped out Custer.

On May 6, 1877, Miles led Brainard and 450 cavalry and infantry troopers in an attack on Sioux Chief Lame Deer. The Army won the Battle of Little Muddy, and, of the five Medals of Honor awarded for the fight, four went to 2nd Cavalry soldiers. The battle with Lame Deer was the last important engagement between the Army and the Indians in the Great Sioux War, but it was not without casualties, including Brainard. He suffered cuts to his hand and a gunshot wound to his right cheek that affected his eye.

After fighting in another Indian campaign against the Bannock tribe from May to August 1878, Brainard volunteered to join a twenty-five-man Army expedition for a two-year exploration of the North Pole.

The primary goal of the expedition was to establish a scientific station at Lady Franklin Bay, Ellesmere Island. Over the planned twenty-four months of the mission, valuable scientific data were collected; many new geographic features were discovered; and north, east, and west "farthest" records were set by sledge parties that included Brainard. Unfortunately, through the misman-agement of planned resupply expeditions from the United States, expedition members were forced to spend an additional winter in disastrous conditions, and most starved to death. When rescuers reached the survivors in June 1884, only six of the twenty-five men who first went to Lady Franklin Bay lived to return home. Brainard was the only surviving member of the sledge parties that set the farthest records.

Those who survived credited Brainard, who had been both the expedition's first sergeant and commissary sergeant, with their survival. As a reward for his courage, example, and leadership, the Army commissioned Brainard as a second lieutenant in his old unit, the 2nd Cavalry. This was highly unusual, and at the time and for many years thereafter, Brainard was the only living Army officer holding a commission awarded for specific distinguished services. He returned to the western frontier after his promotion and served in Arizona, California, and New Mexico.

During the Spanish–American War, then-Major Brainard was the chief commissary of the Department of the Pacific. He later served as chief commissary in the Philippines.

After returning to the United States, Brainard served in the Office of the Commissary General in Washington, D.C., and was promoted to colonel in 1914. During World War I he served as a military attaché to Argentina and was promoted to brigadier general. His last assignment before retiring in 1919 was as military attaché to Portugal.

Some thirteen years later, on January 27, 1933, seventy-six-year-old Brainard was awarded the Purple Heart by the Army for wounds received in action on May 7, 1877. Brainard died at Walter Reed General Hospital in 1946. He is interred at Arlington National Cemetery.[20]

Charles A. Windolph (a.k.a. Wrangel): Purple Heart—June 25–26, 1876

Charles A. Windolph was wounded in action at the battle of Little Bighorn on June 25–26, 1876. He received his Purple Heart from the War Department in 1932.

Born in Bergen, Germany, on December 9, 1851, Windolph immigrated to the United States in 1871, when he was nineteen years old. He settled in Brooklyn, New York, where he appears to have worked as a shoemaker. On November 12, 1871, Windolph enlisted in Company A of the 2nd U.S. Infantry Regiment but deserted less than a year later in Atlanta. He then reenlisted in the 7th U.S. Cavalry as "Charles Wrangel" on July 23, 1872. After President Ulysses S. Grant issued his proclamation of a general amnesty in 1873, however, Wrangel disclosed his status as a deserter along with his true identity. He was restored to duty without punishment.

Then-Private Windolph gained lasting fame during Custer's Last Stand at Little Bighorn on June 25, 1876. As a member of Company H of the 7th U.S. Cavalry, Windolph showed extraordinary heroism under fire in obtaining critical water for the wounded. Along with Sgt. George Geiger, Blacksmith Henry Mechlin, and Saddler Otto Voit, Windolph took up an exposed position outside the cavalry's line of defense in order to draw enemy fire away from fifteen other men who risked their own lives to get water from the river. For four hours, Windolph and his fellow troopers, acting as both decoys and as an attacking force, dodged bullets and laid down a protective covering fire. They accomplished their mission so well that not one of the men who sprinted the eighty yards from the cavalry encampment to the river was killed.

According to an obituary published in the *Deadwood Pioneer-Times* on March 12, 1950, as well as the *Rapid City Journal* on March 11, 1950, Wrangel died in South Dakota on March 11, 1950, at the age of ninety-eight. He is interred at the Black Hills National Cemetery in Sturgis, South Dakota.

SPANISH–AMERICAN WAR (1898)

After the United States declared war against Spain on April 25, 1898, President William McKinley planned to send an expeditionary force to Havana, Cuba. This strategy changed quickly, however, after a small Spanish flotilla arrived off the east coast of Cuba and anchored in Santiago Harbor. The U.S. Navy immediately blocked the entrance to Santiago Bay, and the newly formed V Corps, under the command of Maj. Gen. William Shafter, assembled at Tampa, Florida, and prepared to deploy to Cuba. U.S. Army units arrived off Santiago Bay on June 22, 1898, and began landing twenty miles east of Santiago.

Theodore Roosevelt's dismounted Rough Riders, moving inland on June 23, ran into a large Spanish force at Las Guasimas. After a fierce firefight, the Spanish retreated toward Santiago. U.S. troops continued their advance and, on June 24, were about five miles from Santiago. Directly ahead lay fortified San Juan Hill and the smaller Kettle Hill. On June 30, 1898, after conducting a reconnaissance of enemy positions, Shafter divided his corps, and at dawn the next day, a division under Brig. Gen. Henry Lawton attacked the village of El Caney, while the divisions under Maj. Gen. Joseph Wheeler and Brig. Gen. Jacob Kent assaulted San Juan Hill.

The fighting in Cuba lasted less than a month, beginning on June 22 and ending on July 17. Although U.S. battlefield casualties were 290 killed and 1,600 wounded, more than 2,500 died from yellow fever, malaria, and other tropical diseases.

A small number of veterans applied to the War Department for Purple Hearts on the basis of wounds received in Cuba. Most of the applications were for combat injuries incurred on July 1, 1898.

Hans Villumsen: Purple Heart—July 1, 1898
Born in Denmark, Hans Villumsen served in Company D of the 10th U.S. Infantry, during the war with Spain. He was serving as a sergeant when he was wounded in action at the Battle of Santiago on July 1, 1898. Villumsen was awarded a Purple Heart in 1932. He had previously received the Distinguished Service Medal "for distinguished service at the battle of Santiago."[21]

Joseph Wehr: Purple Heart—July 1, 1898
Joseph Wehr received a gunshot wound to his right hip in the Battle of El Caney, Cuba on July 1, 1898.

Wehr, who served as a private in Company D of the 17th U.S. Infantry, was part of an American force that fought the Spanish at El Caney, a village located about forty miles from Santiago. The enemy garrison at El Caney consisted of three companies of Spanish soldiers and a company of guerrillas—a total of about 520 men. The Spanish were armed with modern Mauser rifles, but they had no artillery.

The American force under General Lawton numbered about 6,600 and included ten regular regiments, the 2nd Massachusetts Volunteers, a cavalry troop, and a battery of artillery.

About 6 AM, the Americans began an artillery bombardment, but this was ineffectual. Soon thereafter, however, the infantry began a slow advance toward the fortified Spaniards. They were in the open and took heavy casualties but continued to advance.

Although the Spanish held El Caney and used well-aimed small-arms fire to inflict serious damage, the overwhelming number of American troops eventually caused the Spanish to abandon El Caney and withdraw from the battle. U.S. losses were 81 killed and 360 wounded. The Spanish lost about 235 men. The 17th Infantry had 4 killed and 27 wounded in action, out of a strength of 506 men.

Wehr was wounded by a bullet to his right hip and subsequently received treatment at the base hospital in Cuba; Fort Monroe, Virginia; and Washington, D.C. He was honorably discharged on the basis of a surgeon's certificate of disability on November 16, 1898.

Wehr applied for a Purple Heart on September 29, 1932, and its award was approved by the Army on November 15, 1932.[22]

PHILIPPINE INSURRECTION (1899–1913)

Prior to the Spanish-American War, Filipino insurgents led by Emilio Aguinaldo had rebelled against Spanish colonial rule in the Philippines. After the United States declared war on Spain in April 1898, Aguinaldo and his guerrilla forces attacked and defeated Spanish garrisons throughout the Philippine islands. They were so successful that when ships bringing Brig. Gen. Thomas Anderson and the soldiers of VIII Corps arrived in Manila Bay on July 1, 1898, Aguinaldo and his men had already surrounded Manila.

Aguinaldo fully expected that the United States would grant his people independence after American forces defeated Spain in the Philippines, but leaders in Washington, D.C., intended to establish a permanent presence in the islands. Determined to prevent another foreign power from ruling his people, Aguinaldo declared war on the United States in February 1899, and his forces began attacking U.S. soldiers.

The Americans initially had considerable success in defeating the guerrillas. But once Aguinaldo and his men retreated into the mountains and jungles of central Luzon, it was a different story. Using their superior knowledge of the difficult terrain, the Filipino insurgents, who lacked firearms, successfully ambushed American patrols, inflicting considerable damage with their spears and long knives.

A vicious guerrilla war lasted for more than two years. It ended only when Army Brig. Gen. Frederick Funston and a small group of U.S. soldiers and Filipino scouts dressed as insurgents gained entry to Aguinaldo's camp and captured the rebel leader. Although some Filipinos continued to resist, organized resistance quickly waned—-at least on Luzon—-and President Theodore Roosevelt declared victory in July 1902.

The Philippine Insurrection had not been without costs. By 1902, 100,000 U.S. troops had fought in the islands in more than 2,800 engagements, and 4,240 had been killed. Another 2,800 were wounded. Moreover, it was not until 1913 that all guerrilla activity ceased, when troops of the 8th Infantry, commanded by then-Capt. John J. Pershing defeated the Moros in the Battle of Bagsak Mountain.[23]

Charles B. Allen: Purple Heart—May 2, 1902

Charles B. Allen was wounded in action during the Battle of Bayan during the Lake Lanao Expedition on the island of Mindanao. He was serving as a private in Company E of the 27th U.S. Infantry. In early 1902 Allen had landed with his fellow soldiers in the 27th U.S. Infantry on Mindanao. Their mission was to attempt to establish friendly relations with the Moros of the region.[24]

Benjamin F. Goldman: Purple Heart—July 3, 1899

Benjamin Franklin Goldman was wounded in his left hand at Taguig, Luzon, Philippine Islands, on July 3, 1899. He was a corporal serving in Company I of the 1st Regiment, Washington Volunteer Infantry. Goldman's Purple Heart was awarded to him on July 30, 1941.[25]

Alvin F. Plottner: Purple Heart—February 28, 1899

Alvin F. Plottner received a gunshot wound to his right shoulder at Caloocan, Philippines, on February 28, 1899.

A private serving in Company A of the 1st Montana Volunteer Infantry, Plottner saw considerable combat during the insurrection. He conducted a "volunteer reconnaissance of enemy positions at Caloocan on February 10, 1899" and "filled canteens under very heavy fire at Malabou on March 25, 1899."[26]

Plottner was living in St. Cloud, Florida, when he applied for a Purple Heart on the basis of his Philippine Insurrection wound. The War Department issued him a Purple Heart on April 6, 1939.

David L. Stone: Purple Heart—1904

David Lamme Stone was wounded in action while fighting Filipino guerrillas in 1904.

Born in Greenville, Mississippi, on August 15, 1872, Stone graduated last in his class at the U.S. Military Academy at West Point in 1898. Commissioned as an infantry officer, Stone saw combat first in Cuba and then in the Philippines, where he was awarded the Silver Star citation for his gallantry in action against the "Insurrectionists." While fighting against the Moro in 1904, Stone was wounded in action.

During World War I, then-Colonel Stone served, first, as assistant chief of staff for personnel of the 3rd Division and, later, as assistant chief of staff for personnel of the Second Army. In these two staff positions, "he performed with distinction ... in the action from July 5 to August 2, 1918, near Chateau-Thierry, and in the advance to the Ourcq River." According to official records, Stone displayed "tireless energy and ability of an unusually high order in supplying troops under most difficult conditions. . . . Aggressive and resourceful, he proved equal to every emergency"[27] and received the Distinguished Service Medal for his efforts. In 1936 then–Major General Stone was commanding the 3rd Division at Fort Lewis, Washington, and from 1937 to 1940, he commanded the Corps Area District of California. After retiring from active duty, Stone remained in Tacoma, Washington, where he died on December 28, 1959 at the age of eighty-seven.

CHINA RELIEF EXPEDITION/BOXER REBELLION (1900–1901)

The Boxers were members of a secret society that sought to eradicate all foreign influences in China. Their movement became increasingly popular at the end of the nineteenth century, and by early June 1900, foreigners in China, especially those living and working in Peking (now Beijing), were in grave danger.

On June 10, 1900, a relief force consisting of 2,100 military personnel from France, Germany, Great Britain, Japan, Russia, and the United States left Tientsin (now Tianjin) for Peking, but the force failed to reach the city because of stiff resistance from the Boxers. Ten days later the rebellion against foreigners culminated with the murder of the German minister in Peking. About 3,500 Westerners and some Chinese Christians subsequently took refuge in the compound where foreign legations had their offices.

To rescue these trapped men and women from the Chinese rebels, an international relief force, including U.S. soldiers, sailors, and Marines, was dispatched to Taku on July 7, 1900. Two battalions of the 9th Infantry participated in an attack on Tientsin, which fell on July 13.

On August 4 an allied force of 19,000 left Tientsin for Peking. The U.S. contingent numbered about 2,500 men and was under the command of Maj. Gen. Adna R. Chafee Sr. Chafee's contingent consisted of the 9th Infantry Regiment, the 14th Infantry Regiment, troopers from the 6th Cavalry and the 5th Artillery, and a Marine battalion.

On August 14, 1900, soldiers from the 14th Infantry attacked the Outer City of Peking, climbed the thirty-foot-high Tartar Wall, planted the first foreign flag ever to fly over that city, and then opened the way for British units to relieve the legation compound. On August 15, members of the 5th Artillery blasted open the gates in an assault on Peking's Inner City.

With Peking in foreign hands, the fury of the Boxer uprising was spent. After extensive negotiations, the Boxer Protocol was signed in September 1901. It ended hostilities and provided that the Chinese would pay reparations to all foreign powers.

While there must have been several awards of the Purple Heart to soldiers wounded during the China Relief Expedition/Boxer Rebellion, only two recipients have been verified—Medal of Honor recipients Calvin P. Titus and Robert H. Von Schlick.

Calvin P. Titus: Purple Heart—August 15, 1900

Calvin Pearl Titus, then serving as a musician in the 14th Infantry, received a "shell wound in neck (slight)" during the attack on Peking on August 15, 1900. He was awarded the Purple Heart by the Department of the Army on February 17, 1955.

Born in Vinton, Iowa, on September 26, 1879, Titus enlisted in the Iowa National Guard in 1898, as he hoped to fight in the Spanish–American War. He saw no action before that conflict ended, however.

Titus remained on active duty by enlisting in the Regular Army's 14th Infantry Regiment, where he served as a bugler in Company E. He sailed to the Philippines with his regiment to serve in the ongoing insurrection, but, when his unit was sent to China to fight the Boxers in the summer of 1900, then-Corporal Titus went with it.

On August 14, 1900, during the heavy fighting in Peking, Titus overheard his commander saying that the thirty-foot-high Tartar Wall needed to be scaled. He answered with the now-famous reply, "I'll try, Sir."

The Americans had no ropes or ladders, but Titus, by holding onto exposed bricks and crevices in the ancient wall, managed to climb to the top. Other soldiers then followed his courageous example, and soon two companies of the 14th Infantry were in control of the wall. Their covering fire subsequently permitted British Army troops to breach the Boxer's stronghold.

According to official military records, Titus was not wounded while scaling the Tartar Wall. He did, however, receive a wound the next day. As a result of this "in line of duty" wound, the Army awarded Titus the Purple Heart more than five decades later.

In 1901 Titus received an appointment to West Point. He had been recommended for the Medal of Honor for his extraordinary heroism in Peking, and he remains the only U.S. Military Academy cadet to receive the Medal of Honor while attending classes at West Point.

After graduating forty-third in the Class of 1905, Titus was commissioned an infantry second lieutenant and assigned to his old unit, the 14th Infantry. He later served as inspector–instructor of the militia of South Dakota and returned to the Philippines for an additional tour of duty in 1913. He returned to the United States in time to join Pershing's Punitive Expedition into Mexico in 1916.

Titus remained in the United States during World War I. He did, however, serve overseas three years with the Army of Occupation of Germany after the war.

After returning from Germany, Titus served as the professor of military science and tactics at Coe College in Cedar Rapids, Iowa. His final assignment, from 1927 to 1930, was at Fort Benning, Georgia, where Titus taught leadership. When he retired as a lieutenant colonel, Titus had served a total of thirty-two years.[28]

Robert H. Von Schlick: Purple Heart—July 13, 1900

Robert Henry Von Schlick was wounded three times in combat near Tientsin on July 13, 1900. Although he was discharged from active duty on October 20, 1900, Von Schlick later received both the Medal of Honor for his extraordinary heroism at Tientsin, as well as a single Purple Heart for his wounds.

Born in Germany on January 2, 1875, Von Schlick enlisted in the U.S. Revenue Cutter Service, the predecessor of the U.S. Coast Guard, in 1889, when he was fourteen years old. He remained with the Revenue Cutter Service through the Spanish–American War and was discharged in San Francisco, California, in May 1899. Less than two months later, on July 5, Von Schlick enlisted as a soldier in Company C of the 9th Infantry. His enlistment records reflect that Von Schlick was five foot nine and had blue eyes, blond hair, and a "ruddy complexion."

Von Schlick was stationed in the Philippines by the end of 1899, but, as he had contracted malaria, he spent much of his time in sick bay. He was not too ill, however, to deploy with the 9th Infantry when it left for China in early June 1900.

On July 13, 1900, then-Private Von Schlick was with the international relief force near Tientsin and was engaged in foraging when a band of Boxers ambushed his party. After the initial firefight, von Schlick saw that a fellow soldier was wounded and lying in an exposed position. Von Schlick consequently ran to the man and was shot and badly wounded while carrying the stricken individual to safety.

Despite the severe wound, Von Schlick "rejoined his command, which partly occupied an exposed position upon a dike, remaining there after his command had been withdrawn." Although he was now alone and presented a "conspicuous target," Von Schlick kept firing his rifle and drew the Boxer's fire while his fellow soldiers withdrew. He continued to fire into the Boxers, killing several, "until he was literally shot off his position by the enemy."[29]

Von Schlick's wounds were so bad that no one expected him to live. One bullet went through his left lung and shattered his collar bone. Another bullet went through his left cheek, breaking his jaw bone and ending up in his neck next to his spine. A third bullet went into his left shoulder, destroying it.

Von Schlick's company commander, 1st Lt. William H. Waldron, nominated Von Schlick for the Medal of Honor on July 19, but this recommendation was either lost or misplaced. Three years later, Von Schlick wrote to the commander of the 9th Infantry and asked about the status of his Medal of Honor. His letter was forwarded to the War Department, which did publish a citation for gallantry in General Orders but took no other action. Ten years later, however, the Army decided to award Von Schlick the Medal of Honor, and this award was announced on June 7, 1913. Von Schlick's award was the fourth and last Army Medal of Honor for the China Relief Expedition/Boxer Rebellion.

Von Schlick worked as a brick mason in San Francisco—using his good right arm—until moving to upstate New York. On January 15, 1910, he married Wilhelmina Adelheit at Syracuse, and they subsequently lived in Ithaca, Batavia, and Buffalo. But Von Schlick then deserted his wife and moved to Portland, Oregon. In 1915, his wife traced him to that city, where they reunited for a short time before Von Schlick again deserted her and moved once more to San Francisco. She followed him to that city also, had him arrested for desertion, but then dropped the charges. Both Von Schlick and his wife then moved—independently—to Los Angeles, California, where they lived for the remainder of their lives.

On July 19, 1932, more than thirty years after the event, the War Department issued a Purple Heart to Von Schlick for the wounds he received in action in China. The old soldier suffered from his injuries the rest of his life and had little or no use of his left arm. Von Schlick died in Los Angeles on July 1, 1941, and he is interred in the Los Angeles National Cemetery.

PUNITIVE EXPEDITION INTO MEXICO (1916–1917)

On March 9, 1916, Mexican warlord Francisco "Pancho" Villa crossed the border with several hundred men and raided the town of Columbus, New Mexico. While troopers in the U.S. 13th Cavalry, stationed nearby, inflicted heavy casualties on Villa and forced him to return to Mexico, President Woodrow Wilson was determined to put an end to such banditry. The president on March 10 ordered the Army to mount an expedition to capture Villa and destroy his forces.

On March 15 Brig. Gen. John J. "Black Jack" Pershing entered Mexico with a force of five thousand men, consisting of four cavalry regiments, two infantry regiments, two field artillery batteries, support units, eight biplanes, and several trucks.

Pershing sent flying cavalry columns after Villa, but the Mexican warlord avoided capture. The most serious firefight occurred at Parral, Mexico, on April 12, 1916, when troopers from the 13th Cavalry clashed with Mexican government troops who also were chasing Villa. This bloody clash merely escalated the conflict and prompted Wilson to call most of the National Guard into service to protect the border.

With American entry into World War I seeming to be more likely, Wilson was finally forced to order Pershing to leave Mexico, and the last troops of the Punitive Expedition were out of Mexico by February 5, 1917.

The number of Purple Hearts awarded to those wounded in action while serving with the Punitive Expedition is not known, but at least two recipients have been identified.

James B. Ord: Purple Heart—April 12, 1916

James Basevi Ord was wounded in action while fighting on horseback at Parra on April 12, 1916.

Born in Mexico, Ord graduated from the U.S. Military Academy in 1915, was commissioned an infantry second lieutenant, and assigned to the 6th Infantry. On April 12, 1916, then–Second Lieutenant Ord was attached to the 13th Cavalry, and was riding with Maj. Frank Tomkins and one hundred men "on a lightning-fast strike deep into Mexico."

Ord and the other troopers expected to stop for a well-needed rest in Parral, a town of some 20,000 inhabitants. When the 13th Cavalry reached Parral, however, they were fired on by Mexican government soldiers loyal to the regime of President Venustiano Carranza. A U.S. cavalry sergeant was killed, and the Americans returned fire, killing an estimated twenty-five Mexicans.

What followed was a running battle, as the cavalry troopers retreated on horseback only to stop periodically to engage their pursuers. At the end of the day, two Americans had been killed and six wounded, including Ord and Tomkins.[30]

According to official records, after Ord was wounded at Parral, "he dismounted from his horse under heavy fire, placed a wounded man on a horse and assisted him from the field." For this act of "exceptionally meritorious service," Ord was awarded the Distinguished Service Medal on September 30, 1918. The Army awarded Ord the Purple Heart for the wounds he received in Mexico on July 7, 1934.[31]

Ord served as an instructor at West Point during World War I and was later a student at the Ecole de Guerre Économique in Paris, France, from 1922 to 1924. He was a military attaché in Paris from 1928 to 1932, and he then served as a military advisor to the Commonwealth of the Philippines. Ord died at Camp John Hay, Philippine Islands, on January 30, 1938.

Frank Tompkins: Purple Hearts—March 9, 1916, April 12, 1916, and September 2, 1918

Maj. Frank Tompkins was twice wounded in action while fighting in Mexico as part of the Punitive Expedition. He was also wounded in action during World War I.

On March 9, 1916, Tompkins, after obtaining permission from his superior, organized a small troop of cavalryman and took off in pursuit of the approximately four hundred Mexicans Pancho Villa had led in the raid of Columbus, New Mexico.

Tompkins and his men crossed the Mexican border after the raiders and, in a series of firefights, killed thirty-two Villistas. Tomkins and another officer were "grazed by Mexican bullets" but there were no other casualties.[32]

The next month Tompkins led two troops of the 13th Cavalry into what was to be the Punitive Expedition's deepest penetration into Mexico—516 miles. At Parral, on April 12, Tompkins and his men also clashed for the first time with Mexican government troops rather than insurgents. According to official documents, Tomkins "requested and received authority to pursue a superior force of bandits into Mexico." He was wounded "early in the pursuit ... but carried on a running fight with the bandits for several miles, inflicting heavy losses on them and stopped the pursuit only when men and horses were exhausted and ammunition reduced to a few rounds per man."[33]

For his extraordinary heroism that day at Parral, Tompkins later received the Distinguished Service Cross. On March 15, 1932, the War Department also awarded him the Purple Heart with oak leaf cluster for the wounds he received in combat on March 9, 1916, and April 12, 1916.

Frank Tompkins received his third Purple Heart for wounds received in action in France on September 7, 1918. Tomkins was still a major when he was wounded during World War I but had retired as a colonel when the Army issued his Purple Heart with two large oak leaf clusters to him on March 15, 1932.

THE UNITED STATES OF AMERICA

TO ALL WHO SHALL SEE THESE PRESENTS, GREETING:

THIS IS TO CERTIFY THAT
THE PRESIDENT OF THE UNITED STATES OF AMERICA
HAS AWARDED THE

PURPLE HEART

ESTABLISHED BY GENERAL GEORGE WASHINGTON
AT NEWBURGH, NEW YORK, AUGUST 7, 1782
TO

Colonel (then Captain) William Alexander, 04632, Artillery

FOR WOUNDS RECEIVED
IN ACTION

in France, 27 July 1918

GIVEN UNDER MY HAND IN THE CITY OF WASHINGTON
THIS   11th   DAY OF   May   1960

Although then-Capt. William D. Alexander was wounded in action in France on July 27, 1918, the Army did not award him a Purple Heart until May 11, 1960, almost ten years after he had retired as a colonel. (Fred L. Borch)

WORLD WAR I (1917–1918)

Since no posthumous awards of the Purple Heart were permitted until World War II, every World War I soldier who received a Purple Heart had survived his combat injuries. While the total number of recipients is not known—the Army has never compiled a list of Purple Heart recipients—193,683 soldiers received "wounds not mortal" while fighting in World War I, and as late as 1942, the War Department estimated that some 186,538 persons were entitled to receive the Purple Heart for wounds received in combat. In fact, the Army awarded 77,958 Purple Hearts from 1932 to early 1942, with the vast majority going to World War I veterans.[34]

William D. Alexander: Purple Heart—July 27, 1918

William Dennison Alexander was wounded in action in France on July 27, 1918. His Purple Heart is unusual because it was not awarded until May 11, 1960, more than forty years after Alexander was injured in combat.

Born in Oklahoma on March 8, 1893, Alexander entered the U.S. Naval Academy in Annapolis, Maryland, in 1911 and graduated in October 1915. He was commissioned as an ensign in January 1916 and served briefly in Washington, D.C., before resigning from the Navy, transferring to the Maryland Army National Guard, and deploying to Eagle Pass, Texas, for service along the Mexican border.

After returning from Texas in September 1916, Alexander applied for a commission as a Regular Army officer and was offered an appointment as a second lieutenant in the field artillery.

Alexander sailed to France in 1917 as part of the American Expeditionary Force and served at the Field Artillery School, Camp de Souge, and in the 3rd Field Artillery Brigade and the 6th Field Artillery Brigade. He took part in the Champagne–Marne campaign and Aisne–Marne campaign and was wounded by poison gas in France on July 27, 1918.

At the conclusion of hostilities, Alexander returned to the United States and completed artillery school at Fort Sill, Oklahoma, in 1919. In the 1920s and 1930s Major Alexander served in a variety of assignments, including assistant professor of military science and tactics at the University of Illinois, Urbana; 6th Field Artillery, Montauk, New York; 7th Field Artillery, Camp Dix, New Jersey; and 10th Field Artillery, Fort Lewis. He also served overseas in the Hawaiian Department.

During World War II, then–Lieutenant Colonel Alexander participated in the Aleutian campaign, seeing combat as an observer in the USS *New Mexico* during the bombardment of Japanese-held Kiska Island, Alaska, in July 1943. He then deployed to the Pacific, where he served twenty-one months as a joint plans officer, including duty on New Guinea, the Solomon Islands, Bismarck Archipelago, and Luzon, Philippines.

After the war then-Colonel Alexander served at the Pentagon, in Washington, D.C., and at Fort Monroe. In 1949 he sailed for Panama and then travelled to San José, Costa Rica, to assume duties as chief of the U.S. Army Mission to Costa Rica. Alexander remained in this assignment until returning to the United States in July 1952. He retired in October and settled in South Carolina.

Only in retirement did Alexander apply for a Purple Heart on the basis of his being wounded in World War I. As his official military personnel file contained medical records showing that he had been injured in a poison gas attack, the Army issued Alexander a Purple Heart medal and Purple Heart certificate on May 11, 1960.

Alexander died at his home on December 18, 1974.[35]

William J. Donovan: Purple Heart—October 14–15, 1918

See chapter 9, "Celebrities: Artists and Entertainers, Politicians, Athletes, and Other Public Figures."

Charles E. Laird: Purple Heart—October 1918

Charles E. Laird was awarded the Purple Heart for meritorious service in performing his duties despite an illness.

During the Meuse–Argonne offensive in October 1918, then–Sergeant Major Laird, "although sick, refused to be evacuated . . . but remained at the front and effectively performed his duties during the entire operation. . . . His efforts attributed [sic] much in maintaining a high state of morale in the Battalion Headquarters Detachment."[36]

This is a most unusual Purple Heart—and a definite exception to policy— as it is for meritorious service and not wounds, and not based on an MSCC.

Douglas MacArthur: Purple Hearts—March 11, 1918, and October 14, 1918

See Chapter 9, "Celebrities: Artists and Entertainers, Politicians, Athletes, and Other Public Figures."

Beatrice A. MacDonald: Purple Heart—August 17, 1917

Beatrice Mary MacDonald was wounded in action in France on August 17, 1917. She was the first female recipient of the Purple Heart for combat wounds.

Born in Canada, MacDonald was living in New York City when the United States entered World War I. She subsequently joined the Army Nurse Corps as a reserve nurse and sailed for France to serve in the American Expeditionary Force.

On the night of August 17, 1917, MacDonald was on duty with a surgical team at the British-run Casualty Clearing Station No. 61. She remained at her post of duty caring for the sick and wounded despite a German night air raid until shrapnel from an exploding bomb pierced her right eye, causing instant blindness.

The Army issued MacDonald a Purple Heart on January 4, 1936. She previously had been awarded the Distinguished Service Cross for extraordinary heroism, the French Croix de Guerre with Bronze Star, the British Military Medal "for conspicuous gallantry . . . in the operating theater until she was wounded," and the British Royal Red Cross (Second Class).[37]

George S. Patton Jr.: Purple Heart—September 26, 1918

See Chapter 8, "Families: Brothers, Fathers and Sons, Husbands and Wives."

Charles W. Ryder: Purple Heart—July 21, 1918

Charles Wolcott Ryder was a remarkable soldier by any measure. He was twice decorated with the Distinguished Service Cross for heroism in World War I and led a division in combat in North Africa and Italy before commanding a corps in the Philippines and Japan in World War II.

Born in Topeka, Kansas, in January 1892, Ryder entered the U.S. Military Academy in 1911 and was in distinguished company when he graduated and received his commission as an infantry second lieutenant on June 12, 1915. His classmates included Omar Nelson Bradley, Dwight David Eisenhower, and James Alward Van Fleet, all of whom would achieve fame as combat leaders in World War II.

After the United States entered World War I in April 1917, Ryder served in France in the 16th Infantry Regiment, 1st Division. According to the 1927 book *American Decorations, 1862–1926*, compiled by the Army Adjutant General, then-Major Ryder received two awards of the Distinguished Service Cross—which is second only to the Medal of Honor in status as a combat decoration—for his gallantry under fire in July 1918 and October 1918.

On July 21, 1918, near Soissons, France, Ryder "took command of the front line units and reorganized them under heavy artillery and machine gun fire." Although he was wounded by the enemy fire, Ryder "remained in command and directed the attack until all objectives had been taken."

Less than three months later, on October 9, 1918, near Fleville, France, Ryder again demonstrated courage under fire. In an attack on an enemy-held hill, "after all his runners had been killed or wounded while trying to establish liaison with the front-line companies, Ryder advanced alone and personally directed operations" despite being under attack from two German machine guns. Later, "he personally led the final assault" on the hill, "thereby making possible the success of the entire attack."

Ryder would later receive the Silver Star for gallantry in action in World War I and the Purple Heart for his wounds.

From 1921 to 1924 Ryder was assigned to West Point, where he was a member of the Brigade Tactical Department. He also served an overseas tour in Tientsin, China, before returning to the U.S. Military Academy in 1937 to assume duties as the commandant of cadets, a position he held until 1941.

With America's entry into World War II, Ryder eagerly sought a combat command and, in May 1942, then–Major General Ryder took charge of the 34th "Red Bull" Infantry Division. He was with the unit when it landed at Algiers in November 1942 as part of Operation Torch, the invasion of North Africa.

Ryder remained in command during the amphibious landings at Salerno, Italy, in September 1943 and saw hard combat in the mountains against the Germans between December 1943 and February 1944. Ryder was still in command when the Red Bulls landed at Anzio in March 1944.

Ryder gave up division command in July 1944, returned to the United States, and then deployed to the Pacific, where he assumed command of IX Corps in the Philippines in September 1944. He served on Leyte, and, after the Japanese surrendered in August 1945, Ryder remained in command. He was with IX Corps when it landed on Hokkaido, Japan, to carry out occupation duties and did not give up command until December 1948.

Ryder then returned to Washington, D.C., to take charge of National Guard and Reserve programs as special assistant to the Army chief of staff. He retired from active duty in 1950 and died at his home in Vineyard Haven, Massachusetts, in August 1960 at the age of sixty-eight years.

Joseph Sink: Purple Hearts—July 29, 1918, and September 28, 1918

Born in Hyde Park, Pennsylvania, Joseph Sink enlisted on April 18, 1917, and served in France with Company L of the 100th Infantry. He was wounded the first time by shrapnel while fighting at Chateau-Thierry on July 29, 1918. Almost two months later, on September 28, then-Private Sink was wounded a second time, by a German machine-gun bullet.

Sink's Purple Heart, with its distinctive and rare "thumbnail-sized oak leaf cluster" denoting a second award, was issued to him by the War Department on March 25, 1933.[38]

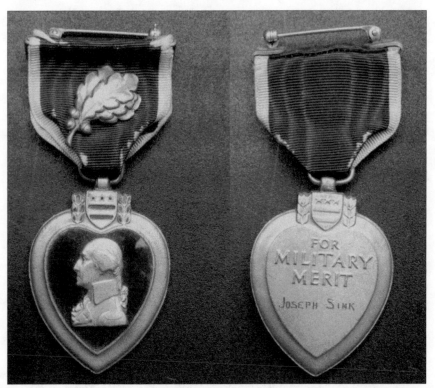

Pvt. Joseph Sink was twice wounded in action during World War I. His second award of the Purple Heart is indicated by the unusual, and rare, thumbnail-size oak leaf cluster used for a brief time by the War Department from 1932 to 1933. (Fred L. Borch)

Leopold Strauss: Purple Heart—1917–1918

Leopold Strauss received his Purple Heart "for services in connection with trench fever experiments" in France. A New York native, Strauss was a private assigned to the American Expeditionary Forces Medical Department's Base Hospital No. 2. The War Department awarded him the Purple Heart on July 7, 1933.

After being honorably discharged in 1919, Strauss returned to New York City, where he became "a wholesale dealer in elastic." Strauss died on October 4, 1952, at Jewish Memorial Hospital after a brief illness. He was fifty-five years old.[39]

CIVILIAN CONSERVATION CORPS (1933–1936)

There was only one recipient of the Purple Heart for meritorious service in peacetime.

Duncan K. Major: Purple Heart—March 9, 1933–July 6, 1936

Then–Brig. Gen. Duncan Kennedy Major received the Purple Heart for three years of peacetime meritorious service involving the Civilian Conservation Corps.

War Department Circular 5, dated January 18, 1937, permitted the award of the Purple Heart as a "junior" Distinguished Service Medal and expressly identified the Civilian Conservation Corps as an example of possible peacetime service meriting a Purple Heart. Nine months after this circular was published, however, it was revoked by War Department Circular 66.

In the meantime, however, one Purple Heart had been awarded—to Major. The citation for the award reads, "For essential service as War Department representative on the Advisory Council of the Director of the Emergency Conservation Work from the inception of the Civilian Conservation Corps March 9, 1933 to July 6, 1936. General Major demonstrated marked ability in the most important work of planning and organizing the Army participation in the Civilian Conservation Corps project."

Army records show that Major was recommended for the Purple Heart by Maj. Gen. H. A. Drum on August 20, 1936, and by Maj. Gen. John Hughes on September 15, 1936. The Army Adjutant General's Decorations Board concurred in the recommendations "per memo" on December 14, 1936, and the Army chief of staff approved the award on January 21, 1937. The Army quartermaster general was directed to issue the Purple Heart to Major on March 2, 1937.[40]

WORLD WAR II (1941–1945)

Joseph Beyrle: Purple Heart—June 1944

Joseph Beyrle is apparently the only soldier who fought for both the United States and the Soviet Union in World War II. He was wounded in action in France while fighting the Germans in June 1944.

Born in Muskegon, Michigan, in August 1923, Beyrle (pronounced "buy early") graduated from high school in June 1942. Although he had won an

MSgt. Llewellyn Chilson was awarded two Purple Hearts in World War II. He also received three Distinguished Service Crosses, two Silver Stars, the Legion of Merit, and the Bronze Star Medal. (National Archives and Records Administration)

athletic scholarship to the University of Notre Dame because, in part, he could run a mile in less than five minutes—fast by the standards of the day—Beyrle decided instead to enlist in the Army in September 1942. He volunteered for parachute training and made his first jump in December 1942.

As historian Thomas Taylor wrote in *The Simple Sounds of Freedom*, then-Corporal Beyrle's amazing experiences began when he was just twenty years old. A "Screaming Eagle" in the 506th Parachute Infantry Regiment, 101st Airborne Division, which is the unit later made famous by the book *Band of Brothers*, Beyrle made two solo parachute jumps into occupied France months before D-day. On both occasions, he was a "paymaster" carrying "bandoliers packed with several hundred thousand dollars of gold for the French Resistance."[41]

Beyrle survived his two solo jumps and, on June 5, 1944, was one of a handful of paratroopers who parachuted into Normandy in advance of the Allied amphibious invasion that would occur in just hours. Beyrle landed on the roof of a church in Saint Come-du-Mont and, although being shot at by the Germans, managed to slide off the roof and set off on his mission. Three days later, however, his career as an American paratrooper came to an abrupt halt when Beyrle crawled over a hedgerow and found himself surrounded by enemy soldiers.

Taken prisoner by the Germans, Beyrle was marched, along with other captured U.S. soldiers, to a holding area. During this journey Beyrle was wounded by shrapnel when he and his fellow Americans were strafed by Allied planes flying overhead.

As Joe Holley wrote in the *Washington Post* in 2004, Beyrle managed to escape during the ensuing confusion but was recaptured. "His dog tags were taken and ended up around the neck of a German soldier who was killed in France while wearing an American uniform." Since the Army graves registration personnel who later recovered the remains of this German assumed that Beyrle in fact had been killed, his parents "received the dreaded telegram about their son's 'death' in September 1944.[42]

Beyrle, however, was not dead. On the contrary, he was shipped to a POW camp in German-occupied Poland. In October 1944 Beyrle escaped, made his way west to Germany, and was recaptured in Berlin. During his captivity, he suffered not only from a lack of food, but also from repeated beatings from the Germans.

In January 1945 Beyrle again escaped from captivity and joined a Red Army tank unit. He fought in numerous engagements alongside Soviet soldiers, serving as a machine gunner on the back of a Sherman tank. Beyrle hoped that fighting with the Red Army would eventually bring him back to U.S. lines, but this did not occur. Rather, after being badly wounded near the Oder River, Beyrle was evacuated by the Soviets to a hospital for treatment. After leaving the hospital, Beyrle eventually made his way to the U.S. Embassy in Moscow. No one believed his story, or that he was, in fact, an American soldier named Joe Beyrle. On the contrary, because the war was still not over, some suspected that he was a Nazi assassin sent to kill the American ambassador. Fingerprints finally established Beyrle's identity.

Beyrle returned to the United States in April 1945 and was reunited with his surprised family, who had thought him dead. He married and then worked for Brunswick Corp. until retiring in 1981. Beyrle died in December 2004 at the age of eighty-one.

Llewellyn M. Chilson: Purple Hearts—February 15, 1944, and April 27, 1945

Llewellyn M. Chilson was wounded in the face by a German shell fragment near Carroceto, Italy, on February 15, 1944, and struck in his right arm by an enemy bullet near Neuberg, Germany, on April 27, 1945.

Born in Ohio on April 1, 1920, Chilson grew up on the streets of South Akron. He may have learned more about fighting than about the three Rs at South High School, where he later said he received his first taste of combat and survival, but not a high school diploma. Chilson said of his youth, "I've always been a fighter. The neighborhoods where I grew up in South Akron were pretty rough."[43]

Sixteen years old in 1936, Chilson became a driver, hauling freight across country in a truck and trailer. He drove about 250 miles a day and made $40 a week, which was considered a good wage at the time. That ended on March 22, 1942, when Chilson, almost twenty-two years old, was drafted. He showed up at Fort Benjamin Harrison, Indiana, weighing 150 lbs. and standing five foot eight.

After infantry and amphibious training, Chilson joined the 179th Infantry Regiment, 45th Infantry Division, the "Thunderbirds." With his division, he landed in Sicily in July 1943, on the Italian mainland in September, and at Salerno and the Anzio beachhead in February 1944.

Chilson was promoted to corporal in April 1944, then to "buck" sergeant and assistant squad leader in May. He was a technical sergeant by August 15, when he waded ashore with his division in southern France during Operation Anvil. By late fall Chilson and his fellow soldiers were fighting in the Vosges Mountains near German-held Denshein, France.

At night on November 24, 1944, German machine-gun and rifle fire halted Chilson's platoon on a mountain road. Chilson set up his own machine gun and advanced alone toward the enemy. He crawled to within sixty feet of the German roadblock, threw two hand grenades, and charged with submachine gun blazing. Chilson killed three Germans and induced nine more to surrender. He was awarded the Silver Star medal.

On March 26, 1945, Chilson was serving as a platoon leader and was with his division at the Rhine River. When the Americans began to cross the river at Gernsheim, the Germans attacked with a furious barrage of rifle and machine-gun fire. The Germans also fired 20-mm cannons at the Americans; although these weapons were designed as antiaircraft artillery they were often used as light artillery.

When another platoon leader was wounded, Chilson took command. He "quickly organized his platoon into a compact, efficient assault force and with vigor and keen judgment led his force along the river bank." In the subsequent firefight Chilson and his soldiers killed 11 Germans and took 225 prisoners. Chilson personally destroyed an ammunition vehicle and two heavy machine guns and made possible the destruction of three enemy flak vehicles. For his extraordinary heroism that day, Chilson would later receive the Distinguished Service Cross.

On March 31, 1945, as Chilson led his platoon near Horsenthal, the Germans opened up with heavy fire from two flak vehicles behind the town. German riflemen and machine gunners began firing at the Americans from positions in front of the town. Chilson ran back three hundred yards through the heavy fire, climbed atop a tank, and rode it back to the front, where he began directing counterfire. With shells exploding and bullets flying around him, he remained in his exposed position to observe the Germans and relay detailed fire orders. His soldiers killed six Germans and captured seven. Chilson received a second Silver Star for his gallantry in action that day.

On April 25, 1945, Chilson and the 45th Division were moving toward Nuernberg, and were near Meilenholen when the Germans opened up with 20-mm cannon fire. Chilson immediately took aggressive action. After spotting the enemy firing position, Chilson got into a jeep and, armed only with a machine gun, drove down the main road and into the town. Then, all alone and very much in an exposed position, Chilson opened fire. At the end of the firefight, Chilson had personally killed forty Germans and knocked out two flak guns and an 88-mm howitzer.

A short time later American soldiers on a reconnaissance mission attempted to take the village of Zell. After 20-mm cannon fire stopped the advance of the U.S. troops, Chilson mounted an abandoned German motorcycle. The vehicle must have been unfamiliar to him, yet he managed to speed out in front of the reconnaissance troops and find six more German 20-mm gun positions. The motorcycle was shot out from under Chilson at pointblank range, but he "hit the dirt, rolled, got to his feet, charged the gun position, and tossed a grenade which killed three members of the enemy gun crew and knocked out the gun." This act of heroism earned Chilson his second Distinguished Service Cross.

Two days later, on April 27, 1945, Chilson's squad was halted by enemy fire from a courtyard in Neuberg. He threw a smoke grenade into the court-yard and attacked with his carbine. "Hit in the right arm by an enemy bullet, he shifted his carbine to his left hand," read a War Department press release about the engagement. "(Chilson) killed two of the enemy before he ran out of ammunition. When a third enemy soldier tried to make his getaway, Sgt. Chilson pursued him, clubbed him into unconsciousness with the butt of his carbine, and took him prisoner. Then, his job finished, he fainted from loss of blood." Chilson would later receive his third Distinguished Service Cross for these acts of extraordinary gallantry under fire.

At a White House ceremony on December 6, 1945, President Truman pinned seven combat decorations on Chilson's chest. No American had ever received so many high-ranking awards at one time. There were three awards of the Distinguished Service Cross, two of the Silver Star medal, one Legion of Merit, and one Bronze Star Medal. Said Truman at the time, "This is the most remarkable set of citations I have ever seen. . . . For any one of these, this young man is entitled to all the country has to offer. . . . This ought to be worth a Medal of Honor."

Chilson did not receive the nation's highest award for valor, but he finished World War II with nearly every other form of recognition the nation could bestow. A fellow soldier in the 45th Infantry Division called him "a fighting machine."

After the war Chilson left active duty and worked for a time as a chemical laboratory assistant in Malvern, Pennsylvania. But he missed the Army and reenlisted in November 1947. He served another seventeen years until retiring as a master sergeant in 1964.

Chilson and his family apparently believed Truman's words about the Medal of Honor. Subsequent investigation showed that Chilson's superior, Lt. Col. Louis K. Hennington Jr., commander of the 179th Infantry Regiment, had, in fact, recommended Chilson for the Medal of Honor on August 3, 1945. But the Army disapproved the recommendation in August 1946, and the result was that Chilson received three awards of the Distinguished Service Cross. Although the Army—urged by Chilson's family and friends—reopened his case in April 1947, the result was the same. As late as the 1980s Chilson's family tried to persuade the Army to award him the Medal of Honor. Their last attempt, requesting relief from the Army Board for Correction of Military Records, also did not succeed.

Chilson died in 1981 at the age of sixty-one and is interred at Mountain View Memorial Park in Tacoma.[44]

Joseph T. Dawson: Purple Heart—June 6, 1944

Joseph Turner Dawson was shot in the leg as he crossed Omaha Beach at Normandy to assault an enemy strongpoint.

During the initial landing on Omaha Beach, Dawson "disembarked under a hail of enemy machine gun and rifle fire and, with the utmost calmness, proceeded to organize a large group of men who were floundering near their bullet-ridden craft and led them ashore."

When Dawson reached dry ground, however, he discovered that his company was pinned down by aimed fire from three German machine guns located beyond a minefield. With no regard for his own well-being, Dawson "moved from his position of cover on to the minefield" so that he deliberately drew the enemy fire. Although he was wounded in the leg by a bullet, this "heroic diversion" allowed Dawson's men to move freely. Once they were in position, Dawson led a successful attack against the enemy stronghold. In addition to the Purple Heart for his injured leg, Dawson also received the Distinguished Service Cross for his extraordinary heroism.[45]

Annie G. Fox: Purple Heart—December 7, 1941

Annie G. Fox, an Army nurse and lieutenant, was the first female recipient of the Purple Heart in World War II. She did not receive the decoration for having been wounded in action. Rather, Fox's Purple Heart was for "outstanding performance of duty and meritorious acts of extraordinary fidelity." According to the citation for her award, "Lt. Fox, in an exemplary manner, performed her duties as head Nurse of the Station Hospital. . . . In addition she administered anesthesia to patients during the heaviest part of the bombardment, assisted in dressing the wounded, taught civilian volunteer nurses to make dressings, and worked ceaselessly with coolness and efficiency, and her fine example of

Maj. Gen. Robert T. Frederick received an unprecedented eight Purple Hearts during World War II. No other American has been awarded so many Purple Hearts in the course of a single conflict. (U.S. Army)

calmness, courage and leadership was of great benefit to the morale of all with whom she came in contact."

Fox was presented her Purple Heart on October 26, 1942, at Hickam Field, Hawaii.[46]

Robert T. Frederick: Purple Hearts—December 5, 1943; January 4, 1944; January 6, 1944; June 3, 1944; June 4, 1944; June 4, 1944; June 4, 1944; and August 15, 1944

Robert Tyron "Bob" Frederick holds the record for the most Purple Hearts, as he was wounded in action eight times during World War II and was awarded the Purple Heart with seven oak leaf clusters. He received an unprecedented three Purple Hearts on the single day of June 4, 1944.

Born in San Francisco on March 14, 1907, Frederick spent a year at Staunton Military Academy in Virginia before entering the U.S. Military Academy in 1924. After graduating from West Point in 1928, Frederick was commissioned as a second lieutenant in the Coast Artillery Corps and spent the next ten years in a variety of locations, including Fort Scott, San Francisco; Fort Amador, Panama Canal Zone; Fort Leavenworth, Kansas; and Fort Shafter, Hawaii.

After a promotion to major in February 1941, Frederick was assigned to the War Plans Division of the Army General Staff as a staff officer, and he reported for duty in Washington, D.C., in September. After being promoted to lieutenant colonel in February 1942, Frederick was selected to create, command, and train a brigade-sized unit of American and Canadian troops that would attack strategic targets in German-occupied Norway.

This commando unit, named the First Special Service Force, was activated at Fort Harrison outside of Helena, Montana, and ultimately consisted of about two thousand highly trained, exceptionally well-conditioned parachute infantrymen. But, by the time Frederick's unit was ready for combat, the mission it had prepared for was cancelled.

The First Special Service Force did, however, take part in the August 15, 1943, landings at Kiska in the Aleutians before deploying first to French Algeria and then Naples, Italy, in November.

In January 1944 Frederick was promoted to brigadier general, and that same month he and the First Special Service Force earned accolades for their fighting prowess at Monte la Difensa, where the soldiers scaled the 3,120-foot-high promontory to attack German defensive positions on the summit. In February, Frederick landed with his brigade at Anzio, where his unit eventually anchored the Allied right flank and earned the moniker "The Devil's Brigade."

Frederick had previously been wounded in Italy on December 5, 1943, January 4, 1944, and January 6, 1944. As he and the First Special Service Force fought near Rome, Frederick was wounded a fourth time on June 3, when "shrapnel whizzed through the left collar of his shirt, ripping out a two inch gash at the base of his neck."[47]

The next day, despite heavy fighting against the Germans, Frederick and his men were the first Allied troops to enter Rome, but not before Frederick was wounded three more times. He was struck by bullets in his thighs and right arm but, despite these serious injuries, refused to be evacuated to a hospital. Frederick's combat injuries on June 4 resulted in the award of an unprecedented three Purple Hearts in one day.[48] In addition to these three Purple Hearts, Frederick also received the Distinguished Service Cross—his second—for extraordinary heroism in the fighting around Rome.

Frederick received his eighth—and final—Purple Heart on August 15, 1944, six days after he had pinned on his second star. On that day Frederick, then in command of the American–British 1st Airborne Task Force, parachuted into France near Saint-Tropez. Frederick and his paratroopers successfully blocked German forces from reaching the French coastline, and this ensured successful Allied landings.

Frederick took command of the 45th Infantry Division in the winter of 1945 and led that unit until the end of the fighting in Europe in May 1945. After a lengthy period of recuperation at Walter Reed Hospital in Washington, D.C., Frederick returned to Europe to command U.S. forces in Austria before returning to the United States to command the 4th Infantry Division and then the 6th Infantry Division from 1949 to 1951.

Frederick returned to Europe in 1951 to command the Joint U.S. Military Aid Group, Greece. He retired in 1952 from the Army and died in November 1970.

While one other individual, Col. David Hackworth, also received eight Purple Hearts for wounds received in action in Korea and Vietnam, no one is likely to equal, much less surpass, the number of Purple Hearts awarded to Bob Frederick for a single war.

Frederick also will be remembered for helping to design the famous V-42 combat knife, which became the trademark weapon of the soldiers in the First Special Service Force. The profile of this knife is featured on the teal blue and yellow colored shoulder sleeve insignia worn by today's U.S. Army Special Forces.

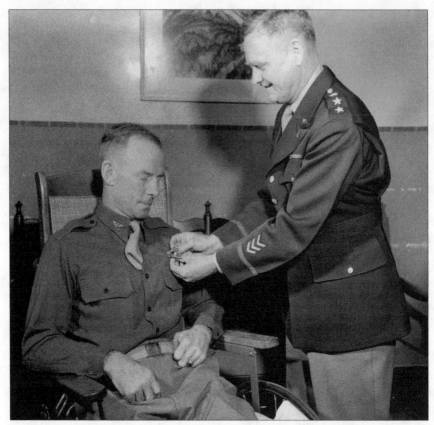

Col. Russell P. "Red" Reeder (shown here being decorated with the Bronze Star Medal) was wounded in action when shrapnel from a German artillery shell shattered his leg in June 1944. (U.S. Army)

Audie Murphy: Purple Hearts—September 14–15, 1944; October 1944; and January 25, 1945

See chapter 9, "Celebrities: Artists and Entertainers, Politicians, Athletes, and Other Public Figures."

Russell P. Reeder: Purple Heart—June 10, 1944

Russell Potter "Red" Reeder was wounded in action in Normandy when shrapnel from a German artillery shell shattered his leg.

Known as Red for the color of his hair, Reeder was born into an Army family at Fort Leavenworth in 1902. In 1913, when he was eleven years old, young Red received the U.S. Treasury's Life Saving Medal for rescuing a child from drowning off the coast of Maine.

After entering the U.S. Military Academy in 1920, Cadet Reeder quickly emerged as an outstanding football and baseball player. So great were his throwing and batting talents that, after graduating in 1926, then–Second Lieutenant Reeder took a leave of absence from the Army to try out with John J. McGraw's New York Giants.

Reeder made the cuts and was offered $5,000 a year to play professional baseball—a very generous salary when compared with the $143 a month he made as an Army officer. But Reeder loved the Army more than he liked the idea of resigning his commission to play ball, and so, no doubt with some regret, he returned to active duty.

At the outbreak of World War II Reeder was a colonel serving in Washington, D.C., on the War Department's staff. In late 1943 he noticed how more and more soldiers in the Army Air Forces proudly wore the ribbon of the Air Medal on their uniforms. This medal, which had been created in May 1942, was being liberally awarded to officer and enlisted aircrew members for meritorious service while in "aerial flight." Realizing that these Air Medals were boosting morale, Reeder was convinced that a "ground medal" counterpart should be created for infantrymen and others fighting the enemy on the ground.

In his off-duty time Reeder prepared a staff study and took it directly to Lt. Gen. Leslie McNair, who was then in charge of the Army's ground forces. McNair agreed with Reeder that the proposed medal was needed, threw his support behind the idea, and got Army Chief of Staff George Marshall to speak personally with President Roosevelt about it. The result was that, in February 1944, President Roosevelt signed an order creating the Bronze Star Medal.

In March 1944 Reeder left the Pentagon to take command of the 12th Infantry Regiment. That unit landed in Normandy on June 6, and Red Reeder was one of the first on the Utah Beach. The next day, when he noticed that a group of his men were hesitant about crossing an open field because of German small-arms fire, Reeder boldly walked into the open with complete disregard for his personal safety. The men immediately got up, followed him across the field, and, thus, flanked the Germans and caused them to withdraw. For this and other examples of personal bravery under fire, General Eisenhower awarded Reeder the Distinguished Service Cross—the first such award to an officer for extraordinary heroism in Normandy.

Three days later, on June 10, Reeder was hit by a German 88-mm shell. Years later, he vividly described what happened:

It shattered my ankle and almost cut off my leg above the knee. I screamed. First Lt. William Mills, although wounded by shell fragments that had pierced his helmet, gave me an injection of morphine from a paratrooper's aid kit. He whipped off his belt and put a tourniquet on my leg. His blood dripped on my face and uniform. A jeep rolled by, carrying four wounded men on stretchers. Two soldiers removed one of the men to make room for me. The morphine was making me heroic. I said, "No, you don't. Come back for me." The driver said, "Sir, this man's a Nazi." "Lay the son-of-a-bitch in the shade," I said.[49]

Reeder survived World War II and left active duty in 1947, when the Army retired all its physically disabled officers. He took a job at West Point as an assistant athletic director and subsequently had a distinguished career coaching football.

Reeder also wrote more than thirty fiction and nonfiction books. One book became a television series and another became a movie called *The Long Gray Line*. His autobiography *Born at Reveille* remains one of the best soldier's memoirs ever published. Red died in 1998 at the age of ninety-five. All in all, Reeder was a remarkable soldier and an Army hero.

George Sakato: Purple Heart—October 30, 1944

George "Machine Gun Joe" Sakato was wounded by shrapnel from enemy mortars while fighting in the Vosges Mountains of eastern France on October 30, 1944.

Drafted in March 1944 Sakato did basic training at Fort Blanding, Florida, and additional training at Camp Shelby, Mississippi, before shipping out from Newport News, Virginia, to an assignment with the all-Japanese American 442nd Regimental Combat Team.

In late October 1944 then-Private Sakato was serving in E Company of the 2nd Battalion and was near Biffontaine, France, in the dense Vosges woods. He and his fellow soldiers were part of a larger fight to rescue the "Lost Battalion" of the 141st Regiment, which was a unit of the 36th (Texas) Infantry Division. This unit had been trapped by German forces and was surrounded for seven days until the 442nd finally broke through enemy lines and rescued their beleaguered comrades.

Before that occurred, however, Sakato had made a heroic one-man charge up a hill on October 29. After his good friend was killed by an enemy bullet, Sakato jumped out of his foxhole. "Mad as hell and crying," he grabbed his

Thompson submachine gun and, while firing from his hips, "hollered to the rest of the platoon to come on."[50] Sakato's assault inspired his unit to follow him, and they overran the German positions on Hill 617, ultimately taking thirty-four prisoners. As for Sakato, he later used an enemy rifle and P38 pistol to stop an organized enemy counterattack, killing twelve Germans, wounding two others, and capturing four. Sakato was later awarded the Distinguished Service Cross for his heroism on October 29, 1944. This award was upgraded to a Medal of Honor in 2001.

On October 30, 1944, Sakato was hit by shrapnel in the back. He later learned that "his life had been saved by his overcoat, which he had folded and stuffed into his backpack. . . . It had absorbed the shock of exploding shrapnel that otherwise would have sliced through his spine."[51] Sakato spent months in hospitals and clinics in England and the United States, recovering from his combat wounds.

S. Donald Singlestad: Purple Heart—April 27–May 1, 1943

Sylvester Donald "Don" Singlestad survived fierce fighting in Tunisia in 1943, where he was wounded in action. He was later decorated for extraordinary heroism in fighting near Monte Casino, Italy, in 1944.

Born on May 9, 1917, in Emmons, Minnesota, Singlestad grew up in relative comfort, as his father was a farmer and small businessman. But the family lost everything in the Great Depression of the 1930s, and Singlestad dropped out of school in seventh grade to help his father plow the family's three-hundred-acre farm. It was to no avail, however, as the local bank foreclosed on the farm, and Singlestad's father went to work for a trucking company while his mother took a job as a cook in a local hotel.

When he was twenty-one years old, Singlestad enlisted in the Minnesota National Guard and became an infantryman. After the Japanese attack on Pearl Harbor, he and Guardsmen from Iowa, Minnesota, and the Dakotas were mobilized as the 34th Infantry Division. The unit earned its nickname of "Red Bull" while in Italy after Germans saw soldiers wearing the unit's unusual shoulder patch—a red steer skull on a black background—and began calling the Northern Plains soldiers Red Bulls.

In January 1942 Singlestad deployed to Ireland with elements of the 34th and began training for the invasion of North Africa. He subsequently landed with Company F of the 2nd Battalion, 135th Infantry Regiment at Algiers and was taken prisoner by the French. Luckily, this imprisonment lasted only about a week, since the French soon surrendered to the Allies.

Then-Capt. Charles A. Wirt was decorated with a Distinguished Service Cross, a Silver Star, a Bronze Star Medal, and two Purple Hearts during World War II. (U.S. Army)

Singlestad trained in Tunisia and participated in the fighting at Faid Pass, Fondouk Pass, and the famous Battle of Hill 609, where he was badly wounded by shrapnel from exploding enemy grenades and spent his 26th birthday in the hospital.

Singlestad next saw combat at Salerno in September 1943, where he waded ashore as part of the third wave of the amphibious landing. In a recent interview, Singlestad explained that he went behind the lines five days later. "I had a Tommy gun (Thompson machine gun) which fired .45 caliber bullets.... I snuck up on a German mortar crew and blew them away.... I then turned the mortar around and started lobbing shells on the Germans."

During hard fighting against the Germans at Monte Casino the following February, Singlestad and one of his squads were surrounded and cut off from the rest of Company F. Then–Technical Sergeant Singlestad fought his way free by moving toward and through the Germans, throwing hand grenades as he advanced. He personally killed at least six enemy troops and wounded several others. Then, when he was out of ammunition, Singlestad used his rifle as a club against the Germans who had surrounded him. According to official records, when Singlestad came "face to face with two Germans, he felled them both with his rifle butt, dived over a rock wall, seized another rifle and continued his advance to his company command past." He subsequently reorganized his platoon and directed artillery fire to repulse an enemy attack. For this extraordinary heroism, Lt. Gen. Mark W. Clark decorated Singlestad with the Distinguished Service Cross in June 1944.

Earlier that same month, shortly before American troops entered Rome, Singlestad had dressed in civilian clothes and gone behind German lines once more to enter Rome with three Italian partisans and an American radioman. Their mission was to set up communications in order to direct air and artillery fire if Rome did not surrender. For this mission, the Italian government later decorated Singlestad with the Italian War Cross for Valor.

After the war Singlestad returned to civilian life. He was successful in the restaurant business and also worked as a sales manager for a large wool company. Today, Singlestad lives in retirement on a lake in Minnesota. He is ninety-one years old.[52]

Charles A. Wirt: Purple Hearts—September 19, 1944, and October 20, 1944

Charles Alvin "Charley" Wirt was twice wounded in action in France during World War II. In addition to two Purple Hearts, he received the Distinguished

Service Cross for extraordinary heroism, the Silver Star for gallantry in action, and the Bronze Star Medal for heroism against the enemy.

Born in Cookeville, Tennessee, on April 16, 1920, Wirt graduated from high school in 1937 and attended Vanderbilt University for one year. But he had always wanted to attend West Point and had enlisted in the Tennessee National Guard while in high school and reached the rank of sergeant. His Guard status allowed Wirt to compete for a presidential appointment to the academy. He was successful and entered the U.S. Military Academy in August 1939.

After graduating in 1943, then–Second Lieutenant Wirt completed infantry officer basic at Ft. Benning and then joined the 66th Infantry Division as a heavy weapons platoon leader. After a year of stateside training with that unit, Wirt volunteered for overseas duty and, in March 1944, joined First Army Group headquarters in England.

After D-day he requested a transfer to a combat unit and joined the 16th Infantry Regiment in Normandy in August 1944. Wirt's official military records show that he was wounded in action—and received two Purple Hearts—in the "vicinity of Muensterbusch, Germany" on September 19 and October 20, 1944. An obituary published in *Assembly* in October 1989 states that "he was wounded twice at Aachen, but not evacuated."[53]

Wirt repeatedly showed tremendous courage and skill in battle while serving as a company commander of Company G of the 16th Infantry in the Ruhr to Rhine operation. On March 1, 1945, when one of his platoons was "impeded by an intense small-arms concentration," Wirt "fearlessly moved across perilous terrain to the unit and, skillfully directing accurate fire, silenced an enemy strongpoint." Wirt later received the Bronze Star Medal for heroism for this gallantry under fire.[54]

Six days later, on March 7, 1945, then–First Lieutenant Wirt was leading his unit near Brenig, Germany, when one of his platoons was held up by an intense small-arms and antiaircraft barrage. His citation for the Silver Star explains that Wirt "fearlessly moved across perilous terrain, summoned friendly tanks, and skillfully guided them to an exposed vantage point . . . with utter disregard for his own safety." Wirt "courageously led a successful attack against the foe and seized an important objective."[55]

On March 10 Wirt's regiment seized and secured Bonn, Germany, shortly after the Ludendorff Bridge across the Rhine at Remagen, Germany, had been captured intact. The 16th Infantry then crossed the Rhine to enlarge the bridgehead at Remagen, only to encounter repeated and fierce German counterattacks.

Two weeks later, on March 24, 1945, then-Captain Wirt was leading Company G as part of a larger attack by the 16th Infantry against German positions. The battle climaxed when Wirt, who was defending Giesbach with his company, successfully held the town against the Germans despite suffering horrendous losses. As his citation for the Distinguished Service Cross explains, when a German counterattack "forced two platoons of his company out of their defensive positions, Capt. Wirt, moving under intense fire from small arms, tank and self-propelled weapons, reorganized these units and led them back into position. Ignoring the increasing danger from the close range of enemy fire, he advanced to within a short distance of an enemy self-propelled weapon and put it out of action with a rifle grenade, killing the five Germans who constituted the crew."

Wirt then displayed truly extraordinary heroism since, as the Germans threatened to overrun his defenses, Wirt ordered his men to take cover while he supplied protective fire, killing ten more of the enemy, and then called artillery fire onto his own position. After a three hour artillery barrage, Wirt "led his reinforced company in a brilliant counter-attack, successfully driving the enemy back with heavy losses, and securing the flank of an entire battalion."[56]

At the end of fighting in Germany, Wirt became the executive officer of 1st Battalion, 16th Infantry and moved to Berlin for occupation duties. After returning to the United States, Wirt was assigned to Fort Benning, where he completed airborne and pathfinder training. Amazingly, he then entered Army aviation training and qualified as both a fixed-wing pilot and a helicopter pilot in 1949 before returning to complete Jumpmaster School and qualify as a senior parachutist in 1950.

During the Korean War, Wirt commanded 2nd Battalion, 38th Infantry, 2nd Infantry Division; 2nd Battalion, 17th Infantry, 7th Infantry Division; and 3rd Battalion, 17th Infantry, 7th Infantry Division. From the Korean peninsula, he transferred directly to Europe to command the U.S. Seventh Army's aviation training center.

Wirt returned to the United States and Fort Leavenworth, where he was involved in Lt. Gen. Hamilton H. Howze's study group examining how the Army could best use helicopters and fixed-wing aircraft in future military operations.

Wirt retired in 1963 as a lieutenant colonel with twenty years of active duty. He worked for General Electric until retiring again in 1970. Wirt died on August 14, 1981, at the age of sixty-one. He is interred at the West Point cemetery.

Col. Russell M. Blair received his first Purple Heart in World War II. He received two more during the Korean War. (U.S. Army)

KOREAN WAR (1950–1953)

Russell M. Blair: Purple Hearts—January 18, 1945; September 21, 1950; and March 2, 1951

Russell M. Blair was wounded twice in Korea, and he was awarded a first and second oak leaf cluster to his first Purple Heart, which he had received for combat wounds in Burma on January 18, 1945.

Born on November 2, 1915, Blair started his Army career in 1934, when he enlisted in the horse cavalry and was stationed with the 13th Cavalry Regiment at Fort Riley, Kansas.

When Blair made sergeant, the Army sent him to the staff of Norwich University, where he taught map reading to the freshman class. When the United States entered World War II, Blair returned to Fort Riley and was commissioned as a cavalry officer. Then–Second Lieutenant Blair became a troop commander with the all-black 10th Cavalry on the Mexican border; American leaders feared that the Japanese might try to invade the United States from Mexico.

Blair later earned a promotion to first lieutenant and then deployed to Burma, where he volunteered for duty in a reconnaissance platoon in the 5307th Composite Unit, which was better known as "Merrill's Marauders." These combat-hardened volunteers under Brig. Gen. Frank Merrill conducted operations against the Japanese army in the jungles of Burma.

On June 13, 1944, when a patrol he was leading was pinned down by a Japanese machine-gun emplacement, Blair crawled alone to the rear of the enemy and killed the gun crew with his carbine. Three days later, Blair crawled under heavy fire to rescue two wounded members of his patrol.

Those two acts of heroism resulted in Lt. Gen. Joseph W. Stillwell approving a battlefield promotion to captain for Blair and awarding Blair the Distinguished Service Cross. In a 2007 letter to the author, Blair wrote that he remembered Stillwell arriving at Merrill's headquarters in Myitkyina, Burma, pinning "the DSC on my shirt" and having "his aide take off my lieut. bars and replace them with captains bars."

After World War II, Blair attended the Command and General Staff College at Fort Leavenworth and the Armor School at Fort Knox, Tennessee. He was in Tokyo when the Korean War broke out in June 1950.

On September 14, 1950, Blair was in Korea in command of 3rd Battalion, 24th Infantry Regiment, an all-black unit in the 25th Infantry Division. According to Army records, Blair and his men were near Haman, Korea, when one of his companies lost all but one of its officers. Realizing the unit's need for leadership, Blair joined the company and, until mid-morning September 15, inspired the unit in several attacks. He "led one platoon in a successful counterattack upon its old position and then covered its withdrawal when the position because untenable."

Blair then organized a perimeter defense of between forty and fifty men and encouraged the soldiers to hold "despite four banzai attacks by over four hundred enemy troops until almost all of their ammunition had been expended." He then covered the disengagement of the company and led the men in fighting their way out of an ambush. This ensured that the main body of troops and the wounded were able to withdraw to safety. According to official records, "the sight of the battalion commander facing death with them ... inspired the reluctant to stay and fight with new-found determination."[57]

For his extraordinary heroism that day, Blair was awarded a second Distinguished Service Cross in January 1951. He also received an oak leaf cluster to his Purple Heart for wounds received in action on September 21, 1950.

Blair was wounded a third time about six months later, on March 3, 1951. He retired from active duty in November 1954 with slightly more than twenty years of active duty. Blair then began a second career in public relations, working for General Motors as a public affairs officer. His knowledge of horses and his own riding skills later resulted in his employment by the New York Military Academy as a riding master.

Despite his retirement from active duty, Blair was not forgotten by the Army. He was inducted into the Army Ranger Hall of Fame in 2003. Blair died at a hospital at Cornwall-on-Hudson, New York, in April 2008 at the age of ninety-two.[58]

David H. Hackworth: Purple Hearts—February 6, 1951; May 31, 1951; September 27, 1951; November 4, 1951; February 12, 1969; March 21, 1969; March 25, 1969; and May 11, 1969

David Haskell Hackworth was wounded four times in combat in Korea and four times in combat in Vietnam. Consequently, he received the Purple Heart with seven oak leaf clusters. This is a record Hackworth shares with fellow soldier Robert T. Frederick (see the World War II profiles above). For more details on Hackworth, see chapter 9, "Celebrities: Artists and Entertainers, Politicians, Athletes, and Other Public Figures."

Lewis L. Millet: Purple Heart—February 7, 1951

Lewis Lee "Red" Millet was wounded by grenade fragments while leading a bayonet charge against strongly held Chinese positions on February 7, 1951.

Born on December 15, 1920, in Mechanic Falls, Maine, Millet joined the Massachusetts National Guard at age seventeen. In 1940 he enlisted in the Army Air Corps, where he was trained as a machine gunner. But, after hearing President Roosevelt say in October 1941 that no Americans would fight on foreign soil, twenty-one-year-old Millett deserted the Army. There was a war on in Europe, and Millett wanted to be a part of it, so he hitchhiked north to Canada and joined the Canadian Army.

By the time Millett sailed for England, America had declared war on Germany, so Millett went to the American Embassy in London and asked to be transferred back to the U.S. Army. In August 1942 he was in Ireland with the 27th Armored Field Artillery, 1st Armored Division.

In November 1942 Millett participated in the Allied invasion of North Africa and saw combat against the Germans in Medjez-el-Bab, Tunisia. He later fought in Italy, where his desertion caught up with him. As Millett explained when interviewed by author Larry Smith for the book *Beyond Glory*, he was court-martialed, found guilty of desertion, and fined $52. "Then, a week later, they made me a second lieutenant in a battlefield commission," Millet said.

After World War II Millett joined the Maine National Guard before returning to active duty in 1949. He was assigned to the 27th Infantry Regiment "Wolfhounds" and sent to Japan. When the Korean War broke out on June 25, 1950, Millett was in Korea. He served as an artillery observer on the ground and in the air. Six months later, then-Captain Millett took command of Company E of the 27th Infantry Regiment.

On February 7, 1951, in the vicinity of Soam-Ni, Millett led his company in an attack against strongly held Chinese positions. He saw that one of his platoons was pinned down by small-arms, automatic, and antitank fire. Placing himself at the head of his two remaining platoons, Millett ordered his soldiers to fix bayonets and led the assault up the hill against the enemy. Millett bayoneted two enemy soldiers and, according to official accounts, "boldly continued on, throwing grenades, clubbing and bayoneting the enemy, while urging his men forward by shouting encouragement." Then, despite having been "wounded by grenade fragments," Millett refused to be evacuated until the objective was taken.

The American charge so demoralized the Chinese that the enemy soldiers who were not killed fled in wild disorder. Historian S. L. A. Marshall later wrote that Millett's bayonet attack "was the most complete bayonet charge by American troops since Cold Harbor" in the Civil War. The location of the 1951 attack, Hill 180, is today part of Osan Air Base, South Korea.[59]

For his gallantry in action that day, Millett received the Medal of Honor, as well as the Purple Heart for his wounds.

After the Korean War Millett attended Ranger School at Fort Benning and, while with the 101st Airborne Division, founded the Army Recondo School, a combat-realistic, small-unit training program for reconnaissance commandos. Millet later served in Vietnam, where he helped establish ranger and commando programs for the South Vietnamese Army.

Millett retired as a colonel in 1973 and settled in California. He died November 14, 2009, at a veterans hospital in California. He had congestive heart failure.[60]

Leonard F. Stegman: Purple Heart—May 20, 1951

Leonard Fernando Stegman was serving as a Roman Catholic chaplain in Korea when he was wounded by enemy rifle fire on May 20, 1951.

Born in Offerle, Kansas, in May 1917, Stegman was one of eighteen children. He graduated from Mary Immaculate Clericate in Garrison, New York, in 1940 and then studied theology for four more years at St. Anthony Seminary in Marathon, Wisconsin. Stegman received a direct commission in the Army Reserve in April 1948, went on active duty in 1950 and completed the officer basic course at the Army Chaplain School at Fort Jackson, South Carolina.

In early November 1950 Stegman deployed to Korea and was assigned to serve as a chaplain with the 15th Infantry Regiment, which was a part of the 3rd Infantry Division. He had only been in country about ten days when an act of selfless heroism earned him the Silver Star.

On November 20 Stegman voluntarily accompanied a battalion that had the mission of clearing out an enemy assembly area near Majon-ni. When elements of the battalion engaged a numerically superior enemy in a firefight and a company commander radioed for a litter jeep to evacuate his wounded, Stegman unhesitatingly volunteered to accompany the jeep to give aid and comfort to the wounded.

He and the occupants of the jeep then proceeded under intense enemy fire to rescue one wounded man. Learning about two more wounded soldiers, Stegman ran another two hundred yards under intense fire to rescue those wounded men.

Five months later, on May 20, 1951, Stegman received his second Silver Star and a Purple Heart. According to the citation for Stegman's Silver Star, the 15th Infantry was attacking up a hill in the face of intense enemy fire. As more and more soldiers were wounded, Stegman realized that additional men were needed to help with evacuating them. Consequently, he "voluntarily left the comparative safety of the battalion aid station and, fearlessly moving forward, assisted a wounded soldier lying in an exposed position." Stegman "dashed across" open terrain to pick the man up and then carried him to a covered position. After rescuing that soldier, Stegman "utilized the protective covering offered by a friendly tank to rescue several other stricken infantrymen." During the rescues, Stegman received a gunshot wound.

In July 1970 Stegman deployed to Vietnam, where he served as a chaplain at the headquarters of U.S. Army, Vietnam. After returning to the United States in July 1971, Stegman was assigned to Third Army, with which he served until 1973. Stegman's last assignment was as a chaplain at the Army's Materiel Readiness Command. Although he was selected for promotion to brigadier general, Stegman declined. With twenty-seven years' active duty, he retired as a colonel in 1977. Stegman settled in Texas, where he was known as Father Len to all in the Archdiocese of San Antonio.[61]

VIETNAM, CAMBODIA, AND LAOS (1958–1975)

The Army awarded 220,521 Purple Hearts to U.S. soldiers and civilians wounded in Southeast Asia between July 1958 and April 1975.[62]

Barry D. Gasdek: Purple Hearts—September 21–22, 1968

Then-Captain Gasdek was wounded twice in Vietnam and awarded two Purple Hearts. His first combat injury occurred on September 21 or 22, 1968, when Gasdek was hit in the leg by shrapnel from a rocket-propelled grenade. His second Purple Heart resulted from a shrapnel wound to his back on September 22, 1968.

Born in Latrobe, Pennsylvania, Gasdek attended Indiana University, where he was an outstanding athlete and lettered four years in football, wrestling, and track. Gasdek had enrolled in the Army Reserve Officers' Training Corps (ROTC), and when he graduated in 1964, he was commissioned as a Regular Army infantry second lieutenant.

After completing training at Fort Benning, Gasdek was assigned to the 4th Armored Division in Bamberg, Germany. His next assignment was to

Vietnam, where he was a company commander and was twice wounded in combat. The citation for Gasdek's Distinguished Service Cross for extraordinary heroism explains how he received both wounds.

On September 21, Gasdek's company was near Duong Da when it came under intense enemy fire. To encourage his men, then-Captain Gasdek "exposed himself to the hail of bullets," fired his weapon, and hurled hand grenades at the enemy. When he learned that there was an armored cavalry troop nearby that could help him and his men, Gasdek took two men and went to direct the armored personnel carriers to the battle site. As he returned with the carriers, Gasdek and his soldiers came under accurate small-arms and mortar fire that wounded him in the leg.

Despite his painful injury, he continued on to his men and organized the evacuation of the wounded to the personnel carriers. The citation explains that Gasdek carried "the most seriously injured man on his back, crawled more than a hundred meters through a murderous barrage to the vehicles, and placed him in the medic track." Then Gasdek returned to the company to ensure that all the wounded had been evacuated and also to gather weapons and radios to keep the enemy from capturing that equipment.

When one of Gasdek's radio operators was killed and the other wounded, Gasdek administered first aid to the injured man and carried the radio equipment himself. He next directed helicopter fire to closer than twenty-five meters from his position, enabling his men to withdraw and establish a night location. The following morning Gasdek led an attack on the enemy, forcing the aggressors from the area. During this second engagement he received a shrapnel wound to his back but, again, refused evacuation to remain with his troops.[63]

After returning from Vietnam Gasdek remained on active duty. He served in a variety of assignments and locations, including Fort Benning; Fort Carson, Colorado; Fort Eustis, Virginia; Hawaii; and Korea. His last assignment was as a professor of military science at the University of Wyoming. Gasdek retired as a lieutenant colonel and lives in Wyoming.

David H. Hackworth: Purple Hearts—February 6, 1951; May 31, 1951; September 27, 1951; November 4, 1951; February 12, 1969; March 21, 1969; March 25, 1969; and May 11, 1969

For more details on Hackworth and his record number of Purple Hearts, see Chapter 9, "Celebrities: Artists and Entertainers, Politicians, Athletes, and Other Public Figures."

Robert C. Knight: Purple Hearts—June 1966, November 1967, and March 1968

Robert C. "Bob" Knight, who served as a helicopter assault pilot in Vietnam, received three awards of the Purple Heart as well as the Distinguished Service Cross for extraordinary heroism.

Born in Maine in 1939, Knight dropped out of high school and enlisted in the Maine National Guard at age sixteen. After six years as an enlisted soldier, including a time as a crew chief on then–Maj. Gen. William C. Westmoreland's helicopter at Fort Campbell, Knight attended Officer Candidate School and was commissioned in 1961. After attending helicopter school at Camp Walters, Texas, and Fort Rucker, Alabama, Knight joined the 1st Armored Division.

In July 1965 then–First Lieutenant Knight arrived in Vietnam and was assigned to the 101st Airborne Division. He then flew UH1H-B "Huey" helicopters out of Soc Trang airfield, located just south of the Mekong River near Can Tho. In June 1966, toward the end of his tour, Knight was flying a "reconnaissance by fire" mission south of Ca Mau.

While diving to make a rocket attack on a suspected enemy position, Knight's helicopter was hit by return fire that apparently severed the fore and aft control rod. As a result, Knight got no response when he tried to pull out of the dive, and his helicopter crashed into a swampy area. Knight was able to get his aircraft level just prior to impact, but his crew chief was killed. Knight and his copilot were able to walk out the front of the helicopter, which had been ripped open by the crash. Knight was badly hurt. An armor-piercing round was imbedded in his upper thigh, and he was medically evacuated to the United States.

A year later, in July 1967, then-Captain Knight returned to Vietnam and the same airfield to rejoin the same unit, which had been redesignated the 336th Assault Helicopter Company. Knight was in charge of a gunship platoon consisting of five Hueys. There were two American aviation units at Soc Trang, but no U.S. ground troops. All airfield perimeter security was the responsibility of a company of South Vietnamese soldiers.

Knight received a second Purple Heart in November 1967, when his airfield was being hit with 75-mm recoilless rounds. He ran from the billets to his helicopter, which was located on the runway approximately one hundred feet away. A round impacted behind Knight, and the concussion knocked him off his feet. He later received medical treatment for lacerations to his hands.

On January 31, 1968, Knight and his fellow Americans knew that an enemy attack was likely, as the Viet Cong had announced that they were canceling a previously agreed upon Lunar New Year cease-fire. So when about two thousand Viet Cong guerrillas launched a coordinated mortar and ground assault on the Soc Trang airfield and nearby city, Knight was ready.

As a hail of bullets struck all around him, Knight dashed to his gunship. Once airborne, he flew low over the enemy positions and located several weapons emplacements from which the Viet Cong were firing 75-mm recoilless rifles. Ignoring the huge volume of fire directed at him, Knight then attacked and destroyed several enemy positions with rockets and machine-gun fire.

In addition to this individual effort, Knight organized his platoon's five gunships in a team and directed their assaults. He made sure sufficient Hueys were in the air at all times. "My concern," said Knight in a recent interview with the author, "was that we would get hammered if too many of us landed at the same time to refuel or pick up more ammunition. So I kept four in the air at all times."

According to official Army records, as the siege on the airfield lifted at dawn, Knight was offered the chance to take a well-deserved rest. He refused and flew with his helicopter platoon toward the adjacent city, where the Viet Cong threatened to overrun vital military positions. Knight and his fellow pilots then used their rockets and machine guns to inflict heavy casualties and were a key factor in repelling the enemy offensive.

By the end of the battle, Knight had flown twenty-eight consecutive hours, and his efforts were recognized with the award of the Distinguished Service Cross.

Knight received his third Purple Heart in March 1968, when, in response to a 75-mm gun attack on his airfield, Knight led a fire team in aerial attacks on the enemy. After suppressing the enemy's fire, Knight returned to the airfield to rearm and refuel. He remembered:

> I was letting the aircraft idle to cool down the exhaust and had my door open, my seat belt off, removed my helmet, and turned off the radios. I had not removed my chest protector. A 75-mm round impacted at a 45-degree angle forward of the helicopter. My door slammed shut, the altimeter spun from zero to over two thousand feet and the helicopter was showered with shrapnel. (Over 40 hit the aircraft). One piece of shrapnel came through the windshield, hit my chest protector and was deflected sideways through my left shoulder muscle. My crew chief exited to the rear of the helicopter and was hit in the buttocks with a piece of shrapnel![64]

After Vietnam, Knight commanded the Army recruiting battalion in New Hampshire. From 1980 to 1982 he also commanded the 1st Battalion, 66th Armor Regiment at Fort Hood, Texas. This seemed only right, as the unit's moniker, the "Iron Knights," matched perfectly with their commander's last name. Knight retired as a lieutenant colonel in 1984 and lives today in Florida.

George S. Patton IV, Purple Heart, September 1968

See chapter 8, "Families: Brothers, Fathers and Sons, and Husbands and Wives."

H. Norman Schwarzkopf: Purple Hearts—January 1966 and May 28, 1970

Herbert Norman Schwarzkopf was twice wounded in Vietnam. He received his first Purple Heart in 1966 while serving as an advisor to a South Vietnamese airborne brigade. His second Purple Heart came in 1970 while Schwarzkopf was in command of an infantry battalion in the 23rd Infantry Division.

Born in New Jersey in August 1934, Schwarzkopf entered West Point in 1952 and was commissioned as an infantry lieutenant when he graduated in 1956. He served two years as a paratrooper in the 101st Airborne Division and two years in Berlin before returning to Fort Benning. After a year at the infantry school, then-Captain Schwarzkopf enrolled at the University of Southern California and, after receiving a master's degree in mechanical engineering, was assigned to teach at West Point in the summer of 1964. He volunteered for Vietnam in 1965 and was assigned as an advisor.[65]

In late January 1966, while riding in an armored personnel carrier in an operation on the Bong Son plains located north of Qui Nhon, then-Major Schwarzkopf was wounded by machine-gun fire in his left arm and face.[66]

Schwarzkopf's second Purple Heart–recognized injury occurred under very unusual circumstances. Back in Vietnam in 1969 as the commander of 1st Battalion, 6th Infantry, 23rd Infantry Division, Schwarzkopf heard that soldiers from his unit had entered a minefield and that one had been badly injured. Schwarzkopf immediately flew to the scene and stayed behind with the wounded trooper after his helicopter lifted off. When another soldier stepped on a mine and began to scream uncontrollably, Schwarzkopf feared that "his cries were causing panic among the troops and that . . . they might break and run."[67]

Schwarzkopf then entered the minefield "one slow step at a time" and, reaching the young trooper, "lay down on him to keep him from thrashing."

But then the artillery liaison officer, who was twenty yards away, stepped on a mine. It blew off the man's right arm and leg, and Schwarzkopf was wounded in the chest from shrapnel.[68]

After 1970 Schwarzkopf served in increasingly important assignments, including command of a brigade in the 9th Infantry Division. He also commanded the 24th Infantry Division at Fort Stewart, Georgia, and I Corps at Fort Lewis before receiving his fourth star and an appointment as commander-in-chief of the U.S. Central Command, Tampa, Florida.

When the United States launched Operation Desert Shield to prevent Iraq from invading Saudi Arabia, Schwarzkopf's staff planned and carried out the deployment of some 765,000 troops from twenty-eight countries, including 541,000 Americans. When Operation Desert Storm began in 1991, Schwarzkopf, as commanding general of the Coalition Forces, followed up a six-week aerial bombardment of Iraq with a ground campaign that began with an amphibious landing in Kuwait. The bulk of Coalition Forces then advanced quickly along the enemy's west flank, and, with their communications and supply lines in disarray, the Iraqis accepted a cease-fire after one hundred hours of ground combat.

For his superb performance in the Persian Gulf, Schwarzkopf later received the Presidential Medal of Freedom and a Congressional Gold Medal. He retired in 1991.

Morris G. Worley: Purple Heart—January 20–21, 1967

Morris G. Worley was wounded by small-arms fire in the face, side, and right arm while fighting the North Vietnamese on January 20–21, 1967.

Then–Sergeant First Class Worley was serving as a Special Forces advisor to a joint American–Vietnamese platoon when he was wounded. At the time, he and his unit were on a combat patrol deep in enemy-held territory. When the point squad he was leading suddenly came under enemy fire, Worley "fearlessly charged the hostile positions, firing his rifle as he ran." These bold actions inspired his fellow soldiers, who assaulted and overcame the insurgents, and captured one North Vietnamese Army (NVA) soldier.

After Worley's unit moved another seventy-five meters down the jungle trail, it was attacked again. According to official records, Worley "dauntlessly moved through a hail of bullets and laid down a devastating base of fire to allow the squad to reach cover." Although Worley had expended all his ammunition by that point, he saw an enemy soldier hiding in the brush a few meters to his front. "Unmindful of the dangers and armed only with a bowie knife . . . Worley darted through the undergrowth and singlehandedly captured the insurgent."

The next day Worley volunteered once again to serve as point man and, while serving in that capacity, "alertly detected an ambush and initiated a fire fight which killed two enemy soldiers."Then,

contemptuous of the intense hostile fire, Sergeant Worley remained on the trail and engaged the North Vietnamese positions. Even when three comrades were killed at his side, he continued to fight until his rifle was shot away and he was severely wounded in the face, side and right arm. Dazed, but undaunted, he drew his pistol with his left hand, emptied the magazine at the enemy, and then threw a grenade which silenced the hostile position. Despite his painful wounds, Sergeant Worley refused to be carried and walked 275 meters to the landing zone where the unit was extracted. His intrepid actions broke three enemy traps, saved many lives and enabled the team to complete its vital mission.[69]

Worley retired from the Army as a sergeant major and lives today in Chapel Hill, North Carolina.

KOREA (1976–1984)

Mark T. Barrett: Purple Heart—August 18, 1976
Arthur G. Bonifas: Purple Heart—August 18, 1976
Capt. Arthur Bonifas and 1st Lt. Mark Barrett were killed by axe-wielding North Korean security guards at Panmunjom, Korea, on August 18, 1976. The next of kin of both soldiers were presented with their posthumous Purple Hearts.[70]

Michael A. Burgoyne: Purple Heart—November 23, 1984
Pvt. Michael Burgoyne was wounded by the North Koreans while he was serving as part of a joint security guard detail within the Joint Security Area, Panmunjom, Korea, on November 23, 1984.[71]

GERMANY (1976–1986)

In the 1970s and 1980s American military personnel stationed in Germany were targets in terrorist attacks by the Baader-Meinhof Gang, which was also known as the Red Army Faction. The group consisted of university students, journalists, and intellectuals who espoused an antiwar, anticapitalist, and anti-imperialist ideology. They struck not only U.S. military interests in Germany, but also German politicians and businessmen, some of whom were killed.

Scores of U.S. soldiers were wounded in Baader-Meinhof terrorist attacks in the 1970s and 1980s but fewer than ten were killed. All received Purple Hearts, including some of the following soldiers.

Joseph W. Gehrke: Purple Heart—June 1, 1976

1st Sgt. Joseph Gerhrke was wounded in an international terrorist attack in Frankfurt on June 1, 1976. The Army awarded him a Purple Heart on March 28, 1984.

Frederick J. Kroesen: Purple Heart—September 15, 1981

Then-Gen. Frederick Kroesen was wounded when terrorists attempted to assassinate him by blowing up his car in Heidelberg on September 15, 1981.

On that day Kroesen and his wife were traveling in an armored-plated Mercedes on their way to the dentist when members of the Baader-Meinhof Gang fired a rocket-propelled grenade and automatic weapons at the car. Kroesen was struck in the neck by glass that shattered when the car was struck. He was treated for his injuries a nearby hospital.[72]

The Army awarded the Purple Heart to Kroesen on March 26, 1984.

Arthur D. Nicholson Jr.: Purple Heart—March 24, 1985

Then-Maj. Arthur Nicholson was killed when a Soviet guard in East Germany shot him. Nicholson was serving as a U.S. Military Liaison Mission officer to the Group of Soviet Forces in Germany at the time of his death.

His posthumous Purple Heart was awarded on March 28, 1985.

Edward F. Pimenthal: Purple Heart—August 8, 1985

Then–Spc. 4 Edward Pimenthal was killed by members of the Baader-Meinhof Gang and the Direct Action terrorist group on August 8, 1985. He was murdered for his military identification card, which terrorists later used to gain access to the Rhein-Main Air Base and plant an explosive device.

Pimenthal's posthumous Purple Heart was awarded on November 21, 1985.

Howard R. Breeden: Purple Heart—November 24, 1985
Charles B. Kennell: Purple Heart—November 24, 1985
Sgt. Howard Breedon, Col. Charles Kennell, and eight other soldiers were wounded in an international terrorist bombing of the Frankfurt Shopping Center Post Exchange facility on November 24, 1985. Their Purple Hearts were awarded on May 16, 1986.[73]

Kenneth T. Ford: Purple Heart—April 5, 1986
James E. Goins: Purple Heart—April 5, 1986
David T. Jackson: Purple Heart—April 5, 1986
Marvin L. Ragin: Purple Heart—April 5, 1986
On April 5, 1986, a bomb exploded in the La Belle disco in West Berlin, a popular hangout for soldiers stationed there. Sgt. Kenneth Ford was killed, and SSgt. James Goins, Spc. 4 David Jackson, and Spc. 4 Marvin Ragin were wounded, along with forty-nine other soldiers. All fifty-three individuals were awarded Purple Hearts.

U.S. and German intelligence concluded that the attack was carried out at the order of Libya's Col. Muammar Qaddafi and was in response to U.S.–Libyan tensions arising out of U.S. Navy operations in the Gulf of Sidra.

FRANCE (1982)

Charles R. Ray: Purple Heart—January 18, 1982
Then–Lt. Col. Charles Ray was killed by a terrorist assassin in Paris on January 18, 1982. He was serving as an assistant Army attaché at the U.S. Defense Attaché Office in Paris when he was killed. The Army awarded Ray a posthumous Purple Heart on July 13, 1984.

LEBANON (1982–1984)

Randall A. Carlson: Purple Heart—September 25, 1982
Then-Maj. Randall Carlson was killed when his jeep hit a landmine near Beirut, Lebanon, on September 25, 1982. He was a member of the UN Truce Supervision Organization, a peacekeeping force, with a duty station in Israel. The Army awarded him a posthumous Purple Heart on September 18, 1984.

Rayford J. Byers: Purple Heart—April 18, 1983
Joseph P. Englehardt: Purple Heart—April 18, 1983
James E. Johnson: Purple Heart—April 18, 1983
Ben H. Maxwell: Purple Heart—April 18, 1983
Mark E. Salazar: Purple Heart—April 18, 1983
Richard Twine: Purple Heart—April 18, 1983

CWO3 Rayford Byers, SSgt. Ben Maxwell, SSgt. Mark Salazar, and MSgt. Richard Twine were killed in an international terrorist bomb attack on the U.S. Embassy in Beirut on April 18, 1983. Maj. Joseph Englehardt and CWO2 James Johnson were wounded by flying debris from the same bomb.

The secretary of the Army approved the award of Purple Hearts to the four deceased soldiers on June 17, 1983. Englehardt and Johnson received their nonposthumous awards in May 1984.[74]

Marcus E. Coleman: Purple Heart—October 23, 1983
Elvin H. Henry: Purple Heart—October 23, 1983
Daniel S. Kluck: Purple Heart—October 23, 1983
James G. Yarber: Purple Heart—October 23, 1983

Spc. 4 Marcus Coleman, 1st Sgt. James Yarber, and Spc. 5 Daniel Kluck were killed, and 1st Sgt. Elvin Henry was wounded, by an international terrorist bomb explosion that destroyed the Marine Battalion Landing Team headquarters near Beirut on October 23, 1983. The Army approved their Purple Hearts on October 31, 1983.

Terry A. Terrell: Purple Heart—September 20, 1984
Kenneth V. Welch: Purple Heart—September 20, 1984

Then-SSgt. Terry Terrell was wounded and then-CWO2 Kenneth Welch was killed in a terrorist attack in Beirut on September 20, 1984. Welch was awarded a posthumous Purple Heart on September 24. Terrell's was awarded the next day.[75]

EL SALVADOR (1983 AND 1989)

Jay T. Stanley: Purple Heart—February 2, 1983

Then-SSgt. Jay Stanley was wounded while a passenger aboard a Salvadoran aircraft hit by hostile fire over El Salvador. He was awarded the Purple Heart on August 31, 1983.

Nelly Aleman-Guzman: Purple Heart—November 21, 1989

While serving as an Army nurse in San Salvador as part of a special medical mission, Nelly Aleman-Guzman was hit in the eyes by glass fragments resulting from a sniper attack on the house in which she was living. As the sniper attack was part of a larger terrorist attack on San Salvador, Aleman-Guzman was awarded the Purple Heart. A major, she was the first active duty nurse to be awarded the Purple Heart since Vietnam.

GRENADA (1983)

The Army awarded 112 Purple Hearts to soldiers who were either killed or wounded in action during Operation Urgent Fury.

GREECE (1984–1985)

Robert H. Judd Jr.: Purple Heart—April 3, 1984

Robert Harold Judd Jr. was wounded when he was shot by two terrorists of the 17 November (a.k.a., Revolutionary Organization 17 November or Epanastatiki Organosi 17 Noemvri) group on April 3, 1984. At the time, then–Master Sergeant Judd was the staff duty officer of the Joint U.S. Military Aid Group, Greece and was on duty driving a government-owned vehicle when he was attacked. Judd's Purple Heart was awarded on April 20, 1984.[76]

Gregory A. Higgins: Purple Heart—February 2, 1985

Then-SSgt. Gregory Higgins was wounded in an international terrorist attack by the National Front in Athens on February 2, 1985. His Purple Heart was awarded July 30, 1986.

HONDURAS (1984 AND 1988)

Jeffrey C. Schwab: Purple Heart—January 11, 1984

Then-CWO2 Jeffrey Schwab was killed on January 11, 1984, after the helicopter he was piloting made a forced landing on a Honduran road near the Nicaraguan border, and insurgents fired on Schwab and his crew. Schwab was killed by a bullet. The other two crewmembers were unharmed.

The Army approved the award of a posthumous Purple Heart to Schwab on January 12, 1984.[77] The Army also awarded Purple Hearts to six other soldiers injured in a terrorist attack in Honduras in July 1988.

NAMIBIA (1984)

Kenneth G. Crabtree: Purple Heart—April 15, 1984
Lt. Col. Kenneth Crabtree was killed by a bomb when he stopped at a gas station in Oshikata, Namibia, on April 15, 1984. The Army concluded that Crabtree's death resulted from an international terrorist attack and awarded him the Purple Heart on April 20, 1984.[78]

BELGIUM (1985)

Michael D. Withers: Purple Heart—January 15, 1985
Then-Sgt. Michael Withers was on duty as a military policeman at the NATO Support Activity in Brussels, Belgium, when a car bomb exploded in front of that building. He was wounded and, as the bomb had been planted by members of the terrorist organization Communist Combat Cells (Cellules Communistes Combattantes), the Army awarded Withers a Purple Heart on July 30, 1986.

SINAI (1988)

Four soldiers serving in the Multinational Force and Observers in the Sinai received Purple Hearts after being wounded when their vehicle struck a landmine.

UNITED KINGDOM (1988)

Twelve soldiers who were passengers on Pan Am Flight 103 were awarded posthumous Purple Hearts after their aircraft was destroyed by a terrorist bomb over Lockerbie, Scotland.

PANAMA (1989–1990)

The Army awarded 233 posthumous and nonposthumous Purple Hearts to soldiers who were killed or wounded in Panama during Operation Just Cause between December 1989 and January 1990.

Grant Gipe: Purple Heart—December 20, 1989

Pfc. Grant Gipe, a paratrooper in the 82nd Airborne Division suffered heat exhaustion during the first hours of the U.S. invasion of Panama and, after receiving medical treatment, was awarded the Purple Heart. After soldiers and veterans groups intensely criticized this award, however, the Army prohibited future Purple Hearts "for combat-related injuries not relevant to enemy action" and specifically identified "heat stroke" as not meriting a Purple Heart.[79]

PERSIAN GULF WAR (1990–1991)

According to the Army Adjutant General, 504 soldiers received Purple Hearts for wounds received in action from January to April 1991.

Rhonda S. Cornum: Purple Heart—February 27, 1991

Rhonda Cornum is one of the few female soldiers to be awarded the Purple Heart, and the only female general officer in any branch of the Armed Forces to be a recipient.

Born in Dayton, Ohio, on October 31, 1954, Cornum grew up in East Aurora, New York. She graduated from Cornell University with a doctorate in biochemistry and joined the Army in 1978. After working at Letterman Army Institute of Research at the Presidio in San Francisco, Cornum entered the Uniformed Services University of the Health Sciences, Bethesda, Maryland, in 1982.

After graduating in 1986 then-Captain Cornum was a general surgery intern at Walter Reed Army Medical Center before becoming a flight surgeon at the Army Aeromedical Center at Fort Rucker.

On the last day of the Persian Gulf War, then-Major Cornum was participating as a flight surgeon in a search-and-rescue mission for a downed Air Force F-16 pilot. When the UH-60 Black Hawk helicopter in which she was flying was hit by Iraqi ground fire, the crippled aircraft plummeted into the desert at a speed greater than 130 knots. An AH-64 Apache helicopter

Brig. Gen. Rhonda L. Cornum is the only female general officer in history to have been awarded a Purple Heart. Then-Major Cornum was wounded in action during the Persian Gulf War in 1991. (U.S. Army)

following the Black Hawk's pilot reported that Cornum's aircraft had exploded in a fireball upon impact and that the crew was presumed dead.

Cornum had only been severely injured, but her first thought was that she might be dead. "When I looked up and saw four or five Iraqi soldiers standing over me . . . carrying AK-47s," Cornum recalled, she knew she had survived.[80] Still, she had two broken arms, a bullet wound to her shoulder, and several other injuries. Cornum was one of three crewmembers who survived the helicopter's downing. All three were taken prisoner by the Iraqis.

In an interview with *Time* correspondent Cathy Booth Thomas in 1992, Cornum acknowledged that she had been sexually assaulted in captivity. It happened in the back of an Iraqi Army truck, as she and an Army sergeant were bumping along a desert road in the dark. An Iraqi soldier pushed Cornum's "muddy, bloodied hair out of her face and kissed her . . . pulling a blanket over them, he unzipped her flight suit and started fondling her."[81]

At five foot six and 115 lbs., and with two broken arms and a bullet in her shoulder, Cornum could not fight back. Moreover, "if she bit her assailant, she worried he'd hit her and break even more bones. . . . She vowed not to scream, but every time he knocked her broken arms, she couldn't stop a scream of pain." According to Cornum, her "main worry wasn't rape" but rather that the American sergeant with her might try to defend her and be shot. "Other than that, it (the sexual assault) didn't make a big impression on me. . . . You're supposed to look at this as a fate worse than death. Having faced both, I can tell you it's not. Getting molested was not the biggest deal of my life."[82]

Cornum was taken first to Basra, then to Baghdad, where she was held prisoner for a week. After her release on March 5, 1991, Cornum's status as a female officer who was a physician and who had suffered as a POW triggered intense media coverage. She published a critically acclaimed memoir titled *She Went to War: The Rhonda Cornum Story* about her experiences in Iraq. Barton Gellman, a *Washington Post* reviewer, wrote that "from its first sentence," the book is "vivid and concrete." Cornum, he added, "displays a resourcefulness and courage that would do credit to any soldier." The *New York Times* listed *She Went to War* as one of the most notable books of 1992.[83]

After returning to the United States, Cornum resumed her military career. She trained in urologic surgery and then served as the staff urologist at Eisenhower Army Medical Center at Fort Gordon, Georgia. She subsequently commanded the 28th Combat Support Hospital at Fort Bragg, North Carolina, and a medical task force in Tuzla, Bosnia, before taking charge of the Army hospital located in Landsthul, Germany.

Promoted to brigadier general in 2008, Cornum is the director of Comprehensive Soldier Fitness, a long-ranging Armywide strategy to increase the psychological strength of the force by training soldiers in the use of resilient thinking skills from the first weeks of basic training. In addition to the Purple Heart, Cornum wears the ribbons of the Distinguished Flying Cross, Bronze Star Medal, Air Medal, and Prisoner of War Medal for her service in Operation Desert Shield and Operation Desert Storm. Soldier, doctor, wife, mother—Cornum is a remarkable person.

Terry L. Plunk: Purple Heart—February 25, 1991
A native of Vinton, Virginia, 1st Lt. Terry L. Plunk was killed while clearing mines at As-Salam Airfield, Kuwait, on February 25, 1991. A 1988 graduate of the Virginia Military Institute, Plunk was the equivalent of class valedictorian at his graduation and the top civil engineering graduate. He was twenty-five years old at the time of his death.[84]

WESTERN SAHARA (1992)

A soldier serving on the UN peacekeeping mission to the Western Sahara was wounded in June 1992 and awarded the Purple Heart.

SOMALIA (1992–1995)

In April 1992, after years of civil war and a decadelong drought left more than half a million Somalis dead from combat, terrorism, disease, and starvation, the UN Security Council established the United Nations Operation in Somalia (UNOSOM). Since its primary mission was providing humanitarian aid, an airlift of food and medical supplies began shortly thereafter. Direct U.S. participation started in July, when President George H. W. Bush authorized American air flights for emergency humanitarian relief as part of UNOSOM's Operation Provide Comfort.

Despite the success of this UNOSOM relief operation, the security situation in Somalia grew steadily worse. In the United States and elsewhere, public distress grew, and on December 4, 1992, President Bush announced the initiation of Operation Restore Hope. Under the terms of a UN resolution, the United States would both lead and provide military forces to a multinational coalition effort that had the mission of providing security, restoring order, and assisting humanitarian organizations in their relief efforts until the situation stabilized enough for the mission to be turned over to a more permanent UN peacekeeping force.

From December 9, 1992, through May 4, 1993, more than 38,000 troops from twenty-one coalition nations—including 28,000 Americans—served in Somalia. These troops succeeded in stabilizing the security situation somewhat, and, on May 4, 1993, a new force called UNOSOM II was established. It was tasked with rehabilitating the political institutions and economy of Somalia, as well as building a secure environment throughout the country.

The ambitious goals UN officials had for Somalia particularly threatened the Mogadishu power base of clan warlord Mohammed Farah Aideed. In June 1993, after twenty-four Pakistani soldiers were killed in an ambush by Aideed supporters, the UN Security Council called for the immediate apprehension of those responsible. This led to U.S. forces being employed in a manhunt for Aideed and his chief deputies. After a series of clashes between armed Somali clans and U.S. Army Rangers and other units, a major engagement occurred on October 3, 1993. About one hundred members of Task Force Ranger, on a mission to capture two top aides of warlord Aideed, were ambushed by Somali gunmen, and two Black Hawk helicopters were shot down. Eighteen Americans and seventy-five others were wounded. Shortly thereafter, President William J. Clinton announced that American participation in UNOSOM II would end on March 31, 1994.[85]

According to the Army's Human Resources Command, a total of 188 Purple Hearts were awarded to soldiers killed or wounded in Somalia between December 1992 and March 1995.

Gary Gordon: Purple Heart—October 3, 1993
Randall Shugart: Purple Heart—October 3, 1993
Then–MSgt. Gary Gordon and then–First Sgt. Randall Shugart were killed in action. In addition to posthumous Purple Hearts, both soldiers were awarded the Medal of Honor—the first awards of the nation's highest military award since the Vietnam War.

IRAQ BLACK HAWK SHOOT-DOWN (1994)

Paul N. Barclay: Purple Heart—April 14, 1994
Cornelius A. Bass: Purple Heart—April 14, 1994
Mark A. Ellner: Purple Heart—April 14, 1994
John W. Garrett: Purple Heart—April 14, 1994
Michael A. Hall: Purple Heart—April 14, 1994
Benjamin T. Hodge: Purple Heart—April 14, 1994
Patrick M. McKenna: Purple Heart—April 14, 1994
Erik S. Mounsey: Purple Heart—April 14, 1994
Richard A. Mulhern: Purple Heart—April 14, 1994
Michael S. Robinson: Purple Heart—April 14, 1994
Rickey L. Robinson: Purple Heart—April 14, 1994
Jerald L. Thompson: Purple Heart—April 14, 1994

On April 14, 1994, two Air Force F-15C Eagle fighters were patrolling the no-fly zone above Kurdish areas of northern Iraq. The pilots mistook two Black Hawk helicopters for Soviet-made Iraqi Hind aircraft and fired upon them. The American helicopters, which were carrying an international team of U.S. military personnel and eleven foreign nationals, exploded in the air and all aboard were killed. The soldiers killed were SSgt. Paul Barclay, Spc. 4 Cornelius Bass, Pfc. Mark Ellner, WO1 John Garrett, WO3 Michael Hall, 1st. Sgt. Benjamin Hodge, Capt. Patrick McKenna, WO1 Erik Mounsey, Col. Richard Mulhern, Spc. 4 Michael Robinson, SSgt. Rickey Robinson, and Col. Jerald Thompson.

The secretary of the Army and the Army Chief of Staff, recognizing that there was no legal authority to award the Purple Heart to soldiers who had been killed in a noncombat, friendly-fire incident, initially declined to award any Purple Hearts. The Air Force concurred. Continued agitation by the families of the deceased, however, caused the Defense Department to signal that it would award the Purple Heart if the Army and Air Force did not. Consequently, the services reversed their decisions and awarded Purple Hearts to those killed in the accident.[86]

HAITI (1994–1995)

The Army awarded three Purple Hearts to soldiers wounded in Operation Uphold Democracy in Haiti between September 1994 and March 1995.

SAUDI ARABIA (1995–1996)

On November 13, 1995, a bomb exploded in the three-story building housing the Saudi Arabian National Guard training center in Riyadh, killing four soldiers and one American civilian and wounding fifty-five military and civilian personnel. The Army subsequently awarded nineteen Purple Hearts to soldiers wounded or killed in the blast.[87] Forty-one Army civilian employees also received Purple Hearts.

Five more Purple Hearts went to soldiers and civilians injured or killed in the Khobar Towers bombing in Dhahran in June 1996.

THE BALKANS: BOSNIA-HERZEGOVINA, CROATIA, KOSOVO, MACEDONIA, AND SERBIA (1995–2001)

The Army awarded a total of sixteen Purple Hearts to soldiers wounded or killed in action in the Balkans between 1995 and 2001.

Martin J. Begosh: Purple Heart—December 30, 1995

Martin John Begosh was wounded in action when his vehicle hit a landmine in the village of Bijela. He was the first soldier to be wounded in action in Bosnia-Herzegovina. Born in Silver Spring, Maryland, Begosh graduated from high school in 1989 and enlisted in the Army as a military policeman in 1992. He served in Somalia for several months and was assigned to Frankfurt, Germany, at the time he deployed to Bosnia as part of Operation Joint Endeavor.

On December 30, 1995, then twenty-three-year-old Specialist Begosh was driving a Humvee in a four-vehicle convoy. He and his fellow policemen from the 709th Military Police Battalion were on a reconnaissance mission to scout and mark roads. But the Americans took a wrong turn, and Begosh ran over an antitank mine on a road going through Bijela, which is about fifteen miles south of the Sava River. He was injured by shrapnel in his right leg and foot.

Maj. Gen. William L. Nash, the commander of the American forces in Bosnia, presented the Purple Heart to Begosh on December 31, 1995.[88]

Richard P. Casini: Purple Heart—June 25, 2001

Richard P. Casini lost his right foot when he stepped on a landmine in Kosovo on June 25, 2000.

A native of Follansbee, West Virginia, then-Sergeant Casini was a twenty-two-year-old cavalry scout with the 1st Cavalry Brigade Reconnaissance Troop, 3rd Infantry Division. On June 25, 2001, he and another soldier were on a mission to stop the cross-border flow of ethnic Albanian guerrillas and their weapons into Macedonia. Casini was outside Basici, Kosovo, about three and a half miles north of the Macedonia border, when he stepped on the mine. He lost his right foot.

Gen. Montgomery Meigs, U.S. Army Europe commanding general, presented the Purple Heart to Casini on June 29, 2001.[89]

Roderick Morgan: Purple Heart—July 13, 1999

Roderick Morgan, a staff sergeant and squad leader in Company B of the 3rd Battalion, 505th Infantry Regiment, was wounded in action in Kosovo on July 13, 1999.

Morgan was on mounted patrol in the city of Ferizaj, Kosovo, when his squad came under fire. He was knocked unconscious when a bullet struck his Kevlar helmet. Shrapnel from the helmet caused ligament damage to his right hand, and he also was treated for a fractured hand.

Gen. Henry H. Shelton, who was then chairman of the Joint Chiefs of Staff, presented the Purple Heart to Morgan in a ceremony in the city square of Ferizaj.[90]

Aaron Quinn: Purple Heart—July 5, 1999

Aaron Quinn, a staff sergeant and squad leader in Company B of the 3rd Battalion, 505th Infantry Regiment, was wounded in action in Kosovo on July 5, 1999.

On the night of July 5 Quinn was on patrol in Ferizaj, Kosovo, and was going through a dark house thought to have people hiding inside. As he rounded a corner, Quinn was "punched in the right eye," and someone tried to take his weapon. When the assailant could not get the weapon, however, he stabbed Quinn in the face. Quinn was treated for a two-inch cut across his right cheek, and he received stitches.

General Shelton presented the Purple Heart to Quinn in a ceremony in the city square of Ferizaj.[91]

Steven Gonzales: Purple Heart—March 31, 1999
Andrew Ramirez: Purple Heart—March 31, 1999
Christopher Stone: Purple Heart—March 31, 1999

Spc. Steven Gonzales, SSgt. Andrew Ramirez, and SSgt. Christopher Stone, all members of the 1st Infantry Division, were captured by Serb forces in Macedonia near the Yugoslav border on March 31, 1999. They were freed thirty-two days later. While in captivity, the three soldiers "were repeatedly beaten in the face, head and body with fists, batons and rifle butts." One soldier "suffered broken ribs, the other a broken nose."

Maj. Gen. David Grange pinned Purple Hearts on all three men at a May 6, 1999, ceremony in Wuerzberg, Germany.[92]

Robert E. Washburn: Purple Heart—February 1, 1996

Then–First Lt. Robert E. Washburn was wounded by a land mine explosion while inspecting a minefield with Serbian soldiers southeast of Tuzla, Bosnia-Herzegovina, on February 1, 1996. Washburn lost part of his foot.[93]

ATTACK ON THE PENTAGON (2001)

On September 11, 2001, terrorists who had hijacked American Airlines Flight 77 crashed the commercial airliner into the Pentagon.[94] While there was no legal basis to award the Purple Heart to soldiers wounded in this incident of domestic terrorism, the Army awarded twenty-two posthumous and thirty-six nonposthumous Purple Hearts to next of kin and victims. The first awards were made at an October 24, 2001, ceremony at Fort Myer, Virginia.[95]

Note that Purple Hearts were awarded for wounds or deaths sustained when the aircraft hit the Pentagon. Consequently, men and women who suffered injuries in the aftermath of the attack were not awarded the decoration because their injuries were not the direct result of the terrorist attack. For example, a person who suffered severe smoke inhalation in the building immediately after the explosion was eligible for the Purple Heart, but an individual who received identical injuries after entering the burning Pentagon to rescue or aid other victims was ineligible.

Christopher D. Braman: Purple Heart—September 11, 2001
SSgt. Christopher Braman, then serving as sous chef and purchasing agent at the General Officer's Mess at the Pentagon, also received the Soldier's Medal for reentering the Pentagon to rescue trapped personnel.[96]

Brian D. Birdwell: Purple Heart—September 11, 2001
When the Pentagon was stuck at 9:37 AM, Lt. Col. Brian Birdwell, a veteran of the Persian Gulf War with nineteen years active duty, was only fifteen or twenty yards away from the blast. He was badly burned in the inferno that engulfed him and suffered burns on 60 percent of his body—40 percent of those were third-degree.

In 2004 Birdwell and his wife wrote *Refined by Fire*, a book about their experiences as 9-11 survivors.[97]

Victor M. Correa: Purple Heart—September 11, 2001
Lt. Col. Victor "Vic" Correa also received the Soldier's Medal for leading people out of the burning Pentagon.

Robert C. Grunewald: Purple Heart—September 11, 2001
Lt. Col. Robert Grunewald also received the Soldier's Medal for noncombat heroism in rescuing at least one civilian coworker in the attack.

Timothy J. Maude: Purple Heart—September 11, 2001

Timothy Maude, who was a lieutenant general and the most senior officer in the Army's Adjutant General's Branch, was killed during the attack and was awarded a posthumous Purple Heart.

Born in Indianapolis, Indiana, in 1947, Maude enlisted in the Army in 1966. He subsequently completed Officer Candidate School in 1967 and was commissioned as a second lieutenant in the Adjutant General's Corps. Maude began his career as a postal officer and subsequently served in personnel and administrative assignments in various locations, including Vietnam, Germany, and Korea. He was fifty-three years old at the time of his death and was interred in Arlington National Cemetery.

Maude was the most senior officer to be awarded the Purple Heart since World War II. Lt. Gen. Lesley McNair had been awarded a posthumous Purple Heart after being killed by friendly fire in France in 1944.

AFGHANISTAN (2001–)

Operation Enduring Freedom, the U.S. and allied invasion of Afghanistan, officially began on October 11, 2001. As of August 2009, more than 850 U.S. personnel had been killed and more than 3,300 wounded in action. Despite these numbers, however, Army Human Resources Command reported that only 2,665 Purple Hearts have been awarded as of April 1, 2009.[98] Recipients include the following.

Brian Craig: Purple Heart—April 15, 2002
Justin Galewski: Purple Heart—April 15, 2002
Jamie Maugans: Purple Heart—April 15, 2002
Jeffrey Pugmire: Purple Heart—April 15, 2002

Brian Craig, Justin Galewski, and Jamie Maugans, who were all staff sergeants, were killed, and Sgt. Jeffrey Pugmire was wounded, while conducting explosive-clearing operations in Kandahar, Afghanistan, on April 15, 2002. The soldiers were all qualified in explosive ordnance disposal (EOD) and were members of the California-based 710th Ordnance Company, a subordinate unit of the 52nd Ordnance Group based at Fort Gillem, Georgia. The EOD team's mission in Afghanistan was to identify and then dispose of deadly munitions left behind by the Taliban.[99]

Laura M. Walker: Purple Heart—August 18, 2005

Then–First Lt. Laura Walker was riding in a Humvee near Delak, Afghanistan, when an improvised explosive device (IED) exploded under her vehicle, killing her and another soldier. At the time of her death, Walker was conducting a public affairs mission for Task Force Peacemaker.

The daughter of Brig. Gen. Keith C. Walker, Laura Margaret Walker was born on June 16, 1981, and graduated from SHAPE American High School in Belgium. She then entered West Point, where she excelled as a leader and athlete. As captain of the women's handball team, Walker led her fellow cadets to a national collegiate championship.

After graduating in 2003 and receiving a commission in the Corps of Engineers, then–Second Lieutenant Walker was assigned to Fort Lewis and deployed to Iraq with the 555th Combat Engineer Group in February 2004.

Walker returned to Fort Lewis in April 2004 and subsequently took charge of a platoon in Company B of the 864th Engineer Combat Battalion (Heavy), 555th Maneuver Enhancement Brigade (Provisional). She deployed with that platoon to Afghanistan in March 2005. When Walker was killed on August 18, 2005, she gained the unwanted distinction of becoming the first female soldier killed in action in Afghanistan.[100]

PHILIPPINES (2002)

Mark W. Jackson: Purple Heart—October 2, 2002

Mark Wayne Jackson, a Special Forces soldier assigned to Fort Lewis, was killed when a nail-laden bomb fastened to a motorcycle exploded outside a karaoke bar and restaurant in Zamboanga, Philippines.

A native of Glennie, Michigan, First Sergeant Jackson was assigned to the 1st Special Forces Group and was part of a 260-member special operations task force deployed to the southern Philippines when he was killed. The task force was part of a long-term security agreement with the Philippine government and was conducting humanitarian assistance work such as helping to refurbish hospitals and schools, dig wells, and treat Filipinos in need of immediate medical treatment in Zamboanga.

Gen. Hermogenes Ebdane, the Philippine national police chief, blamed the al-Qaida-linked Abu Sayyaf terrorist group for the attack.[101]

IRAQ (2003–)

Operation Iraqi Freedom, the U.S.-led invasion of Iraq, officially began on March 19, 2003. Although combat against Saddam Hussein's forces was over by the time President George W. Bush announced "mission accomplished" on May 1, 2003, the fighting continued through the short-lived U.S. occupation and the reestablishment of an Iraqi government in June 2004.

As of August 2009, more than 3,460 U.S. military personnel had been killed in action, and more than 31,000 had been wounded. Despite these numbers the Army Human Resources Command reported that only 20,744 Purple Hearts have been awarded to soldiers as of April 1, 2009.[102]

Travis Atkins: Purple Heart—June 1, 2007

SSgt. Travis Atkins was killed in the town of Abu Sarnak when a suicide bomber detonated an explosive device. Atkins was awarded a posthumous Purple Heart.

A native of Great Falls, Montana, the thirty-one-year-old Atkins was a member of Company D of the 2nd Battalion, 14th Infantry Regiment, 2nd Brigade Combat Team, 10th Mountain Division. On June 1, 2007, while he was conducting route security in Abu Sarnak, Atkins apprehended and began to search a group of suspected insurgents.

One of the men resisted and engaged Atkins in hand-to-hand combat. As Atkins attempted to subdue the man, he realized that the insurgent was trying to trigger a suicide vest that he was wearing under his clothing. Despite Atkins' efforts, the insurgent reached his vest. Atkins then tackled the suicide bomber and pinned the man to the ground while shielding his fellow soldiers from the imminent explosion. Atkins' action saved the lives of three other Americans. For his extraordinary heroism, Atkins also was awarded a posthumous Distinguished Service Cross.[103]

Tammy L. Duckworth: Purple Heart—November 12, 2004

Tammy Ladda Duckworth was wounded when the helicopter she was piloting was hit by a rocket-propelled grenade on November 12, 2004. She suffered severe damage to her right arm and lost both her legs.

Born in Bangkok, Thailand, to an American father and a Thai mother, Duckworth settled with her family in Hawaii. She received her bachelor of arts degree from the University of Hawaii in 1989 and, while in graduate school at George Washington University in 1990, joined the Army ROTC. She subsequently obtained an Army Reserve commission and qualified as a helicopter pilot. Duckworth later joined the Illinois National Guard and deployed to Iraq as a Black Hawk pilot in 2004.[104]

Jessica D. Lynch: Purple Heart—March 23, 2003

See chapter 9, "Celebrities: Artists and Entertainers, Politicians, Athletes, and Other Public Figures."

Max Ramsey: Purple Heart—March 1, 2006

Max Ramsey was wounded by an IED while on patrol in Ramadi, Iraq.

Ramsey, enlisted in the Army in 2004 and deployed to Iraq with the 1st Battalion, 506th Infantry Regiment. On March 1, 2006, then–Private First Class Ramsey was traveling in a Humvee in Ramadi. After the gunner in his vehicle dismounted to help set up an observation post, Ramsey moved from his seat behind the driver into the turret. Shortly thereafter, a 155-mm artillery round exploded, ripping through the Humvee and severely injuring Ramsey's left leg.

Although Ramsey's leg was amputated by doctors at the combat support hospital in Baghdad, he was returned to duty at Fort Campbell on March 1, 2007. For the next two years, Ramsey served on the 101st Airborne Division's Parachute Demonstration Team. Sergeant Ramsey, an avid skydiver, had completed about 350 jumps prior to enlisting in the Army; since losing his leg, he has completed some 600 descents. Ramsey left active duty in summer 2009.[105]

Nancy Romero: Purple Heart—March 12, 2004

See chapter 8, "Families: Brothers, Fathers and Sons, and Husbands and Wives."

David Romero: Purple Heart—April 2004

See Chapter 8, "Families: Brothers, Fathers and Sons, and Husbands and Wives."

Jessica Sarandrea, Purple Heart, March 3, 2009

Then-Spc. Jessica Sarandrea was killed in action when insurgents attacked her forward-operating base in Mosul. She was "walking from her office when she was hit by shrapnel from incoming mortar fire."[106]

A resident of Miami, Florida, Sarandrea enlisted in August 2005 as a unit supply specialist and deployed from Fort Hood to Iraq in December with the 3rd Brigade Special Troops Battalion, 3rd Heavy Brigade Combat Team, 1st Cavalry Division.

Sarandrea was twenty-two years old at the time of her death. Her husband, Sgt. Alejandro "Alex" Sarandrea, was serving in Iraq at the same time. Shortly after her death, Sarandrea's husband told the *Miami Herald* that the two had met in Kuwait during a prior deployment. The Sarandreas had much in common, as they were both the same age and both from Miami. "I know what a wonderful person she was," said Alex Sarandrea. "I will always carry her memory in my heart."[107]

In addition to the Purple Heart, Sarandrea was awarded a posthumous Bronze Star Medal. She previously had been awarded the Army Commendation Medal and Army Good Conduct Medal.

Sarandrea's cremated remains were interred at Arlington National Cemetery on June 8, 2009. She became the 550th service member killed in Afghanistan or Iraq to be buried at Arlington.

CHAPTER 3

Sailors: Spanish–American War to Afghanistan and Iraq

During World War II the Navy awarded Purple Hearts to two sailors wounded in action during the Spanish–American War, and these two recipients, who received their medals some forty-five years after being injured in the Battle of Manila Bay, are the earliest known naval Purple Heart recipients.

While the precise number of Purple Hearts awarded to sailors wounded or killed in action since 1898 is not known, probably about 80,000 sailors have received the decoration, with the majority going to those with World War II service. Sailors have received Purple Hearts for combat injuries sustained in the following armed conflicts, terrorist attacks, or other military operations:

- Spanish–American War (1898)
- Philippine Insurrection (1899–1911)
- China Relief Expedition/Boxer Rebellion (1900–1901)
- Veracruz (1914)
- World War I (1917–1918)
- China, Nicaragua, and the Atlantic (1927–1941)
- World War II (1941–1945)
- Korean War (1950–1953)
- Vietnam, Cambodia, and Laos (1962–1975)
- USS *Liberty* (1967)
- USS *Pueblo* (1968)
- Guatemala (1968)

- Korea (1974)
- Lebanon (1978)
- Puerto Rico (1979)
- Turkey (1980)
- Lebanon (1983–1984)
- El Salvador (1983)
- Grenada (1983)
- Greece (1983)
- Lebanon (1985)
- USS *Stark* (1987)
- Italy (1988)
- Persian Gulf War (1991)
- Somalia (1993)
- Cambodia (1993)
- Haiti (1994)
- The Balkans (1994–1999)
- Attack on the Pentagon (2001)
- Afghanistan (2001–)
- Iraq (2003–)

SPANISH–AMERICAN WAR (1898)

John Davis: Purple Heart—May 11, 1898
John Davis was wounded in action near Cienfuegos, Cuba, on May 11, 1898. He retired from the U.S. Navy as a lieutenant commander and was awarded the Purple Heart on March 9, 1943.

William Sneath: Purple Heart—May 1, 1898
William Sneath was wounded in action when he was hit in the head by a recoiling 5-inch gun during the Battle of Manila Bay in the Philippines.

Sneath enlisted in the Navy in 1892 and was honorably discharged in 1900, after serving in the USS *Raleigh*, USS *Olympia*, USS *Potomac*, and USS *Chesapeake*. In 1902 he joined the Providence, Rhode Island, police force and served there for thirty years. Over the years, Sneath represented Rhode Island at a number of official functions relating to Adm. George Dewey and the Spanish–American War. Sneath died in 1960.

SN William Sneath's officially engraved Purple Heart is unique. It is the only Purple Heart awarded to a sailor wounded in action during the Battle of Manila Bay in 1898. (FJP Auctions Inc.)

In 1958, Sneath described his role at Manila Bay to a news reporter:

At 10:15 Dewey's fleet stood in to silence the land batteries. The USS *Raleigh* steamed along delivering broadsides at the remaining fort on Sangley Point. At 20 minutes past 12, a white flag went up near Cavite and the bombardment ceased.

The USS *Boston* and USS *Concord* remained off the navy yard while the rest of the fleet proceeded to the city to silence the fort there. Just as we got in range the white flag went up. It was all over.

The Spanish fleet of six cruisers, five gunboats and two transports were either sunk or burned. Casualties were heavy as many of the ships were double manned. There were no American ships or lives lost. Only eight of our men were wounded. I was one of the eight.

I was No.2 captain of a six inch gun on the *Raleigh*. During the battle, our No.1 captain was in sick bay so I took over his position. I had fired about eight rounds when Lieut. Hugh Rodman, who later became an admiral, came in and told me to take my regular position. He took over as gun captain.

On one shot, I was just hooking the lanyard into the primer which set off the fuse. He pulled it before I had a chance to get out of the way. When the gun recoiled I was hit on the forehead. It split my head open and from then on until the end of the battle I was covered with blood. Later it took 12 stitches to close the wound. I still have the wound on my forehead. Years later I got the Purple Heart Medal.[1]

While official contemporary reports do not verify Sneath's injuries, the Navy clearly accepted their validity when issuing him the Purple Heart on January 15, 1944. Sneath's medal was officially hand-engraved "William/Sneath/Sea./USN."

Sneath's award is the earliest known Purple Heart given for a naval action.

PHILIPPINE INSURRECTION (1899–1911)

After the United States claimed possession of all the Philippines in January 1899, some 40,000 Filipino guerrillas led by Emilio Aguinaldo refused to accept American sovereignty. Consequently, the Filipino nationalists ratified a new constitution, declared an independent republic, and began a bloody war against their new colonial masters.

The poorly armed and badly trained insurgents could not stand against the mobility and firepower of the Americans, however, and Aguinaldo and his forces were soon defeated and forced to flee into the hills on Luzon. Aguinaldo was captured in March 1901, and most organized resistance to U.S. rule ceased by June 1902. Some 100,000 U.S. soldiers, sailors, and Marines were needed to quell the insurrection, and despite the end of fighting around Manila and the island of Luzon, U.S. pacification operations against the Moros in the southern Philippines did not end until 1913.

Henry D. Cooke: Purple Heart—March 7, 1906

Henry David Cooke was wounded in action in the assault on Bud Dajo, Island of Jolo, Philippine Islands, on March 7, 1906. Born in Washington, D.C., on September 21, 1879, Cooke graduated from the U.S. Naval Academy in Annapolis, Maryland, in 1903. He received his commission as an ensign on February 3, 1905.

During World War I, then-Commander Cooke commanded the USS *Allen* and was awarded the Navy Cross "for distinguished service in the line of his profession as commanding officer." His citation for the decoration lauds his work "operating in the war zone and protecting vitally important convoys of troop and cargo ships through the area of submarine activity" and his "prompt and efficient action in contacts with enemy submarines on March 11 and March 16, 1918."[2]

Cooke retired as a captain on June 30, 1939, but returned to active duty in June 1941 as a rear admiral. The Navy awarded him the Purple Heart on November 2, 1943. Cooke retired a second time at the end of World War II and died in East Hills, New Jersey, on July 7, 1958.

Lee Herliss: Purple Heart—June 11, 1902

Lee Herliss was wounded by enemy fire on June 11, 1902. He was serving as a lieutenant (junior grade) in the U.S. Naval Reserve when the Navy awarded him the Purple Heart on July 29, 1943.

CHINA RELIEF EXPEDITION/BOXER REBELLION (1900–1901)

The United States had maintained a naval presence in East Asian waters as early as 1835, with sailors protecting American lives and property during the many uprisings that shook Imperial China. During the Boxer Rebellion at the turn of the twentieth century, attacks were again directed against foreigners living in China.

In June 1900 Chinese insurgents surrounded the legations in Peking and began a two-month siege. To rescue the beleaguered Westerners, an international relief force including U.S. sailors and Marines slowly fought its way inland while the USS *Newark* and USS *Monocacy* stood off Taku Bar. Both warships landed Marines and Bluejackets to help with the retaking of the walled city of Tientsin from the Boxers, and the ships continued to provide logistic support to the multinational force fighting to relieve Peking.

As the weeks wore on and the crisis in northern China grew, additional warships were dispatched to Tientsin by Asiatic Station Commander Rear Adm. George Remey. The legations were relieved in late August 1900, and the fury of the Boxer uprising was spent.

John McCloy: Purple Hearts—June 22, 1900, and April 22, 1914

John McCloy, who was wounded on June 22, 1900, is one of only a handful of Americans who have been awarded two Medals of Honor.

Born in Brewster, New York, on January 3, 1876, McCloy had a boyhood desire to go to sea and joined the Merchant Marine when he was fifteen years old. In March 1898, twenty-two-year-old McCloy enlisted in the Navy and served in the USS *Columbia* in West Indian waters during the war with Spain. His earlier experiences at sea apparently caused his superiors to believe he was ready for challenges not ordinarily given to a new sailor since, while "in charge of a Navy tug in 1898," McCloy "saved two men from drowning and rescued the entire crew of a schooner in a hurricane off the Florida Keys."

In 1899 McCloy was assigned for duty in the Philippines, and he was serving in the USS *Newark* during June 1900, when that warship participated in the rescue of Westerners during the Boxer Rebellion. For his "distinguished conduct in the presence of the enemy in the battles of 13, 20, 21, 22 June 1900, while with the relief expedition under Vice Adm. (Sir Edward) Seymour," then-Coxswain McCloy was awarded the Medal of Honor.[3] Seymour was a Royal Navy admiral and, as the ranking officer in the eight-nation Allied relief force, had command of the entire expedition; McCloy's American superior was Capt. Bowman H. McCalla, who had command of the sailors in the *Newark*. For wounds he had received on June 22 at the taking of Tsku Arsenal on the Pei Ho River, the Navy awarded McCloy the Purple Heart on August 5, 1943.

In April 1901 McCloy reenlisted and served in USS *Manila* and the USS *Alliance*. In 1905 then-Boatswain McCloy received orders to USS *Galveston* and was serving in that ship when she escorted the remains of naval hero John

Lt. John McCloy was wounded in action in China in 1900 and again in Mexico in 1914. He was awarded two Purple Hearts for those combat injuries and two Medals of Honor for his extraordinary heroism in both locations. (Naval Historical Center)

Paul Jones back to the United States. He later served in the USS *Hancock*, USS *Fish Hawk*, and USS *Lebanon*. He also had shore duty in Key West, Florida.

In 1914 then-Chief Boatswain's Mate McCloy was serving in the USS *Florida* and was the beachmaster for the landing force in the seizure and occupation of Veracruz. He was wounded in action a second time at Veracruz and received a second Medal of Honor and a second Purple Heart.

The citation for the second Medal of Honor states that McCloy led a flotilla of "three picket launches along the Veracruz sea front, drawing Mexican fire and enabling cruisers to save our men on shore." General Orders No. 177, published by the Navy Department on December 14, 1915, provides additional details on McCloy's heroism that day:

> Chief Boatswain McCloy led a flotilla of three picket launches, mounting 1-pounders along the sea front of Veracruz in front of the (Mexican) naval school and customhouse. The launches drew the combined fire of the Mexicans in that vicinity and thus enabled the cruisers to shell them out temporarily and save our men. The conduct of Chief Boatswain McCloy was eminent and conspicuous, and although shot through the thigh during this fire, he remained at his post as beachmaster for 48 hours until sent to a hospital ship by the brigade surgeon.[4]

After recuperating from his wounds at the New York Naval Hospital, McCloy returned to sea duty in USS *Tennessee* and then USS *Maine*. In late 1916 he served as assistant to the captain of the yard at the Boston Navy Yard in Massachusetts.

After the United States entered World War I, McCloy obtained a temporary commission as an ensign and commanded the USS *Ontario*. In early 1918 he took command of USS *Favorite* and was promoted to lieutenant in the summer of 1918.

In January 1919, then-Lieutenant McCloy commanded the newly commissioned minesweeper USS *Curlew* and on November 11, 1920, was awarded the Navy Cross for his "exceptionally meritorious and distinguished service . . . in the important and hazardous work of clearing the North Sea of mines."[5]

In early 1921 McCloy took command of USS *Cormorant*. He returned to shore duty at the New York Navy Yard in February 1922 but took command of USS *Lark* in November 1923. Before he retired as a lieutenant in October 1928, McCloy also served in the USS *Patoka*, USS *Memphis*, and USS *Dobbin*.

In April 1942 McCloy was advanced on the retired list to lieutenant commander. He had lived in New York before moving to Leonia, New Jersey, where he died on May 25, 1945, at the age of sixty-nine years. He is buried in Arlington National Cemetery.[6]

Joseph K. Taussig: Purple Heart—June 20, 1900
See chapter 8, "Families: Brothers, Fathers and Sons, and Husbands and Wives."

VERACRUZ (1914)

On April 9, 1914, nine U.S. sailors were briefly detained by Mexican forces at Tampico, Mexico. Less than two weeks later, President Woodrow Wilson learned that a German ship carrying a large supply of munitions was scheduled to arrive in Veracruz, and Wilson decided this delivery must not be successful. Consequently, on April 21 Wilson directed Secretary of the Navy Josephus Daniels to have U.S. naval forces stop the German ship.

The Navy had three principal ships off Veracruz—the USS *Florida*, USS *Utah*, and USS *Prairie*—along with several smaller vessels. The *Florida* and *Utah* were battleships, and the *Prairie* was a transport carrying a battalion of Marines. Rear Adm. Frank E. Fletcher, who was in overall command of U.S. naval forces off Veracruz, was ordered to seize the customhouse in the town.

Shortly before noon, steam-powered launches towing whaleboats filled with U.S. troops entered the inner harbor of Veracruz. There were 502 Marines from the *Prairie* and 285 sailors from the *Florida*. They landed unopposed and quickly occupied the railway yard, power plant, and post and telegraph office.

At the customhouse, however, the Americans ran into stiff opposition from Mexican forces armed with machine guns. In the meantime, additional sailors from the *Utah* landed, and by noon on April 22, American forces were in control of Veracruz. Seventeen sailors and Marines and had been killed, and sixty-three had been wounded. Mexican casualties were about eight hundred dead and wounded. A number of sailors subsequently received Purple Hearts for the wounds they received in combat at Veracruz, including the following.

Arthur Burnside: Purple Heart—April 22, 1914
Arthur Burnside was wounded in action on April 22, 1914, while attached to USS *Chester*.

Walter L. Hawk: Purple Heart—April 22, 1914
Walter L. Hawk was wounded in action on April 22, 1914, while part of the landing force at Veracruz. He was attached to the USS *Minnesota*. Hawk retired from the Navy as a lieutenant commander and received his Purple Heart from the Navy on April 9, 1943.

James P. Lannon: Purple Heart—April 22, 1914
James Patrick Lannon was wounded during the engagement at Veracruz. Born on October 12, 1878, in Alexandria, Virginia, Lannon graduated from

the U.S. Naval Academy in 1902 and was commissioned as an ensign in 1904. On April 22, 1914, while attached to the battleship USS *New Hampshire*, then-Lieutenant Lannon "assisted a wounded man under heavy fire, and after returning to his battalion was himself desperately wounded." For this "extraordinary heroism in battle," Lannon was awarded the Medal of Honor and was cited for "distinguished conduct" in General Orders No. 177, which was published by the Navy Department on December 4, 1914.

During World War I then-Commander Lannon served as commanding officer of the USS *Nashville* and "for exceptionally meritorious and distinguished service in the line of his profession" was awarded the Navy Cross. The citation for that decoration lauds Lannon's having "engaged in the important, exacting and hazardous duty of escorting mercantile convoys in the Mediterranean Sea through waters infested with enemy submarines."

Lannon received his Purple Heart from the Navy Department on June 4, 1943. When he retired as a rear admiral in 1947, Lannon had served at both sea and shore stations in the United States, Europe, and Asia. Lannon died on March 13, 1953, and is interred at Arlington National Cemetery.[7]

Paul A. Stevens: Purple Heart—April 22, 1914

Paul Augustus Stevens was wounded in action at Veracruz while attached to the USS *Henry T. Allen*. The Navy awarded Stevens his Purple Heart on July 8, 1943.

Born on February 22, 1890, in Crisfield, Maryland, Stevens attended public schools in Dover, Delaware, from 1896 to 1906 before transferring to a preparatory school in New Haven, Connecticut. He was at Yale University for one year before entering the Naval Academy in 1909.

After graduating from Annapolis in 1913, Stevens served "on all surface types except carriers, and in all waters from Turkey to China and Tasmania to Spitsbergen." He was a student at the Naval War College from 1925 to 1926, and when the United States entered World War II, Stevens provided valuable service in both the Atlantic and Pacific. He was commended for his work during the amphibious invasion of North Africa in 1942 and awarded the Legion of Merit for his work in New Guinea in 1944.

Stevens retired as a captain at the end of World War II and died in Mahoning County, Ohio, on October 16, 1969.

WORLD WAR I (1917–1918)

According to the Navy Department, 431 sailors were killed, and 819 sailors were wounded, in combat in World War I. Consequently, Purple Hearts to naval personnel for this conflict were relatively rare.

Sailors wounded while serving with Pershing's American Expeditionary Force were eligible to apply to the War Department for Purple Hearts, and more than a few did receive Army-issued decorations. When the Navy obtained its own legal authority to award the Purple Heart in 1942, however, sailors who had been wounded in 1918 could apply directly to the Navy Department for the decoration. But, because the Navy issued the Purple Heart retroactively only upon request, it estimated in 1958 that only about eighty Purple Hearts had been awarded to sailors wounded in World War I.[8]

Frederick R. Hook: Purple Heart—June 16, 1918

Frederick Hook, an officer in the Navy Medical Corps was "gassed in action against an enemy of the United States." The Navy awarded then-Captain Hook the Purple Heart on July 29, 1943.

Roger G. Osterheid: Purple Heart—September 5, 1918

Roger Osterheid was wounded in action on September 5, 1918, while attached to the USS *Mount Vernon*. The Navy awarded then–Lieutenant Commander Osterheid the Purple Heart on July 10, 1943.

Frank Tousig: Purple Heart—November 6, 1918

Frank Tousig was wounded in the ankle by either a bullet or shrapnel at the Battle of Blanc Mont Ridge on November 6, 1918. The Navy awarded then–Chief Pharmacist Tousig the Purple Heart on June 24, 1944.

Charles Turnier: Purple Heart—November 9, 1918

Charles Turnier was wounded in action on November 9, 1918, while serving in the USS *Saetia*.

The *Saetia* was a Naval Overseas Transportation Service vessel operating in the Atlantic during World War I. On October 24, 1918, having unloaded her cargo, the ship left Bordeaux, France, for Philadelphia. At 8:30 AM on November 9, the *Saetia* struck a German mine and sank ten miles from the Fenwick Island Lightship off the mid-Atlantic coast of the United States. All hands survived, but thirteen men were injured, including Turnier. The Navy awarded then–Lieutenant Commander Turnier of the U.S. Naval Reserve a Purple Heart on January 30, 1945.

CHINA, NICARAGUA, AND THE ATLANTIC (1927–1941)

China (1927)

Micszlav Rutyna: Purple Heart—April 16, 1927

Micszlav Rutyna was wounded on April 16, 1927, while serving in the USS *Preble*. A *Clemson*-class destroyer, the *Preble* was on patrol duty on the Yangtze River and Whangpoo River in China, which meant that it routinely escorted merchant vessels and also transported American and foreign refugees to safety.

On several occasions, Chinese factions fired on the *Preble* from shore. On April 16, 1927, while "answering gunfire" on the Yangtze River, Rutyna was wounded. The Navy awarded then-Ensign Rutyna the Purple Heart on May 6, 1944.[9]

Nicaragua (1928)

Oliver Llewellen Young: Purple Heart—May 13–14, 1928

Oliver Young, who served in the Navy Hospital Corps, was wounded in action while fighting against an organized bandit group near Pena Blanca, Nicaragua, on May 13–14, 1928. The Navy awarded then–Lieutenant (junior grade) Young a Purple Heart on January 10, 1944.

China (1937)

In December 1937 the gunboat USS *Panay* was on patrol in the Yangtze River in China. Her crew consisted of four officers and forty-nine enlisted men, and the *Panay* was armed with two 3-inch guns and eight Lewis .30-caliber machine guns.

The *Panay* was part of a larger American naval presence called the Yangtze Patrol that had been on the Yangtze since the early 1900s. Standard Oil Company operated tankers on the waterway, and the need to protect them and other U.S. merchant shipping from bandits, pirates, and warlords required a U.S. Navy presence. The *Panay* was one of six shallow-draft gunboats—it drew only about five feet of water—that had been constructed in Shanghai in 1926–1927. The others were the USS *Guam*, USS *Luzon*, USS *Mindanao*, USS *Oahu*, and USS *Tutuila*.

The Japanese had been in China since their invasion of Manchuria in 1931. Six years after that invasion, an incident between Japanese and Chinese forces near the Marco Polo Bridge southwest of Peking caused an escalation of violence, and by the end of August 1937, there was full-scale war between Japanese and Chinese forces.

After Japanese imperial forces moved against Nanking in November 1937, killing, raping, and otherwise brutalizing more than 300,000 Chinese civilians, it was clear that the *Panay* and other U.S. ships on the Yangtze might become targets in the ongoing combat, even though the Americans were neutral in the conflict.

Hoping to reduce the chance of attack on the *Panay*, Lt. Cdr. James J. Hughes, the boat's commander, had the crew mark the *Panay* by placing large American flags across her upper deck awnings. Additionally, when the ship was anchored at Nanking at night, she was illuminated, and a spotlight shone on a large six-by-eleven-foot American flag flying from a pole.

With this as background, the *Panay* found herself under way on December 9, 1937, carrying not only her crew, but also a small group of civilians who were being evacuated from Nanking for their own safety. There were eleven Americans, including four U.S. embassy employees, and four foreign nationals. At least eight of the evacuees were journalists, including the well-known cameraman Norman Alley of Universal News and Eric Mayell of Fox Movietone.

On December 11 the *Panay* was steaming in a convoy consisting of three Standard Oil tankers. It was a mutually beneficial arrangement: The *Panay* provided the tankers with protection, while the tankers provided her with fuel. The next day, after passing a British-flagged tanker that had been sunk by an aerial bombardment and was still on fire, the *Panay* dropped anchor twenty-eight miles above Nanking. About 1:40 PM, Japanese aircraft appeared in the skies above the American gunboat and, without warning, released a string of bombs. Chief Quartermaster John Lang, on duty with Hughes in the pilot-house, was wounded in the blast from the first bomb.

While the crew did manage to return fire, the *Panay*'s light armament was configured for ship-to-shore combat and not to repel an air attack. Consequently, the sailors did no harm to their Japanese attackers. On the other hand, the Japanese bombs had found their mark, and within minutes, the *Panay* was sinking. The last of her crew abandoned ship about 3:00 PM, and she rolled to starboard and sank about an hour later. Meanwhile, the Japanese also had attacked the oil tankers traveling with the *Panay*, setting two of the three aflame.

As for the *Panay*'s crew and passengers, two sailors and one civilian died from wounds received in the attack. The survivors managed to make it to shore. Twenty-seven were wounded, fourteen so badly that they could only be moved by stretcher. The survivors had been lucky enough to land in territory controlled by the Chinese army and were subsequently rescued by a party led by the British gunboats HMS *Bee* and HMS *Ladybird*.

Historians today generally agree that the Japanese attack on the *Panay* was deliberate while differing about the reasons for the attack and the extent of Japanese culpability. In any event, the Japanese government issued a note of apology before the *Panay*'s survivors reached Shanghai. In that note the Japanese insisted that the *Panay* had been bombed by mistake. While no one believed this was true because Alley had filmed the attack with his 16-mm camera and had visual proof that the Japanese planes had flown at masthead height, President Franklin D. Roosevelt did not want to go to war with Japan over the *Panay*. Consequently, he accepted the apology, and the Japanese paid nearly half a million dollars in compensation.[10]

As for the crew members, a number received the Navy Cross and Navy Distinguished Service Medal. None received Purple Hearts, however, because the medal was still exclusively an Army award. Additionally, once World War II began and the Navy obtained the legal authority to award the Purple Heart, the *Panay* attack was forgotten in the rush of other more-dramatic events.

In the early 1990s, however, the Navy's leadership decided it was not too late to honor the crew of the *Panay*. On October 28, 1992, the Navy approved Purple Heart awards to the following members of the *Panay* crew who were killed or wounded in the attack:

- Lt. Arthur F. Anders
- Lt. (j.g.) John W. Geist
- COX Walter Cheatham
- WT2 Fon B. Huffman
- Lt. Cdr. James J. Hughes
- QMC John H. Lang
- EM1 Carl H. Birk
- COX Edgar W. G. Hulsebus
- MM2 A. Kozak
- RM3 J. T. Murphy
- RM2 R. Peterson
- SN1 Charles S. Schroyer
- FN1 Marcus V. Williamson
- RM1 A. R. Wisler

Because few survivors remained, most of these decorations were presented to relatives. At least one, however, went to a living recipient—Fon Huffman.

Then-WT2 Fon B. Huffman received a one-inch shrapnel wound to his right shoulder during the Japanese attack on the USS *Panay* in 1937. He received his Purple Heart almost fifty-five years later. (Nick T. Spark)

Arthur F. Anders: Purple Heart—December 12, 1937

Lt. Arthur F. Anders, who was the *Panay's* executive officer, was severely wounded during the bombing. He was suffering from loss of blood and was unable to speak, but he remained at his duty station, directing fire of the *Panay's* machine guns and supervising abandon-ship operations. Being unable to talk, he gave his orders and commands in writing.

Fon B. Huffman: Purple Heart—December 12, 1937

Fon Birdell Huffman received a one-inch shrapnel wound in his right shoulder. Almost fifty-five years later, he received his Purple Heart.

Born in Truro, Iowa, Huffman grew up on a farm and enlisted in the Navy when he was sixteen years old. He was twenty-four years old and an experienced watertender second class on the *Panay* when she was attacked. Huffman's job was to man the boiler room and ensure that the oil was hot and the boilers were making steam to power the gunboat.

In a recent letter to the author, Huffman's daughter, Nancy Ferguson, explained that her father received $1,200 from the Navy as his share of compensation paid by the Japanese. Huffman spent $800 of his proceeds on a brand-new Chevrolet.

Huffman retired as a chief boiler technician in 1949 after serving twenty years in the Navy. In addition to the *Panay*, he served in the USS *Lexington*, USS *Augusta*, USS *Texas*, USS *Stack*, USS *Hawkins*, and USS *Thomas*. Huffman was the last survivor from the *Panay* crew. He died at his daughter's home in Arizona on September 4, 2008, at the age of ninety-five.

James J. Hughes: Purple Heart—December 12, 1937

James Joseph Hughes was wounded by shrapnel during the aerial attack on the *Panay*.

Born in New York in 1898, Hughes graduated from the U.S. Naval Academy in 1918 but was officially a member of the Class of 1919. He had considerable experience on the Yangtze River Patrol prior to taking command of the *Panay* in June 1936 as a thirty-eight-year-old lieutenant commander. Hughes was intelligent and had a reputation for stern judgment. As historian Darby Perry wrote in *The Panay Incident*, Hughes had "pushed himself through a number of courses that a professional naval officer would need for advancement and a Yangtze Patrol officer might need for survival when operating independently and with almost unlimited authority deep inside China."[11]

Hughes had suffered a badly broken femur but remained on active duty during World War II until he was medically retired as a lieutenant commander. He died on November 24, 1953, and is interred at Arlington National Cemetery.

Atlantic (1941)

Prior to the Japanese attack on Pearl Harbor and America's official entry into World War II, the destroyers USS *Kearny* and USS *Reuben James* engaged in combat with German submarines in the North Atlantic. Sailors killed and wounded on both U.S. warships would later be awarded the Purple Heart.

On October 16, 1941, the *Kearny* was escorting a convoy in the North Atlantic when German submarines attacked three of the merchant ships. The *Kearny* immediately dropped depth charges, but the Germans struck back. At the beginning of midwatch the next day, a torpedo launched by the submarine *U-568* hit the *Kearny* on her starboard side.

The *Kearny*'s crew confined flooding to the forward fireroom, and the ship remained afloat until she could reach Iceland on October 19. A total of eleven sailors were killed in the attack. Twenty-two other men were wounded in action, including the ship's commanding officer.

The *Reuben James*, a World War I–era *Clemson*-class destroyer, sailed with four other warships from Newfoundland on October 23, 1941. She was escorting an eastbound convoy when she was torpedoed by the German submarine *U-522* on October 31, 1941. After being struck by the torpedo, the *Reuben James'* bow exploded when a magazine blew up. The bow sank immediately, and the ship's aft section sank five minutes later.

Of the 159 sailors in the destroyer, only 44 survived. The singer-songwriter Woody Guthrie later authored and sang "The Sinking of the *Reuben James*."[12]

In 1943 the Navy began awarding posthumous Purple Hearts to the next of kin of the men who had been killed on the *Kearny* or *Reuben James*. Those who had been wounded in action also received the decoration. Some Purple Heart recipients from these engagements include the following individuals.

▶ **USS *Kearny***

Louis T. Bobe: Purple Heart—October 17, 1941
Louis Thomas Bobe, who previously served in the USS *Denebola*, was serving as a gunner's mate second class in the *Kearny* when she was torpedoed. "Commended for his attention to duty during and following the action" on October 17, Bobe also received the Purple Heart for wounds received that day.[13] The Navy mailed the decoration to Bobe's home in Montgomery, Alabama, and he received it on February 9, 1945.

Anthony L. Danis: Purple Heart—October 17, 1941
Anthony Lee Danis was the commanding officer of the *Kearny*. Because he was wounded in action, the Navy awarded then-Captain Danis the Purple Heart on August 2, 1943.

Herman A. C. Gajeway: Purple Heart—October 17, 1941
Then WT1 Herman Augustus Charles Gajeway was killed in action when the torpedo struck the *Kearny*'s forward fireroom. While his remains were never recovered, the Navy presented a Purple Heart to Gajeway's father on February 13, 1945.

▶ **USS** *Reuben James*

Heywood L. Edwards: Purple Heart—October 31, 1941
Then–Lt. Cdr. Heywood Lane Edwards was killed in action. Born in 1906 he graduated from the U.S. Naval Academy in 1926 and was in command of the *Reuben James* when she was sunk. The Navy presented Edwards' posthumously awarded Purple Heart to his wife on March 5, 1945.

Benjamin Ghetzler: Purple Heart—October 31, 1941
Then–Lt. Benjamin Ghetzler was killed in action. Ghetzler's posthumous Purple Heart was presented to his wife in Annapolis on May 27, 1943.

Ralph W. H. Kloepper: Purple Heart—October 31, 1941
　　Then-SM3 Ralph William Henry Kloepper, who had previously served in the USS *Denebola*, was killed in action. On February 14, 1945, his father was informed by letter that he would receive Kloepper's posthumously awarded Purple Heart. This decoration, along with the American Defense Service Medal and World War II Victory Medal, were mailed to Kloepper's father in February 1947.

Joseph Molnar: Purple Heart—October 31, 1941
Then-FN1 Joseph Molnar survived the sinking of *Reuben James* and was rescued. Interestingly, he was serving as a chief machinist's mate in the *Kearny* when the Navy awarded him the Purple Heart on January 27, 1945.

Howard V. Wade: Purple Heart—October 31, 1941
Then-Ens. Howard Voyer Wade was killed in action. Wade's posthumous Purple Heart was presented to his father in Glen Ridge, New Jersey, on May 29, 1943.

WORLD WAR II (1941–1945)

Between the Japanese attack on Pearl Harbor in December 1941 and end of hostilities in August 1945, the U.S. Navy expanded to more than 3.4 million men and women. By the end of World War II, roughly 36,950 sailors had been killed in combat, and another 37,778 had been wounded. About 75,000 posthumous and nonposthumous Purple Hearts eventually were awarded to naval personnel and their next of kin for action during the conflict.

Since the Navy continues to award the Purple Heart to eligible World War II–era upon request, the precise number of awards may never be known. In 1958, however, the Navy estimated that it had awarded 9,440 Purple Hearts to sailors who were nonmortal battle casualties between 1941 and 1945.[14]

John F. Kennedy: Purple Heart—August 2, 1943
See chapter 9, "Celebrities: Artists and Entertainers, Politicians, Athletes, and Other Public Figures."

Reinhardt J. Keppler: Purple Heart—November 12–13, 1942
Reinhardt John Keppler was wounded in action while serving in the USS *San Francisco* at Guadalcanal on the night of November 12–13, 1942. Because he died from his injuries three days later, Keppler's family received his posthumous Purple Heart and Medal of Honor.

Born in Ralston, Washington, on January 22, 1918, Keppler was the son of German immigrants. After graduating from high school, he enlisted in the Navy on February 19, 1936. Keppler subsequently reenlisted in April 1940 and was assigned to the heavy cruiser USS *San Francisco*.

Keppler saw action at Pearl Harbor, Bougainville, and New Guinea. On the night of November 12, 1942, then-BM1 Keppler was one of the many sailors fighting fires on the *San Francisco*, which had been badly damaged by gunfire from Japanese battleships and an enemy torpedo plane that had crashed on the ship's aft machine-gun platform.

As fires raged below deck, Keppler single-handedly tried to extinguish a large fire in the ship's hangar. Ignoring the constant rain of enemy shells, Keppler walked into the blaze, using the water in his fire hose to cut a path. At one point, he was badly wounded by enemy shrapnel, but, although in great pain and mortally wounded, Keppler refused to seek medical treatment. He succeeded in extinguishing the fire in the hangar and continued to fight other fires until collapsing from loss of blood.

For Keppler's "extraordinary heroism and distinguished courage" in the *San Francisco*, he was posthumously awarded the Medal of Honor. According to the citation for this award, Keppler "saved the lives of several shipmates who otherwise might have perished." He also "labored valiantly in the midst of bursting shells, persistently directing fire-fighting operations and administrating to wounded personnel."[15]

Keppler died of his wounds on November 15, at the age of twenty-four. Keppler is buried at Golden Gate National Cemetery in San Bruno, California.

Albert L. Sullivan: Purple Heart—November 13, 1942
Francis H. Sullivan: Purple Heart—November 13, 1942
George T. Sullivan: Purple Heart—November 13, 1942
Joseph E. Sullivan: Purple Heart—November 13, 1942
Madison A. Sullivan: Purple Heart—November 13, 1942

See chapter 8, "Families: Brothers, Fathers and Sons, and Husbands and Wives."

Franklin Van Valkenburgh: Purple Heart—December 7, 1941

Franklin Van Valkenburgh, the captain of the USS *Arizona*, was killed in action during the Japanese attack on Pearl Harbor. His family received his posthumous Purple Heart and Medal of Honor.

Born in Minneapolis, Minnesota, on April 5, 1888, Van Valkenburgh entered the U.S. Naval Academy in 1905 and graduated in 1909. His initial service was in battleships, punctuated by a tour with the Asiatic Squadron from 1911 to 1914.

Van Valkenburgh was the engineering officer of the USS *Rhode Island* during World War I, and he also served in the battleships USS *Minnesota* and USS *Maryland* during that time. After being promoted to commander, he served in the Office of the Chief of Naval Operations in Washington, D.C., from 1928 to 1931 and then commanded the destroyer USS *Talbot* and Destroyer Squadron Five.

In February 1941 then-Captain Valkenburgh took command of the *Arizona*. On December 7, 1941, he was on the bridge of his battleship when a direct bomb hit on the bridge killed him. For his "conspicuous devotion to duty and extraordinary courage" that day, Van Valkenburgh was posthumously awarded the Medal of Honor. His next of kin also received his posthumously awarded Purple Heart.[16] The Navy named the destroyer USS *Van Valkenburgh* in his honor when she was commissioned in 1944.

Bert V. Webb: Purple Heart—November 1942

Bert V. Webb was serving as a sailor in the submarine USS *Chatot* when, "during action" in November 1942, he was "knocked against bulkhead, injuring knee, shin and ankle." The Navy awarded him a Purple Heart on September 13, 1944.[17]

Stafford M. Wheeler: Purple Heart—April 13, 1945

Lt. Stafford Manchester Wheeler, a naval reservist serving in the Medical Corps, was killed in Yugoslavia on April 13, 1945, when he stepped on an enemy land mine. Wheeler was a member of the USA Typhus Commission.

Albert H. Wilson Jr.: Purple Heart—June 6, 1942

Albert H. Wilson Jr. was in the USS *Yorktown* and was part of a salvage party when he was wounded in action. According to Navy records, the wound occurred when Wilson was "knocked down by a falling hatch when the ship (*Yorktown*) was struck by a torpedo." After Wilson requested that he be awarded a Purple Heart and enclosed proof of medical treatment, the Navy awarded him the decoration on June 5, 1944.[18]

KOREA (1950–1953)

Four hundred seventy-five sailors were killed and 1,576 were wounded in the fighting on and around the Korean peninsula between June 1950 and the end of hostilities in 1953. It follows that slightly more than two thousand Purple Hearts could have been awarded for the Korean War, but the exact number of awards may never be known. In 1958, the Navy estimated that it had awarded about four hundred Purple Hearts to sailors who had been nonmortal battle casualties between 1950 and 1953.[19]

Billy E. Cochran: Purple Heart—June 16, 1951

Billy Edward Cochran was reported missing in action near the island of Yo Do, Korea, in June 1951, and presumed to have died in March 1955.

Then–Lieutenant (junior grade) Cochran served as a photographic interpretation officer and assistant intelligence officer on the staff of the Seventh Fleet during the Korean War. From September 1950 until March 1951, he "spent long arduous hours interpreting photographs of enemy installations in order to obtain the most suitable targets and to assess battle damage." Cochran also interviewed North Korean and Chinese POWs and collected "enemy documents while a member of the Seventh Fleet intelligence team at Wonsan, Korea," and "assisted directly in the locating of enemy mine fields."[20]

On June 14, 1951, Cochran, in the company of a Republic of Korea Marine coxswain, left the island of Yo Do in a U.S. Army boat to return two mechanics to their ship after the mechanics had made preliminary repairs to an Army vessel. According to a letter from the Bureau of Naval Personnel, "Billy became confused as to his directions and headed south at a high rate of speed toward enemy held territory."[21] Later, the boat in which Cochran was travelling was located on a beach near Hwangto-do. Efforts to intercept and recover the vessel were not successful, and Cochran was never seen again.

The Navy initially carried Cochran as missing in action, but declared him to be dead on March 1, 1955, "for purposes of termination of pay and allowances." As a letter to his parents explained, the Navy was "most reluctant" to declare that Cochran was deceased. But, "in view of the lack of official information indicating he survived and of the length of time that has elapsed since he was reported missing in action," the Navy "reluctantly concluded" Cochran was deceased.

The Navy awarded Cochran a posthumous Purple Heart on June 9, 1955, and presented an officially engraved medal and certificate to his parents shortly thereafter. Despite this official action by the Navy in 1955, the Defense Prisoner of War/Missing Personnel Office currently shows Cochran as a POW on its roll of personnel still missing from the Korean War.[22]

Donald E. Mason: Purple Heart—October 12, 1952

Donald E. Mason was wounded while administering to wounded Marines during fierce combat in Korea in 1952.

Born in Indiana in 1933, Mason dropped out of high school and joined the Navy in 1950. After completing basic training at Great Lakes, Illinois, he went to sea on the cruiser USS *Albany* and participated in cruises in the Mediterranean, South America, Scandinavia, and the Caribbean. While at sea, Mason decided he wanted to go to Hospital Corps Training School, and he volunteered to work in the ship's sick bay. This work would later pay big dividends.

After completing hospital school in Portsmouth, Virginia, in 1952, Mason volunteered for Field Medical Service School at Camp Pendleton, California. After four weeks of medical schooling and four weeks of Marine training, then-Hospitalman Mason deployed to South Korea. He landed in August

Navy nurses Lt. Barbara Wooster (left), Lt. Ruth A. Mason (center), and Lt. (j.g.) Ann D. Reynolds (right) are decorated with the Purple Heart after being wounded in action in Saigon on Christmas Eve, 1964. They were the first women to be awarded the Purple Heart in Vietnam. (Naval Historical Center)

1952 and immediately went online with Company B of the 1st Battalion, 7th Marine Regiment, 1st Marine Division. On October 12, 1952, Mason and another corpsman accompanied eighty-four Marines on a raid against Chinese forces above the 38th parallel.

The unit departed friendly lines at 9 PM and moved 2 ½ miles with the intent of attacking the enemy. Instead, the Marines stumbled into Chinese trenches, and a bloody firefight erupted. Grenades, heavy machine-gun fire, and automatic weapons fire pinned down the Americans for four hours. Throughout the engagement Mason "unhesitatingly moved about the devastated area to administer first aid and lend words of encouragement to the many wounded Marines," even though he had been painfully wounded.[23]

After he was temporarily blinded by flash burns from a grenade, Mason continued to minister to casualties. When told that a Marine was seriously wounded and could not be moved, Mason asked to be led to the side of the man, where he applied a difficult splint by sense of touch.

In a 2007 interview with the author, Mason said that his success in Korea was due to his training aboard the *Albany*. "That really helped me," Mason recalled. "Because I had more experience. . . . For example, I had already done a lot of suturing. . . . That put me ahead of the game."

In addition to receiving the Purple Heart, Mason was decorated a year later with the Navy Cross. But it was a bittersweet event because, of the eighty-six men who had gone on the raid, 40 percent were casualties. Two Marines were killed, nineteen were litter-wounded, and another fourteen sustained wounds that did not require hospitalization.

After Korea, Mason returned to Indianapolis to finish high school. He graduated in 1954 and briefly attended Indiana University before returning to the Navy as a hospital corpsman. Over the next twenty years, Mason served in various assignments, including three more tours with the Marines and a long tour in Southeast Asia detailed to the State Department.

After retiring from the Navy as a master chief hospital corpsman in February 1977, Mason had a second career as a Foreign Service Officer. He retired a second time in May 1994 and now lives in Texas.

VIETNAM, CAMBODIA, AND LAOS (1962–1975)

Navy casualties for Vietnam were 1,605 killed in action and 4,178 wounded. It follows that the Navy awarded more than 5,600 Purple Hearts to service members who took part in the conflict.[24]

Frances L. Crumpton: Purple Heart—December 24, 1964
Ruth A. Mason: Purple Heart—December 24, 1964
Ann D. Reynolds: Purple Heart—December 24, 1964
Barbara Wooster: Purple Heart—December 24, 1964

Lt. Frances Crumpton, Lt. Ruth Mason, Lt. (j.g.) Ann Reynolds, and Lt. Barbara Wooster were wounded in Saigon on Christmas Eve 1964, when Viet Cong saboteurs blew up the Brink Bachelors Officer Quarters. Two Americans were killed, and more than one hundred personnel were wounded.

The four Navy nurses refused treatment for their own wounds while continuing to attend to the other wounded. They were the first females to receive the Purple Heart in Vietnam.[25]

Robert J. Flynn: Purple Hearts—August 21, 1967, and January 1970

Robert J. Flynn, an A-6 bombardier–navigator, was shot down over North Vietnam in 1967 and spent the next 2,032 days as a POW in the People's Republic of China. Flynn's experience was unique for two reasons: He was the only naval flyer to be held captive by the Chinese, and all his imprisonment was in solitary confinement.

Born in September 1937 in La Crosse, Wisconsin, Flynn grew up in Houston, Minnesota, a town of fewer than one thousand residents. After graduating from high school in 1955, Flynn entered the University of Minnesota, but he left his studies early to join the Navy in July 1958. He completed training as a bombardier-navigator and joined Heavy Attack Squadron Eight (VAH-8) in February 1961. In 1963 Flynn was reassigned to Attack Squadron 42 (VA-42), known as the "Green Pawns" at Naval Air Station Oceana.

VA-42 became the first fleet squadron to receive the A-6A Intruder, and Flynn joined twenty-seven other pilots and bombardier-navigators as part of the Fleet Introduction Team transitioning to this new twin-engine jet attack plane. He and his colleagues subsequently instructed other attack squadrons on operating the new A-6.

In 1966 then-Lieutenant Flynn deployed to Vietnam, where he joined Attack Squadron 85 (VA-85) and flew fourteen missions off the USS *Kitty Hawk*. In 1967 Flynn joined Attack Squadron 196 (VA-196) aboard the USS *Constellation*.

On August 21, 1967, Flynn was on his seventy-first combat mission as the bombardier-navigator in an A-6 piloted by Cdr. James L. "Jimmy" Buckley. Theirs was one of four aircraft whose mission was to strike the Duc Noi rail yard, four miles north of Hanoi.

Flynn explained in a 2008 interview that while he and Buckley were successful in reaching the target, they were shot down east of Hanoi, about twenty miles from the border with China by a MiG-19 using an air-to-air missile. "We were not over Chinese territory and never violated Chinese airspace," said Flynn. On the contrary, "I landed in North Vietnam but was turned over to the Chinese by the North Vietnamese . . . probably because there was a significant Chinese soldier presence in this border area."

Buckley had been killed in the shootdown. Flynn survived but suffered severe spinal compression fractures during his ejection from the A-6.

Flynn was taken by the Chinese to Beijing and was held in solitary confinement for the next five and a half years. During the winter months,

Cdr. Robert J. Flynn, an A-6 bombardier-navigator, was shot down over North Vietnam and spent the next 2,032 days as a prisoner of war in China. He was awarded two Purple Hearts for his combat wounds. (U.S. Navy)

Flynn suffered freezing temperatures because he had no warm clothing. He also was repeatedly tortured by the Chinese, who demanded that Flynn sign a "confession" that he was a "culprit" and a "criminal" who had violated "sacred Chinese airspace." Despite the half decade of isolation and three separate episodes of excruciatingly painful handcuff torture—one lasting two months in 1970—Flynn steadfastly refused to cooperate.

The Chinese released Flynn on March 15, 1973, and he was reunited with his wife and children. He subsequently served as a squadron commander and, finally, as the director of aviation warfare training at the Naval Education and Training Command headquarters in Pensacola, Florida, before taking a medical retirement in 1985.

For his extraordinary heroism in captivity, Flynn was awarded the Legion of Merit and three Bronze Star Medals, each with the V Combat Distinguishing Device. His other awards include the Distinguished Flying Cross and two Purple Hearts.[26]

James B. Stockdale: Purple Hearts—September 9, 1965, and September 1969

See chapter 9, "Celebrities: Artists and Entertainers, Politicians, Athletes, and Other Public Figures."

USS *LIBERTY* (1967)

On June 8, 1967, Israeli aircraft and torpedo boats attacked the USS *Liberty*, which was operating in international waters in the Mediterranean. Israel was at war with Egypt, Jordan, and Syria in what has become known as the Six-Day War because the conflict lasted only from June 5 until June 10. The *Liberty* was in the area to gather intelligence about the conflict.

Thirty-one sailors were killed and 168 men were wounded. The Israel Defense Forces (IDF) has steadfastly maintained that the episode was a tragic friendly-fire incident, but others believe the attack was premeditated. Official investigations conducted by both the Israeli and U.S. governments, however, concluded that the attack was an accident.[27]

The Navy approved Purple Hearts for all the sailors and Marines on the *Liberty* who were killed or wounded prior to September 1967. Recipients included the following.

William L. McGonagle: Purple Heart—June 8, 1967

William Loren McGonagle, then serving as the *Liberty*'s captain, was wounded during the air attack, but he remained in command on the ship's bridge. Born November 19, 1925, McGonagle was a Wichita, Kansas, native who enlisted in the Navy in 1944. He served in World War II and Korea before taking command of the *Liberty* in April 1966.

While McGonagle was awarded the Purple Heart for his serious injuries, his extraordinary heroism on June 8 also resulted in McGonagle receiving the Medal of Honor. His citation reads in part:

Although severely wounded during the first air attack, Captain (then Commander) McGonagle remained at his battle station on the badly damaged bridge and, with full knowledge of the seriousness of his wounds, subordinated his own welfare to the safety and survival of his command. Steadfastly refusing any treatment which would take him away from his post, he calmly continued to exercise firm command of his ship. Despite continuous exposure to fire, he maneuvered his ship, directed its defense, supervised the control of flooding and fire, and saw to the care of the casualties. Captain McGonagle's extraordinary valor under these conditions inspired the surviving members of the *Liberty*'s crew, many of them seriously wounded, to heroic efforts to overcome the battle damage and keep the ship afloat. Subsequent to the attack, although in great pain and weak from the loss of blood, Captain McGonagle remained at his battle station and continued to conn his ship for more than seventeen hours. It was only after rendezvous with a United States destroyer that he relinquished personal control of the *Liberty* and permitted himself to be removed from the bridge. Even then, he refused much needed medical attention until convinced that the seriously wounded among his crew had been treated.

After recovering from his wounds, McGonagle commanded the ammunition ship USS *Kilauea* and also commanded the Naval ROTC unit at the University of Oklahoma.

Captain McGonagle retired from active duty in 1974 and died on March 3, 1999, at his home in Palm Springs, California. He is interred at Arlington National Cemetery.[28]

USS *PUEBLO* (1968)

On January 23, 1968, the USS *Pueblo* and its crew were attacked and seized by North Korean submarine chasers and torpedo boats. This was the first capture of an American naval vessel since World War II, and the sailors and Marines in the *Pueblo*'s crew suffered greatly until their release eleven months later, on December 23, 1968.

The basic facts are not in dispute. While America's armed forces focused their efforts in Vietnam—there were some 500,000 military personnel in Southeast Asia in 1968—military operations continued elsewhere in the world. The *Pueblo*, a Navy auxiliary general environmental research vessel being used for military intelligence gathering, was operating off the North Korean coast. While the North Koreans insist that the *Pueblo* entered their territorial waters, most historians believe she was in international waters. There is no question, however, that the *Pueblo* was eavesdropping on Soviet and North Korean signals traffic when she was attacked. Although the ship was lightly armed and could not have withstood an all-out assault, the *Pueblo* was unable to put up any fight whatsoever because her ammunition was below deck, and her guns were encased in cold-weather tarpaulins.

The *Pueblo*'s crew, commanded by Cdr. Lloyd M. Bucher, consisted of six naval officers, seventy-three enlisted naval personnel, two enlisted Marines, and two civilian oceanographers. DC3 Duane D. Hodges was killed in the attack and was awarded a posthumous Purple Heart. Eight other sailors, including Bucher, were wounded in the attack and also received Purple Hearts.[29] Additionally, each of the men wounded in the initial attack received a second Purple Heart for the wounds they suffered at the hands of the North Koreans during captivity.

While Bucher and the *Pueblo*'s crew were starved and repeatedly tortured, negotiations for their release got under way and culminated in the release of the Americans just before Christmas Day 1968. With Bucher in the lead, the *Pueblo* crew walked across the Demilitarized Zone into South Korea.

The secretary of the Navy, having determined that the entire crew had been tortured and otherwise injured while imprisoned by the North Koreans, directed that Purple Hearts be awarded to the entire crew. This was highly unusual, and no crew before or since has had every member awarded the Purple Heart for wounds received while in captivity.

The Navy subsequently convened a court of inquiry, and that body faulted Bucher for surrendering the *Pueblo* without firing a shot and recommended that he and another officer be court-martialed. Secretary of the Navy John H. Chafee, however, declined to adopt this recommendation, believing that no useful purpose would be served by legal action. As a result, Bucher was able to finish his naval career as a commander and retired in 1973. He wrote *Bucher: My Story* (Doubleday and Co., 1970) before he died in 2004 at the age of seventy-six.

Cdr. Lloyd M. Bucher was awarded two Purple Hearts for the wounds he received while serving as skipper of the USS *Pueblo*. (Naval Historical Center)

Today, some informed observers insist that Bucher should not have surrendered the *Pueblo* and could have resisted. Others, however, insist that he did all he could and that the Navy could have sent help that would have prevented the disaster. In a 1989 letter published in two magazines, Bucher himself said that "the story of the *Pueblo*, in a nutshell, is one of a naval officer, his crew and his ship. . . . Things went bad, and the Navy abandoned them."[30]

In retrospect, it is clear that the *Pueblo's* capture was part of a larger North Korean plan to foment trouble in South Korea, and, in fact, North Korean troops had attempted the assassination of South Korea's president just days earlier. The struggle on the Korean peninsula, of course, was part of the larger Cold War then waging between America and the Soviet Union.

While the crewmembers of the *Pueblo* have long since returned to American soil, the ship itself remains captive in Pyongyang, North Korea, where it is a major tourist attraction.[31] *Pueblo* crew members receiving the Purple Heart included the following.

Lloyd Bucher: Purple Hearts—January 23, 1968, and
     January 24–December 23, 1968
Charles H. Crandlell: Purple Hearts—January 23, 1968, and
     January 24–December 23, 1968
Timothy L. Harris: Purple Hearts—January 23, 1968, and
     January 24–December 23, 1968
Duane D. Hodges: Purple Heart—January 23, 1968
Peter M. Langenberg: Purple Hearts—January 23, 1968, and
     January 24–December 23, 1968
Wendell G. Leach: Purple Hearts—January 23, 1968, and
     January 24–December 23, 1968
Edward R. Murphy: Purple Hearts—January 23, 1968, and
     January 24–December 23, 1968
Steven J. Robin: Purple Hearts—January 23, 1968, and
     January 24–December 23, 1968
Steven E. Woelk: Purple Hearts—January 23, 1968, and
     January 24–December 23, 1968

GUATEMALA (1968)

Harry L. Greene: Purple Heart—January 16, 1968
Ernest A. Munro: Purple Heart—January 16, 1968
On January 16, 1968, Lt. Cdr. Ernest Munro, RMCS Harry Greene, and two other American military men were travelling in a sedan in Guatemala City when they were attacked by three terrorists firing machine guns. Munro, who was serving as chief of the U.S. military mission's naval section, was killed almost instantly by the fusillade. Greene was wounded in the attack.[32] The

secretary of the Navy awarded Purple Hearts to both men on April 5, 1968. Munro's medal was presented to his next of kin. Greene received his award at Walter Reed General Hospital on April 22, 1968.[33]

KOREA (1974)

Robert M. Ballinger: Purple Heart—November 20, 1974

Cdr. Robert Ballinger was killed while on a mission to investigate tunnels built by the North Koreans in the southern portion of the Demilitarized Zone. He was killed by an explosion of dynamite placed in the tunnel by the North Koreans. The secretary of the Navy awarded Ballinger a posthumous Purple Heart on February 3, 1975.[35]

Franklin G. West: Purple Heart—March 3, 1974

Lt. Cdr. Franklin West was wounded by North Korean soldiers in Panmunjom, Korea, on March 3, 1974. The secretary of the Navy awarded him the Purple Heart on October 29, 1974.[34]

LEBANON (1978)

Robert E. Nelson: Purple Heart—March 15, 1978

Robert E. Nelson was wounded in his left arm by shrapnel while serving as an unarmed UN observer in Lebanon on March 15, 1978.

Then-Lieutenant Nelson was a member of the UN Truce Supervisory Organization and was manning an observation post at the village of Maroun Al Ras. On the night of March 14–15, 1978, the village was assaulted by the IDF as part of Israel's invasion of Lebanon up to the Latani River. The Israelis attacked with air support, tanks, and artillery and swept directly over the bunker in which Nelson had taken refuge.

About 6 AM on March 15, while Nelson and his Canadian Army colleague were "attempting to identify themselves as unarmed observers, an IDF soldier fired a short burst, 5–10 rounds, through the door of our bunker. The rounds ricocheted off the concrete walls; one lodged in Lt. Nelson's flak jacket. Many smaller pieces, wounded him in the left arm near his elbow and his leg."[36]

Nelson was given first aid by the Israelis and, subsequently, had the shrapnel removed by UN medical staff in Beirut.

PUERTO RICO (1979)

Cottie A. Allen: Purple Heart—December 3, 1979
John R. Ball: Purple Heart—December 3, 1979
Allen Bush: Purple Heart—December 3, 1979
Bradley Clark: Purple Heart—December 3, 1979
Cynthia C. Edwards: Purple Heart—December 3, 1979
Joseph R. Key: Purple Heart—December 3, 1979
Monique A. Ritter: Purple Heart—December 3, 1979
Richard D. Sauter: Purple Heart—December 3, 1979
Sandra L. Seaton: Purple Heart—December 3, 1979
Warren C. Smith: Purple Heart—December 3, 1979
Emil E. White: Purple Heart—December 3, 1979
Debra J. Whitehurst: Purple Heart—December 3, 1979

On December 3, 1979, Puerto Rican terrorists ambushed a Navy bus near San Juan. The bus had seventeen unarmed sailors aboard, all of whom were travelling to work. Two of the sailors—CTO1 John Ball and RM3 Emil White—were killed, and the ten others named above were wounded.

Since this attack was not by an "enemy" or the result of a "hostile foreign force," the legal basis for awarding the Purple Heart was highly questionable; note that the "international terrorist attack" category did not yet exist. Yet, on March 31, 1980, the secretary of the Navy awarded the Purple Heart to sailors killed and wounded in the incident.[37]

TURKEY (1980)

Sam A. Novello: Purple Heart—April 16, 1980
Sam A. Novello was assassinated by terrorists as he left his home in the Levent neighborhood of Istanbul, Turkey, on April 16, 1980.

Born in Erie, Pennsylvania, Novello had enlisted in the Navy in 1942. At the time of his murder, then–Master Chief Boatswain's Mate Novello was serving as the Istanbul representative of the U.S. Navy Section, Joint U.S. Military Mission for Aid to Turkey. He was a hard hat diver and worked with Turkish Navy units to improve their salvage, amphibious, and demolition operations.

Novello and his Turkish driver were both killed instantly by four gunmen, who fired more than one hundred rounds of ammunition and then fled on motorcycles. The Marxist-Leninist Armed Propaganda Squad, a branch of the Turkish Peoples' Liberation Party-Front, claimed responsibility for the killings.[38]

On April 24, 1980, Secretary of the Navy Edward Hidalgo approved the award of a posthumous Purple Heart to Novello. Novello also received a posthumous Legion of Merit.

LEBANON (1983–1984)

Daniel J. Pellegrino: Purple Heart—April 18, 1983
IS1 Daniel Pellegrino was wounded during the bombing of the U.S. Embassy in Beirut on April 18, 1983. The secretary of the Navy awarded Pellegrino a Purple Heart on November 16, 1984.[39]

Eugene H. Cole: Purple Heart—August 29, 1983
EOC Eugene Cole was wounded on Green Beach, Beirut, while attempting to spot positions of hostile forces. He was awarded the Purple Heart on April 19, 1984.[40]

Lee A. Cloninger: Purple Heart—October 19, 1983
Lt. Lee Cloninger was injured by a car bomb while travelling with a Marine convoy in Beirut on October 19, 1983. He was awarded the Purple Heart on March 23, 1984.

David E. Worley: Purple Heart—October 23, 1983
David Edward Worley died in the infamous Beirut bombing of October 1983 in which 241 troops, mostly Marines, were killed. A native of Maryland, then twenty-five-year-old Worley was a hospital corpsman and had deployed to Beirut with Camp Lejeune–based Marines. Worley's wife and two sons were presented his posthumously awarded Purple Heart.

EL SALVADOR (1983)

Albert A. Schaufelberger III: Purple Heart—May 25, 1983
Albert A. "Al" Schaufelberger III was shot and killed by a terrorist in San Salvador, El Salvador, on May 25, 1983.

A 1971 graduate of the U.S. Naval Academy, Schaufelberger was SEAL-qualified and had served in Japan, Thailand, the Philippines, and Korea prior to arriving in El Salvador in August 1982. At the time of his murder then–Lieutenant Commander Schaufelberger was serving as the Navy representative to the U.S. Military Group, El Salvador. His chief mission was to advise the El Salvadoran Navy on how best to interdict the flow of arms to guerrilla forces operating in El Salvador. Consequently, he advised the Salvadorans on patrol boat operations and maintenance, boat repair, and supply support administration.

According to contemporary media accounts, Schaufelberger was killed while seated in his armored, U.S. embassy–provided Ford Maverick. He was parked on the ground of the Central American University in San Salvador and was waiting for his girlfriend. It was about 6:30 PM. As Schaufelberger's girlfriend approached his car, she saw a white Volkswagen Microbus pull up. Three men got out of this bus, and one of them ran to the open window of Schaufelberger's car and fired four small-caliber bullets into Schaufelberger's head. The thirty-three-year-old American was killed instantly.[41]

On May 26, 1983, a recorded message, purportedly from Popular Forces of Liberation insurgents, claimed that Schaufelberger had been killed as "an answer to the criminal intervention of Yankee imperialism."[42] Secretary of the Navy John F. Lehman Jr. awarded Schaufelberger a posthumous Purple Heart and Legion of Merit on June 3, 1983.[43]

GRENADA (1983)

Donald K. Erskine: Purple Heart—October 25, 1983

Donald Kim Erskine received a bullet wound to his right arm during combat in Grenada as part of Operation Urgent Fury.

During the early morning hours of October 25, 1983, then-Lieutenant Erskine "twice engaged the enemy and . . . took ten wounded prisoners of war without casualty to his assault element." After establishing a defensive perimeter, he was attacked by a "numerically superior force" using automatic weapons, rocket-propelled grenades, and 20-mm cannon fire. "Although painfully wounded . . . and closely pursued by a large enemy force," Erskine "courageously directed his men in evasion and escape maneuvers which resulted in the safe extraction of his entire force."[44]

On January 26, 1984, the secretary of the Navy awarded Erskine a Purple Heart for the combat injuries he suffered on October 25 and a Silver Star for extraordinary heroism.

GREECE (1983)

George Tsantes Jr.: Purple Heart—November 15, 1983

George Tsantes Jr. was assassinated by terrorists in Athens, Greece, while on his way to work in an automobile.

Captain Tsantes, a U.S. Naval Academy graduate who had served as an engineering officer in nuclear-powered surface ships, was in Greece as the chief of the Naval Section, Joint U.S. Military Advisory Group. On November 15, 1983, he was en route to his office from his home in a northern suburb when a gunman on a motor scooter fired a .45-caliber pistol into the car in which Tsantes was riding. A bullet struck Tsantes "below the heart," killing him instantly. The driver of the car, who was also shot, died later in a hospital.[45]

The Greek terrorist group 17 November claimed responsibility for the murder, and Tsantes was posthumously awarded the Purple Heart by Secretary of the Navy Lehman in February 1984.

LEBANON (1985)

Robert D. Stethem: Purple Heart—June 15, 1985

Robert D. Stethem was shot in the head by terrorists during the hijacking of an airliner in Beirut on June 15, 1985.

Born in November 1961 in Waterbury, Connecticut, Stethem enlisted in the Navy after graduating from high school in 1980. In June 1985, then-Steel-worker Second Class Stethem was a Navy Seabee and was working on a project at the Naval Communication Station at Nea Makri, Greece. On June 14, 1985, he boarded TWA Flight 847 in Athens for a flight to the United States to see family and friends.

After the flight departed Athens, however, it was hijacked by the militant Shiite group Hezbollah, who forced the pilot to fly first to Algiers, and then to Beirut. Hezbollah demanded that Israel release 766 Lebanese and Palestinian prisoners held by Israel. When these demands were not met, Stethem was singled out because of his U.S. military status, brutally beaten, and then killed. The hijackers dumped his body on the tarmac at the Beirut airport.[46]

Stethem was posthumously awarded the Purple Heart and the Bronze Star Medal for heroic achievement. He is interred at Arlington National Cemetery and the destroyer USS *Stethem* was named in his honor.

USS *STARK* (1987)

On May 17, 1987, two Exocet antiship missiles fired by an Iraqi fighter struck the guided missile frigate USS *Stark*. The first Iraqi missile penetrated the portside hull but did not detonate. The second missile entered at almost the same point and then exploded. Thirty-seven U.S. sailors were killed, and twenty-one were injured.

Although she was on fire and listing badly, the *Stark* was brought under control by her crew and sailed to Bahrain for temporary repairs. The ship was later fully repaired in Mississippi and returned to service until she was decommissioned in May 1999.

While the Iraqi pilot's attack on the *Stark* was intentional, the extent to which the Iraqi government authorized it—if at all—remains unanswered. A court of inquiry, however, concluded that the frigate's commanding officer, Capt. Glenn R. Brindel, had failed to perform his duty satisfactorily. Brindel was relieved from command and recommended for court-martial. He was, however, permitted to retire after accepting nonjudicial punishment for dereliction of duty.[47]

Recipients of the Purple Heart for the *Stark* debacle included the following sailors.

John A. Ciletta Jr., Purple Heart, May 17, 1987
SN John Ciletta, a native of Brigantine, New Jersey, was killed in the attack. He is interred at Arlington National Cemetery.

Christopher DeAngelis: Purple Heart—May 17, 1987
ET3 Christopher DeAngelis, a Dumont, New Jersey, native, was killed in the attack. He is interred at Arlington National Cemetery.

ITALY (1988)

Stanley Lawson: Purple Heart—April 14, 1988
Francisco A. Navalta: Purple Heart—April 14, 1988
Charles F. Roberts: Purple Heart—April 14, 1988
Craig L. Trent: Purple Heart—April 14, 1988
On April 14, 1988, about 8 PM, a terrorist bomb exploded in a car parked across from the Naples USO club. A number of sailors were injured, and the secretary of the Navy approved the award of Purple Hearts to ET3 Stanley Lawson, EMC Francisco Navalta, FCCS Charles Roberts, and ET3 Craig Trent.

PERSIAN GULF WAR (1991)

Six sailors were killed in action during Operation Desert Storm between January 17 and February 28, 1991, and at least nine were wounded. All received Purple Hearts, including the following.[48]

Clarence D. Connor: Purple Heart—January 17, 1991
HM Clarence D. Connor was the first individual to receive the Purple Heart in Operation Desert Storm. On January 17, 1991, he was a corpsman attached to the 1st Reconnaissance Battalion, 1st Marine Division and was on a patrol near the Kuwait border when he was hit in the back by shrapnel from Iraqi artillery fire. He was knocked to the ground when a two-by-one-half-inch piece of shrapnel tore a three-inch hole in his trapezius muscle and severed a nerve in his right shoulder. The shrapnel in Connor's wound was so deep that the twenty-one-year-old sailor was medically evacuated to a rear hospital for surgery.

Maj. Gen. James M. Myatt, the commanding general for the 1st Marine Division, congratulated Connor on earning the war's first Purple Heart. The decoration was presented to Connor on January 28, 1991.[49]

Patrick K. Connor: Purple Heart—February 2, 1991
Barry T. Cooke: Purple Heart—February 2, 1991
Patrick Kelly Conner and Barry T. Cooke were killed in action during a strike mission against Iraqi warships.

Lieutenant Commander Cooke was the pilot, and Lieutenant (junior grade) Conner was the bombardier-navigator, of an A-6 Intruder that took off from the deck of the USS *Theodore Roosevelt* on February 2, 1991. After the aviators did not return from their mission, search-and-rescue efforts located aircraft wreckage off the coast of Kuwait. Initially, both men were declared missing in action, but, after Conner's remains were recovered, the status of both men was changed to killed in action.

Connor, a native of Columbia, Missouri, was twenty-five years old at the time of his death. He was a 1987 graduate of the University of North Carolina at Chapel Hill and received his commission through Naval ROTC. Connor's remains were buried at Arlington National Cemetery in April 1991.

The next of kin of both Cooke and Connor received the men's posthumous Purple Hearts.

William T. Costen: Purple Heart—January 18, 1991
Charles J. Turner: Purple Heart—January 18, 1991

William Thomas Costen and Charles J. Turner were killed in action on January 18, 1991, when their A-6 Intruder was shot down over Iraq.

Lieutenant Costen was a pilot flying off the aircraft carrier USS *Ranger.* He and Lieutenant Turner, a navigator-bombardier, were asked to fly combat missions on Iraqi targets in the first wave of offensive strikes. When they did not return from their mission on January 18, 1991, both men were listed as missing in action. In March 1991, after the Iraqis returned Costen's remains and Turner's body was recovered sometime later, the status of both men was changed to killed in action.

A native of Independence, Missouri, Costen grew up in St. Louis and graduated from the University of the South in Sewanee, Tennessee. He had been in the Navy six years and was twenty-seven years old at the time of his death. Turner, a native of Richfield, Minnesota, was twenty-nine years old at the time of his death and left a wife and six-month-old son.

Costen's and Turner's next of kin received the men's posthumous Purple Hearts.

Robert J. Dwyer: Purple Heart—February 8, 1991

Lt. Robert J. Dwyer was killed when his F/A-18 Hornet was shot down on a bombing mission over Iraq. A native of Worthington, Ohio, Dwyer was thirty-two years old at the time of his death. His wife received his posthumous Purple Heart.

Michael S. Speicher: Purple Heart—January 17, 1991

Michael Scott Speicher was killed in action when his F/A-18 Hornet was shot down on the opening day of the war. His was the first Navy aircraft lost in combat in the Persian Gulf War.

Born in July 1957 in Kansas City, Kansas, Speicher graduated from Florida State University before joining the Navy and qualifying as a naval aviator. On January 17, 1991, then–Lieutenant Commander Speicher took off from the deck of the USS *Saratoga* in order to fly a bombing mission over Iraq. He was shot down either by a surface-to-air missile or by an air-to-air missile fired by an Iraqi MiG-25.

The day he was shot down, Speicher was listed as missing in action. On March 22, 1991, his status was changed to killed in action/body not recovered, and his next of kin were presented his posthumous Purple Heart.

After Speicher's family and others insisted that he had been captured alive and might be held prisoner, the secretary of the Navy changed Speicher's status back to missing in action in 2001, and then to missing in action/captured in 2002.[50] After the 2003 invasion of Iraq and a subsequent investigation failed to provide any evidence that Speicher was still alive, however, the Navy once more reversed course and, in March 2009, listed Speicher as missing in action. In July 2009 Speicher's remains were discovered in Anbar Province, Iraq, which means his memorial headstone in Arlington National Cemetery will be changed to reflect that he was killed in action.

Robert Wetzel: Purple Heart—January 17 1991

Then-Lt. Robert Wetzel was wounded when his A-6E Intruder attack plane was shot down on the first night of the war. He suffered two broken arms and was taken prisoner by the Iraqis.[51]

SOMALIA (1993)

Jarin Connell: Purple Heart—March 25, 1993

On the night of March 25, 1993, then-HM Jarin Connell had treated a Somalian for a gunshot wound and was medevacing the injured man to the military hospital at the airport. While en route to that destination, Connell was struck in the neck by a spear or blowgun dart that caused two puncture wounds.

The tip of the projectile penetrated almost 1½ inches into Connell's neck, and the force of the impact caused him to be ejected from the back of a moving truck. Connell broke his right arm as a result of the fall and also lost consciousness for about five minutes.

Connell's puncture wound required two days hospitalization, and he lost the use of his arm for two weeks. The commandant of the Marine Corps awarded him the Purple Heart on July 31, 1995.[52]

John Gay: Purple Heart—October 3, 1993
Howard Wasdin: Purple Heart—October 3, 1993

Then-SMC John Gay and HT1 Howard Wasdin were both wounded while temporarily assigned to Task Force Ranger, a one-hundred-man unit ambushed by Somali gunmen on October 3, 1993. They were in Mogadishu and on a mission to capture two top aides of the Somali warlord Mohammed Farah Aideed at the time they were attacked and wounded. The secretary of the Navy awarded both Gay and Wasdin Purple Hearts.

CAMBODIA (1993)

Stephen J. Corley: Purple Heart—September 7, 1993

Stephen Corley was wounded when the vehicle in which he was a passenger hit an antitank mine in Cambodia.

Then-Lieutenant Corley was assigned to the UN Transitional Authority in Cambodia as a military observer. About 8 AM on September 7, 1993, Corley was riding in a UN vehicle traveling to Angkor Thom District, Siem Reap Province, in support of Operation Paymaster. An incident report from the senior U.S. military observer dated September 15, 1993, informed the commander of the U.S. Military Observer Group that Corley had "sustained multiple shrapnel wounds, contusions, and a ruptured left ear drum."[53]

Secretary of the Navy John H. Dalton awarded the Purple Heart to Corley on November 5, 1993.

HAITI (1994)

Jose Joseph: Purple Heart—September 24, 1994

While serving in Cap Haitien, Haiti, on September 24, 1994, then-FA Jose Joseph received a gunshot wound in his left calf. The chief of naval operations awarded Joseph a Purple Heart for this combat injury on October 18, 1994.

THE BALKANS: BOSNIA-HERZEGOVINA, CROATIA, KOSOVO, MACEDONIA, AND SERBIA (1994–1999)

Michael W. Watkins: Purple Heart—March 8, 1994

On March 8, 1994, Lt. Michael W. Watkins was aboard a Spanish CASA 212 aircraft en route from Zagreb, Croatia, to Split, Croatia. He was injured in an explosion which was the result of ground fire directed at the airplane.

On July 27, 1994, Navy Secretary Dalton approved the award of a Purple Heart to Watkins.

ATTACK ON THE PENTAGON (2001)

On September 11, 2001, terrorists flew a hijacked airliner into the Pentagon. While there was no legal basis for awarding Purple Hearts to military personnel wounded in the attack because the event was not an international terrorist attack and because the hijackers were not enemy belligerents, the Navy awarded the Purple Heart to a small number of sailors, including the following men and women.

Sarah Cole: Purple Heart—September 11, 2001

Sarah Cole, an intelligence specialist and seaman, was in her office in the Pentagon and was wounded when the impact of the hijacked airliner "blew out the wall in front of her and threw a metal filing cabinet against her body, leaving her with an inch-and-a-half gash in her left shoulder and a mild concussion." Although the "force of the crash blew her and several others completely out of the office," which was located on the first floor of the Pentagon's D Ring, Cole ignored her own injuries and assisted in initial rescue efforts.[54] The Navy awarded her the Purple Heart in late 2001.

Charles E. Coughlin: Purple Heart—September 11, 2001

Charles E. Coughlin was "hit by debris" during the attack on the Pentagon and "slammed his head into a door while scrambling around in the dark and smoky building helping others to escape." The Navy awarded him the Purple Heart for these injuries in late 2001.

Coughlin retired from the Navy as a commander and later was prosecuted for mail fraud in U.S. District Court. Federal prosecutors claimed that Coughlin "falsely claimed he suffered a debilitating injury" as a result of the 9-11 attacks and "used it as an excuse to apply for aid from the Justice Department's victim compensation fund." He collected some $300,000. In April 2009 a federal judge declared a mistrial after a jury acquitted Coughlin of three counts of mail fraud and deadlocked on four other charges.[55]

Patrick Dunn: Purple Heart—September 11, 2001

Then-Cdr. Patrick Dunn was working in the Navy Command Center in the Pentagon when he was killed. Dunn's widow received his posthumously awarded Purple Heart.

A native of Fords, New Jersey, and the son of a police officer, Dunn was a 1985 U.S. Naval Academy graduate. He was a surface warfare officer and had served in the amphibious ship USS *Inchon*, the frigate USS *Montgomery*, and the aircraft carrier USS *Theodore Roosevelt*. Sadly, Dunn's first child—a girl—was born six months after his death.[56]

Kevin Schaeffer: Purple Heart—September 11, 2001

Then-Lt. Kevin Schaeffer was in his office in the Pentagon when "everything just exploded," and he was badly burned. The Navy awarded him the Purple Heart in late 2001.

As Schaeffer remembered it, he saw an orange fireball. "I could feel my hair and head on fire," he later told *Army Times*. "I ran my fingers through my hair, rolled on the floor to put myself out. When I stood, the space was dark, black. There was smoke and rubble."

Burns covered more than 40 percent of Schaeffer's body, including third-degree burns to his hands, arms, and back. He also had severe lung damage, which was caused by inhaling jet fuel in the instant before his office exploded. During a lengthy hospitalization, Schaeffer twice went into cardiac arrest, but he was revived. Although his doctors did not think he would survive his second cardiac event, Schaeffer beat the odds. He was medically retired from the Navy in October 2002.[57]

AFGHANISTAN (2001–)

Mark L. Donald: Purple Heart—October 25, 2003

Mark Donald was wounded by shrapnel in the mountains near Shkin, Afghanistan, on October 25, 2003. A New Mexico native, Donald joined the Marine Corps after graduating from high school in 1985 but then transferred

Navy SEAL Lt. Mark Donald was wounded by shrapnel while fighting in Afghanistan in October 2003. He received a Purple Heart, as well as a Navy Cross for extraordinary heroism. (U.S. Navy)

to the Navy to become a corpsman. In 1989 he completed SEAL training and joined SEAL Team 2. Donald was commissioned in 2000 as a physician's assistant.

On October 25, 2003, then-Lieutenant Donald was part of a mounted convoy on a mission against al-Qaida and the Taliban. The Americans and their Afghan allies were ambushed, and a "hammering eight-hour firefight" followed. Despite "ripping" small-arms, machine-gun, and rocket-propelled grenade fire, Donald got out of his truck shooting, pulled a wounded Afghan commander into cover behind the vehicle's engine block, and then pulled out a trapped American. Donald then covered the wounded with his own body and returned fire. While the al-Qaida and Taliban fire "was heavy enough at points to rip through his clothing and gear and hit his weapon," Donald still managed to treat the wounded.

Later that day, after a joint unit sweeping the area was attacked, Donald "ran 200 meters between opposing forces, exposing him to withering and continuous machine gun and small arms fire, to render medical treatment to two wounded personnel, one Afghan and one American." Then, despite being wounded by shrapnel, Donald organized the surviving Afghan soldiers and led a fighting withdrawal.

For his combat wounds Donald received a Purple Heart. In April 2007, the SEAL medical specialist also was awarded the Navy Cross for his extraordinary heroism that day in October 2003.[58]

Marcus Luttrell: Purple Heart—June 28, 2005

Marcus Luttrell was wounded in action on June 28, 2005, while engaged in combat with Taliban fighters in the mountainous Hindu Kush region.

After enlisting in the Navy and graduating from Basic Underwater Demolition/SEAL (BUD/S) Class 228, then–Petty Officer Marcus Luttrell and three teammates from SEAL Team 10 were assigned to a reconnaissance mission in the Hindu Kush region, and their objective was to gather intelligence on Taliban movements in the area. Luttrell's team was discovered and engaged by more than two hundred Taliban fighters. He was the only survivor of this contact, and, during the rescue mission that followed, sixteen Special Forces personnel, including eight SEALS, died when their helicopter was shot down.

Luttrell received the Navy Cross in 2006 and subsequently wrote an account of his experiences called *Lone Survivor*.[59]

IRAQ (2003–)

Michael J. Pernaselli: Purple Heart—April 24, 2004
A native of Monroe, New York, PO1 Michael Pernaselli was conducting waterborne security operations and was attempting to board a dhow—a small lateen-rigged Arabian boat—when it exploded, killing him instantly. Pernaselli was twenty-seven years old. His family received his posthumous Purple Heart.

Christopher E. Watts: Purple Heart—April 24, 2004
A native of Knoxville, Tennessee, PO2 Christopher Watts was in the same boat with Petty Officer Pernaselli and was also killed in the explosion. Watts was twenty-eight years old. His family received his posthumous Purple Heart.[60]

CHAPTER 4

Airmen: World War I to War on Terrorism

The Aeronautical Division of the Army Signal Corps accepted the Army's first airplane, a Wright Flyer, on August 2, 1909. Consequently, it should come as no surprise that the first Purple Hearts awarded to airmen after the revival of that decoration in 1932 were for combat injuries received while fighting in the skies over France during World War I. Since that time, however, airmen have received Purple Hearts for wounds in the following armed conflicts, international terrorist attacks, and other military operations:

- World War I (1917–1918)
- World War II (1941–1945)
- Korea (1950–1953)
- Soviet Union (1952)
- Cuba (1962)
- Vietnam (1964–1975)
- Cambodia (1975)
- Libya (1986)
- Persian Gulf War (1990–1991)
- Somalia (1993–1994)
- Iraq (1994)
- The Balkans (1994–1995)
- Saudi Arabia (1996)
- Attack on the Pentagon (2000)
- Afghanistan (2001–)
- Iraq (2003–)

The vast majority of Purple Hearts were awarded to airmen wounded or killed during World War II.

WORLD WAR I (1917–1918)

At least one member of the Army Air Service received a Purple Heart decades after being wounded in combat over France.

John W. Van Heuvel: Purple Heart—July 16, 1918

John W. Van Heuvel, a first lieutenant and pilot assigned to the 91st Aero Squadron, was wounded on July 16, 1918. The official history of the squadron states that Van Heuvel was wounded during "a spectacular event" on July 16:

> Lt. Guilbert, pilot, with Lt. Seymour, observer, and Lt. Van Heuvel, pilot, and Lt. Hirth, observer, were attacked soon after crossing the lines at Pont-a-Mousson, by four Fokkers. Lt. Hirth was almost immediately shot dead and Lt. Heuvel "creased" on each side of his head (by enemy bullets). He was knocked unconscious and did not come to until he had dropped over 4,000 meters when he found himself on our side of the lines in a steep dive with the motor full on. He (Van Heuvel) managed to land on the field, and a few minutes later was joined by the other plane which had finally emerged with combat with sixteen bullet holes in the wings and fuselage.[1]

WORLD WAR II (1941–1945)

On June 20, 1941, less than six months before the Japanese attack on Pearl Harbor, Army Chief of Staff Gen. George C. Marshall formally established the U.S. Army Air Forces (USAAF). By early 1942 the USAAF was one of the Army's three coequal commands, and its expansion over the next three years was truly remarkable.

In 1938 there were roughly 20,100 airmen in Army uniforms. By the time major military operations ended in August 1945, the USAAF had grown to more than 1.9 million airmen out of a total Army of more than 8 million troops, and it had almost 80,000 aircraft.

Casualties were heavy for airmen in World War II: 40,061 killed (17,021 of whom were officers) and more than 75,000 wounded in action. All were eligible for the Purple Heart.[2]

Joseph Bernard: Purple Heart—July 9, 1944
Charles Watson: Purple Heart—July 9, 1944
William Winston: Purple Heart—July 9, 1944

Gunfire from Messerschmitt Bf 109 fighters wounded SSgt. Joseph "Joe" Bernard and Sgt. Charles "Charlie" Watson in their legs, and Sgt. William "Billy" Winston in both hands, while the three airmen were on a bombing mission on July 9, 1944. Bernard was an armorer-gunner, Watson was the left waist gunner, and Winston was the ball turret gunner on a B-17 Flying Fortress. They were on their 14th combat mission—a long-range, high-altitude strike on German oil refineries in Ploesti, Romania.

Approaching the target, Bernard was in the bomb bay and arming the plane's bombs. "Our altitude that day was 27,500 feet," said Bernard. "The ambient temperature at that altitude was 53° below zero Fahrenheit." He was just beginning to feel the cold when, abruptly, he was slammed around "like a sardine in a can" by gunfire that knocked out one of the bomber's engines and damaged the other three.

Bernard's crew was a long way from their base at Foggia, Italy. The pilot's concern was to keep up with the formation and continue to the target. Bernard was also concerned about Winston and Watson, both of whom were injured and burned. Amid all this, there was a higher priority: German fighters swarmed around the B-17, guns blazing, ready to finish off the Fortress and its ten-man crew. "Our pilot aggressively called for help from the American fighter aircraft that were part of our protective escort," said Bernard.

A furious gun battle unfolded between the bomber and the Bf 109s. "Winston, Watson and I were credited with shooting down two Bf 109s and with a 'probable kill' of a third," said Bernard. "During this encounter, I received a direct hit of a 20-mm German projectile that exploded on contact with my right leg. I felt a flash of heat and looked down to see why I was off balance. I saw my boot on the floor hanging from the leg zipper of my heated suit. At the end of my stump was a large ball of frozen blood."

Bernard sat down and cut open the leg of his heated suit and applied two tourniquets and sulfa powder to the stump where his foot had been. Hoping to stay mobile to help his buddies, he swallowed several sulfa tablets and gave himself a shot of morphine. "The enemy aircraft responsible for my predicament came up from below us," said Bernard. "I gave him several bursts of my gun, completely oblivious to my being on only one leg. I hit him several times and saw my tracers bounce off his armor-plated underbelly."

After long minutes of pandemonium, a formation of USAAF P-38 Lightning fighters appeared and chased the Germans away. The unique horror of war aboard a damaged bomber had only begun, however. Bernard went to Watson's aid, cut open his bloody pants leg, and applied a tourniquet and sulfa powder. "Winston in his ball turret was screaming uncontrollably," Bernard said. "He said he had been blinded and couldn't move. I went over to the turret and proceeded to hand-crank the turret until I could get it opened. I wiped the blood off and found Winston's face devoid of wounds. He had been wounded in both hands." Again: tourniquets and sulfa.

Bernard and his buddies wrapped themselves in parachutes for protection from the bitter cold while their pilot nursed their crippled bomber homeward. Due in part to Bernard's extraordinary efforts, the B-17 returned safely to Foggia that day. The B-17, riddled with bullet holes, skidded off the runway, and ambulances raced crewmembers to the hospital. A priest administered last rites to Bernard.

Bernard was awarded a Silver Star for saving his fellow airmen. He lost his right leg just below the knee and received a Purple Heart for this and other wounds. Today Joe Bernard, 84, lives with his family in Gainesville, Virginia.[3]

George C. Kenney: Purple Heart—September 12, 1942

George C. Kenney received the Purple Heart for "a singularly meritorious act of essential service" in using instantaneous-fuse parachute bombs to attack Japanese aircraft. This award is one of 272 Purple Hearts awarded for merit—and not for wounds—during World War II.

Born in 1889 Kenney was awarded both the Distinguished Service Cross and Silver Star as an aviator during World War I. In the 1930s then–Lieutenant Colonel Kenney was assigned to the Air Corps Tactical School, where he focused his attention on improving low-altitude bombing. The problem was that the ground absorbed much of the blast of small, light bombs. Kenney realized that reducing the rate of fall of such bombs by merely installing a parachute in their tails would greatly increase bombing effectiveness. The slower rate of fall would give the bombs enough time to arm and allow the aircraft dropping the bomb sufficient time to escape the target area before detonation. Moreover, the bombs would explode before hitting the ground, resulting in greater blast damage because airbursts produce more fragments that travel farther and wider than do groundbursts.

After assuming command of General MacArthur's Air Forces in Southwest Asia in July 1942, then–Major General Kenney decided that the

Gen. George Kenney received his Purple Heart for an "act of essential service" in World War II. His award was one of 272 Purple Hearts made for merit, rather than wounds, during World War II. (National Archives and Records Administration)

parafrag bombs he helped develop were ideal aerial weapons against Japanese aircraft parked on New Guinea airfields. Parafrag bombs were brought from storage in the United States to Australia and, on September 12, 1942, were employed with tremendous success against aircraft on an enemy airfield near Buna, New Guinea. Kenney received the Purple Heart for his role in that attack on September 15, 1942.[4]

Kenney retired as a four-star general and died in 1977.

James Kunkle: Purple Heart—September 16, 1944

James Kunkle was severely wounded when he was shot down while flying a P-38 Lightning in combat over France.

Born in Pennsylvania in 1922, James Kunkle moved to West Hollywood, California, as a boy and graduated from Beverly Hills High School in 1940.

When the Army lowered the age restriction for pilot training, Kunkle left Cumnock College in Los Angeles and joined USAAF pilot class 44-A. After completing training at Williams Field, Arizona, Kunkle received his pilot wings and a commission in January 1944.

After arriving in England then–Second Lieutenant Kunkle flew with the 401st Fighter Squadron, 370th Fighter Group. His first mission was an armed reconnaissance flight across the English Channel shortly after the June 6, 1944, D-day invasion at Normandy. Kunkle and his fellow pilots attacked German trains, trucks, and airfields.

Since they were part of the Ninth Air Force, Kunkle's squadron moved to France after D-day, and by July 1944, they were operating from Cardonville Airfield, designated A-3, near Omaha Beach. A month later, when the Germans were trapped in the Falaise Pocket, Kunkle flew close air support missions, strafing and dive-bombing enemy troops as they withdrew from the Allied counterattack. He flew as many as three missions a day.

Kunkle was wounded in action on September 16, 1944. "We were up over Aachen, Germany," he remembered. "The 1st Infantry Division was trying to take the city. We were there to support the Army. My 401st Fighter Group was providing top cover for two squadrons down on the deck. . . . I was number four in the last flight. I noticed separate gaggles of German aircraft coming in at our five or six o'clock position. I thought they were attacking my entire group but when I broke into them, they stayed with me."

It was supposed to be an armed reconnaissance mission, but it quickly became a dogfight, with Kunkle the lone American flyer. According to official records, after Kunkle was unable to reach his flight leader on the radio, he "alone unhesitatingly pulled away from his formation and vigorously attacked the enemy, immediately destroying one of his (the enemy's) aircraft." Although this aerial victory and a subsequent one were officially confirmed, Kunkle does not know which of the two types of German fighter—a Folke-Wulf Fw 190 or a Bf 109—he shot down.

Any celebration was short-lived. Luftwaffe fighters attacked Kunkle from the rear. The German pilots "started walking their cannon shells up my left wing," Kunkle said.' He was aware of heat and smoke. "On the P-38, the cold air vent was down by your left knee," he explained. "Your main and reserve fuel tanks also were on the left side, where that duct is, and they hit both tanks. The flame looked like a blowtorch coming through the air vent into the cockpit." For an instant, there was very little smoke, but then it began to fill the canopy.

Kunkle was badly burned on his face, neck, and hands. He nevertheless continued to attack the German fighters that seemed to be all around him. He fired at several and shot one down. Then, when his P-38's main fuel tank exploded, Kunkle broke off from combat.

He jettisoned his canopy and either jumped or was blown out of the cockpit. He was at four thousand feet when he bailed out, and the only thing he remembers about his fall was that he was tumbling while his parachute was flapping at his back. Kunkle feared that if he opened his parachute too early, German ground troops would fire at him. Consequently, he pulled the ripcord when the ground looked close. Although he was sure that he would be captured and become a POW, Kunkle was lucky. He landed on the Allied side of the rapidly eastward-moving front line. Soldiers of the 1st Infantry Division, amid the fight to take Aachen, saw Kunkle's dogfight, watched him fall from the sky, and rescued him.

Kunkle never flew again in Europe. He was badly burned and spent months in hospitals recovering. For his combat injuries, he was awarded a Purple Heart. In February 1945 Gen. Carl "Tooey" Spaatz, the U.S. air commander in Europe, also decorated Kunkle with the Distinguished Service Cross for his heroism in the air.

Kunkle left active duty in 1948, a few months before the U.S. Air Force became an independent branch of the Armed Services.[5]

H. Michael O'Shea: Purple Heart—February 25, 1944

Henry Michael "Mike" O'Shea was wounded in action when he bailed out of his B-17 over Germany on February 25, 1944.

Born in Philadelphia on July 13, 1915, then sixteen-year-old O'Shea dropped out of high school and went to work as an elevator operator to feed his family after his father was killed in an accident. After World War II broke out, O'Shea enlisted in the Army Air Corps and graduated from flight school as a single-engine pilot. He became the pilot of a four-engine, ten-man B-17 bomber because the Army's Eighth Air Force was losing a lot of pilots and O'Shea "was breathing and willing" to be a replacement.

After arriving in England he was assigned to the 92nd Bomb Group (Heavy), which flew missions out of Poddington. Then-Lieutenant O'Shea wrote to his mother that he and his crew had flown their first mission over Germany and returned safely. He failed to tell her that his B-17 had flown a daylight mission without fighter escorts and that his plane made it back to base with two of its four engines out and more than five hundred bullets in its fuselage.

On January 11, 1944, O'Shea flew his fifteenth mission, which turned out to be both harrowing and rewarding. Approaching the target, his B-17 "was subjected to repeated savage assaults by enemy fighters and encountered intense antiaircraft fire." O'Shea, however, kept his position in the bomber formation and released his bombs. According to official records, just after the bombs were dropped, one of the engines on O'Shea's B-17 "was knocked out by flak" and his aircraft was

> riddled by fire from enemy fighters. . . . When forced to leave the formation, Lt. O'Shea's plane became the object of concentrated attacks by hostile fighters. During the running battle which ensured, Lt. O'Shea maneuvered his plane so expertly that his gunners were able to destroy four of the enemy fighters and the balance were finally eluded. Shortly after crossing the coast of Europe on his return journey, another engine became disabled and burst into flames. Though it appeared inevitable that the crippled bomber would have to be abandoned, he flew it back to England and made a safe landing.[6]

For his extraordinary achievement in the air that day, O'Shea was awarded the Distinguished Flying Cross.

In early February 1944 O'Shea transferred from England to Italy and joined the 301st Group, Fifteenth Air Force. He did not know it at the time, but his days as an airman were near an end. O'Shea flew his twenty-fourth and last mission on February 25, 1944.

On that day O'Shea's B-17 was one of sixty-five bombers on a mission to hit Regensburg, Germany. The Americans had no fighter cover, which was unfortunate since O'Shea and his crew saw more enemy fighters that day than they had seen on any other mission—more than three hundred Bf 109s. But, while they were harassed by those enemy fighters for the entire ninety-minute flight from Italy to Regensburg, O'Shea and his crew were lucky to be free of any direct assault. The Bf 109s focused on other B-17s.

After releasing bombs over Regensburg, however, O'Shea and his B-17 took heavy flak, which knocked out two left motors and ruptured the left-wing gas tank. As the plane filled with liquid gasoline, another B-17 that had also been damaged by enemy flak hit O'Shea's plane. The collision caused the tail gunner turret section to break off with the unconscious gunner still strapped in and embed itself in the wing of O'Shea's B-17.

While the other American bomber went into a spin and fell to earth, O'Shea managed to keep control of his B-17. He also sounded the alarm for his crew to bail out, and they did. O'Shea, however, stayed at the controls until the tail gunner regained consciousness and could escape. Only then did O'Shea bail out—behind his copilot—but his plane was then so low to the ground that his parachute did not deploy properly. O'Shea was badly injured when he landed.

No one had seen O'Shea bail out, and so he initially was reported as missing in action and presumed dead. But O'Shea had survived and, after being captured by the Germans, was sent to a hospital for treatment. After being discharged from the German hospital, O'Shea spent the remainder of the war in the Stalag Luft 1 POW camp in Barth, Germany. He played chess and cards to pass the time with famous airmen like Francis "Gabby" Gabreski, who was the top Allied ace in Europe with twenty-eight confirmed kills, and Medal of Honor recipient John Morgan.

On May 1, 1945, O'Shea and his fellow airmen were freed when advancing Soviet troops overran their prison camp. The Americans were taken to a captured airfield, flown to France, and then put aboard a ship that sailed to New York City. On November 8, 1945, the War Department issued O'Shea a Purple Heart for the injuries he had suffered during his February 25, 1944, bailout.

After the war, O'Shea returned to civilian life, married, raised a family, and had a successful career as a bond trader at Drexel and Co. in Philadelphia. He died in Santa Monica, California, on May 18, 1993.[7]

Robert E. Shepard: Purple Heart—May 21, 1944
See chapter 9, "Celebrities: Artists and Entertainers, Politicians, Athletes, and Other Public Figures."

KOREA (1950–1953)

The Air Force suffered 1,238 killed and 368 wounded in action during the Korean War.[8] Two Purple Heart recipients were the following pilots.

George A. Davis Jr.: Purple Heart—February 10, 1952
George Andre Davis Jr. was killed in action when his F-86 Sabre jet was shot down by a Chinese MiG on February 10, 1952.

An experienced pilot who was a P-47 fighter ace with 266 combat missions in World War II, Davis arrived in Korea in late October 1951. A month later he became the war's fifth jet ace by downing three MiGs and two Chinese bombers. Davis shot down six more enemy jets in December—four on December 13 alone.

On February 10, 1952, Davis took off from Seoul with seventeen other F-86s. He was in command of the 334th Squadron, 4th Fighter Interceptor Group, and his mission that day was to provide cover for U.S. fighter-bombers attacking railway lines near the Chinese border. While in the air, Davis and his wingman saw a dozen MiG-15s coming from the northeast, and he and his wingman went after the enemy planes. Davis quickly scored two kills, and the Chinese aircraft retreated. But then the MiGs regrouped and returned to attack the Americans.

Davis could have escaped to safety, but he instead slowed down to attack a third MiG. At 32,000 feet, Davis maneuvered behind this enemy jet, but before he could fire, another MiG "swooped in on the Sabre from seven o'clock and scored a direct hit. Davis' jet exploded into a ball of flames as it careened into an icy mountainside" thirty miles south of the Yalu River.[9]

In addition to the Purple Heart, Davis received a posthumous Medal of Honor and promotion to lieutenant colonel.

Charles J. Loring Jr.: Purple Heart—November 22, 1952

Charles Joseph Loring Jr. was killed in action when he intentionally crashed his F-80 Shooting Star into an enemy artillery position.

Born October 2, 1918, Loring enlisted in the USAAF March 1942 and flew fifty-five missions as a fighter pilot with the 35th Fighter Group in Europe. For his extraordinary achievement in the air in World War II, Loring was awarded the Distinguished Flying Cross.

In May 1952 then-Major Loring arrived in Korea and joined the 8th Fighter Bomber Wing as squadron operations officer. He subsequently served in both the 36th Squadron and 80th Squadron, and he led fifty-one artillery-strafing missions between June and November.

On November 22, 1952, then-thirty-four-year-old Loring was piloting an F-80 on a close air support mission in support of the Army's X Corps, which was locked in a furious battle with Chinese troops near Sniper Ridge, North Korea. As he attacked the enemy, intense antiaircraft fire scored a direct hit on his aircraft, and his F-80 was badly damaged. Three other F-80s flying with Loring "deployed around him to cover his withdrawal . . . but Loring made no attempt to retreat. . . . Instead, he forced his smoking plane back around and deliberately aimed the plummeting aircraft at the heart of the harassing artillery position. . . . Moments later, the bomb-laden Shooting Star crashed to earth directly on target."[10]

For sacrificing his life in order to destroy enemy gun emplacements, Loring was awarded a posthumous Purple Heart and a posthumous Medal of Honor.

SOVIET UNION (1952)

On October 22, 1995, the Air Force presented Purple Hearts to the next of kin of the pilot and eleven crewmembers of an RB-29 reconnaissance bomber, all of whom were killed when their aircraft was shot down by two MiG-15 fighters. The RB-29 was on a "ferret" mission when it went down near Vladivostok, off the eastern coast of the Soviet Union, on June 13, 1952.

Until 1993 the Air Force considered the twelve Air Force personnel on the RB-29, who were members of the 91st Strategic Reconnaissance Squadron, to be noncombat losses. It told the families of the missing that "the plane and its crew simply vanished." Forty-one years after the incident, however, Russian documents were released showing that the RB-29 was shot down.[11]

The next of kin of the following airmen received a posthumously awarded Purple Heart and a Distinguished Flying Cross:

- SSgt. Roscoe Becker, crew
- SSgt. Eddie R. Berg, crew
- SSgt. William A. Blizzard, crew
- SSgt. Leon F. Bonura, crew
- Maj. Samuel Busch, pilot
- MSgt. William B. Homer, crew
- 1st Lt. Robert J. McDonnell
- SSgt. Miguel W. Monserrat, crew
- MSgt. David L. Moore, crew
- A1C Danny H. Pillsbury, crew
- 1st Lt. James Scully
- Capt. Samuel Service, copilot

CUBA (1962)

Rudolph Anderson Jr.: Purple Heart—October 27, 1962

Rudolph Anderson Jr. was killed in action when his U-2 spy plane was shot down by a Cuban surface-to-air missile during the Cuban Missile Crisis.

Between October 15, 1962, and October 27, 1962, then-Major Anderson flew an unescorted, unarmed U-2 on aerial reconnaissance missions over Cuba. He took photographs that provided U.S. military officials with "conclusive evidence of the introduction of long-range offensive missiles into Cuba." Anderson was killed on October 27 when he was shot down.[12]

Anderson's widow was presented with his posthumously awarded Purple Heart in November 1962. At the same time she also received his posthumously awarded Air Force Cross—the first to be awarded to any airman.

VIETNAM (1964–1975)

The Air Force suffered 1,738 killed and 931 wounded in action in the Vietnam War.[13] Some recipients of the Purple Heart included the following fliers.

Fred V. Cherry: Purple Hearts—October 22, 1965, and August 15, 1967–November 15, 1967

Fred Vann Cherry was wounded in action when the F-105 Thunderchief he was piloting was shot down over North Vietnam by a surface-to-air missile.

A native of Suffolk, Virginia, Cherry enlisted as an airman in the Air Force in 1951. After qualifying as a pilot, he flew F-84G Thunderjets during the Korean War from 1953 to 1954. From 1960 to 1965 then-Major Cherry saw service in Japan and Southeast Asia.

On October 22, 1965, while flying his fiftieth mission over North Vietnam, Cherry was shot down and injured. Imprisoned in Hanoi, Cherry was placed in a cell with Navy Lt. Porter Halyburton. Although the two men initially distrusted each other—Halyburton did not know the Air Force had African American pilots, and Cherry suspected his cellmate of being a French spy for the Vietnamese—their relationship became extremely close. When medical neglect cause Cherry's injuries to become badly infected, Halyburton saved Cherry's life by feeding him and helping him with his other bodily needs.

The North Vietnamese, recognizing that Cherry was the senior-ranking black POW, tried to stir up racial animosity between Cherry and his fellow

In October 1965 Col. Fred V. Cherry (right) was wounded in action when the F-105 he was piloting was shot down over North Vietnam by a surface-to-air missile. Cherry was held as a prisoner of war in Hanoi until February 1973. (National Archives and Records Administration)

white prisoners. Cherry, however, resisted. As he told some University of Maryland students in 1989, the North Vietnamese "tried to make me different. . . . They tried to exploit me. . . . They knew we had a race problem back home. And they used it to try and turn me against white POWs in the camp." At one point, his captors had him listen to a recording by well-known Black Power advocate Stokely Carmichael and asked him to make a similar tape. According to Cherry, his jailers thought that "if they could get the first and most senior black POW to denounce the war, they could play that tape to young black soldiers in the field and get them to drop their weapons."[14]

Unfortunately for Cherry, his resistance to these North Vietnamese plans resulted in severe torture and almost two years of solitary confinement. Cherry was tortured daily for ninety-three straight days at one point, between August 15 and November 15, 1967. But he never submitted, and, according to fellow

Col. Philip J. Conran was wounded while engaged in ground combat in Laos in October 1969. He was a major when awarded his Purple Heart. (U.S. Air Force)

prisoner of war Jeremiah Denton, the North Vietnamese eventually "gave up on" Cherry."[15]

After his release in February 1973, then-Colonel Cherry attended the National War College and the Defense Intelligence College of the Defense Intelligence Agency in Washington, D.C. He retired as a colonel in 1981 and today lives in Virginia.

In addition to his two Purple Hearts, Cherry was awarded the Air Force Cross. The citation for that award—second only the Medal of Honor—states that it was for "extraordinary heroism" in demonstrating "strong personal fortitude and maximum persistence in the face of severe enemy harassment and torture between August 15 and November 15, 1967" and notes that Cherry suffered "critical injuries and wounds" during this time.[16]

Philip J. Conran: Purple Heart—October 6, 1969

Phillip J. "Phil" Conran was wounded in the leg by enemy rifle or mortar fire after he crash-landed his helicopter in Laos on October 6, 1969.

Born in Hartford, Connecticut, in 1937, Conran graduated from Fordham University and was commissioned as a second lieutenant in 1958. After receiving his pilot's wings in 1960, Conran served as an air rescue aircraft commander and as an Air Force ROTC professor of aerospace studies before deploying to Vietnam in July 1968. It was during this combat tour and while serving as a special operations helicopter gunship commander that then-Major Conran was awarded the Purple Heart and Air Force Cross.

At 10:45 AM on October 6, 1969, five helicopters carrying U.S and friendly troops left Vietnam for a camp in Laos. Conran was the aircraft commander of the number two helicopter in the formation. After being told that the landing zone was clear, the helicopters started their approach in trail formation. The lead aircraft was shot down while landing, and its crew members abandoned the helicopter and took up defensive positions on the ground. Conran immediately climbed out of the range of the enemy's small-arms fire, assumed command of the remaining four helicopters, and then directed fire from two escorting A-1E Skyraiders on to the enemy.

By this time Conran was running low on fuel. He had two choices: He could return to a safe area and refuel—leaving his fellow airmen—or he could attempt to rescue the downed crew and reinforce the friendly soldiers on the ground. Concluding that the twenty-six friendly soldiers would not be able to provide sufficient protection for the downed helicopter crew, Conran decided to land his helicopter.

Although he selected what he thought was the safest approach route, Conran's helicopter was severely damaged by enemy fire while attempting to land. He probably could have broken off his approach and returned to a safe area at that point, but Conran elected instead to land and unload the friendly troops from his helicopter, who joined the fight.

As Conran began to take the downed crewmembers aboard his helicopter, enemy small-arms fire ripped through the main rotor transmission and cockpit of his helicopter. With takeoff now impossible, Conran and his crew abandoned the aircraft.

For the rest of the day, Conran repeatedly exposed himself to enemy fire to obtain essential ammunition and food from the downed helicopters. After an HH-3E Jolly Green Giant attempting to rescue Conran and the other airmen was driven off by an intense barrage of automatic weapons fire, enemy mortar rounds began falling into the friendly positions. Conran exposed himself, located the enemy mortar crew, and called in an airstrike to destroy it. Later, while trying to strengthen defenses, Conran was severely wounded in the leg. He did not mention this injury until he had lost all feeling in his leg and felt that, if a rescue helicopter were to arrive to extract them, he might not be able to make it to the aircraft on his own and would need help. In spite of the seriousness of his leg wound, Conran refused to allow anyone else to expose himself to enemy fire to examine his injury.

Just before nightfall, two Jolly Green Giants were able to complete a successful rescue of all forty-four personnel. As Conran appeared to be chiefly responsible for the survival of the men on the ground, he was recommended for the Medal of Honor.

After his Southeast Asia tour, Conran served in a variety of assignments and locations, including as executive officer and commander of an Air Force satellite control facility and as inspector general for Air Force Systems Command.

Conran retired from the Air Force as a colonel in 1988 after logging more than five thousand flying hours, three hundred of which were during combat. He then had a successful career in private industry until retiring again. Today, he lives in California.[17]

George E. Day: Purple Hearts—August 26, 1967; September 1967; and July 16–October 14, 1969

George Edward "Bud" Day was wounded four times and received four Purple Hearts. He is the most highly decorated living American, having been awarded nearly seventy military decorations and awards, including the Medal of Honor.

Born in Sioux City, Iowa, in February 1925, Day dropped out of high school and joined the Marine Corps in 1942. He then served thirty months in the South Pacific as a noncommissioned officer. He received an appointment as a second lieutenant in the Air National Guard in 1950 and entered jet pilot training when called to active duty in the Air Force in 1951. Day served tours in the Far East as a fighter-bomber pilot during the Korean War, and, in 1955, he survived a no-chute bailout from a burning jet fighter in England.

In April 1967 then-Major Day was assigned to the 31st Tactical Fighter Wing at Tuy Hoa Air Base, Republic of Vietnam. He later moved to Phu Cat Air Base, where he organized and became the first commander of the "Misty Super FACs," an F-100F Super Sabre squadron.

On August 27, 1967, Day was shot down while flying a forward air control mission over North Vietnam. After his F-100 was hit by an enemy 57-mm

The most highly decorated living American, Col. George E. "Bud" Day has received more than seventy Air Force decorations and medals, including the Medal of Honor. He also has been awarded four Purple Hearts. (U.S. Air Force)

shell, Day's plane rolled into an inverted dive and headed for the ground. Day ejected immediately. He was seriously injured, and when he regained consciousness, Day was staring into the barrel of a rifle held by a young North Vietnamese guard.

From that point on, thinking "of little except escape," Day worked to convince his captors that he was not an escape risk. One week after being shot down, and having faked internal injuries so that the enemy guards would be less vigilant in watching him, Day untied the cheap rope that bound his hands and feet and slipped away under cover of darkness. Surviving only on berries and an uncooked frog, Day evaded capture by the North Vietnamese for an incredible fourteen days. The only U.S. POW to escape from North Vietnam, Day managed to cross back into South Vietnam. He was shot and recaptured by the North Vietnamese, however, when he was within two miles of a U.S. Marine Corps outpost.

Day spent the next sixty-seven months as a POW in Hanoi. Described by a fellow prisoner as "one of the toughest men alive," Day was brutally and repeatedly tortured by the North Vietnamese.[18] His worst experience occurred between July 16, 1969, and October 14, 1969, when the enemy applied "maximum torture and punishment . . . to obtain a detailed confession of escape plans, policies and orders of the American senior ranking officer in the camp." Day withstood this abuse "and gave nothing of value to the Vietnamese, although he sustained many injuries and open wounds to his body."[19]

When released from captivity in 1973, Day cited his positive attitude and faith in God as the keys to his survival. Returning to active duty as a colonel, Day hoped for a succession of top military assignments commensurate with his extensive fighter experience and years of combat leadership. In 1977, however, after being offered a "nonpromotable, nonflying job," Day elected to retire.[20]

In addition to his four Purple Hearts, Day holds the Medal of Honor, Air Force Cross, Air Force Distinguished Service Medal, Silver Star, Legion of Merit, Distinguished Flying Cross, Air Medal with nine oak leaf clusters, and the Bronze Star with V device and two oak leaf clusters. Day also has 4,500 hours of single-engine jet time and more than 5,000 hours of flying time.

Today, Day is a trial attorney and has his own law firm in Florida.

Pollard H. Mercer Jr.: Purple Heart—January 14, 1968

Pollard Hugh "Sonny" Mercer Jr. was wounded in action in North Vietnam on January 14, 1968. He died of his injuries in the Philippines six days later, on January 20.

This officially machine-engraved Purple Heart spells out the recipient's name in all capital letters that are 1/16 inch in height. It was presented to the surviving family members of Maj. Pollard H. Mercer Jr. after Mercer's death in January 1968. (Fred Borch)

Born on June 30, 1932, in Winnfield, Louisiana, Mercer was an EB-66C Destroyer pilot. On January 14, 1968, he was on his seventy-ninth combat mission when he was shot down over North Vietnam by a MiG fighter. Then-Major Mercer and his seven member crew ejected Some survived, but search-and-recovery efforts were stymied by bad weather.

Three days later, on January 17, Mercer and two of his fellow crewmembers were rescued by helicopter and were immediately transported to the 432nd Air Force Tactical Dispensary in Udorn, Thailand.

Mercer's injuries were serious. He had a fractured right femur, large soft tissue injuries to his thighs and arms, and numerous abrasions and contusions. Consequently, Mercer was airlifted from Thailand to the Air Force hospital at Clark Air Base on Luzon, Philippines, where he could receive better medical care. The prognosis for recovery was good, but Mercer took a sudden turn for the worse, dying of his injuries on January 20, 1968. His death was attributed to a blood clot and cardiac arrest.[21]

Mercer's officially engraved Purple Heart was presented to his widow, along with a posthumous Silver Star and Distinguished Flying Cross.

CAMBODIA (1975)

The Air Force had two killed and six wounded in the rescue of the SS *Mayaguez* in May 1975. All received the Purple Heart.

Jon D. Harston: Purple Heart—May 15, 1975

On May 15, Jon Harston was a flight mechanic aboard a CH-53 Sea Stallion helicopter in the first wave of the assault on Koh Tang Island to recover the container ship *Mayaguez*. Then–Staff Sergeant Harston's helicopter was shot down by antiaircraft fire from the island, and it crashed just offshore in shallow water. Harston was wounded in the leg, but he managed to escape from the burning helicopter. Despite his wound, he returned to the fiery aircraft, reentered it, and dragged three Marines to safety.

As the survivors of the crash swam away from the beach, Harston provided covering fire. He returned to the helicopter again to pull out another wounded Marine. While swimming out to deeper water, he kept himself and two wounded Marines afloat with his damaged life preserver until they were all rescued by a Navy destroyer approximately three hours later.

In addition to the Purple Heart, Harston also was awarded the Air Force Cross for his extraordinary heroism that day.[22]

LIBYA (1986)

On April 14–15, 1986, Air Force and Navy aircraft attacked targets in Tripoli, Libya. One Air Force plane and its crew of two were lost. Both men were awarded posthumous Purple Hearts.

PERSIAN GULF WAR (1990–1991)

The Air Force awarded thirty Purple Hearts to airmen either killed or wounded in action during Operation Desert Storm. Some recipients include the following individuals.

William F. Andrews: Purple Heart—February 27, 1991

William Andrews was wounded in action when he broke his leg after ejecting from his F-16 on February 27, 1991.

Then-Captain Andrews was shot down about thirty miles northwest of Basra, Iraq, while leading an F-16 flight against heavily defended armor and mechanized forces. He was a member of the 10th Tactical Fighter Squadron, located at Hahn Air Base, Germany, and was on his 35th mission.

As he explained to an interviewer in March 1991, Andrews dropped below the clouds for a closer look at his target and was hit by a surface-to-air missile. "It hit my plane violently, throwing it out of control immediately. If I had hesitated at all, I wouldn't have survived."[23] Within a short time of landing on the ground, Andrews was surrounded by Iraqi soldiers. He had a broken leg and decided to surrender. He had, however, put his survival radio into operation and was in contact with the remaining F-16s in his flight. Consequently, when the Iraqis were within twenty feet of his location and Andrews saw that the Iraqis were launching more surface-to-air missiles, he radioed his fellow airmen that they must quickly drop decoy flares, make hard turns, and dive to elude and outmaneuver the climbing missiles. They did, and no F-16s were hit.

The Iraqis, however, were furious and began shooting at Andrews. He dropped his radio, and the Iraqis "blew it to pieces with their automatic rifles." Andrews was taken prisoner and, although he managed to slip away from his captors later than evening, was subsequently recaptured and taken to Baghdad.

He was released on March 4, 1991, when the Red Cross arrived to take charge of all American prisoners. After extensive orthopedic care, Andrews returned to flying status in May 1991.

In addition to receiving a Purple Heart for his broken leg, Andrews also was awarded the Air Force Cross for his extraordinary heroism in warning his fellow airmen of the danger they faced from Iraqi surface-to-air missiles.[24]

Thomas C. Bland Jr.: Purple Heart—January 31, 1991
John P. Blessinger: Purple Heart—January 31, 1991
Paul G. Buege: Purple Heart—January 31, 1991
Barry M. Clark: Purple Heart—January 31, 1991
Arthur Galvan: Purple Heart—January 31, 1991
William D. Grimm: Purple Heart—January 31, 1991
Robert K. Hodges: Purple Heart—January 31, 1991
Damon V. Kanuha: Purple Heart—January 31, 1991
James B. May II: Purple Heart—January 31, 1991
John L. Oelschlager: Purple Heart—January 31, 1991
Mark J. Schmauss: Purple Heart—January 31, 1991
Dixon L. Walters Jr.: Purple Heart—January 31, 1991
Paul J. Weaver: Purple Heart—January 31, 1991

First Lt. Thomas C. Bland Jr., SSgt. John P. Blessinger, SMSgt. Paul G. Buege, Sgt. Barry M. Clark, Capt. Arthur Galvan, Capt. William D. Grimm, TSgt. Robert K. Hodges, Sgt. Damon V. Kanuha, MSgt. James B. May II, SSgt. John L. Oelschlager, SSgt. Mark J. Schmauss, Capt. Dixon L. Walters Jr., and Maj. Paul J. Weaver were crewmembers on a special operations mission when their AC-130 gunship was shot down on January 31. Initially listed as missing in action, the airmen's status was changed to killed in action after their aircraft was found off the coast of Kuwait on March 6, 1991.

Donnie R. Holland: Purple Heart—January 18, 1991
Maj. Donnie R. Holland was killed when his F-15 was shot down over Iraq. Initially listed as missing in action, his status was changed to killed in action on March 22, 1991. Holland was forty-two years old and was survived by a wife and five children.

Thomas F. Koritz: Purple Heart—January 18, 1991
Maj. Thomas F. Koritz was killed when his F-15 was shot down over Iraq on January 18, 1991. Initially listed as missing in action, his status was changed to killed in action on March 22. He was thirty-seven years old at the time of his death.

MSgt. Timothy A. Wilkinson was wounded in a firefight in Mogadishu, Somalia, on October 3, 1993. In addition to a Purple Heart, which he received while he was a technical sergeant, Wilkinson also was awarded an Air Force Cross for extraordinary heroism. (U.S. Air Force)

SOMALIA (1993–1994)

U.S. Air Force C-141 and C-130 aircraft carrying food and medical supplies began flying daily relief sorties into Somalia as part of a massive UN humanitarian aid mission in July 1993. As more and more humanitarian aid flowed into the area, however, the security situation grew steadily worse. As a result, the United Nations authorized an armed security force for Somalia, and by May 1993, some 38,000 men and women, including 28,000 U.S. personnel, were in country as part of Operation Restore Hope.

By mid-1993 the United Nations decided that the relief mission was too limited. Consequently, the U.N. Security Council established a peacekeeping force in Somalia and tasked it with rehabilitating the political institutions and economy of Somalia. In part to accomplish these goals, U.S. special forces set out to capture Somali warlord Mohammed Farrah Aideed from Mogadishu on October 3, 1993.

The mission, involving about one hundred members of Task Force Ranger, was supposed to last about an hour, but it went horribly awry. Americans on the ground were ambushed by Somali gunmen, and two Black Hawk helicopters were shot down. Eighteen U.S. soldiers lost their lives, and another seventy-five sustained wounds.

During this brutal firefight airman Tim Wilkinson participated in the rescue of a downed Army helicopter crew. Wilkinson is apparently the only Air Force recipient of a Purple Heart for action in Somalia.

Timothy A. Wilkinson: Purple Heart—October 3, 1993

Timothy Wilkinson was wounded in action while rescuing the crew of a downed Army helicopter on October 3, 1993.

A pararescueman with the 24th Special Tactics Squadron, based at Pope Air Force Base, North Carolina, then–Technical Sergeant Wilkinson "conducted a fast rope insertion into the crash site." Although under extremely heavy fire from the Somali fighters, he "repeatedly exposed himself to intense small arms fire and grenades" to clear debris, provide emergency medical treatment to the survivors, and extract the dead and wounded members of the crew from the wreckage."

During an eighteen-hour period, Wilkinson also "broke cover on three separate occasions to locate and provide emergency medical treatment to three Ranger casualties," which required him to cross a forty-five-meter-wide open area "blanketed with intense fire from small arms and rocket propelled grenades."

Wilkinson later received a Purple Heart for the wounds he received during the rescue, which took place as part of the longest sustained firefight involving U.S. combat forces in more than twenty years. He also was awarded the Air Force Cross, becoming the first enlisted airman to receive this decoration since the Vietnam war.[25]

Wilkinson retired from the Air Force as a master sergeant in July 2001.[26]

IRAQ (1994)

Laura A. Piper: Purple Heart—April 14, 1994

Two Air Force F-15C Eagle fighters mistook Army Black Hawks carrying American military personnel and friendly foreign nationals for Soviet-made Iraqi Hind helicopters and shot the helicopters down on April 14, 1994. All aboard were killed, including Air Force 2nd Lt. Laura A. Piper.

The secretary of the Air Force initially determined that Piper could not receive a Purple Heart because her death resulted from a noncombat, friendly-fire incident. Facing pressure from the families of the deceased, and recognizing that the Defense Department would likely award Piper a Purple Heart if the Air Force did not, the Air Force secretary reversed his decision and made the award to Piper.[27]

THE BALKANS: BOSNIA-HERZEGOVINA, CROATIA, AND KOSOVO (1994–1995)

Air Force personnel participated in the North Atlantic Treaty Organization's (NATO) Operation Deny Flight from November 1994 to December 1995. During one of these missions, which were intended to enforce a no-fly zone over Bosnia, two Air Force noncommissioned officers were wounded while searching for two downed French pilots in Bosnia. Both Americans later were awarded Purple Hearts.[28]

SAUDI ARABIA (1996)

Sandra J. Beneway: Purple Heart—June 25, 1996

On June 25, 1996, terrorists exploded a tanker truck containing at least 20,000 lbs. of explosives near the eight-story Khobar Towers building in Dhahran. At the time, a large number of soldiers and airmen from the 4404th Wing (Provisional) were housed in this structure. The blast killed 19 military personnel and wounded more than 350 men and women.

Then-Captain Beneway was injured in the eye and arm and was subsequently awarded a Purple Heart.

ATTACK ON THE PENTAGON (2001)

Noe Sepulveda: Purple Heart—September 11, 2001

Then-MSgt. Noe Sepulveda was serving in the Air Force Directorate of Plans and Programs when he was wounded in the terrorist attack on the Pentagon. Air Force Chief of Staff Gen. John Jumper presented Sepulveda with his Purple Heart on April 15, 2002.

AFGHANISTAN (2001–)

Since the beginning of military operations in Afghanistan in October 1991, Air Force personnel have seen heavy combat. Two early Purple Heart recipients were combat controller TSgt. John A. Chapman and pararescueman SrA. Jason Cunningham, both of whom were killed in action during ground combat on March 4, 2002. Both airmen received posthumous Purple Hearts and Air Force Crosses.[29]

Other Purple Heart recipients include the following Air Force members.

Timothy Bowles: Purple Heart—March 15, 2009
SSgt. Timothy Bowles, a tactical vehicle mechanic with the Nangarhar Provincial Reconstruction Team, was killed when a roadside bomb exploded near his vehicle. He was on a patrol to check on a local school. A native of Tucson, Arizona, the twenty-four-year-old Bowles had deployed to Afghanistan in November 2008 from Elmendorf Air Force Base, Alaska.[30]

Timothy Davis, Purple Heart, February 20, 2009
SSgt. Timothy Davis, a twenty-eight-year-old combat controller, was killed by a bomb in Afghanistan. He was a member of the 23rd Special Tactics Squadron, which operates out of Hurlburt Field, Florida. In addition to his posthumous Purple Heart, Davis' widow, Meagan, also received his posthumous Bronze Star for valor.[31]

Ashton L. M. Goodman: Purple Heart—May 26, 2009
Mark E. Stratton: Purple Heart—May 26, 2009
SrA. Ashton Goodman and Lt. Col. Mark Stratton were killed when their vehicle struck a roadside bomb near Bagram Airfield in Afghanistan.

An Indiana native, Goodman enlisted in July 2006 and was a vehicle operator dispatcher based at Pope Air Force Base. She had previously served in Iraq before deploying to Afghanistan. At the time of her death, she was working on a reconstruction team based in the mountainous Panjshir province.

Stratton, who grew up in Foley, Alabama, graduated from Texas A&M University in 1991 and received an Air Force commission through the ROTC program. He had served as a senior navigator in RC-135 reconnaissance aircraft and worked as an executive assistant for the deputy director for politico-military affairs (Asia) on the Joint Staff in the Pentagon before deploying to Afghanistan. At the time of his death, Stratton was the chief of the reconstruction team on which Goodman was serving.

The next of kin of both Goodman and Stratton received their posthumous Purple Hearts.[32]

Zachary J. Rhyner: Purple Heart—April 6, 2008

Then-SrA. Zachary J. Rhyner received his Purple Heart after being wounded in the leg by a bullet in the rocky Shok Valley, which sits about one hundred miles northeast of Kabul, Afghanistan, on April 6, 2008.

On that day, while assigned as a special tactics combat controller, Rhyner landed by helicopter near a village in Nuristan Province, Afghanistan. He and his special forces teammates were on a mission to capture "high-value insurgents" located in the village. While climbing "near vertical terrain to reach their objective," Rhyner's team was "attacked in a well-coordinated and deadly ambush."

The Americans were pinned down by "devastating sniper, machine gun and rocket-propelled grenade fire (that) poured down on them from elevated and protected positions on all sides." Rhyner, without concern for his own well-being, "placed himself between the most immediate threats and provided suppressive fire with his M-4 rifle." Then, despite a gunshot wound to his left leg, Rhyner withstood enemy fire to control eight Air Force fighters and four Army attack helicopters in making more than fifty close air strikes, several within one hundred meters of Rhyner's position.

For his extraordinary heroism during the six-and-a-half-hour battle, Rhyner—since promoted to staff sergeant—also was awarded the Air Force Cross. Rhyner became the first living airman since 2001 to receive that award, and only the twenty-fifth enlisted man in Air Force history to be so recognized.[33]

Roslyn L. Schulte: Purple Heart—May 20, 2009

Roslyn L. Schulte was killed when a roadside bomb exploded and hit her convoy, which was travelling to Bagram Airfield. She was the first female graduate of the U.S. Air Force Academy to be killed in either Afghanistan or Iraq.

A St. Louis, Missouri, native, First Lieutenant Schulte graduated from the academy in 2006, where she played on the lacrosse team. She was assigned to the Pacific Air Forces 613th Air and Space Operations Center at Hickam Air Force Base, Hawaii, and had been on duty in Kabul for about three weeks when she was killed. At the time of her death, the twenty-five-year-old Schulte had been "working with local military officials in an intelligence capacity," and was travelling to Bagram to participate in a Joint Task Force intelligence sharing conference.[34]

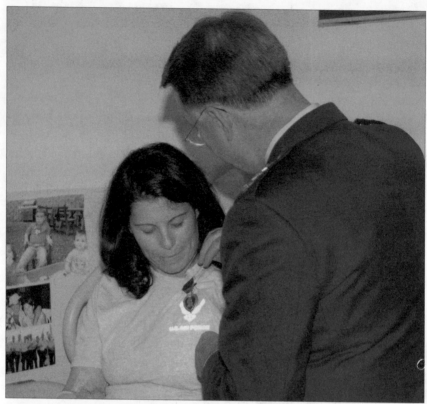

SrA. Diane Lopes, an Air Force Reserve security forces apprentice, was wounded in action at Kirkuk Air Base, Iraq, in early September 2007. In this photograph, Air Force Lt. Gen. John A. Bradley pins the Purple Heart on Lopes at Walter Reed Army Medical Center on September 28, 2007. (U.S. Air Force)

IRAQ (2003–)

Since the U.S. invasion of Iraq in 2003, airmen have participated in both air and ground operations against Iraqi forces and insurgents. Purple Heart recipients include these airmen.

Joshua Bellin: Purple Heart—January 13, 2008

Then-SrA. Joshua Bellin was wounded when his vehicle was struck by an IED. He "would later be diagnosed with a concussion as a result of the blast" and awarded a Purple Heart.[35]

A native of Lomira, Wisconsin, Bellin was on his third deployment to Iraq and was traveling to a convoy support center on October 13, 2008, when his truck was struck. Bellin and another airman "still managed to keep moving another two or three miles until they were out of the kill zone." As a result of his injuries, Bellin was put on light duty and restricted from completing missions for two weeks.

Navy Adm. Eric T. Olson, the commander of U.S. Special Operations Command, presented a Purple Heart to Bellin at a July 8, 2008, ceremony at Hurlburt Air Force Base.[36]

Diane Lopes: Purple Heart—September 21, 2007

Diane Lopes was wounded in her right arm and left leg by shrapnel from a mortar shell. At the time, she was off-duty and taking a walk.

Then–Senior Airman Lopes was part of a thirteen-person security team from the 920th Security Forces Element stationed at Kirkuk Air Base, Iraq. An Air Force reservist, Lopes had been in Iraq for less than a month when she was wounded. As she later told an interviewer, "At first, I wasn't sure what happened. . . . I heard it coming and remember turning toward it. I heard a boom and felt a compression wave go right through me. Initially, I thought I was on fire and dropped to the ground in case I had to put myself out. Then I tasted blood in my mouth and within a second it hit me: 'I just got bombed!'"

Within ninety seconds of being hit, Lopes was rushed to the medical facility on Kirkuk Air Base. She had initial surgery at Balad Air Base and was then medically evacuated to Landstuhl Regional Medical Center in Germany. She received her final medical care—and her Purple Heart—at Walter Reed Army Medical Center. Air Force Reserve Command Commander Lt. Gen. John A. Bradley pinned the decoration on Lopes on September 28, 2007.[37]

CHAPTER 5

Marines: Spanish–American War to Afghanistan and Iraq

arines have been awarded Purple Hearts for wounds received in combat as early as the Spanish–American War in 1898, although these decorations were not issued until the 1940s. While the majority of Marine Corps Purple Hearts have gone to men killed or wounded while fighting in World War II, Marines have also received Purple Hearts for wounds incurred during the following armed conflicts, international terrorist attacks, and other military operations:

- Spanish–American War (1898)
- China Relief Expedition/Boxer Rebellion (1900–1901)
- World War I (1917–1918)
- Nicaragua (1927–1933)
- World War II (1941–1945)
- China (1945–1947)
- Korea (1950–1953)
- Cuba (1962)
- Vietnam (1964–1973)
- USS *Liberty* (1967)
- USS *Pueblo* (1968)
- Philippines (1972)
- SS *Mayaguez* (1975)
- Iran (1979)
- Pakistan (1979)
- Lebanon (1982–1984)

- Grenada (1983)
- Germany (1984)
- El Salvador (1985)
- Persian Gulf Tanker Escort Operations (1987–1988)
- Panama (1989)
- Lebanon (1990)
- Persian Gulf War (1990–1991)
- Somalia (1992–1995)
- Kenya (1998)
- Afghanistan (2001–)
- Iraq (2003–)
- Haiti (2004)

SPANISH–AMERICAN WAR (1898)

James D. Bourke: Purple Heart—June 13, 1898

James D. Bourke was wounded in action at the Battle of Guantánamo on June 13, 1898.

Born in Ireland in 1874, he enlisted in the Marine Corps on December 23, 1896, and was a private in Company D of the 1st Battalion, U.S. Marines in Cuba. In early 1932 Bourke applied to the War Department for his Purple Heart, and it was issued to him because he had been a Marine "serving in the Army" when he was wounded in combat.[1]

CHINA RELIEF EXPEDITION/BOXER REBELLION (1900–1901)

John T. Myers: Purple Heart—July 3, 1900

John Twiggs Myers was badly wounded by a spear while engaged with Chinese fighters during the Boxer Rebellion.

Born on January 29, 1871, in Wiesbaden, Germany, Myers came to the United States in 1876. Myers was an American citizen whose father had served in the Confederate Army during the Civil War. Disillusioned after the South's defeat, the father took his family to Germany in the later half of the 1860s. The younger Myers entered the U.S. Naval Academy in 1887, and after graduating in 1892, continued to hold the rank of naval cadet until he received an appointment as an assistant engineer in August 1894. About six months later, however, Myers transferred to the Marine Corps and accepted an appointment as a second lieutenant on March 6, 1895.

In May 1898 Myers joined the Marine detachment aboard the USS *Charleston* and sailed a few days later for the Philippines. Before reaching that destination, however, the sailors and Marines stopped at Guam, which was still under Spanish control. On June 21, 1898, Myers accompanied the captain of the *Charleston* ashore as the head of a landing party of sixteen sailors and thirty Marines. The Americans subsequently took the Spanish garrison on the island prisoner.

After arriving in the Philippines, Myers transferred to the USS *Baltimore*. He subsequently commanded several landing expeditions, including a hundred-man force that took over the naval station at Subic Bay on December 10, 1899, one day after it had been seized by the Army.

After briefly serving in the USS *Oregon*, then-Captain Myers was detached to the USS *Newark* in May 1900. On May 29, the day after E. H. Conger, the American minister in Peking, requested an armed American force for the protection of foreigners then in danger from the Boxers, Myers set out for Peking as commander of a unit of forty-eight Marines and three sailors from the *Oregon* and the USS *Brooklyn*. The Americans—along with British, French, Italian, Japanese, and Russian Marines—reached Peking on May 31, 1900.

Three weeks later serious fighting broke out on the walls of the legations as thousands of Boxers, armed with swords, spears, clubs, and stones, tried to overwhelm the small number of foreign troops in Peking. After the Boxers suffered a number of heavy losses in ill-advised attacks, however, they changed their tactics and began building a tower on the ancient wall above the American legation. Since the tower would give the Chinese insurgents the ability to fire on the troops and civilians below, the tower had to be destroyed. Myers was selected to lead the assault.

At 3 AM on July 3, 1900, Myers led an attacking force consisting of fourteen American, sixteen Russian, and twenty-five British Marines. In the vicious hand-to-hand fighting that followed, Myers was badly wounded by a spear. Two U.S. Marines and one Russian were killed, and several other men were wounded. But the tower was seized and destroyed, and as many as fifty Boxers were killed. The British minister in Peking hailed the action as "one of the most successful operations of the siege, as it rendered our position on the wall, which had been precarious, comparatively strong."[2] In fact, the Chinese were so discouraged by the success of the attack that they agreed to a truce on July 16.

For his extraordinary heroism while leading the assault on the Boxers' tower, Myers received a brevet promotion to major, and President William F. McKinley mentioned Myers by name in a speech to Congress in February 1901. Many years later, Myers would also receive a Purple Heart from the Navy Department.

A relief column reached Peking in August, and Myers was evacuated the following month to the U.S. Naval Hospital in Yokohama, Japan, since he was not only suffering from the spear wound to his leg, but also from typhoid fever. After returning to the United States he spent time serving at Bremerton, Washington; Newport, Rhode Island; and Washington, D.C. Myers later returned to the Philippines, where he was in command of the 1st Marine Regiment until 1907. He then transferred to the USS *West Virginia* as commander of its Marine detachment.

After graduating from the Army War College in 1912, Myers took command of the Marine Barracks in Washington, D.C., but this tour of duty was interrupted by deployment with the 2nd Provisional Marine Regiment to Santo Domingo and, then, deployment with the 2nd Regiment, 2nd Provisional Marine Brigade to Guantánamo Bay.

In 1914 Myers took command of the 1st Battalion, 4th Marine Regiment, which was then located at Mare Island, California. He and his men subsequently sailed with the USS *South Dakota* to the west coast of Mexico during a period of heightened tension between the United States and Mexico. But, while sailors and Marines operating in the Gulf of Mexico did land at Veracruz, Myers and his regiment did not leave their battleship after entering Mexican waters.

In June 1916 then–Lieutenant Colonel Myers was assigned to the Atlantic Fleet as fleet Marine officer and counterintelligence officer on the staff of the fleet's senior commander. He served in these roles for most of World War I. In November 1925 Myers took command of the 1st Marine Brigade in Haiti and did not return from that tour of expeditionary duty until January 1928, when he was assigned to Marine Corps headquarters in Washington, D.C. After serving on various boards, he was named assistant to the major general commandant in April 1930, and served in that position until February 1933.

Myers retired from the Marine corps as a major general in February 1935 at the age of sixty-four. He had forty years of service, nearly ten of which were spent at sea. Myers was promoted on the retired list to lieutenant general in 1942, when Congress authorized such promotions for Marines who had been specially commended for heroism in combat. In addition to a Purple

Heart for his wounds during the China Relief Expedition/Boxer Rebellion, Myers received the Marine Corps Brevet Medal, Spanish Campaign Medal, Philippine Campaign Medal, China Campaign Medal, Marine Corps Expeditionary Medal, Mexican Service Medal, and World War I Victory Medal.

Myers died at his home in Coconut Grove, Florida, on April 17, 1952. He is interred at Arlington National Cemetery.[3]

WORLD WAR I (1917–1918)

Many Marines who had been wounded while serving with Pershing's American Expeditionary Force applied to the War Department for Purple Hearts after the award was revived in 1932. An unknown number—perhaps as many as five hundred—received Army-issued Purple Hearts in the 1930s.

After the Navy received its own legal authority to issue the Purple Heart in December 1942, Marines could apply directly to the Navy Department for the award. And they did, but how many is, again, not known. According to a 1950 memorandum from the Navy's Medals and Awards Division, 9,520 Marines had been nonmortal battle casualties in World War I.[4]

Wilburt S. Brown: Purple Heart—October 4, 1918

Wilburt Scott Brown received a gunshot wound in the right elbow while fighting in France on October 4, 1918. He was serving as a private in 20th Company, 5th Marine Regiment and fought in the St. Mihiel offensive of September 12–16, 1918, and the Meuse–Argonne offensive of October 1–4, 1918. On the basis of Brown's service in the American Expeditionary Force, the Army issued him a Purple Heart on October 12, 1938.

Born in Beverly, Massachusetts, on December 20, 1900, Brown grew up in Roxbury, just south of Boston, and enlisted in the Marine Corps on May 28, 1918. His enlistment papers show that he had blue eyes, light brown hair, and a ruddy complexion. Brown was six foot two and 185 lbs.—both well above average for the time.

After completing training at the Recruit Depot at Parris Island, South Carolina, Brown sailed for Europe and was wounded in action a month before the war ended. In July 1920 then-Sergeant Brown was discharged from the Marine Corps so he could accept appointment to the U.S. Naval Academy. He was, nonetheless, discharged from Annapolis in August 1922 for "inaptitude."

Maj. Gen. Wilburt S. Brown received a gunshot wound to his right elbow while fighting in France on October 4, 1918. (U.S. Marine Corps)

His official military personnel file contains a personal statement in which Brown explains he was discharged "as a result of a charge of drunkenness while ashore on liberty in Fort-de-France, Martinique, during a practice cruise, and a similar indiscretion committed the year before in Lisbon, Portugal." Brown's record also contains evidence that he was found guilty of drunkenness at a general court-martial in 1921.

As Brown was committed to a life in uniform, however, he reenlisted in the Marine Corps immediately after leaving the Naval Academy, and on February 19, 1925, then-Corporal Brown was commissioned from the ranks as a second lieutenant. Interestingly, the commanding officer of the Marine Corps Schools detachment at Quantico, Virginia, concluded that Brown was "intelligent, willing, and a man of excellent habits . . . good officer material." Moreover, wrote the commanding officer, "it is the opinion of the undersigned that his mistakes as a midshipman have been outweighed by his service as a Marine."[5]

In February 1927 Brown sailed for Nicaragua with the 5th Marine Regiment. He fought in several engagements against rebel bandits and was recommended for the Navy Cross for his extraordinary heroism. On January 19, 1928, for example, while leading an advance guard of a force of Marines, then–Second Lieutenant Brown "was challenged by a bandit sentry on the outskirts of Buena Vista. . . . Lt. Brown shot the sentry and with the two squads of his advance force utterly routed the bandit force of not less than 30 rifles, who were prepared to ambush the Marines."

Brown, however, did not receive the Navy Cross. Instead, he was awarded a letter of commendation by the secretary of the Navy for "splendid professional ability displayed while in combat . . . between October 1927 and January 1928 in Nicaragua." Brown also received the Nicaraguan Medal of Merit with silver star. Brown's letter of commendation was "elevated" to the Navy and Marine Corps Medal in 1952.

Brown returned to the United States from Nicaragua in May 1929 and subsequently served in the USS *Saratoga*, at the Marine Barracks in the Navy Yard at Mare Island, and at the Marine Barracks on Guam. Returning from Guam in July 1935, Brown first commanded an artillery battery at Quantico before taking charge of a 155-mm battery in San Diego. In June 1939 he took command of the Marine detachment aboard the battleship USS *Pennsylvania* and remained in that assignment until July 1941, when he returned to San Diego.

During the first half of World War II Brown served as an artillery and naval gunfire instructor at Coronado, California, and at Morro Bay, California. He was a pioneer in the coordination of naval gunfire, artillery, and air support. In October 1944 Brown deployed to the Pacific, where he organized and briefly commanded the 15th Marine Regiment, 6th Marine Division. He then took command of the 11th Marine Artillery Regiment, 1st Marine Division, serving in that capacity during the Okinawa campaign and in China at the war's end. Brown received the Legion of Merit with Combat *V* for outstanding service at Okinawa and a second Legion of Merit for his service in China.

Returning from China in October 1946, Brown was assigned to the Air University at Maxwell Field, Alabama, as an instructor in amphibious warfare and the coordination of fire and air support. In June 1949 Brown left Maxwell Field for Camp Lejeune, where he took command of the 10th Marine Artillery Regiment, 2nd Marine Division.

Then-Colonel Brown deployed to Korea in April 1951, where he commanded the 1st Marine Regiment, 1st Marine Division, until his return to the United States in December 1951. He was decorated with the Silver Star Medal for gallantry in action near Yanggu, Korea, during June 2–3, 1951. As his citation explains:

When one of his assault battalions was subjected to an accurate enemy mortar and artillery barrage which inflicted heavy casualties, including four company commanders and ten other officers, Col. Brown proceeded to the area in the face of the murderous fire and skillfully reorganized the battalion, enabling it to continue the attack. Moving to an exposed position in full view of the enemy and under continuous hostile mortar and artillery fire, he directed his men in seizing all assigned objectives and in inflicting a serious defeat upon a tenacious enemy.[6]

In August 1952 Brown pinned on his first star and was assigned to Camp Pendleton, where he was commanding general of Force Troops, Fleet Marine Force, Pacific. When he retired on December 1, 1953, Brown was promoted to major general. He had thirty-five years of service and had seen combat in World War I, Nicaragua, World War II, and Korea.

After retiring from active duty, Brown earned a PhD in history from the University of Alabama. His *Amphibious Campaign for West Florida and Louisiana, 1814–1815* was published in 1969.[7] Brown died in Birmingham, Alabama, in December 1968.

Brig. Gen. Robert L. Denig was wounded while leading his men in attacks against German machine-gun nests in France on October 3, 1918. (National Archives and Records Administration)

Robert L. Denig Sr.: Purple Heart—October 3, 1918

Robert Livingston Denig Sr. was wounded while leading his men in cleaning enemy machine guns and snipers out from the area around Medeah Farm in France, on October 3, 1918.

Denig was born on September 29, 1884 in Clinton, New York. The son of a Navy officer, he became acquainted with naval service early in life and attended grade school in Japan for several years while his father was serving with the U.S. Asiatic Fleet. In 1900, while attending high school in Sandusky, Ohio, Denig joined the Sixth Ohio Regiment of the National Guard. He later attended St. John's School in Manlius, New York, and the University of Pennsylvania for two years beginning in 1903.

In 1905, on this twenty-first birthday, Denig was appointed a second lieutenant in the Marine Corps. Denig reported to Marine Officer's School for training, but his studies were interrupted almost immediately when he was ordered to deploy to Cuba. Denig landed in Nuevitas, Cuba, in September 1906, but he returned home the next month.

After finishing his basic officer's education in 1907, Denig reported for duty in the battleship USS *Missouri*, where he served with the Marine detachment until December 1909. After a brief period of service in Annapolis and recruiting duty in St. Paul, Minnesota, Denig deployed to Olongapo, Philippines, for a three-year tour.

After America entered World War I, then-Major Denig sailed with the 5th Marine Regiment and arrived in France in July 1917. Denig probably wanted to stay with his fellow Marines, but he and four other Marine officers "joined" the Army's 3rd Division when that unit arrived in France short of experienced senior officers. Denig took command of the soldiers of the 1st Battalion, 30th Infantry Regiment and commanded his Army unit in June and early July 1918 before returning to the 6th Marines for several weeks.

On July 30, 1918, Denig took to soldiering once again, assuming command of the Army's 3rd Battalion, 9th Infantry, 2nd Division. In September 1918 then–Lieutenant Colonel Denig led his unit at St. Mihiel, and on October 3 he demonstrated extraordinary heroism in the assault at Medeah Farm, near Mont Blanc. Denig was badly wounded but refused to be evacuated until his battalion had achieved its objective. For his gallantry that day, the Army awarded Denig its Distinguished Service Cross—a decoration second only to the Medal of Honor. He later received the Navy Cross for the same action, and after the Army revived the Purple Heart in 1932, Denig applied for and received that decoration as well.

After returning to the United States in December 1918, Denig served in a variety of increasingly important assignments, including duty with the 2nd Brigade in Santo Domingo and service with the Guardia Nacional in Nicaragua. For his outstanding performance of duty in that last assignment during the 1931 earthquake, Denig was awarded Nicaragua's Presidential Medal of Merit. Denig initially retired from the Marine Corps as a brigadier general on June 30, 1941.

When World War II broke out, however, Denig was immediately recalled to active duty to serve as the first director of Marine Corps public relations. In that newly created job, Denig was in charge of overall publicity efforts for the Corps between 1941 and 1945. Denig ensured that photographers and correspondents were near the action and that they produced positive images of and stories about Marines in combat.

Having served more than forty years, Denig retired a second time in December 1945. He died in Los Altos, California, in July 1979, a few months shy what would have been his 95th birthday.[8]

Robert G. Robinson: Purple Heart—October 14, 1918

While serving as an aerial observer in an air raid over Belgium, Robert Guy Robinson was shot thirteen times and wounded in the chest, leg, and stomach.

Born in Wayne, Michigan, on April 30, 1896, Robinson enlisted as a private in the Marine Corps on May 22, 1917, slightly more than a month after the United States entered World War I. His enlistment paperwork reflects that he was five foot five-and-a-half inches, 142 lbs., and had blue eyes, brown hair, and a "ruddy" complexion. At the time he joined the Corps, Robinson was living in Chicago and working as a "mechanic."[9]

After training at Port Royal, South Carolina, and at Quantico, Robinson sailed to France in July 1918 as part of the newly created 1st Marine Aviation Force. That small unit, commanded by Marine Maj. Alfred A. Cunningham, entered combat in October 1918, just one month before the war ended. The Marine aviators carried out deep interdiction bombing, supply runs, and observation missions.

Robinson and the rest of his unit had trained on Curtiss JN-4, or "Jenny," biplanes before going overseas, but in combat they flew the two-seat British-made DH-4 biplanes. Built as bombers, the DH-4s had initially entered service with Great Britain's Royal Flying Corps in March 1917, but the American Expeditionary Force subsequently purchased the aircraft for use by Army and Marine pilots.

Then-Cpl. Guy Robinson was an aerial observer in the rear seat of a biplane when he was severely wounded by enemy gunfire. He later received a Purple Heart for those injuries and a Medal of Honor for his extraordinary heroism in the air. (U.S. Marine Corps)

On October 8, 1918, then-Corporal Robinson was an aerial observer in the rear seat of a DH-4 and, "in company with planes from Squadron 218, Royal Air Force ... took part in an air raid."[10] Robinson's job as the "back seater" was to serve as an extra pair of eyes while also manning the .30-06-caliber Lewis automatic machine gun mounted on a ring near him. He performed heroically that day. When Robinson's plane was attacked by nine German scout planes, he managed to down one with his Lewis gun.

With a cyclic rate of between five hundred and six hundred rounds a minute, the machine gun was a valuable defensive weapon for the DH-4, and Robinson again proved his skills with it less than a week later during an air raid over Pitthan, Belgium. His citation for the Medal of Honor explains that on October 14, 1918, Robinson's "plane and one other became separated from their formation on account of motor trouble and were attacked by 12 enemy scouts."

Robinson immediately engaged the enemy and shot down one German plane. But then, Robinson "was struck by a bullet which carried away most of his elbow" and, at the same time, his own gun jammed. Acting "with conspicuous gallantry and intrepidity"—and great presence of mind—Robinson managed to clear the jammed machine gun with his remaining good hand and returned to the fight. Despite intense pain and a useless left arm, he fought off the enemy scouts "until he collapsed after receiving two more bullet wounds, one in the stomach and one in the thigh."

By the end of the dogfight, Robinson had taken a baker's dozen of German bullets, and his left forearm was hanging loosely by a single tendon. But he was still alive, and his luck held. After the pilot, Marine 2nd Lt. Ralph Talbot, landed the DH-4 in Belgium, the surgeon general of the Belgian Army successfully reattached Robinson's arm.

For his extraordinary heroism on October 8 and 14, 1918, Robinson was recommended for both the Army Distinguished Service Cross and the Navy Distinguished Service Medal. In December 1919, however, he received the Medal of Honor, becoming the first noncommissioned officer in Marine Corps history to receive the award for heroism in the air. Talbot also received the Medal of Honor, but he never lived to have it bestowed upon him because he was killed in a test-flight crash in late October 1918.

Robinson returned from Europe in January 1919 and left active duty as a gunnery sergeant that July. He received an appointment as a reserve second lieutenant and remained in the Marine Corps Reserve until May 1923, when he retired fully. In September 1936 Robinson was retroactively was promoted to first lieutenant.

Robinson died in October 1974 at his home in Michigan. He is buried in Arlington National Cemetery.

NICARAGUA (1927–1933)

In 1912 Adolfo Diaz, then-president of Nicaragua, requested that the United States "guarantee with its forces security for the property of American Citizens in Nicaragua and that it extend its protection to all the inhabitants of the Republic."[11] As a result of this request, Marines soon arrived in Managua and, except for a nine-month period in 1925, the Corps was present in Nicaragua until 1933.

Although there was a Marine presence in Nicaragua prior to World War I, there do not appear to have been Purple Hearts awarded for wounds received in action until 1927, when guerrillas led by General Augusto C. Sandino battled both U.S. Marines and the conservative regime then in power. Sandino's forces suffered repeated losses in their engagements with the Marines, but he evaded capture and emerged as a national hero. After a liberal government took power in 1932 and President Roosevelt announced that a "Good Neighbor Policy" would govern American relations in the Western Hemisphere, the United States withdrew all its military forces from Nicaragua in January 1933.

In the 1940s a very small number of Purple Hearts were awarded to Marines for wounds received while conducting military operations in Nicaragua during the 1920s and 1930s.[12]

Harry D. Hutchcroft: Purple Heart—May 17, 1932

Harry D. Hutchcroft was wounded by a gunshot to his thigh while fighting bandits near Sisin, Nicaragua.

Hutchcroft served in the Army during World War I, but after being honorably discharged in 1919, he enlisted in the Marine Corps. On June 10, 1930, then-Sergeant Hutchcroft was one of several Marines riding along with the transport SS *Fairfax* when she collided with the tanker *Pinthis* off the Massachusetts coast. A fire started on the *Fairfax*, and Hutchcroft helped battle the blaze and aided women and children passengers to get to safety. For his gallant and conspicuous conduct that day, the secretary of the Navy awarded Hutchcroft a Special Letter of Commendation on August 22, 1930.

Less than two years later Hutchcroft was serving as a second lieutenant in Nicaragua. While on patrol with the Guardia National near Sisin, Hutchcroft's unit "had contact with a bandit group estimated at 50 and thought to include

Guardia mutineers from the town of Kisalaya." The Marines captured one Thompson machine gun and two Browning automatic rifles. Apparently the only casualty was Hutchcroft "who received a bullet wound to the thigh."[13]

Hutchcroft remained in the Marine Corps during World War II but saw no overseas service. In 1944 while assigned to the 18th Defense Battalion, Hutchcroft applied for the newly created Navy Commendation Ribbon on the basis of his 1930 letter from the secretary of the Navy. The Navy Board of Decorations and Medals decided instead, however, that Hutchcroft should receive the Navy and Marine Corps Medal. He received that medal in a ceremony at Camp Lejeune in May 1944.

Hutchcroft retired as a major in 1955. In addition to his Purple Heart for wounds received in Nicaragua and his Navy and Marine Corps Medal for heroism while in the *Fairfax*, Hutchcroft also was awarded the Marine Corps Good Conduct Medal, World War I Victory Medal for his earlier service as a soldier, Second Nicaraguan Campaign Medal, American Campaign Medal, American Defense Service Medal, and World War II Victory Medal.

WORLD WAR II (1941-1945)

There were 19,733 Marine battle deaths between the Japanese attack on Pearl Harbor in December 1941 and the end of combat operations in the Pacific in August 1945. Another 68,207 Marines were wounded in action during World War II.[14] While this means that more than 88,000 Marines were eligible for a posthumous or nonposthumous Purple Heart, how many actually were awarded is not known.

In any event, Marines initially awarded Navy Purple Hearts received only the ribbon; no Purple Heart medal was available until May 1943, when the Bureau of Naval Personnel mailed out Purple Hearts to the next of kin of Marines killed in action at Pearl Harbor, in the Philippines, and in the battles of Coral Sea and Midway.[15]

John Basilone: Purple Heart—February 19, 1945

John Basilone was killed in action on Iwo Jima on February 19, 1945. His widow, Marine Sgt. Lena Mae Basilone, received his posthumously awarded Purple Heart and Navy Cross. John Basilone had already been awarded the Medal of Honor for his extraordinary heroism at Guadalcanal in October 1942, becoming the first enlisted Marine to receive America's highest award for combat heroism in World War II.

Sgt. John Basilone was killed in action on Iwo Jima on February 19, 1945. His widow received his posthumously awarded Purple Heart. (U.S. Marine Corps)

Born in Buffalo, New York, in November 1916, Basilone was the son of an Italian immigrant father and one of ten children. Basilone enlisted in the Army when he was eighteen years old, served a tour as a soldier in the Philippines, and, after being honorably discharged, went to work as a truck driver in Reisterstown, Maryland.

In July 1940 Basilone enlisted in the Marine Corps in Baltimore, Maryland. He trained at Quantico, Parris Island, and New River, North Carolina—which later became Camp Lejeune. Basilone also served at Guantánamo Bay before deploying to the Pacific.

On October 24, 1942, Basilone, known to his fellow Marines as "Manila John" because of his earlier soldiering in the Philippines, was serving with 1st Battalion, 7th Marines, 1st Marine Division in the Lunga area of Guadalcanal. He was in charge of two sections of heavy machine guns and was fighting "valiantly" against a "savage and determined" Japanese attack. According to the citation for his Medal of Honor, after the enemy had put one of Basilone's gun sections out of action, leaving only two men able to carry on, Basilone moved "an extra gun into position, placed it in action and then, under continual fire, repaired another and personally manned it, gallantly holding his line until replacements arrived."

Later, "with ammunition critically low and the supply lines cut off, Sgt. Basilone, at great risk of his life and in the face of continued enemy attack, battled his way through hostile lines with urgently needed shells for his gunners, thereby contributing in large measure to the virtual annihilation of a Japanese regiment."

Basilone apparently killed a total of thirty-eight Japanese that day with either a machine gun or his pistol. Said Marine Pfc. Nash W. Phillips, of Fayetteville, North Carolina, who was in the same unit as Basilone on Guadalcanal, "Basilone had a machine gun on the go for three days and nights without sleep, rest or food. . . . He was in a good emplacement, and causing the Japs lots of trouble, not only firing his machine gun but also using his pistol."[16]

On February 19, 1945, then–Gunnery Sergeant Basilone again proved his fighting skills during the landings on Iwo Jima. While serving as the leader of a machine-gun section in Company C of the 1st Battalion, 27th Marines, 5th Marine Division, Basilone "shrewdly gauged the tactical situation" and then "defied the smashing (Japanese) bombardment" to work his way around the flank and single-handedly destroy an enemy blockhouse with "grenades and demolitions." He later "repeatedly exposed himself to the blasting fury of exploding shells" and rescued a friendly tank that had been trapped in an enemy minefield and was under intense Japanese mortar and artillery fire. Tragically, Basilone was killed a short time later by an exploding mortar round, but his gallantry on February 19 was recognized with a posthumous award of the Navy Cross.

Basilone is interred at Arlington National Cemetery, and he has not been forgotten. In 1949 the destroyer USS *Basilone* was commissioned in his honor, and the U.S. Postal Service issued a stamp bearing his likeness in 2005.

Evans F. Carlson: Purple Hearts—1918 and June 15–July 9, 1944

Although Evans Fordyce Carlson was wounded in action while serving as a soldier in France in World War I, he received his first Marine Corps Purple Heart for injuries he incurred during the Battle of Saipan between June 15, 1944, and July 9, 1944. Consequently, he is listed as a World War II Marine Corps recipient.

Born on February 26, 1896, in Sidney, New York, Carlson, who later became famous as the leader of Carlson's Raiders, started his military career in the Army when he dropped out of high school in 1912 and joined the Army. He was sixteen years old in 1912, but he excelled as a soldier in the Philippines and Hawaii. When he was honorably discharged after completing a four-year enlistment, Carlson was a top sergeant.

He spent less than a year as a civilian before reenlisting and then serving under Pershing during the Punitive Expedition into Mexico. Carlson also served with Pershing in France and was wounded in action. Commissioned as a second lieutenant in May 1917, Carlson finished the war as a captain in Germany with the Army of Occupation.

Despite his obvious success as a soldier, Carlson enlisted as a Marine private in 1922. His experience in the Army, however, meant that he was able to secure an appointment as a Marine second lieutenant in 1923. Carlson then served at Quantico; Culebra, Puerto Rico; and Pensacola, where he took aviation training. From 1927 to 1929, he was a China Marine in Shanghai.

In 1930 then–First Lieutenant Carlson arrived in Nicaragua to serve as an officer in the Guardia Nacional. For gallantry in leading twelve Marines against one hundred bandits, Carlson was awarded his first Navy Cross. He also was commended for his bravery following the 1931 Managua earthquake and for his performance of duties as a chief of police in Nicaragua from 1932 to 1933.

After a brief stay in the United States in 1933, Carlson was assigned once again to Shanghai, but he shortly thereafter transferred to the Marine detachment in Peking, China. He returned home in 1936 for Marine Corps schooling at Quantico.

Carlson returned to Asia for his third tour as a China Marine in 1937. Because he had previously studied Chinese, Carlson's new assignment was serving as a military observer with Nationalist Chinese forces under Chiang Kai-shek. According to the Marine Corps History Division, Carlson traveled "thousands of miles through the interior of China, often on foot and horseback over the most hazardous terrain" and "lived under the primitive conditions of native troops."[17] The experience proved invaluable, however, because it allowed Carlson to learn the tactics of Japanese soldiers.

After returning home in 1938, Carlson was so alarmed about Japanese aggression in Asia that he resigned his commission in order to be able to write and speak freely about the danger. In 1941, however, Carlson requested to be recommissioned and was appointed as a major. The next year he was given command of the 2nd Marine Raider Battalion and promoted to lieutenant colonel. For his superb leadership of that unit during the raid on Makin Island on August 17, 1942, Carlson was awarded a second Navy Cross. Just months later, he received a third Navy Cross for "heroism and distinguished leadership" on Guadalcanal.[18]

After returning briefly to the United States for medical treatment following the Guadalcanal invasion, then-Colonel Carlson returned to the Pacific to serve as an observer on Tarawa. Sometime between June 15, 1944, and July 9, 1944, he was wounded on Saipan while attempting to rescue a wounded enlisted Marine from a front-line observation post.

Carlson's wounds from Saipan caused him to take medical retirement on July 1, 1946. He was advanced to brigadier general for having been "specially commended for the performance of duty in actual combat."[19] He died in Portland, Oregon, on May 27, 1947, at the age of fifty-one.

Raymond G. Davis: Purple Heart—September 1, 1944

Raymond Gilbert Davis was wounded in action during the landings on Peleliu on September 1, 1944.

Davis, who received the Medal of Honor for heroism at Chosin Reservoir, Korea, in 1950, was born in January 1915 in Fitzgerald, Georgia. After graduating from high school in 1933, Davis attended the Georgia School of Technology—now Georgia Tech—and earned a BS in chemical engineering in 1938. Although he had been a member of the Army ROTC while in college and was commissioned in the Army Reserve, Davis resigned that commission to accept an appointment as a Marine second lieutenant in June 1938.

After completing the Marine Officers' Basic School in May 1939, Davis joined the Marine detachment in the USS *Portland*. After a year of sea duty in the Pacific, he was assigned to Quantico, where he received weapons and artillery instruction. Prior to America's entry into World War II, Davis also did brief tours of duty at Guantánamo Bay, Parris Island, and New River.

After deploying to the Pacific in June 1942, Davis participated in the August 7–9, 1942, Guadalcanal–Tulagi landings. In October 1943, then-Major Davis took command of the 1st Special Weapons Battalion, 1st Marine Division and led that unit at New Guinea and Cape Gloucester. In April 1944, while on Cape Gloucester, Davis was named commanding officer of the 1st Battalion, 1st Marines, 1st Marine Division.

On September 1, 1944, Davis landed with his battalion at Peleliu. Despite being wounded during the first hour of the landings, he refused evacuation and remained with his men. According to the citation for his Navy Cross, Davis repeatedly showed bravery under fire. On one occasion, when heavy casualties and point-blank Japanese cannon fire had allowed the enemy to break through Marine lines, Davis personally rallied and led his men in fighting to reestablish defensive positions.

Shortly after being promoted to lieutenant colonel in October 1944, Davis returned Quantico, where he first served as tactical inspector for the Marine Corps Schools before being named chief of the Infantry Section, Marine Air-Infantry School.

In July 1947 Davis joined the 1st Provisional Marine Brigade on Guam. He returned home two years later to take up his new assignment as the inspector-instructor for the 9th Marine Corps Reserve Infantry Battalion in Chicago.

In August 1950 Lieutenant Colonel Davis took command of the 1st Battalion, 7th Marines, 1st Marine Division. From December 1–4, 1950, during the exceptionally heavy fighting and brutally cold temperatures at Chosin Reservoir, Davis again showed that he was an exceptional Marine. According to his citation for the Medal of Honor, Davis "boldly led his battalion into the attack" against overwhelming odds. During the four-day battle that followed, his leadership and heroism were key factors in saving a rifle company from annihilation and opening a mountain pass for the escape of two trapped Marine regiments. At one point Davis was knocked to the ground when a shell fragment struck his helmet and two bullets pierced his clothing, but he got up and fought his way forward at the head of his men.

Almost two years later, on November 24, 1952, President Truman presented Davis a Medal of Honor in a White House ceremony. Prior to that event, however, Davis finished his tour of combat duty in Korea. He was awarded two Silver Stars for gallantry in action for exposing himself to heavy enemy fire while leading and encouraging his men in the face of strong enemy opposition. Davis also received the Legion of Merit with Combat V and the Bronze Star Medal with Combat V.

After returning to the United States in June 1951, Davis served in a variety of positions at Marine Corps headquarters in Washington, D.C. He was promoted to colonel in 1953. During the 1950s Davis served in a variety of assignments and locations, including assistant G-2 while at headquarters and chief of the Analysis Branch of the U.S. European Command headquarters in Paris.

After being promoted to brigadier general in July 1963, Davis served as assistant division commander for the 3rd Marine Division, Fleet Marine Force, on Okinawa from October 1963 until November 1964. He was promoted to major general in November 1966 and deployed to Vietnam, where he served as commanding general of the 3rd Marine Division from May 1968 until April 1969. He returned to the United States in May 1969 and was promoted to lieutenant general in July 1970.

In March 1971 Davis received his fourth star and assumed duties as assistant commandant of the Marine Corps. When he retired in March 1972, he had more than thirty-three years of active duty. His Medal of Honor, Navy Cross, two Silver Stars, Legion of Merit with Combat V, Bronze Star with Combat V, and Purple Heart speak volumes about the quality of his service.

Davis died of a heart attack on September 3, 2003, at the age of eighty-eight.[20]

James L. Day: Purple Hearts—May 14–15, 1944; October 1952–June 1953; and June 1966–May 1967

James Lewis "Jim" Day received the Medal of Honor and six Purple Hearts in three wars—a record no other Marine has equaled or exceeded. Amazingly, Day did not receive his highest honor until 1998, some fifty-three years after the events that merited the Medal of Honor. As for Day's record number of Purple Hearts, Mr. Doug Sterner, an expert in American military awards, confirmed that "Day has the record for the most Purple Hearts (made) to a Marine. . . . He was awarded six for wounds received in combat in World War II, Korea, and Vietnam."[21]

Born in East St. Louis, Illinois, in October 1925, Day enlisted in the Corps in 1943 and saw action in the Marshall Islands and on Guam. On May 14,

Maj. Gen. James L. Day holds the record for the most Purple Hearts awarded to a Marine, with six. (U.S. Marine Corps)

1945, nineteen-year-old then-Corporal Day was in the middle of fighting for a hill called Sugar Loaf on Okinawa. According to official records, Day led several other Marines to a shell crater on the slope of the hill and then fought off a fierce Japanese attack. That night, he helped repel three more enemy assaults on his position. Then, after his fellow Marines were wounded, Day braved heavy fire to escort them to safety.

The next day only Day and another Marine—who was wounded—were still in their foxhole. Despite repeated assaults, Day continued the fight, even after he was badly burned by white phosphorous and injured by shrapnel. Three days later, when Day was finally relieved, he was still alive. More than one hundred Japanese lay dead around his foxhole.

Day received a commission after the war and completed officer's training at Quantico in September 1952. He subsequently deployed to Korea and, in addition to being twice wounded in action, received two Silver Stars for gallantry while serving with Company C of the 1st Battalion, 7th Marines and with the 1st Reconnaissance Company.

Returning to the United States then–First Lieutenant Day served first at the Marine Corps Supply Center in Barstow, California, before taking command of a company at Camp Pendleton in July 1954. Day also commanded a 4.2-inch mortar company on Okinawa from 1957 to 1958.

In April 1966 then-Major Day deployed for the first time to Vietnam, where he commanded the 1st Battalion, 9th Marines, 3rd Marine Division. When he returned to the United States in June 1967, Day received a promotion to lieutenant colonel and was given two more battalion commands at Camp Pendleton.

After graduating from the Army War College in 1972, Day returned to Vietnam to serve as operations officer for the 9th Marine Amphibious Brigade, III Marine Amphibious Force. Day was promoted to colonel in November 1973, and he received his first star in 1976. In 1980 Day was promoted to major general and assumed command of the 1st Marine Division. When he retired from active duty in December 1986, he was in command of Marine Corps Base, Camp Butler on Okinawa and also served as the deputy commander for Marine Corps Bases, Pacific and Okinawa Area Coordinator.

During a career that had spanned more than four decades, Day had been awarded three Silver Stars, the Legion of Merit with Combat *V*, a Bronze Star Medal Combat *V*, and six Purple Hearts. But his most important decoration was still to come. According to the *Los Angeles Times*, the original paperwork recommending Day for the Medal of Honor for his heroism at Sugar

Loaf had been lost in 1945 and was only rediscovered in 1980, when a retired Marine "found faded carbon copies of the recommendation among his World War II memorabilia."[22]

It took another eighteen years until, on January 20, 1998, President Clinton presented the Medal of Honor to Day in a White House ceremony. Sadly, Day died of a heart attack only months later, on October 28. He was buried in Fort Rosecrans National Cemetery outside of San Diego.[23]

Emil Elias: Purple Heart—February 19–20, 1944

Emil Elias was first severely wounded by shrapnel from a Japanese hand grenade and was later also shot through the chest by the enemy. He survived both wounds and received a Purple Heart and Navy Cross.

Born January 14, 1920, Elias enlisted in the Marine Corps on November 18, 1942. Then-Corporal Elias was in a foxhole on Eniwetok Atoll in the Marshall Islands on the night of February 19, 1944, when the Japanese infiltrated Marine lines. Elias was severely wounded when an enemy soldier tossed a grenade into his defensive position. Despite suffering excruciating pain, Elias kept silent because he believed that a groan or cry from him might attract other Marines to come to his assistance and, thus, endanger their lives. As a result, "he feigned death from 10 PM until dawn of the following day, during which period he was searched eleven times by the Japanese and was shot through the chest to ensure his death." When his fellow Marines reached Elias at daylight, his only words were, "I feel much better now."[24] For this "act of superb heroism, of iron self-control, and of complete unselfishness," Elias was awarded a Navy Cross.

Elias was honorably discharged on October 28, 1945, and died on September 4, 1983.

Timerlate Kirvin: Purple Heart—June 15,1944
Samuel J. Love Sr.: Purple Heart—June 15, 1944

SSgt. Timerlate Kirvin and Cpl. Samuel Love were among the first African American Marines to be decorated with the Purple Heart. Both men were wounded on June 15, 1944, while fighting the Japanese during the Battle of Saipan. While both Kirvin and Love were serving in support companies, and consequently should not have seen combat, the fierce fighting on Saipan caused support personnel to be drawn into battle.

The historical significance of the Purple Hearts awarded to Kirvin and Love is clear when one remembers that when the United States entered World

Cpl. Emil Elias was severely wounded by shrapnel from a Japanese hand grenade and also suffered a gunshot wound through his chest. He survived to receive a Purple Heart and Navy Cross. (U.S. Marine Corps)

SSgt. Timerlate Kirvin and Cpl. Samuel J. Love Sr. were among the first African American Marines to be decorated with the Purple Heart. (National Archives and Records Administration)

War II, the Marine Corps did not have a single black officer or enlisted man in its ranks. Yet, while the Corps—unlike the Army and Navy—had never before allowed African Americans to enlist, by the end of the war, more than 19,000 blacks had served in the Marine enlisted ranks. There were no African American Marine officers during World War II.[25]

Peter J. Ortiz: Purple Heart—March 1943

See chapter 9, "Celebrities: Artists and Entertainers, Politicians, Athletes, and Other Public Figures."

Lewis B. Puller: Purple Heart—November 8, 1942

See chapter 8, "Families: Brothers, Fathers and Sons, and Husbands and Wives."

CHINA (1945–1947)

Roughly fifty-five Purple Hearts were awarded to Marines serving in China between 1945 and 1947. The earliest Purple Hearts went to three Marines wounded by rifle fire when their reconnaissance patrol was attacked by up to fifty Chinese communist guerrillas near Tientsin, China, on October 6, 1945. The last Purple Heart was a posthumous decoration awarded to a Marine killed in an ambush by Chinese communists outside Tientsin on Christmas Day 1947.[26]

Three verified China Marine Purple Heart recipients who also were awarded Silver Stars for gallantry in action on the day they were wounded are profiled below.

Jacob P. Jereb: Purple Heart—April 5, 1947

Then-Pfc. Jacob Jereb was wounded by automatic weapons and grenade fire near Hsin-Ho, China, on April 5, 1947.

A native of Cleveland, Ohio, Jereb was serving in Company C of the 1st Battalion, 5th Marines, 1st Marine Division (Reinforced) when a large number of Communist forces "penetrated his sentinel point at the ammunition supply point." Despite the intense automatic and grenade fire directed at him, Jereb immediately returned fire and directed "an accurate stream of small-arms fire at the onrushing attackers until he fell, wounded by the hostile fire."[27] The Navy later awarded Jereb both the Purple Heart and the Silver Star.

Alfred E. Perkey: Purple Heart—April 5, 1947

Alfred E. Perkey was killed in action by Communist forces near Hsin-Ho, China, on April 5, 1947.

Born in Sprague, West Virginia, Perkey was serving as a private first class in Company C of the 1st Battalion, 5th Marines, 1st Marine Division (Reinforced) when the truck in which he was a passenger was attacked by "a large group of . . . dissident Chinese forces." Although he and his fellow Marines initially "disembarked" from the vehicle under a "barrage of small arms, automatic weapons and grenade fire," Perkey soon returned and climbed back on the truck. He then "unloaded two mortars, a machine gun and ammunition for all weapons, successfully placed one of the mortars in action and, after firing several wounds, was mortally wounded by an enemy hand grenade and fell at his post."[28]

Perkey's next of kin received his posthumously awarded Purple Heart and Silver Star.

Peter R. Stankiewicz Jr.: Purple Heart—April 5, 1947

Peter Stankiewicz was wounded "in action against dissident forces" near Hsin-Ho, China, on April 5, 1947.

A native of Chicago, then–Private First Class Stankiewicz was serving in Company C of the 1st Battalion, 5th Marines, 1st Marine Division (Reinforced). When he heard rifle and grenade fire near his sentinel point and the ammunition supply point, Stankiewicz "unhesitatingly pressed forward and engaged in a fire fight with an overwhelming number of dissident forces." Despite being pinned down and having been "seriously wounded by an enemy grenade," Stankiewicz "delivered accurate and concentrated rifle fire and succeeded in diverting the advance until reinforcements arrived."[29]

The Navy subsequently awarded Stankiewicz both a Purple Heart and a Silver Star for gallantry in action.

KOREA (1950–1953)

Official reports list 4,270 Marines killed in action during the Korean War. Another 23,744 Marines suffered nonmortal casualties. But, while 4,270 posthumous Purple Hearts were awarded, the Navy reported in 1958 that only about 5,930 Purple Hearts had been awarded to the 23,744 Marines who were apparently eligible for the decoration on the basis of their nonmortal combat wounds.[30]

Second Lt. John T. Chamberlain was killed in action when the AU-1 Corsair he was flying was shot down on March 29, 1953. Chamberlain's officially hand-engraved Purple Heart was presented to his parents. (Fred Borch)

John T. Chamberlain: Purple Heart—March 29, 1953

Then–Second Lt. John Chamberlain was killed in action in Korea on March 29, 1953. He was an aviator with the 1st Marine Air Wing and was piloting an AU-1 Corsair on a bombing mission when he was shot down. Chamberlain initially was carried on his unit's duty list as missing in action, but the Marine Corps changed his status to killed in action in April 1953.

Chamberlain's officially hand-engraved Purple Heart was presented to his parents.

Wesley L. Fox: Purple Hearts—June 8, 1951; February 22, 1969; and October 1967–May 1969

Wesley Lee Fox was awarded his first Purple Heart in Korea, when he was wounded by "light metal and wood shrapnel" on June 8, 1951.[31] He was wounded three more times in Vietnam, and received three more awards of the Purple Heart, as well as a Medal of Honor.

Born in Virginia in September 1931, Fox "was not motivated to do well in schoolwork," so he quit school in ninth grade and worked as a farmer.[32] In August 1950, however, inspired to serve his country, Fox enlisted in the Marine Corps.

After completing recruit training at Parris Island in October 1950, Fox served briefly at Camp Lejeune before sailing to Korea and fighting as a rifleman in Company I of the 3rd Battalion, 5th Marines, 1st Marine Division. On September 8, 1951, Fox and his squad were assaulting an enemy position when he was wounded by a concussion grenade thrown by a Chinese soldier. Fox's left hand, arm, and foot "felt as though red-hot needles were sticking in them," and he was evacuated to the U.S. Naval Hospital in Bethesda, Maryland, for treatment.

After the Korean War, Fox remained in the Corps and served in a variety of assignments and locations, including Marine Aircraft Group 11 in Japan; 3rd Battalion, 5th Marines in Korea; and Marine Corps Recruit Depot, San Diego.

In 1961 then–Technical Sergeant Fox qualified as a military parachutist, and the following year he completed Underwater Swimmers School at Subic Bay. In May 1964 he was promoted to gunnery sergeant. Then, while serving in the Office of the Provost Marshal at Supreme Headquarters Allied Powers Europe in Paris, Fox decided to apply for a commission as an officer. His application was accepted, and on May 27, 1966—ten days after he had been promoted to first sergeant—Fox pinned on the gold bars of a second lieutenant.

Col. Wesley L. Fox received his first Purple Heart in Korea, and three more in Vietnam. He also was awarded the Medal of Honor for his extraordinary heroism in battle. (U.S. Marine Corps)

In August 1966 Fox took command of a platoon in the 2nd Force Reconnaissance Company based at Camp Lejeune. A year later he deployed to Vietnam, and, from October 1967 until November 1968, he served as an advisor to a South Vietnamese Marine battalion.

In November 1968 then–First Lieutenant Fox took command of Company A, 1st Battalion, 9th Marines. While with that unit on February 22, 1969, he was wounded when a rocket-propelled grenade "exploded against a bush two feet behind" him and he received shrapnel to his left leg and shoulder.[33] His extraordinary heroism that same day later resulted in Fox being awarded a Medal of Honor in a White House ceremony on March 2, 1971.

According to the official citation for that decoration, after Fox's company "came under intense fire from a large well concealed enemy force," he moved "to a position from which he could assess the situation and confer with his platoon leaders." But, as Fox and his Marines "departed to execute the plan he had devised, the enemy attacked," and "Fox was wounded along with all of the other members of the command group, except the executive officer."

Despite his injuries, Fox fought through heavy enemy fire, personally destroyed one enemy position, and "calmly ordered an assault against the hostile emplacements." Then, after his executive officer was mortally wounded, Fox "reorganized the company and directed the fire of his men as they hurled grenades against the enemy and drove the hostile forces into retreat." Although wounded again in this final assault, "Fox refused medical attention, established a defensive posture, and supervised the preparation of casualties for medical evacuation."[34]

After returning home in 1969, Fox served in a number of key assignments before retiring as a colonel with forty-three years of active duty in September 1993. He then served as deputy commandant of cadets at Virginia Tech in Blacksburg, Virginia, until retiring a second time in 2001. Fox's autobiography, *Marine Rifleman*, was published in 2003.

Donald N. Hamblen: Purple Heart—May 4, 1952

Donald Hamblen was wounded in his left leg during a mortar barrage, and also shot in the right shoulder, on May 4, 1952. While he made a complete recovery from these combat injuries, Hamblen lost his left leg in a parachuting mishap ten years later. He remained on active duty, however, and later wrote an autobiography about this experiences.

Born in Maine in July 1932, Hamblen enlisted in the Marine Corps in February 1950 and completed recruit training at Parris Island. In late

November 1951 he shipped out to Korea to serve as a rifleman in Company D of the 2nd Battalion, 5th Marines, 1st Marine Division.

On May 4, 1952, Hamblen was wounded in his left leg in a Chinese mortar attack. As he was being carried back toward friendly lines by a four-man litter team, Hamblen and his fellow Americans were ambushed by a squad of Chinese infantrymen. Hamblen spilled from the litter onto the ground, and, as he lay there helplessly, the Chinese shot him in the shoulder. But he did not die, and when his fellow Marines later found him and brought him to the battalion aid station, medics removed two pieces of shrapnel from his leg and a rifle bullet from his right shoulder.[35]

After returning to the United States in November 1952, Hamblen completed airborne, pathfinder, and scuba training and served in a variety of assignments and locations. On September 21, 1962, disaster struck after then–Staff Sergeant Hamblen had parachuted from an aircraft flying over Camp Pendleton. Strong winds blew him into high-tension power lines, and his canopy became entangled in the wires. When Hamblen's presence caused these 69,000 volt lines to touch, he was badly injured. Doctors later amputated his left leg about six inches below the knee.

After being fitted with a prosthesis, Hamblen worked hard to return to active duty. He successfully passed a Marine Corps physical readiness test consisting of a fireman's carry, twenty-foot rope climb, and three-mile run and was permitted to remain in the Corps. He also requalified as a parachutist and later served in Vietnam at Military Assistance Command, Vietnam. Hamblen has claimed in his autobiography and elsewhere that he repeatedly accompanied Special Operations Group teams on combat missions, including a March 1967 mission into North Vietnam. He has also claimed that he was wounded in combat in both North Vietnam and South Vietnam on three occasions.[36]

Hamblen left Vietnam in November 1969 and retired from the Marine Corps on March 1, 1970.

Jimmie E. Howard: Purple Hearts—August 15, 1952; October 3, 1952; and June 16, 1966

Medal of Honor recipient Jimmie Earl Howard was wounded twice in Korea in 1952 and once in Vietnam in 1966. He was awarded three Purple Hearts.

Born in Burlington, Iowa, on July 27, 1929, Howard enlisted in the Marine Corps on July 12, 1950, when he was twenty years old. After completing recruit training at the Recruit Depot in San Diego in January 1951, Howard received advanced infantry training and then deployed to Korea, where he served as a forward observer with the 4.2-inch Mortar Company of the 1st Marines, 1st Marine Division.

On August 15, 1952, then-Corporal Howard was wounded in combat with the Chinese. He was wounded again on October 3, 1952. By the time he left Korea in April 1953, Howard had two Purple Hearts and a Silver Star for gallantry in action.

Howard remained on active duty over the next ten years and served in a variety of assignments and locations, including tactics instructor with the 2nd Infantry Training Regiment at Camp Pendleton, squad leader in the Marine detachment in the USS *Oriskany*, squad leader in the 1st Force Reconnaissance Company at Camp Pendleton, and instructor for the Counter-Guerrilla Warfare Course of the 1st Marine Division at Camp Pendleton.

In June 16, 1966, thirty-seven-year-old Staff Sergeant Howard—now married and the father of six children—was in Vietnam and serving as a platoon leader with Company C, 1st Reconnaissance Battalion, 1st Marine Division. On that day he was leading an eighteen-man reconnaissance patrol in Quang Tin Province when the patrol was attacked by a North Vietnamese battalion. Howard was wounded in the fierce firefight that followed, during which Howard and his fellow Marines defended a perimeter measuring only twenty meters in diameter. While Howard later received a third Purple Heart, his extraordinary heroism under fire that day also was later recognized with the award of the Medal of Honor.

Howard was the sixth Marine to be awarded a Medal of Honor for combat in Vietnam, and he received it from President Lyndon B. Johnson in a White House ceremony on March 21, 1967. According to the citation for his award, after his platoon was attacked by the numerically superior enemy, Howard "immediately organized his platoon to personally supervise the precarious defense . . . and . . . repeatedly exposed himself to enemy fire while directing the operation of his small force." Then, despite mounting casualties and his own severe wounds from an enemy grenade, Howard "continued to set an example of calmness and courage . . . and moving from position to position, he inspired his men with dynamic leadership and courageous fighting spirit." He also successfully directed friendly aircraft and artillery strikes on the North Vietnamese positions. Then, when helicopters arrived to medically evacuate the Marines, Howard directed them away so that he could call in additional air strikes on the enemy in order to make the landing zone as secure as possible.[37]

At the end of the action, at least thirty of the enemy were dead. Six Marines out of the eighteen in the platoon also had been killed. Every surviving Marine had been wounded, and each received a Purple Heart. Also, in addition to the Medal of Honor awarded to Howard, four Marines received a Navy Cross for their gallantry under fire.

After returning to the United States, Howard was promoted to gunnery sergeant. He retired from active duty in March 1977 and died in November 1993.

CUBA (1962)

Paul E. Kessler: Purple Heart—November 3, 1962
Robert E. Mehaffie: Purple Heart—November 3, 1962
John S. Turner: Purple Heart—November 3, 1962
Sgt. Paul Kessler, LCpl. Robert Mehaffie, and Pvt. John Turner were wounded by an exploding land mine on November 3, 1962.

All three Marines were members of Company A of the 2nd Pioneer Battalion, 2nd Marine Division, which had landed at Guantánamo Bay on October 18, 1962, as part of President Kennedy's "show of force" during the Cuban Missile Crisis. On November 3, as they and other Marines resurveyed a U.S. minefield located at Leeward Point, a landmine exploded. Kessler, a native of Indiana, Pennsylvania, and Mehaffie, of Frederick, Maryland, each lost both legs. Turner, of Sharpsburg, Maryland, lost one leg and suffered multiple shrapnel wounds in the other. All three men received the Purple Heart. Their awards are unusual, given the lack of any direct hostile acts by Cuban forces and the accidental nature of the explosion.[38]

VIETNAM (1964–1973)

A total of 13,070 Marines were killed in Vietnam, and another 51,392 Marines wounded in action.[39] Among those receiving Purple Hearts were the following members of the Corps.

Thomas A. Richards: Purple Heart—June 5–6, 1969
While Thomas Richards was wounded twice on the night of June 5–6, 1969, he received one Purple Heart because of the contemporaneous nature of the combat wounds.

Richards enlisted in 1967 and completed recruit training in San Diego. He subsequently served in Vietnam as a fire team leader, squad leader, and platoon guide in Company H of the 2nd Battalion, 9th Marines, 3rd Marine Division. He was a twenty-two-year-old corporal fire team leader for Hotel Company when injured. His platoon came into contact with a company-size Viet Cong force who were occupying well-camouflaged positions on a cliff overlooking a trail and began pouring heavy fire onto the Marines.

With bullets flying everywhere, Richards regrouped his platoon and led a counterattack. He prompted, prodded, and encouraged others, and he also organized a defensive perimeter. Richards helped counter Viet Cong attacks and moved wounded Marines to areas of relative safety. Although wounded by an enemy grenade, Richards insisted on staying with his men.

When a machine-gun crew ran low on ammunition, Richards made several trips to obtain more, exposing himself to heavy enemy fire. Then, when the machine gunner and assistant machine gunner were wounded, Richards dashed to the gun position. Exposed to the brunt of the Viet Cong attack, he fired burst after burst at the enemy, causing them to falter long enough for the Marines to repulse the attack and preventing the Marine perimeter from being penetrated.

For his extraordinary heroism that night, Richards was awarded a Navy Cross. He retired as a lieutenant colonel in 1995 and lives today in San Diego.[40]

John W. Ripley: Purple Heart—January–February 1967

John Walter Ripley was wounded in action near the demilitarized zone between North Vietnam and South Vietnam while commanding a company in the 3rd Battalion, 3rd Marine Regiment.

Known as "Rip" to his friends, Ripley was born in West Virginia on June 29, 1939. He grew up in Radford, Virginia, and, after graduating from high school in 1957, enlisted in the Marine Corps. After completing recruit training at Parris Island, Ripley completed the Naval Academy Preparatory School and then entered the U.S. Naval Academy. He graduated in 1962 and was commissioned as a Marine second lieutenant.

After completing the Basic School, Ripley was assigned to the aircraft carrier USS *Independence*. After returning from a year of sea duty, he joined 2nd Battalion, 2nd Marines, in which he served as a rifle and weapons platoon commander. Ripley also successfully completed basic parachutist, scuba, Ranger, and Jumpmaster training.

He first went to Vietnam in October 1966 as a captain and company commander of Company L of the 3rd Battalion, 3rd Marine Regiment. While with Lima 3/3 near the demilitarized zone, Ripley was wounded in action and decorated with a Purple Heart. He also received a Silver Star for his gallantry during an attack against an NVA regimental command post.

In October 1969 Ripley was chosen to be an exchange officer to the British Royal Marines. He was one of the last U.S. Marines to go through training with Royal Marine recruits and was later deployed to Singapore and northern Malaya with them. He spent several months on campaign in the jungle with the Gurkha Rifles and received additional training in demolitions.

At the end of his two years with the Royal Marines, Ripley had developed a set of fighting skills possessed by few U.S. Marines. He returned to Vietnam in 1971 and served as the lone advisor to the Third South Vietnamese Marine battalion. While assigned to that unit, Ripley was awarded the Navy Cross for his heroism in destroying a key bridge on Easter Sunday 1972.

After leaving Southeast Asia the next year, he served in a variety of assignments. He commanded 1st Battalion, 2nd Marines from 1979 to 1981 and graduated from the Naval War College in 1982. Ripley then served on the joint staff before going to the Naval Academy as Senior Marine and director of the Division of English and History.

In 1988 Ripley took command of the 2nd Marine Regiment at Camp Lejeune. After completing that tour, he commanded the Navy–Marine Corps ROTC at Virginia Military Institute.

Ripley retired as a colonel in 1992. He then became the president of Southern Virginia College in Buena Vista, Virginia, and later took over as president of Hargrave Military Academy in Chatham, Virginia. In 1999 Ripley returned to the Marine Corps as the civilian director of Marine Corps History and Museums Division.

Ripley became the first Marine officer to receive the Distinguished Graduate Award from the Naval Academy in 2002, and he left his history and museums position in 2005. He died on October 28, 2008, at his home in Annapolis. Ripley was sixty-nine years old at the time of his death.[41]

USS *LIBERTY* (1967)

On June 8, 1967, Israeli naval and air forces attacked the intelligence ship USS *Liberty*, killing 34 Americans killed and wounding another 170. For additional details on the attack on the naval vessel, see chapter 3, "Sailors: Spanish–American War to Afghanistan and Iraq." The chief of naval operations approved the Purple Heart for all uniformed personnel who were injured during the attack or died as a result of their injuries prior to September 1967.[42] Two Marine recipients are Jack Raper and Edward Rehmeyer.

Jack L. Raper: Purple Heart—June 8, 1967

Born in Cedartown, Georgia, in August 1944, then-Sgt. Jack Lewis Raper had been on active duty in the Corps since August 1962. He was killed in the Naval Security Group Department spaces on *Liberty* and is interred at Arlington National Cemetery.

Edward E. Rehmeyer III: Purple Heart—June 8, 1967

Born in York, Pennsylvania, in September 1945, then-Cpl. Edward Emory Rehmeyer III had been on active duty in the Corps since October 1964. He was killed in the Naval Security Group Department spaces on *Liberty*.

USS *PUEBLO* (1968)

On January 23, 1968, North Korean forces surrounded and boarded USS *Pueblo* in international waters in the Sea of Japan. For more on the attack, see chapter 3, "Sailors: Spanish–American War to Afghanistan and Iraq." Two Marines and seventy-nine sailors were in the *Pueblo* when she was captured. Both Marines were awarded Purple Hearts. One recipient was Robert Chicca.

Robert J. Chicca: Purple Hearts—January 23, 1968, and January 23–December 22, 1968

Robert Chicca, a Marine sergeant, was wounded in action when the *Pueblo* was captured by the North Koreans. He subsequently received a second Purple Heart, as did the entire *Pueblo* crew, for wounds received in captivity.

PHILIPPINES (1972)

Sidney T. James: Purple Heart—1972

Sgt. Sidney James was serving as a Marine security guard at the U.S. Embassy in Manila when he was wounded during an attack by a terrorist group in 1972. The Navy awarded him a Purple Heart that year.[43]

SS *MAYAGUEZ* (1975)

In May 1975, less than two weeks after the fall of Saigon, Cambodian gunboats seized the U.S. merchantman SS *Mayaguez* in international waters off the Cambodian coast. President Gerald R. Ford denounced the capture as an "act of piracy" and quickly authorized U.S. forces to rescue the crew and recapture the ship.

On May 15, 1975, at the end of a fierce battle with Khmer Rouge forces, a total of forty-one Americans had been killed or were missing, including fourteen Marines. Another thirty-five Marines were wounded in action.[44] All casualties received either posthumous or nonposthumous Purple Hearts, including the following.

Gary L. Hall: Purple Heart—May 15, 1975
Joseph N. Hargrave: Purple Heart—May 15, 1975
Danny G. Marshall: Purple Heart—May 15, 1975
All three Marines listed were mistakenly left behind when U.S. forces withdrew after their firefight with the Khmer Rouge. The three men had been manning a machine gun on the perimeter, and, in the chaos on the beach, failed to board the last evacuation helicopter. All three were declared missing in action and presumed dead prior to being awarded posthumous Purple Hearts.

IRAN (1979)

Garry Downey: Purple Hearts—February 11, 1979, and February 14, 1979
Kenneth Kraus: Purple Heart—February 14, 1979
Sgt. Garry Downey and Sgt. Kenneth Kraus were serving as Marine security guards at the U.S. Embassy in Teheran when they were wounded during attacks on the facility by Iranian guerrillas. Downey was wounded on February 11, 1979, and February 14, 1979, and received two Purple Hearts. Kraus, who was wounded on February 14, received one Purple Heart.

PAKISTAN (1979)

Steven J. Crowley: Purple Heart—November 21, 1979

Cpl. Steven Crowley was serving as a Marine security guard at the U.S. Embassy in Islamabad when he was killed by sniper fire. The Navy awarded Crowley a posthumous Purple Heart.

LEBANON (1982-1984)

U.S. forces first landed in Beirut in August 1982 as part of a multinational force (MNF) to oversee the evacuation of Palestine Liberation Organization and Syrian soldiers trapped by Israeli forces. The MNF withdrew in mid-September but returned a few days later when a civil war broke out. U.S. forces were completely withdrawn by February 26, 1984.

The most Marine casualties during the action in Lebanon occurred on October 23, 1983, when a suicide bomber drove a truck loaded with the equivalent of 12,000 lbs. of TNT into the four-story barracks where more than three hundred U.S. troops were sleeping. The resulting blast and fireball killed 220 Marines and wounded another 151.[45] All received Purple Hearts, including the following Marines.

Davin M. Green: Purple Heart—October 23, 1983

Then-LCpl. Davin Green was killed in the Beirut bombing. Born July 16, 1963, he grew up in Baltimore and enlisted in July 1981. Green had married just forty-eight hours before shipping out for Beirut. His widow received his posthumously awarded Purple Heart.

Charles J. Schnorf: Purple Heart—October 23, 1983

Then–First Lt. Charles Jeffrey Schnorf was killed in the Beirut bombing. He was twenty-four years old at the time of his death and is interred at Arlington National Cemetery.

GRENADA (1983)

Three Marines were killed, and fifteen were wounded, during Operation Urgent Fury in October 1983. All were awarded Purple Hearts.

Timothy D. Howard: Purple Heart—October 25, 1983
Jeb F. Seagle: Purple Heart—October 25, 1983
On October 25, 1983, Capt. Timothy Howard's AH-1 Cobra was hit by antiaircraft fire, and he and his copilot, Capt. Jeb Seagle, were both wounded. Howard's right arm was useless, and his right leg was broken. Despite his wounds, Howard managed to land the damaged helicopter. When Seagle regained consciousness, he dragged Howard away from the burning Cobra.

Howard was later rescued by a CH-46 Sea Knight helicopter, but Seagle, who had gone looking for help, was killed by small-arms fire.[46]

GERMANY (1984)

Rudolfo Hernandez: Purple Heart—February 7, 1984
Then-LCpl. Rudolfo Hernandez was killed in a terrorist attack in Germany on February 7, 1984. Hernandez's next of kin received his posthumously awarded Purple Heart.

EL SALVADOR (1985)

Bobby J. Dickson: Purple Heart—June 20, 1985
Thomas T. Handwork: Purple Heart—June 20, 1985
Patrick R. Kwiatkowski: Purple Heart—June 20, 1985
Gregory H. Webber: Purple Heart—June 20, 1985
Sgt. Bobby Dickson, Sgt. Thomas Handwork, Cpl. Patrick Kwiatkowski, and Cpl. Gregory Webber were assigned to duty at the U.S. Embassy in San Salvador. While off-duty, they were shot and killed by guerrillas in an outdoor café near the embassy. The Marine Corps awarded each man a posthumous Purple Heart, and President Reagan placed the medals on their caskets.[47]

Miles N. Kaiser: Purple Heart—June–August 1985
Miles N. Kaiser was wounded in action in the summer of 1985 while training government soldiers to track guerrillas.

A native of Liberty, New York, then-Sergeant Kaiser was assigned to the 4th Marine Amphibious Brigade when he deployed to El Salvador as a trainer. While teaching a team of soldiers how to set an ambush, Kaiser was injured by shrapnel after a Salvadoran soldier set off a "Bouncing Betty" land mine.

Kaiser had previously served as a Marine security guard at U.S. embassies in Paris; Casablanca, Morocco; Cairo, Egypt; and Beirut. He also served in the elite 2nd Reconnaissance Battalion.

Retired Marine Gen. Alfred M. Gray presented the Purple Heart to Kaiser on June 13, 1996.[48]

PERSIAN GULF TANKER ESCORT OPERATIONS (1987–1988)

From 1987 to the end of 1988, during the final stages of the Iran–Iraq War, U.S. naval and other forces protected eleven reflagged Kuwaiti tankers and other U.S.-flagged merchant ships in the Persian Gulf from possible attack by Iranian forces. The name for the operation was Earnest Will.

Purple Hearts were awarded to two Marines killed when the USS *Samuel B. Roberts* struck an Iranian mine on April 14, 1988.[49]

PANAMA (1989)

Operation Just Cause was one of the shortest military operations in U.S. military history. Within seventy-two hours of the outbreak of hostilities on December 20, 1989, all major combat operations ended. About 26,000 military personnel took part in Just Cause, including 650 Marines. Given the small number of personnel involved, only five Purple Hearts were awarded—two posthumously and three to Marines who survived their wounds.

Robert Paz: Purple Heart—December 16, 1989

Four days before the beginning of military operations, then–First Lt. Robert Paz was killed at a Panama Defense Forces roadblock when the Panamanians fired on the car carrying him and three other Marines. Paz was the son of U.S. missionaries, and he had decades of ties to Panama. His next of kin were presented his posthumously awarded Purple Heart.

Paz's death—and the arrest and brutal beating of a U.S. Navy officer and his wife shortly thereafter—were key factors President Bush considered when launching Just Cause in order to apprehend Panamanian strongman Manuel Noriega and eliminate Noriega's Panama Defense Forces.[50]

LEBANON (1990)

William R. Higgins: Purple Heart—July 6, 1990

William Richard "Rich" Higgins was taken hostage in Lebanon in February 1988 by a terrorist group said to have ties with Hezbollah. He was repeatedly tortured by his captors and, later, murdered by them. While his body was dumped into the streets of Beirut on December 23, 1991, Higgins was declared by the U.S. Defense Department to have died on July 6, 1990.

Higgins was born in Danville, Kentucky, in January 1945. During his college years at Miami University in Oxford, Ohio, Higgins participated in the Naval ROTC program and was commissioned in the Marine Corps in 1967. He served in Vietnam in 1968 with Company C of the 1st Battalion, 3rd Marines and saw combat as a rifle platoon leader. Higgins returned to Vietnam in 1972 as an advisor to a South Vietnamese Marine battalion.

In February 1988 then–Lieutenant Colonel Higgins was serving in Beirut as the chief of Observer Group Lebanon and as senior military observer in the UN Military Observer Group, UN Truce Supervision Organization. He was pulled from his vehicle by armed men while driving on a coastal highway in southern Lebanon and never seen alive again. A year and a half after he was taken hostage, a videotape released by his captors showed that Higgins had been hanged by the neck and was dead.

Higgins was posthumously awarded the Purple Heart and, after a long campaign by his widow, then–Marine Lt. Col. Robin Higgins, the Navy also posthumously awarded Higgins a Prisoner of War Medal.

Higgins was not forgotten. In April 1999 a guided missile destroyer was commissioned as the USS *Higgins* in his honor, and his widow published a book about him in 2000.[51]

PERSIAN GULF WAR (1990–1991)

Twenty-four Marines were killed, and ninety-two were wounded, during Operation Desert Storm.[52] Some Purple Heart recipients include the following Marines.

Stephen E. Bentzlin: Purple Heart—January 30, 1991
Ismael Cotto: Purple Heart—January 30, 1991
Michael E. Linderman Jr.: Purple Heart—January 30, 1991
David T. Snyder: Purple Heart—January 30, 1991

Stephen Bentzlin, Ismael Cotto, Michael Linderman, and David Snyder all died in fighting around the Saudi border town of Khafji on January 30, 1991.

A native of Yellow Meadow, Minnesota, then–Lance Corporal Bentzlin was twenty-three years old at the time he was killed in action. His wife received his posthumously awarded Purple Heart.

A native of Bronx, New York, then-Corporal Cotto was twenty-seven years old at the time he was killed in action. He was survived by a wife and daughter.

Born in Douglas, Oregon, then–Lance Corporal Linderman was nineteen years old when he was killed in action. His wife received his posthumously awarded Purple Heart.

A native of Kenmore, New York, then–Lance Corporal Snyder was twenty-one years old when he was killed in action.

SOMALIA (1992–1995)

On December 9, 1992, a small group of Marines waded ashore on the beach near Mogadishu. They were the first ground troops ashore in Operation Restore Hope, and by the following month, more than 11,000 U.S. Marines, soldiers, sailors, and civilians were in Somalia. Before the Marines temporarily departed Somalia in May 1993, two had been killed on January 12, 1993, and January 26, 1993, and another fifteen had been wounded in action.[53] All these Marines received Purple Hearts.

After the deadly October 1993 attack on U.S. forces, a small number of Marines returned to Somalia. The last Marines from the 13th Marine Expeditionary Unit (Special Operations Capable) departed Mogadishu for good on March 3, 1995.

KENYA (1998)

On August 7, 1998, terrorists bombed the U.S. Embassy in Nairobi, Kenya. This was part of a coordinated multinational attack, and a car bomb exploded at the U.S. Embassy in Dar es Salam, Tanzania, at the same time. A total of 257 people were killed, including 11 Americans. More than 4,000 people were wounded.

Jesse N. Aliganga: Purple Heart—August 7, 1998

Jesse Nathaniel Aliganga was the only Marine killed in the bombing attack. Another Marine was wounded.

After graduating from high school in Tallahassee, Florida, in 1994, Aliganga enlisted in the Marine Corps. He completed recruit training at Parris Island and then qualified as a communications specialist. Aliganga subsequently served with the 3rd Marine Division on Okinawa and with the 1st Force Service Support Group at Camp Pendleton.

In early 1998, after completing training at the Marine Security Guard School, Quantico, then-Sergeant Aliganga began a tour of duty as a security guard at the U.S. Embassy in Kenya. He was on duty when he was killed on August 7, 1998, and was awarded the Purple Heart posthumously. Aliganga is interred at Arlington National Cemetery.[54]

Daniel Briehl: Purple Heart—August 7, 1998

Daniel Briehl was the only Marine wounded in the terrorist attack on the U.S. Embassy in Kenya. He suffered three broken ribs and numerous cuts and bruises.

A native of Lorain, Ohio, Briehl was waiting in a car outside the embassy when a grenade exploded and gunfire erupted. He got out of the vehicle and was running toward the embassy's main entrance when there was a huge explosion that propelled glass shards and chunks of concrete through the air. As Briehl entered the building, he fell down an elevator shaft and was seriously injured. Despite his wounds he ushered six people up darkened stairs and away from falling debris. He repeatedly ran back into the wreckage to rescue more survivors.

For his injuries Briehl was decorated with a Purple Heart by Marine Lt. Col. Dennis Sabal at a ceremony in Nairobi on January 9, 1999. Briehl also was awarded a Navy and Marine Corps Medal for his heroism in risking his life to save others wounded in the bombing.[55]

AFGHANISTAN (2001–)

Since their arrival in Afghanistan in October 2001, Marines have suffered more than one hundred dead and wounded in combat operations against Taliban or al-Qaida fighters. Recipients of the Purple Heart for action in Afghanistan include the following Marines.

Brady A. Gustafson: Purple Heart—July 21, 2008

Brady Gustafson was wounded in his left leg by shrapnel from a rocket-propelled grenade near the Afghan village of Shewan.

A native of Eagan, Minnesota, then-twenty-year-old Lance Corporal Gustafson was serving as a turret gunner in a mine-resistant ambush protected (MRAP) vehicle when his squad was ambushed by Taliban fighters. As blood gushed from his leg, and while another Marine applied a tourniquet, Gustafson identified enemy positions and engaged them with his M-240B machine gun.

Although machine-gun fire impacted around him, Gustafson remained steadfast and fired more than four hundred rounds of concentrated fire on the enemy. His effective fire suppression allowed Marines in a second burning vehicle to safely dismount and escape the kill zone and almost certain death. According to official reports, Gustafson "braved the effects of shock and reloaded his weapon twice ... before he allowed himself to be pulled from the turret and receive medical treatment."

After being medically evacuated, Gustafson was awarded a Purple Heart for his July 21, 2008, combat injury. On March 27, 2009, he also was awarded a Navy Cross at a ceremony at Marine Corps Air Ground Combat Center Twentynine Palms, California.[56]

Anthony L. Viggiani: Purple Heart—June 3, 2004

Anthony Lester Viggiani was wounded in the leg by rifle fire while battling Taliban insurgents in Zabul Province, Afghanistan.

Born in Strongsville, Ohio, Viggiani enlisted in the Marine Corps in 1998 and, after completing twelve weeks of basic training and six weeks of infantry training, was sent to the Marine Security Forces School in Chesapeake, Virginia. Viggiani subsequently served as a guard with the Maine detachment at Camp David, Maryland, from October 1999 to February 2002. Viggiani was then assigned to Company C of the 1st Battalion, 6th Marine Regiment based at Camp Lejeune. Two years later he deployed with that unit to Afghanistan.

On June 3, 2004, then-Sergeant Viggiani and members of his unit were conducting a cordon and search operation in a remote area of Afghanistan when they spotted about twenty armed enemy fighters fleeing the village of Khabargho. While Viggiani led a pursuit after the insurgents, two Marines were wounded by enemy machine-gun fire. In the face of continued hostile fire, Viggiani ran one hundred yards to rescue the two wounded Marines. On the way he killed several Taliban who were firing on the Marines from a concealed cave.

Then-LCpl. Joseph B. Perez was wounded in his torso and stomach by gunfire on April 3, 2003. He was later awarded both a Purple Heart and a Navy Cross. (U.S. Marine Corps)

After Viggiani was seriously wounded in the leg, his first sergeant called for a medical evacuation helicopter. Viggiani refused to go, saying, "I ain't damn going. . . . I ain't leaving my boys." When he told his commanding officer the same thing, Viggiani was allowed to remain with his squad after a Navy corpsman treated and field-dressed his wound.

Viggiani continued to lead his troops until the insurgents were routed. In all, fourteen insurgents were killed, and Viggiani accounted for more than a few of them. Viggiani left Afghanistan in September 2004 and was assigned to Parris Island as a senior drill instructor in May 2005.

For his combat wound Viggiani was awarded a Purple Heart. He received a Navy Cross on February 24, 2006, for his extraordinary heroism under fire.[57]

IRAQ (2003–)

Since their arrival in Iraq in March 2003, more than five hundred Marines have been killed in combat, and more than five thousand have been wounded.

Erin Liberty: Purple Heart—June 23, 2005

Erin Liberty was wounded by an IED while riding in a convoy near Fallujah on June 23, 2005. She is one of only a handful of female Marines to be decorated with the Purple Heart.

A native of Niceville, Florida, then–Lance Corporal Liberty was an ammunition technician serving with the Ammunition Company of 2nd Supply Battalion, 2nd Force Service Support. On the day she was injured an IED detonated about six feet from the seven-ton truck in which she sat. The bomb consisted of five 155-millimeter incendiary rounds and a few propane tanks, and Liberty sustained second- and third-degree burns to her hands and broke a cervical vertebra in her neck.

Joseph B. Perez: Purple Heart—April 4, 2003

Then-LCpl. Joseph Perez was wounded by gunfire in the torso and stomach on April 3, 2003.

Born in Houston, Texas, Perez enlisted in the Marine Corps after graduating from high school. He was serving as a rifleman with Company I of the 3rd Battalion, 5th Marines, 1st Marine Division and was advancing with his platoon into Baghdad when the platoon came under intense enemy fire. Perez, who was the point man for the lead squad—and therefore its most exposed member—received the majority of the fire. Yet he continued to fire his M-16 rifle at the enemy and led a charge down an Iraqi trench, destroying the enemy with rifle fire and hand grenades. He also fired an AT-4 rocket into a machine-gun bunker, killing four Iraqi soldiers and allowing his squad to seize the position.

As Perez continued to battle the enemy, he was wounded in the torso and shoulder by enemy rifle or machine-gun fire. Despite these injuries, Perez remained with his men and directed his squad so that it was able to reorganize and destroy the enemy.

Perez was awarded a Purple Heart and a Navy Cross for extraordinary heroism.[58]

HAITI (2004)

Will Hamilton: Purple Heart—March 2004

Then-Pfc. Will Hamilton was wounded by gunfire in a firefight in Port-au-Prince in early March 2004.

A native of Murfreesboro, Tennessee, then nineteen-year-old Hamilton was a rifleman assigned to Company L of the 3rd Battalion, 8th Marine Regiment and deployed to Haiti on February 29, 2004. Shortly after arriving, he and his squad began conducting patrol operations throughout the capital city.

On the night he was wounded, Hamilton was returning from a patrol and was "in an area thought to be friendly when the ambush occurred." As he remembered, "We got down the hill, and our security element had already passed the building. . . . Firing started going off. . . . I had no cover at all. . . . I had a 13-foot wall to the right of me and I couldn't do anything. . . I got up against the wall, got down, and started sighting in, and then all of the sudden I felt a huge shock wave go right through me."[59]

A bullet entered Hamilton's left arm about two inches above his wrist, traveled along the bone, and exited his elbow. After receiving first aid Hamilton was medically evacuated to Miami, Florida, where doctors repaired his bones with metal plates and reconnected his damaged nerves. He was discharged two days later.

Maj. Gen. Stephen Johnson, 2nd Marine Division commanding general, presented a Purple Heart to Hamilton in a ceremony at U.S. Marine Corps Forces South headquarters.

CHAPTER 6

Coast Guardsmen: World War I to Afghanistan and Iraq

A mong members of the U.S. Armed Forces, Coast Guard personnel have been awarded the fewest Purple Hearts. The earliest Coast Guard recipients of the decoration were the crew of the USS *Tampa*, which sank with all hands on board during World War I. The majority of Purple Hearts went to Coast Guardsmen killed and wounded during World War II. A small number of Coast Guard personnel also were awarded the Purple Heart in Vietnam, and a few received the decoration after being wounded while conducting port security operations during Operation Iraqi Freedom.

Purple Hearts have been awarded to Coast Guardsmen in the following conflicts and military operations:

- World War I (1917–1918)
- World War II (1941–1945)
- Vietnam (1965–1975)
- Iraq (2003–)

WORLD WAR I (1917–1918)

The only World War I Coast Guard recipients of the Purple Heart were the crewmembers of the cutter *Tampa*, which was sunk by a German U-boat on September 26, 1918.

After the United States entered World War I in April 1917, the 190-foot-long, 1,100-ton Coast Guard cutter *Tampa* was temporarily transferred from the Treasury Department to the U.S. Navy and redesignated the USS *Tampa*. In early November she began ocean escort duty operations in the North Atlantic. Over the next ten months, the *Tampa* took part in eighteen convoys and escorted some 350 allied ships. Her eighteenth convoy began on September 17, 1918, when the *Tampa* left Gibraltar for the United Kingdom.

In the afternoon of Thursday, September 26, while in the Celtic Sea off the southwestern coast of Cornwall, England, Capt. Charles Satterlee, the skipper of the *Tampa*, received permission to detach from the convoy and proceed alone on a course for Wales. About 7:30 PM, the *Tampa* was sighted by Imperial German Navy submarine *U-91*. The U-boat's captain fired one stern torpedo that hit the *Tampa* portside amidships. The American steamship sank with all hands on board, representing the greatest single loss in combat for the U.S. Navy and Coast Guard during World War I. One hundred eleven Coast Guardsmen, including Captain Satterlee, four Navy sailors, ten British sailors, and five civilians were killed.

In 1999 James C. Bunch, a retired Coast Guard master chief, recommended that the crew of the *Tampa* be awarded posthumous Purple Hearts, and Coast Guard Commandant James M. Loy approved the recommendation. These Purple Hearts are highly unusual because they were made ninety years after the event. Some of the medals were presented to relatives of the deceased crew by Loy and Secretary of Transportation Rodney E. Slater during a special ceremony at Arlington National Cemetery on November 11, 1999. The then-current officers and crew of the Coast Guard medium-endurance cutter *Tampa*—the fourth to carry the name—also were present to accept the posthumous awards. Some Purple Hearts also were presented to surviving relatives in a ceremony in Tampa, Florida, in January 2001.[1]

The following were among the 111 Coast Guard recipients.

James M. Fleury: Purple Heart—September 26, 1918

SN James Marconnier Fleury was the only Coast Guardsman whose body was recovered and identified. He was buried with full military honors at Lamphey Churchyard in Wales. Fleury's family later brought his body home and buried him in a cemetery on Long Island, New York.

Charles E. Galvin: Purple Heart—September 26, 1918

Charles Emmitt Galvin was a Tampa native. His nephew, Edwin T. Galvin, accepted Charles Galvin's posthumous Purple Heart in a ceremony in Tampa in January 2001.[2]

Homer B. Sumner: Purple Heart—September 26, 1918
Wambolt Sumner: Purple Heart—September 26, 1918

Homer B. Sumner was a seaman and Wambolt Sumner was a ship's writer. Their cousin, Jack C. Edwards, accepted their posthumous Purple Hearts in January 2001.

Charles Satterlee: Purple Heart—September 26, 1918

Charles Satterlee was a career Coast Guard officer and in command of the *Tampa* when she was torpedoed.

Born on September 14, 1875, in Gales Ferry, Connecticut, Satterlee received an appointment as a cadet to the School of Instruction of the Revenue Cutter Service on November 19, 1895. Three years later, in January 1898, Satterlee was commissioned as a third lieutenant.

Prior to the Spanish–American War, Satterlee served as a line officer in the U.S. Revenue Cutter Service ship *Levi Woodbury*. After hostilities began Satterlee and his cutter conducted operations with Rear Adm. William T. Sampson's North Atlantic Squadron, with the *Levi Woodbury*'s primary mission being blockading the port of Havana.

Satterlee was promoted to second lieutenant in 1899 and to first lieutenant in 1905. He reached the rank of captain shortly after the establishment of the Coast Guard in January 1915 and took command of the cutter *Miami* in December. At the time he took over the *Miami*, Satterlee had more than twenty-two years of service, of which more than fifteen were at sea.

When the *Miami* was renamed the *Tampa* in February 1916, Satterlee remained as her captain, and when the United States declared war on Germany in April 1917, Satterlee found himself once again serving with the Navy. After the *Tampa* was torpedoed, Satterlee went down with his ship. His body was never recovered. In addition to a posthumous Purple Heart, Satterlee also was posthumously awarded a Navy Distinguished Service Medal.

SN1 Donald J. Anderson was serving in the Coast Guard Cutter *Muskeget* when the ship disappeared without a trace in September 1942. Anderson's officially hand-engraved Purple Heart was presented to his next of kin. (Fred Borch)

WORLD WAR II (1941-1945)

On December 7, 1941, 29,000 military and civilian personnel served in the Coast Guard. Less than three years later, there were 175,000 regulars and regular reservists in the Guard.[3] By the end of the war, 241,093 men and women had served in Coast Guard.[4] The Coast Guard's official Website states that 957 Purple Hearts were awarded to Coast Guard personnel in World War II, including 574 posthumous awards.[5]

Donald J. Anderson: Purple Heart—September 1942

Then-SN1 Donald Anderson was serving in the Coast Guard Cutter *Muskeget* when the ship disappeared without a trace in early September 1942. The cutter had been on weather station in the North Atlantic and was likely sunk by a German submarine. One hundred seventeen men were lost, including Anderson. His next of kin received his posthumously awarded Purple Heart.

Douglas C. Denman: Purple Heart—August 30, 1942

Douglas C. Denman was severely wounded by shrapnel during the Japanese air attack on the USS *Calhoun* on August 30, 1942.

A native of Tallapoosa, Georgia, Denman was serving as a coxswain in the *Calhoun* and manning Boat No. 4 when the Japanese launched a night-time aerial bombardment. Although he was badly wounded by the first two bombs to strike the ship, Denman persisted in remaining on duty and, with the aid of a shipmate, carried two injured men to the bow of his lifeboat and floated them clear. Together, Denman and his shipmate also threw overboard thirty kapok life jackets and called them to the attention of the survivors struggling in the water. In addition to receiving a Purple Heart for the wounds he suffered, Denman also received the Silver Star for gallantry in action.[6]

Joseph Gerczak: Purple Heart—December 26, 1943

Joseph Gerczak was mortally wounded by shrapnel in a Japanese aerial attack on his ship on December 26, 1943.

Seaman 3rd Class Gerczak was serving in the *LST-66* during the initial assault against enemy-held Borgen Bay, New Britain, near New Guinea. When seven Japanese dive-bombers suddenly attacked while his ship was in the bay awaiting the formation of the task unit whose other members were then on the beach unloading cargo, Gerczak immediately manned his battle station. He was the first to open fire when the planes came in and struck from starboard, and he poured his drums of ammunition into the attackers. Gerczak successfully downed two Japanese planes, which crashed into the sea near his ship.

With his ship struck by bomb fragments, each bursting successively closer, Gerczak continued delivering a steady stream of bullets against the enemy until he was fatally struck down when a violent blast silenced his weapon and forced shrapnel into his gun shield. In addition to a posthumous Purple Heart, Gerczak's next of kin also received his posthumous Silver Star.[7]

Warren G. Gill: Purple Heart—September 1943

Warren G. Gill was wounded by enemy gunfire during the amphibious invasion of Salerno, Italy, in September 1943.

A native of Lebanon, Oregon, Gill was serving as a lieutenant, junior grade, and had command of an assault flotilla during the amphibious invasion of Salerno. Although severely wounded by heavy enemy gunfire while directing the lowering of small boats from his ship, Gill steadfastly remained at his post. He continued to give important last-minute instructions to his officers and men before collapsing as a result of his injuries. Gill later received a Purple Heart for his wounds and a Navy Cross for his extraordinary heroism.[8]

Ralph E. Martin: Purple Heart—January 8, 1945

SN2 Ralph Eugene Martin was killed in action in the Pacific on January 8, 1945.

Martin was serving as a member of a gun crew for the USS *Callaway* and, while manning his station, was killed when his ship was struck by a Japanese suicide plane. Before he was killed, Martin "unhesitatingly relinquished all chance of escape as the plane plunged toward the target and remaining steadfastly at his gun, continued to direct his fire with unrelenting fury upon the enemy until carried away with his weapon by the terrific impact." Martin posthumously received both a Purple Heart and a Silver Star.[9]

Lloyd M. Morris: Purple Heart—November 1942

A native of Vallejo, California, BMC Lloyd M. Morris was the first Coast Guard recipient of the Purple Heart. He was wounded in action during amphibious landing operations in North Africa.

SN3 Douglas A. Munro was killed in action on September 27, 1942. Munro's parents received his posthumously awarded Purple Heart and Medal of Honor. (U.S. Coast Guard)

Douglas A. Munro: Purple Heart—September 27, 1942

Douglas Albert Munro was killed in action on September 27, 1942. In addition to a posthumous Purple Heart, Munro received a Medal of Honor, making him the only Coast Guardsman in history to receive America's highest decoration for combat valor.

Born in Vancouver, Canada, in October 1919, Munro grew up in the small mountain town of Cle Elum, Washington. He enlisted in the Coast Guard in September 1939. Munro spent his first eighteen months in uniform at Coast Guard Base, Staten Island, New York, where he served aboard the cutter *Spencer*.

In early 1941 Munro transferred to the attack transport USS *Hunter Liggett*, which needed his expertise as a signalman. Munro subsequently deployed to the Pacific. In August 1942 he waded ashore with the Marines in the bloody amphibious landing at Tulagi, which sits twenty miles from Guadalcanal in the Solomon Islands.

Having survived Tulagi, Munro moved to Lunga Point Base on Guadalcanal, which was the staging area for troop movements along the coast. A month later Munro was in charge of ten Higgins Boats—lightly armed landing craft—that were transporting Marines led by then–Lt. Col. Lewis B. "Chesty" Puller. The vessels landed three companies of Marines in the Point Cruz area, where the U.S. troops intended to establish a new patrol base.

After five hundred Marines landed, Munro and the boats returned to Lunga Point Base. Shortly thereafter the Marines ran into a large Japanese force that threatened to push the Americans off the beach. Munro now volunteered to lead the boats back to the beach to evacuate the Marines. It promised to be a risky mission because the plywood Higgins boats had no weapons larger than .30-caliber machine guns.

Historian Edward F. Murphy wrote in *Heroes of World War II* that Munro "ordered his nine (other) boats to stay put while he drove his own boat shoreward to reconnoiter the scene."[10] Despite the hail of Japanese bullets, Munro went into the beach area and picked up thirty wounded Marines. After transferring these men to another boat, Munro returned to the beach with three more boats to pick up more Marines. According to his Medal of Honor citation, Munro signaled still other boats to land to rescue the Marines, "and then in order to draw the enemy's fire and protect the heavily loaded boats, he valiantly placed his craft with its two small guns as a shield between the beachhead and the Japanese."

When the evacuation was nearly complete, Munro was cut down by enemy fire. He spoke his last words to his shipmate, SM3 Raymond Evans. "Did we get them all off?" Munro asked. Evans replied: "Yes." Munro smiled, then died.[11]

Munro's parents accepted his Medal of Honor in a White House ceremony hosted by President Roosevelt on May 24, 1943.

Raymond O'Malley: Purple Heart—June 10, 1943

Raymond O'Malley, who was serving as a first class seaman, was wounded during the sinking of the Coast Guard Cutter *Escanaba* in the North Atlantic on June 10, 1943. He was one of only two survivors.

In mid-1943 the *Escanaba* was escorting vessels from Greenland to Newfoundland and back. Just after 5 AM on June 10, a terrific explosion ripped through the cutter, and O'Malley, who was on the bridge, was blown to the overhead and had his head cut open. Only his grasp on the ship's wheel kept him from greater injury. O'Malley made his way to the wing of the bridge, putting on his life preserver as he went. As he got out of the door, he saw that the afterdeck was in splinters and the main mast was falling overboard. Moments later, he was swept overboard into the frigid waters of the North Atlantic.

The explosion and sinking of *Escanaba* occurred in about three minutes. While some believe she was torpedoed by a German U-boat, no submarine claimed the kill. Consequently, it is more likely that she was sunk by a drifting mine.

Coast Guard Commandant Russell R. Waesche later presented a Purple Heart to O'Malley.[12]

Carl U. Peterson: Purple Heart—June 10, 1943

Carl U. Peterson was killed in action when the *Escanaba* sank in the North Atlantic on June 10, 1943.

Peterson, who was a lieutenant commander and in command of *Escanaba*, was a career officer who graduated from the U.S. Coast Guard Academy in 1930. Prior to his death he and the crew of *Escanaba* had gained renown for rescuing 133 survivors of the U.S. Army Transport *Dorchester*, which had been torpedoed and sunk in the North Atlantic on February 3, 1943. In addition to a Purple Heart, Peterson also was awarded a posthumous Legion of Merit for his valiant efforts in the rescuing the crew of the *Dorchester*.

James A. Powers: Purple Heart—June 6, 1944

James A. Powers was wounded in action during the initial D-day assault into Normandy.

A native of Ozone Park, New York, Powers was serving as a second class seaman in LCM (3) *PA13-1*. During the initial assault on Normandy, his craft received two direct hits from German shells while unloading at the beach. One shell struck the gun shield just forward of Powers, and he was wounded in his face and hands. Despite these injuries, Powers "willingly and efficiently carried out his duties refusing to leave his craft for medical aid until it was hoisted from the water."[13]

Powers later received the Purple Heart and the Bronze Star with Combat *V.*

John C. Scheuerman: Purple Heart—September 9, 1943

SN1 John C. Scheuerman was killed in action during the amphibious invasion of Sicily.

A native of Columbus, Ohio, Scheuerman was serving in the *LCI(L)-319* on September 9, 1943. As his landing craft approached the assault beachhead in the Gulf of Salerno, Scheuerman saw a German fighter plane begin a strafing attack. Despite the danger Scheuerman "unhesitatingly manned his battle station" and used his antiaircraft gun to direct accurate gunfire against the plane. Although Scheuerman was "mortally wounded before he could deliver effective fire, he remained at his post in the face of imminent death, thereby contributing materially to the protection of his ship against further attack."

In addition to a posthumous Purple Heart, Scheuerman received a Silver Star for his gallantry in action.[14]

VIETNAM (1965–1975)

About eight thousand Coast Guard personnel served in Southeast Asia between 1965 and 1975, with seven men receiving posthumous Purple Hearts after being killed in action, and another sixty receiving the decoration for their combat wounds.[15]

David G. Brostrom: Purple Heart—August 11, 1966
Richard H. Patterson: Purple Heart—August 11, 1966
Jerry Phillips: Purple Heart—August 11, 1966

David G. Brostrom and Jerry Phillips were killed, and Richardson Patterson was wounded, when U.S. Air Force aircraft mistakenly strafed and bombed the Coast Guard Cutter *Point Welcome* on the night of August 11, 1966. The attack occurred while the cutter was on patrol between North Vietnam and South Vietnam.

Lieutenant, junior grade, Brostrom was in command of the *Point Welcome* at the time of the attack, and he and Engineman Second Class Phillips were the only two Coast Guardsmen to be killed. Patterson, who was wounded by shrapnel, subsequently received both a Purple Heart and a Bronze Star Medal for heroism in aiding the *Point Welcome*'s surviving crewmembers. Patterson retired from the Coast Guard as a boatswain's master chief.[16]

Jack C. Rittichier: Purple Heart—June 9, 1968

Jack Columbus Rittichier was killed in action when his helicopter was shot down during a rescue mission on June 9, 1968.

Born on August 17, 1933, in Akron, Ohio, Rittichier graduated from Kent State University in 1957 and entered the U.S. Air Force. He qualified as a pilot in December 1958 and subsequently served as a B-47 Stratojet bomber pilot with the Strategic Air Command.

In September 1963 Rittichier accepted a commission in the U.S. Coast Guard and, after serving in Elizabeth City, North Carolina, and at Selfridge Air Force Base outside of Mount Clemens, Michigan, Rittichier volunteered for exchange duty with the U.S. Air Force 37th Aerospace Rescue Recovery Squadron in Da Nang, Vietnam.

On June 9, 1968, a Marine Corps fighter pilot who had ejected from his A-4 Skyhawk lay on the ground alongside the Ho Chi Minh Trail just inside the Laos border with a broken arm and leg. This was an area held by North Vietnamese troops, and the enemy used the injured man as bait to lure U.S. Air Force Jolly Green Giant rescue helicopters within killing range.

The first helicopter on the scene made three rescue attempts before leaving to refuel. Lieutenant Rittichier then tried a pickup but was driven off by heavy enemy gunfire. As Rittichier returned for a second attempt, bullets "punched his aircraft and it began to burn. . . . He tried to pull away, but the Jolly Green would not rise. . . . The helicopter settled to the ground and exploded. . . . Within 30 seconds a ball of fire consumed the aircraft."[17]

For many years, the Defense Prisoner of War/Missing Persons Office listed Rittichier as missing in action, with the additional classification of killed in action—body not recovered. After his crash site was located in 2003 and his remains recovered and positively identified, however, Rittichier was interred at Arlington National Cemetery.

In addition to a posthumous Purple Heart, Rittichier was awarded a Silver Star by the Air Force. His other decorations include three awards of the Distinguished Flying Cross and four Air Medals.

Robert J. Yered: Purple Heart—March 7, 1968

Robert J. Yered was wounded by shrapnel during a Viet Cong rocket and mortar attack on Cat Lai Army Terminal on March 7, 1968.

Located about eight miles due east of Saigon, the facility at Cat Lai was a major water terminal and the primary ammunition offloading point for the southern and delta areas of South Vietnam. Engineman First Class Yered served as the Coast Guard's safety advisor at the terminal.

In addition to a Purple Heart, Yered also received a Silver Star for gallantry in action during an earlier enemy attack. On February 18, 1968, when the terminal "was subjected to an intense enemy rocket, mortar and small arms attack," one of the rocket rounds struck a barge loaded with several hundred tons of mortar ammunition. The blazing barge threatened to destroy three other ammunition ships containing more than 15,000 tons of high explosives. Yered, "without regard for his personal safety, exposed himself to the enemy fusillade as he helped extinguish the fire on the burning barge" and his heroism "averted total destruction of the ammunition ship" and the terminal.[18]

IRAQ (2003–)

While Coast Guard personnel participated in a variety of military operations after Vietnam, including the invasions of Grenada and Panama (1989), as well as the Persian Gulf War, no Coast Guard personnel were decorated with the Purple Heart during the post-Vietnam era until 2004.

Nathan B. Bruckenthal: Purple Heart—April 24, 2004
Joseph T. Ruggiero: Purple Heart—April 24, 2004

DC3 Nathan B. Bruckenthal was killed, and BM3 Class Joseph Ruggiero was wounded, in a waterborne suicide attack against the Khawr Al Amaya Oil Terminal near Basra on April 24, 2004.

In the early evening hours of April 24, a dhow approached the security zone around the oil terminal pumping station, and Bruckenthal, Ruggiero, and five sailors boarded an inflatable boat to investigate. Their actions were considered routine enforcement of the security zone around the oil terminal, but as the Americans were about to board the dhow, it exploded. Bruckenthal became the first Coast Guardsman to die in action since Vietnam, and two of the sailors also died.[19]

Born in Stony Brook, New York, on July 17, 1979, Bruckenthal enlisted in the Coast Guard in January 1999 and had served on the *Point Wells* prior to attending Damage Controlman "A" School. At the time of his death, Bruckenthal was a member of Tactical Law Enforcement Team South, which was based at Coast Guard Air Station Miami, and was on his second deployment to Iraq. In addition to a posthumous Purple Heart, Bruckenthal was awarded a posthumous Bronze Star Medal and a Combat Action Ribbon. He was interred at Arlington National Cemetery in May 2004.

Ruggiero, a native of Revere, Massachusetts, received his Purple Heart from Vice Adm. James Hull, commander, Coast Guard Atlantic Area, during a May 4, 2004, ceremony in Miami.

CHAPTER 7

Civilians: World War II to the War on Terrorism

I n early 1943 General Eisenhower requested authority to award the Purple Heart to three civilian war correspondents who were wounded during the fighting in North Africa. With this request in mind, Secretary of War Henry L. Stimson obtained express authority from President Roosevelt for the Army and the Navy to award Purple Hearts to "accredited civilian personnel who are wounded by enemy action while serving in any capacity."[1]

In fact, some Purple Hearts had previously been awarded by the Army to civilian firefighters who suffered wounds during the Japanese attack on Pearl Harbor on December 7, 1941. Neither Eisenhower nor Stimson—nor Roosevelt—appeared to be aware of those awards, however. In any event, from 1942 until 1997, when Congress enacted legislation restricting the Purple Heart to U.S. military personnel, civilians accompanying Army, Navy, Air Force, and Marine Corps personnel in an official capacity were eligible for the Purple Heart under the same criteria applicable to uniformed men and women.

A total of about one hundred Purple Hearts were awarded to war correspondents, photographers, Red Cross volunteers, U.S. civil service employees, and other civilians for wounds received in the following conflicts, military operations, and terrorist attacks:

- World War II (1941–1945)
- Vietnam (1966–1972)
- USS *Liberty* (1967)

- Lebanon (1983)
- Greece (1985)
- Germany (1985)
- Malta (1985)
- Somalia (1993)
- Saudi Arabia (1995–1996)

WORLD WAR II (1941–1945)

American Field Service

Richard G. Decatur: Purple Heart—February 15, 1944
Richard G. Decatur, an American Field Service employee from Needham, Massachusetts, was wounded in action at Anzio on February 15, 1944. The Army awarded him a Purple Heart on April 25, 1944.[2]

Glendining Frazer: Purple Heart—February 15, 1944
Glendining Frazer, an American Field Service employee from Philadelphia, was wounded in action at Anzio on February 15, 1944. The Army awarded him a Purple Heart on April 25, 1944.[3]

War Correspondents
While 37 war correspondents were killed during World War II and another 112 were wounded, only a handful of those individuals received a Purple Heart.[4] Together, the Army and Navy probably awarded fifteen to twenty Purple Hearts to newspapermen, photojournalists, and other war correspondents between 1942 and 1945.

Michael Chinigo: Purple Heart—July 10, 1943
Michael "Mike" Chinigo, wounded in action in Sicily, was an International News Service (INS) correspondent who accompanied U.S. troops as they waded ashore.

An Albanian-born U.S. citizen, Chinigo (pronounced "Kinigo") spoke fluent Italian. He also was well educated, having attended Yale University and the University of Rome, Italy. Prior to America's entry into World War II, Chinigo had been a newspaper correspondent for Hearst's INS and lived in Rome.

On July 10, 1943, Chinigo "landed with the first group of assault troops on the shore of Sicily." As an "accredited correspondent" assigned to the 3rd Infantry Division, he was probably expected to focus on gathering and reporting news. Chinigo, however, did much more. "Disregarding his personal safety," Chinigo's Silver Star citation states, "he moved forward with advance troops, under heavy enemy fire, interrogating prisoners as they were taken, and assisted the wounded." Later, despite being "wounded in the wrist and arm by Nazi shellfire," Chinigo moved ahead and "accompanied a patrol which entered Palermo in advance of the occupation." According to official records, he "contacted the Chief of Police, and met with him to inform the Italian troops that the American forces had taken the city." Finally, "accompanying a patrol on another occasion, he entered Messina prior to its occupation, and returned with two truckloads of Italian prisoners."

For his "absolute disregard for personal safety, (and) his voluntary actions and willingness to be of service above and beyond call of duty (that) reflect the highest credit upon himself and his profession," the Army awarded Chinigo a Purple Heart for his combat wounds and a Silver Star for his gallantry under fire.[5]

Chinigo remained with the 3rd Infantry Division after it landed on the Italian mainland in September 1943 and was still working as an accredited war correspondent when the division landed at Anzio in January 1944. He also worked as a technical advisor for the 1945 film *The Story of G. I. Joe*, which starred Burgess Meredith as war correspondent Ernie Pyle. Chinigo remained in Italy after the war, returning to Rome, where he became the INS bureau chief. During this time he became friendly with Italian film director Roberto Rossellini and was cast by Rossellini as the internment camp boss in the 1950 Italian-language film *Stromboli*.

The movie, starring Swedish actress Ingrid Bergman, received decidedly mixed reviews. But the affair between Rossellini and Bergman that began during the making of the film was front-page news in the United States. After the Italian film director and Swedish actress wed, Chinigo's friendship with the newlyweds resulted in his being the first to obtain photographs of their baby son, Renato, in the birth clinic in June 1950. This was a coup for Chinigo and the Hearst papers since photographers had offered 5 million lire ($8,000) for exclusive pictures of mother and child and, when refused, had tried to bribe the Catholic nuns operating the clinic to get access to Bergman and Renato. Chinigo, however, got eleven exclusive 35-mm photographs for nothing.[6]

Raymond Clapper: Purple Heart—February 2, 1944

On February 2, 1944, war correspondent Raymond "Ray" Clapper was on the aircraft carrier USS *Bunker Hill*. At about 10 AM he took off as a passenger in an airplane piloted by Lt. Cdr. Frank Whittaker to observe a bombing strike against Japanese forces on Eniwetok. Whittaker's aircraft and the other planes taking part in the mission were over the target an hour later, and as they were forming up to return to the *Bunker Hill*, Whittaker's wingman collided with him. Both planes went down into an Eniwetok lagoon in flames, and Clapper was killed in the crash.

On January 15, 1945, the director of Navy Public Affairs recommended Clapper for the Purple Heart. He wrote that "as Ray Clapper went to the Pacific at the invitation of the Secretary of the Navy it seems only fitting that the Navy should honor him with the Purple Heart Medal (sic) posthumously."[7] The Navy Department Board of Decorations and Medals agreed and the Navy secretary approved a posthumous Purple Heart for Clapper on January 26, 1945.

Joe James Custer: Purple Heart—August 9, 1942

United Press International (UPI) war correspondent Joe Custer "lost the use of one eye during action on the USS *Astoria*" on August 9, 1942.[8] The Navy engraved Custer's name on a Purple Heart and sent that medal and a certificate to him via the commandant of the 3rd Naval District on January 19, 1945.

Leo S. Disher: Purple Heart—November 8, 1942

Leo Disher, a writer for UPI, was covering the North African landing from a Coast Guard cutter when he "received numerous injuries." He was later decorated with a Purple Heart by Army Maj. Gen. Lloyd R. Fredendall.[9]

Charles H. McMurtry: Purple Heart—October 26, 1942

Charles McMurty, a "civilian war correspondent" was wounded "in enemy action" on October 26, 1942 while riding along with the USS *Hornet*. The Navy engraved a Purple Heart with his name and sent that medal and a certificate to him via the commander in chief of the Pacific Fleet on January 19, 1945.

Ernest T. Pyle: Purple Heart—April 18, 1945

Ernest Taylor Pyle, who was killed by Japanese machine-gun fire while accompanying elements of the Army's 77th Infantry "Statue of Liberty" Division, was the most famous war correspondent of World War II. He is also, arguably, the most famous civilian recipient of the Purple Heart.

Ernest T. Pyle was the most famous war correspondent of World War II. Although he was killed by Japanese machine-gun fire in 1945, the Army did not award Pyle a Purple Heart until 1983. (National Archives and Records Administration)

Known to family and admirers as "Ernie," he smoked Bull Durham tobacco and rolled his cigarettes with one hand. There was nothing pretentious about the man. Born in Dana, Indiana, on August 3, 1900, Pyle served in the Naval Reserve during World War I and attended Indiana University before embarking on a career as a newspaperman. Sent to England in 1940 to report on the bombing of London, Pyle subsequently covered the invasions of North Africa, Sicily, and Italy in 1943, and of Normandy in 1944. His winning personality and front-line reporting made him popular with both combat troops and Americans back home. Pyle won a Pulitzer Prize for journalism in 1943.

An appreciation of Pyle written by the Indiana Historical Society cites this example of his care and concern for everyday soldiers: "The Hoosier reporter's columns not only described the soldier's hardships, but also spoke out on his behalf. In a column from Italy in 1944, Pyle proposed that combat soldiers be given 'fight pay' similar to an airman's flight pay. In May of that year, Congress acted on Pyle's suggestion, giving soldiers 50 percent extra pay for combat service, legislation nicknamed 'the Ernie Pyle bill.' "[10]

While on the Italian front, Pyle also wrote his most famous column. The *Washington Daily News* devoted its entire January 10, 1944, front page to that description of the death of Capt. Henry T. Waskow of Belton, Texas. Later that month Pyle covered the Anzio landing while suffering from anemia and narrowly escaped death. Pyle's luck ran out on April 18, 1945, when he was struck by enemy bullets while accompanying the 77th Infantry Division on the island of Ie Shima, near Okinawa.

A movie about Pyle's wartime career, *The Story of G. I. Joe*, was in production while he was still alive, but Pyle never saw the completed version. The movie covered his time with the 18th Infantry Regiment in North Africa and Italy, and many critics consider it to be one of the best nondocumentary war films ever made. A *New York Times* reviewer described *The Story of G. I. Joe* as a "hard-hitting, penetrating drama of the footslogging soldier" and an "eloquent motion picture."[11]

On April 28, 1983, thirty-eight years after Pyle lost his life, Secretary of the Army John O. Marsh awarded a Purple Heart to Pyle. Today, that decoration and its accompanying certificate are on display at Pyle's boyhood home, which has been dedicated as the Ernie Pyle State Historic Site.

Pyle is buried at the National Memorial Cemetery of the Pacific at Punchbowl on the island of Oahu, Hawaii.

Jack Singer Jr.: Purple Heart—September 15, 1942

Jack Singer Jr., an accredited correspondent with INS, was killed in action on the USS *Wasp* when that vessel was sunk on September 15, 1942. The Navy sent Singer's posthumous Purple Heart to his father on February 17, 1945.

John Thompson: Purple Heart—July 9–10, 1943

John Thompson, wounded in action when landing by parachute as part of the Allied airborne invasion of Sicily on the night of July 9–10, 1943, was a newspaperman with the *Chicago Tribune*. According to an article in *Time* magazine, "big, bearded, 35-year-old" Thompson "parachuted out of a night sky into Sicily, landed in an olive tree, twisted a knee, (and) cracked a rib." The Army awarded Thompson a Purple Heart in November 1943.[12]

Herbert K. Wheeler: Purple Heart—February 20, 1945

Herbert Keith Wheeler, a war correspondent with the *Chicago Times*, was wounded on Iwo Jima on February 20, 1945. He was awarded a Navy Purple Heart on June 20, 1945.

Fire Department: Hawaii

On June 13, 1942, the Army awarded six Purple Hearts to Honolulu Fire Department firemen who were injured while fighting blazes caused by the Japanese attack on Pearl Harbor on December 7, 1941.[13]

As existing Army regulations provided that any person "serving *in* the Army"—emphasis added— might be awarded the Purple Heart, there was no legal basis to award Purple Hearts to these civilian firemen. Nonetheless, the following six men received the decoration while responding to fires caused by the Japanese attack:

Gorge Correa: Purple Heart—December 7, 1941
John A. Gilman: Purple Heart—December 7, 1941
Moses Kalilikane: Purple Heart—December 7, 1941
Frederick Kealoha: Purple Heart—December 7, 1941
Patrick McCabe: Purple Heart—December 7, 1941
Soloman Naauao Jr.: Purple Heart—December 7, 1941

On December 7, 1984, the Army awarded three more posthumous Purple Hearts to the following firefighters:

John Carreira: Purple Heart—December 7, 1941
Thomas Macy: Purple Heart—December 7, 1941
Harry T. L. Pang: Purple Heart—December 7, 1941

John Carreira and Thomas Macy, both captains in the Honolulu Fire Department, were killed "when a Japanese bomb flattened a hangar in which they were trying to keep American planes from catching fire."[14] The hangar was located on Hickam Field. Pang, who was a hoseman in the Honolulu Fire Department, also was killed while fighting fires during the Japanese attack on Oahu.

Police and Paramilitary Personnel: Guam

The Navy awarded a small number of Purple Hearts to civilian policemen and paramilitary personnel wounded while fighting the Japanese on Guam.

Vincente L. Borja: Purple Heart—May 1, 1945

A native of Guam, Vincente Lujan Borja was wounded in enemy action on May 1, 1945, while attached to the Guam Police Force. The Navy awarded him a Purple Heart on March 14, 1946.

Jesus Cruz: Purple Heart—December 8–10, 1941

A native of Guam, Jesus Cruz was killed in enemy action during the Japanese attack and occupation of Guam in December 1941. He was attached to the Insular Force, Guam, at the time of his death. The Navy awarded Cruz a posthumous Purple Heart on March 14, 1946.

Juan Lujan: Purple Heart—January 8, 1945

A native of Guam, Juan Lujan "received wounds in enemy action ... while on the Guam Police Force."[15] The Navy awarded him a Purple Heart on March 14, 1946, and a medal, certificate, ribbon bar, and lapel pin were sent to Lujan care of "The Island Commander" on April 12, 1946.

Antonio P. Manibusan: Purple Heart—March 14, 1946

Patrolman First Class Antonio Pangelinan Manibusan was shot and killed by Japanese soldiers while participating in "an officially authorized patrol" of the Guam Police Force Combat Patrol in the municipality of Yigo, Guam, on March 14, 1946.[16] Manibusan's death—months after Japanese forces officially surrendered—occurred because some enemy soldiers on Guam either did not receive notification of the surrender or did not believe it and, consequently, continued to fight. The last Japanese soldier to surrender on Guam was Corporal Shoichi Yokoi, who gave himself up in January 1972.[17] The Navy awarded Manibusan a posthumous Purple Heart on September 9, 1946.

Joaquin C. Rabon: Purple Heart—August 22, 1944

A resident of the village of Barrigada, Guam, Joaquin Cepeda Rabon "was killed while serving as a civilian scout on an authorized patrol with the Third Marine Division on 22 August 1944."[18] The Navy awarded Rabon a posthumous Purple Heart on February 24, 1947.

V. S. Sablan: Purple Heart—December 8–10, 1941

V. S. Sablan was "killed in enemy action during the Japanese attack and occupation of Guam 8–10 Dec 1941 while attached to the Insular Force, Guam."[19] The Navy awarded him a posthumous Purple Heart on March 14, 1946.

Other Civilians

William L. Benedict: Purple Heart—December 7, 1941

On January 7, 1944, the Army awarded a Purple Heart to "Mr. William L. Benedict, civilian employee, Quartermaster Corps, United States Army, for wounds received during the Japanese attack on Oahu, 7 December 1941."[20]

Benehakka Kanahele: Purple Heart—December 7, 1941

Benehakka "Benjamin" Kanahele, a resident of the Hawaiian island of Niihau, was shot twice by a Japanese pilot on December 7, 1941.

On the afternoon of December 7, a Japanese Zero fighter crashed on Niihau, which is located some 130 miles from Oahu. A local Hawaiian named Kaleohano captured the enemy pilot and seized his papers. Kaleohano and the rest of the local residents decided to hold the Japanese flyer until they could turn him over to the authorities. Their plan was to put the pilot on the sampan that made a weekly trip to and from Oahu, but, in the chaos after the attack on Pearl Harbor, the boat did not arrive.

In the meantime, an ethnic Japanese Niihau resident named Harada, who had been acting as an interpreter for the captured pilot, decided to ally himself with the man. Harada and the pilot then stole a shotgun and pistol, salvaged the crashed Zero's machine guns, and took control of the island as the local people hid in the fields. They also burned down the home belonging to Kaleohano, the Hawaiian who had initially taken the pilot captive.

The Japanese "occupation" of Niihau was short-lived. After Kanahele and another islander successfully stole the ammunition for the guns, Kanahele and his wife tried to ambush the pilot and the collaborating Harada but failed. Undeterred, the Kanaheles "bravely made a grab for the guns pointed at them and a four-cornered melee developed, during which (Benjamin) Kanahele was shot twice."

Enraged, Kanahele seized the pilot by the leg and neck and flung him against a stone wall, killing him. Harada, the Japanese interpreter who had been struggling with Kanahele's wife, broke free of her, grabbed the shotgun, and then committed suicide. The wounded Kanahele survived and, nearly four years later, was awarded a Purple Heart in ceremonies at Fort Shafter, Hawaii.[21]

Since no U.S. forces were involved in the episode on Niihau, there was no legal basis for Kanahele to receive a Purple Heart. But he did because of a very liberal interpretation of the phrase "serving in any capacity" language of Army Regulation 600-45.

VIETNAM (1966–1972)

The Army and Navy awarded a total of twenty-two Purple Hearts to civilians wounded or killed in action in Vietnam. Two recipients were American Red Cross employees; the remainder were Department of the Army, Department of the Navy, Department of State, and Department of Transportation civil service employees.

Neil M. Clark Jr.: Purple Heart—September 25, 1970
Neil Clark was an American Red Cross employee. The Army awarded him a Purple Heart after he was wounded in action.

Eugene Halsey: Purple Heart—July 1967
Eugene Halsey, a civil service employee working for the Navy, was wounded in a Viet Cong attack in July 1967. The secretary of the Navy approved the award of a Purple Heart to Halsey on April 19, 1968.[22]

James D. Holland: Purple Heart—December 7, 1967
A retired Army colonel who returned to Vietnam as an employee with the U.S. Agency for International Development, James Holland was wounded in a Viet Cong mortar attack on December 7, 1967. At the time he was

assigned to the Civil Operations and Revolutionary Development Support Program. Holland was awarded his Purple Heart by the Military Assistance Command, Vietnam.

Joseph Zaremba: Purple Heart—February 19, 1968

Joseph Zaremba was a thirty-five-year-old Federal Aviation Agency employee who "sustained shrapnel wounds to his back" from an exploding enemy rocket while waiting for a flight at Tan Son Nhut Air Base in Vietnam. The Army awarded him the Purple Heart on May 30, 1970.[23]

USS *LIBERTY* (1967)

Donald L. Blalock: Purple Heart—June 8, 1967
Allen M. Blue: Purple Heart—June 8, 1967

After Israeli fighters attacked the USS *Liberty* in June 1967, the chief of naval operations approved the award of the Purple Heart to 31 sailors and Marines killed in action and to 168 personnel wounded in action in that unprovoked attack. One civilian—Allen M. Blue—was killed and one—Donald L. Blalock—was wounded; both received Purple Hearts.

LEBANON (1983)

Sally Johnson: Purple Heart—April 18, 1983
William R. Sheil: Purple Heart—April 18, 1983

On April 18, 1983, a suicide car bomb exploded outside the U.S. Embassy in Beirut, killing sixty-three people, seventeen of whom were Americans. The Army awarded Purple Hearts to both Sally Johnson and William Sheil, who were civilian employees of the embassy.

GREECE (1985)

On February 2, 1985, a bomb exploded at a popular nightclub for U.S. Air Force personnel stationed at the airbase in Glyfada, Greece, near Athens. Fifty-five Americans were injured, but there were no deaths. The Air Force later awarded a Purple Heart to one civilian employee who was injured in the attack.

GERMANY (1985)

On August 8, 1985, a car bomb exploded in a parking lot at Rhein-Main Air Base, near Frankfurt, Germany. Both the German Red Army Faction and the French Action Directe terrorist groups claimed responsibility for the attack. The Air Force later awarded a Purple Heart to one of its civilian employees who was wounded in the blast.

MALTA (1985)

On November 23, 1985, gunmen belonging to Abu Nidal's Arab Revolutionary Brigade hijacked an EgyptAir jet flying from Cairo to Athens. The terrorists forced the aircraft to land in Malta and, subsequently, began shooting American and Israeli passengers. The hijacking ended when Israeli commandos stormed the plane, but not before sixty passengers were dead and twenty were wounded. Later, the U.S. Air Force awarded a Purple Heart posthumously to a civilian employee who had been killed on November 25.

SOMALIA (1993)

Edward C. Gaumer: Purple Heart—July 20, 1993

Edward Gaumer received gunshot and shrapnel wounds while working as a civilian employee in Mogadishu. A civil service employee and quality assurance specialist for the Defense Contract Management Command (International), Gaumer was in Somalia for less than twenty-four hours and "was being indoctrinated in the requirements of his job by touring various worksites in the area" when he got wounded.

At about 11:30 AM on July 20, 1993, the vehicle in which Gaumer was a passenger came under fire by Somali insurgents. Sitting in the backseat, Gaumer was hit by gunshot and shrapnel in his left ankle. He also suffered a severed tendon in his right foot. Navy Secretary John Dalton approved the award of a Purple Heart to Gaumer on December 13, 1993.[24]

SAUDI ARABIA (1995–1996)

On November 13, 1995, an explosion ripped through a three-story building in Riyadh, Saudi Arabia. Nineteen soldiers and forty Department of the Army and Department of Defense civilians were either wounded or killed. All were working in the Army Materiel Command's Program Management Office for the Saudi Arabian National Guard Modernization Program. Civilians receiving the Purple Heart included:

- Jim H. Allen, posthumous
- William J. Combs, posthumous
- Michelle D. Hainsworth
- Pauline B. Robinson
- Wayne P. Wiley, posthumous

Robert E. French: Purple Heart—June 25, 1996

Robert French was a civil service employee working in Saudi Arabia when he was wounded in the terrorist attack on Khobar Towers on June 25, 1996.[25]

A quality control specialist with the Army Signal Command's 504th Signal Battalion, then-sixty-year-old French had been installing a local area network in Dhahran. He was in his room at the time of the explosion. The blast shattered a sliding glass door, and shards of glass and metal became embedded in his arm and leg.[26]

Families: Brothers, Fathers and Sons, and Husbands and Wives

G iven that military and naval service often runs in families, it has not been unusual for more than one person in a family to have received a Purple Heart. But some family recipients are better known than others, and not all recipients from the same family have been male.

BROTHERS

Albert L. Sullivan, Navy: Purple Heart—November 13, 1942
Francis H. Sullivan, Navy: Purple Heart—November 13, 1942
George T. Sullivan, Navy: Purple Heart—November 13, 1942
Joseph E. Sullivan, Navy: Purple Heart—November 13, 1942
Madison A. Sullivan, Navy: Purple Heart—November 13, 1942

The unenviable record for the most Purple Hearts awarded to the greatest number of family members belongs to the Sullivans, five of whom were killed when the cruiser in which they were serving was sunk during the naval Battle of Guadalcanal during World War II.

The Sullivan brothers were all born in Waterloo, Iowa. George Thomas was born in December 1914, Francis Henry in February 1916, Joseph Eugene in August 1918, Madison Abel in November 1919, and Albert Leo in July 1922. Their sister, Genevieve Marie, was born in February 1917.

Life during the Great Depression was tough for the Sullivans, when jobs were scarce. The two oldest brothers, George and Frank, served in the Navy in

The Sullivan brothers—from left to right, Joseph, Francis, Albert, Madison, and George—were serving in the USS *Juneau* at the time of her commissioning ceremonies at the New York Naval Shipyard on February 14, 1942. All the brothers were lost with the ship following the November 13, 1942, Battle of Guadalcanal. (Naval Historical Center)

the 1930s, but all five brothers were together and working in Iowa when the Japanese attacked Pearl Harbor on December 7, 1941. Angered by the death of a friend who was serving in the USS *Arizona*, the brothers decided to enlist in the Navy on the stipulation that the service permit them all to be assigned together. The Navy agreed, and on January 3, 1942, the five Sullivans enlisted in Des Moines. When they finished training at Great Lakes, the brothers deployed to the Pacific and were assigned to the cruiser USS *Juneau*.

On November 8, 1942, a Navy task force of five cruisers and eight destroyers left New Caledonia in support of American efforts to bring supplies to Marines at Guadalcanal, who were engaged in bitter fighting with the Japanese. Near Savo, an island located just north of Guadalcanal, a furious battle erupted between the Americans and Japanese warships. The enemy

Gen. Mark W. Clark was severely wounded while fighting in France during World War I. His son Maj. William D. Clark was wounded three times during the Korean War. (U.S. Army)

ships were also in the area to resupply their troops on Guadalcanal. In the thirty-minute slugfest that followed, several cruisers were crippled or sunk, including the light cruiser *Juneau*, in which the five Sullivan brothers were serving. She was hit by a Japanese torpedo on the port side near the forward fireroom. The shockwave from the explosion buckled the deck, shattered the fire control computers, and knocked out power. Although she remained afloat, the *Juneau* limped from the battle, down by the bow and struggling to maintain eighteen knots.

The *Juneau* rejoined surviving American warships at dawn on November 13 and zigzagged to the southeast with two other cruisers and three destroyers. Unfortunately, the Americans then crossed paths with the Japanese submarine *I-26*. The submarine fired three torpedoes at the USS *San Francisco*. None hit that cruiser, but one passed beyond and struck the *Juneau* on the port side very near the previous hit. The ensuing magazine explosion blew the light cruiser in half, killing most of the *Juneau*'s crew.

Fearful of another submarine attack, the American task force did not stay to check for survivors. More than one hundred of the *Juneau*'s crew did survive initially, including George Sullivan, but exposure, exhaustion, and shark attacks whittled down the survivors. Only ten men were eventually rescued from the water eight days after the sinking. George Sullivan was not among them.[1]

News of the deaths of all five brothers became a rallying point for war bond drives and other patriotic campaigns, as well as the 1944 movie *The Sullivans*. Their sister Genevieve enlisted in the Naval Reserve as a recruiter and, with her parents, visited two hundred manufacturing plants and shipyards under Navy auspices. By January 1944, the three surviving Sullivans had spoken to more than a million workers in sixty-five cities and reached millions of others over the radio.

The Navy has named two warships after the five Sullivan brothers. In February 1943 the Navy assigned the name *The Sullivans* to a destroyer under construction. That ship was commissioned on September 30, 1943, and served the Navy until final decommissioning in January 1965. In 1977 the decommissioned destroyer was donated to the city of Buffalo as a memorial. The second USS *The Sullivans* was built in Bath, Maine, and launched in August 1995.

Misconceptions about the aftereffects of the Sullivan brothers' deaths abound. Contrary to myth, Congress never enacted any law to prevent family members from serving together. Nor has any president issued any executive order forbidding assignment of family members to the same ship. Current Navy policy, unchanged since 1942, is that brothers or members of the same family may serve in the same ship following approval of their request to do so by the Department of the Navy.

FATHERS AND SONS

Mark W. Clark, Father, Army: Purple Heart—June 14, 1918
William D. Clark, Son, Army: Purple Heart—October 7, 1951

Mark Wayne Clark was severely wounded while serving in France on June 14, 1918. His son, William Doran Clark, was wounded three times in Korea, including on October 7, 1951.

Born at Madison Barracks, New York, on May 1, 1896, Mark Clark graduated from West Point in April 1917 and, like many of his classmates, sailed to France to take part in World War I. On June 14, 1918, then-Captain Clark was serving with the 11th Infantry Regiment, 5th Division when he suffered wounds during the Aisne–Marne offensive. After recovering from his injuries, Clark served on the First Army staff during the St. Mihiel offensive and the Meuse–Argonne offensive. When World War I ended Clark remained in Europe, serving with the Third Army during the occupation of Germany.

Clark returned to the United States in 1919 and completed a number of staff and training assignments before being promoted to major in 1933. He then served briefly with the Civilian Conservation Corps before attending the Army War College. Promoted to lieutenant colonel in 1940, Clark then skipped a rank and pinned on the stars of a brigadier general in August 1941.

After the Japanese attack on Pearl Harbor, Clark deployed to Great Britain, where he was commander of U.S. forces. As a lieutenant general, Clark was General Eisenhower's deputy in North Africa and, on October 22, 1942, demonstrated both pluck and daring when he and a few other men landed by submarine in Algeria to conduct negotiations with Vichy French commanders. As a result of these fairly successful negotiations, French resistance to Operation Torch, the November 1942 Allied invasion of North Africa, was relatively light.

In January 1943 Clark was given command of the newly formed Fifth Army, which consisted of American, British, and Polish troops, and he was with these soldiers when they landed at Salerno on September 9, 1943. On September 14, five days after wading ashore, Clark performed an act of extraordinary heroism at the Salerno bridgehead. According to official records, Clark went to the front and "with complete disregard for his personal safety [and while] under enemy artillery and automatic weapons fire, stopped time and time again to talk to front line riflemen and leaders of front line units, telling them that their line must be held at all costs." Additionally, after "discovering 18 German Mark IV tanks" approaching his area, Clark quickly located a tank destroyer battalion and "personally issued instructions" that "resulted in the destruction of six of the enemy tanks." For these acts of extraordinary gallantry in combat, Clark was awarded a Distinguished Service Cross.[2]

In June 1944 Clark's Fifth Army liberated Rome, but his subsequent efforts in Italy were largely overlooked by the American public after the Allied invasion of Normandy. Still, Clark received his fourth star and command of 15th Army Group in December 1944.

After World War II General Clark commanded U.S. Forces, Austria before returning to the United States in 1947 to take command of Sixth Army. In 1949 he moved to Fort Monroe, where he assumed command of

Army Field Forces in 1949. He deployed to Korea in May 1952 and succeeded Gen. Matthew B. Ridgeway as commander in chief of the Far East Command and UN Command. Clark remained in Korea through the armistice negotiations with the Chinese and North Koreans. Clark then retired from the Army in October 1953 and later served as the president of The Citadel in Charleston, South Carolina. He retired again in 1965 and died in April 1984.[3]

The War Department issued Clark a Purple Heart on March 5, 1932. In addition to this decoration and a Distinguished Service Cross, Clark also received a variety of high-level awards, including four Army Distinguished Service Medals, a Navy Distinguished Service Medal, a Legion of Merit, and a Bronze Star Medal.

★ ★ ★

Born in Georgia on March 21, 1925, William Clark followed in his father's footsteps and graduated from the U.S. Military Academy in 1945. Commissioned as an infantry second lieutenant, the younger Clark first served in the Mediterranean with U.S. troops in Trieste, Italy, before returning to West Point as the aide-de-camp to the superintendent. In 1951 Clark deployed to Korea, where he served first at IX Corps headquarters before taking command of a company and serving as a battalion executive officer in the 9th Infantry.

On October 7, 1951, Clark was with his unit in the vicinity of Mungdung-ni, Korea, when a "friendly infantry company" was engaged in an attack against "a numerically superior hostile force occupying heavily fortified hill positions." As the friendly soldiers neared their objective, the company commander and all company officers were wounded by enemy mortar, artillery, and small-arms fire. As a result the soldiers, most of whom were inexperienced and under fire for the first time, became disorganized.

According to official records, Clark realized "that the confusion of the men might result in their annihilation and that, without an organized effort, the attack was lost." Consequently, Clark "immediately rushed forward through the heavy enemy fire and assumed command of the faltering friendly troops." He then rallied the men and led them forward in a renewed attack. Despite being wounded by enemy fire, Clark refused to be evacuated and continued to direct the friendly troops, urging "them onward with words of encouragement." Clark's "great tactical skill and complete disregard for his personal safety so inspired the friendly troops that they swept forward and routed the hostile force from the hill with heavy casualties."[4]

Gen. George S. Patton Jr. was wounded in action in September 1918. His son George S. Patton IV was wounded in action in September 1968. Both were awarded Purple Hearts. (U.S. Army)

In addition to receiving a Purple Heart for the injuries he received on October 7, Clark also was awarded a Distinguished Service Cross. He later received two more Purple Hearts and two Silver Stars for wounds and gallantry in action. Clark completed a final tour of duty as a major on the staff and faculty of the Infantry School at Fort Benning before taking a medical retirement in 1955.

George S. Patton Jr., Father, Army: Purple Heart—September 26, 1918
George S. Patton IV, Son, Army: Purple Heart—September 1968
George Smith Patton Jr. was wounded in action in France on September 26, 1918. His son, George S. Patton IV, was wounded in combat in Vietnam fifty years later.

George Smith Patton Jr. was born in San Gabriel, California, on November 11, 1885. He suffered from dyslexia but worked hard to overcome that disability. In 1903 Patton began his college studies at the Virginia Military Institute but left after one year to enter the U.S. Military Academy. After graduating from

West Point in 1909 after being held back because of poor marks in mathematics, he was commissioned as a second lieutenant of cavalry. Then-twenty-six-year-old Patton was a superb athlete and took part in the 1912 Olympics in Stockholm, Sweden, finishing fifth in the modern pentathlon. He then remained in Europe to study at the French Cavalry School in Saumur. After returning to the United States in 1913, Patton reported to Fort Leavenworth, where he designed a saber that was later adopted as a weapon by the Army and taught a course in swordsmanship.

In 1916 then–First Lieutenant Patton deployed with General Pershing into Mexico, where Patton saw his first combat. Having impressed Pershing, Patton sailed with him to Europe in 1917 and began studying tank tactics with the Allies. Patton established a tank school in Bourg, France, trained the first American tank crews and commanders, and led a 345-tank brigade into combat at Meuse–Argonne. On September 26, 1918, Patton was severely wounded in his leg by a gunshot, and his heroism also resulted in an award of a Distinguished Service Cross and a temporary promotion to colonel.

After the war Patton reverted to his prewar rank of captain. For the next twenty years, he served with the horse cavalry but, having seen tanks in action, became an apostle of armored warfare. In 1939 then–Brigadier General Patton took command of the 2nd Brigade, 2nd Armored Division at Fort Benning. During maneuvers in Louisiana in 1941, he performed so well that, after America's entry into World War II, General Marshall chose him to command the Western Task Force during the Allied invasion of North Africa.

After his success in North Africa, Patton commanded the U.S. Seventh Army during the invasion of Sicily in 1943 and received his second Distinguished Service Cross for "personally directing the movement of reinforcements" to stop a German breakthrough at Gela on July 11.[5] But Patton nearly destroyed his career when he visited a field hospital and, encountering a soldier suffering from battle fatigue, slapped him for alleged cowardice.

Following the Normandy invasion, Eisenhower gave Patton command of the U.S. Third Army, and Patton quickly showed that Eisenhower's trust in him was not misplaced. On August 1, 1944, Patton's forces broke out of Normandy, smashed through German defenses, and helped encircle 100,000 enemy soldiers in the Falaise Gap, forcing them to surrender.

Patton continued to press hard against the Germans, and his tanks reached the Meuse River on August 31. But, having outrun their fuel supply, they stopped. While Patton argued that an all-out attack on the Siegfried Line was now required and that the Allies could then roll into Germany itself, Eisenhower instead opted for a more orderly advance against the enemy.

In December 1944 the Germans struck back in what became known as the Battle of the Bulge. As the U.S. lines crumbled in Belgium, Patton came to the rescue by disengaging his forces in front, rotating them to the north, and then striking the Germans in the flank. This brilliant maneuver also enabled elements of the Fourth Armored Division to relieve the besieged airborne forces holding out in Bastogne.

In January 1945 Patton was on the offensive and crossed the Rhine River into Germany on March 22. When Patton halted at the Elbe River on May 5, 1945, he and his army had crossed France, Belgium, Luxembourg, Germany, Austria, and Czechoslovakia and had liberated or conquered 81,522 square miles of territory. In October 1945 Patton assumed command of the Fifteenth Army in American-occupied Germany. Then, on December 9 of that year he suffered injuries as the result of an automobile accident and died twelve days later. Patton is buried among the soldiers who died in the Battle of the Bulge in Hamm, Luxembourg.

Today, Patton is accepted as one of the greatest military commanders in history, and the 1970 film *Patton*, starring George C. Scott in the title role, cemented his heroic image in popular culture. The movie won seven Academy Awards, including the statuettes for Best Actor and Best Picture.

George Smith Patton IV—there was no "III," and the younger Patton dropped the "IV" later in life—was born in Massachusetts on December 23, 1923. Patton was twenty-two years old and in his last year at the U.S. Military Academy in December 1945 when his father was killed in a traffic accident in Germany. After being commissioned in June 1946, Patton completed the Infantry Officer Basic Course at Fort Benning and then joined a constabulary unit in Augsburg, Germany. He subsequently served at the 7767th Tank Training Center in Vilsek and as a platoon leader and executive officer in Company C of the 63rd Heavy Tank Battalion, a unit organic to the 1st Infantry Division in Germany.

After completing the advanced class at the Armor School at Fort Knox, Patton served as an instructor before deploying to Korea in February 1952. Then-Captain Patton was a company commander in the 140th Tank Battalion, 40th Infantry Division, saw heavy combat, and was decorated with a Silver Star for gallantry and a Bronze Star Medal.

Patton did two tours of duty in Vietnam. His first was at Military Assistance Command, Vietnam, from April 1962 to April 1963, and he spent much of that tour "concentrating on the organization of paramilitary forces … their ranks filled primarily by the Montagnard tribes."[6] Patton returned to Vietnam for his second tour in 1967 as chief of the Army's force development study group, which was located at Long Binh. After six months in that staff position, then-Colonel Patton took command of the 11th Armored Cavalry "Blackhorse" Regiment. He remained with that unit until returning to the United States in April 1969.

During his time in command, the unit's motto was "Find the Bastards and Pile On," and Patton was in the thick of fighting. In September 1968 his extraordinary heroism in combat resulted in Patton receiving two awards of the Distinguished Service Cross, another Silver Star, and another Bronze Star Medal. He also was wounded in action and received a Purple Heart.[7]

Patton's first Distinguished Service Cross was for gallantry during a battle with the North Vietnamese near Chanh Luu on September 5, 1968. According to the citation for the award, Patton was in his command-and-control helicopter when he

saw a force of fifty-eight hostile soldiers attempting to escape his troops' encirclement. Col. Patton immediately directed his door gunners to engage the communists and ordered his pilot to land in the vicinity of the enemy element. As the aircraft touched down it was damaged by an intense barrage of hostile fire from a deep, well concealed ravine.

Aided by helicopter gunships, Col. Patton led an assault against the North Vietnamese positions which forced the enemy to withdraw. A three-man rocket propelled grenade team remained behind to cover their retreat. When a platoon of infantry arrived to assist him, Colonel Patton led a squad into the ravine and directed an assault on the hostile position. During the fierce engagement Colonel Patton captured one of the aggressors, and the other two were killed as they tried to flee the ravine.[8]

Patton's second Distinguished Service Cross was awarded for heroism under fire on September 24, 1968, while elements of the Blackhorse Regiment and South Vietnamese Rangers conducted a sweep around the village of Chanh Luu. The citation for this award reads, in part:

Intense automatic weapons and rocket-propelled grenade fire from a house destroyed an assault vehicle and wounded several men, including the Rangers' commanding officer.

Seeing that the Ranger unit was beginning to lose momentum, Colonel Patton had his command and control helicopter land in the middle of the embattled area and left the ship to rally the Vietnamese soldiers.

Exposing himself to the hostile fire raking the area, he maneuvered them back to a supporting position near the enemy stronghold and directed his troops to more defensible terrain, while personally engaging the communists with his grenade launcher. He then led a charge which destroyed the house and revealed a heavily fortified bunker that had been concealed by the building.

Ordering his men to lay down a base of fire, Colonel Patton crawled through the open terrain until he was at the fortification's entrance and hurled a grenade inside. When the enemy in the extensive and well protected bunker continued to resist, he assaulted a second time with two other men and placed TNT in the emplacement, annihilating the position.[9]

After Vietnam, then–Brigadier General Patton served as an assistant division commander for the 4th Armored Division before being promoted to major general and taking command of the 2nd Armored Division in 1975. This was the same tank division his father had led in North Africa during World War II.

In 1977, three years before he retired from active duty, Patton was asked whether he felt overshadowed by his father, who gained fame for his exploits in North Africa, Sicily, and France and who was introduced to new generations of Americans through George C. Scott's movie portrayal. "I've never worried about it," Patton told the interviewer. "I've been too busy."[10]

Patton retired from active duty in August 1980, having served in the Army for thirty years. He died at his farm outside Hamilton, Massachusetts, on June 27, 2004, at the age of eighty. Patton is interred at Arlington National Cemetery.

"Chesty" B. Puller, Father, Marine Corps: Purple Heart—November 8, 1942
Lewis B. Puller Jr., Son, Marine Corps: Purple Hearts—September 1968 and October 11, 1968

Lewis "Chesty" Burwell Puller was wounded by Japanese artillery fire while commanding the 1st Battalion, 7th Marines near the mouth of the Metapona River on Guadalcanal on November 8, 1942.

Born in West Point, Virginia, on June 26, 1898, Puller briefly attended the Virginia Military Institute before enlisting in the Marine Corps in August

Lt. Gen. Lewis B. "Chesty" Puller received one Purple Heart during World War II. His son Lewis "Lew" B. Puller Jr. received two Purple Hearts in Vietnam. (U.S. Marine Corps)

1918. The war ended in Europe before Puller could get overseas, so he served several months as an instructor at Parris Island. In June 1919 Puller received a commission as a second lieutenant but was unable to remain on active duty because of postwar reductions in the size of the Corps. He consequently reenlisted and shipped out to Haiti, where he served as an acting lieutenant in the Gendarmerie d'Haiti, a paramilitary force created to fight revolutionary peasants known as "cacos." Most of the Gendarmerie officers were U.S. Marines, while most of the enlisted personnel were Haitians.

Puller returned to the United States in March 1924 and was commissioned as a second lieutenant. He subsequently attended flight school at Pensacola but did not earn his wings. This is one of the few occasions that Puller failed at anything.

After a two-year tour of duty in Hawaii, Puller deployed to Nicaragua, where he served as a captain in the Guardia Nacional, another native constabulary. Except for a period of schooling from 1931 to 1932 at Fort Benning, Puller was in Nicaragua from 1928 to 1933, and his aggressive patrolling and heroism under fire earned him the nickname "El Tigre" (The Tiger) and the award of two Navy Crosses.

In February 1933 Puller sailed for China, where he joined the Marine detachment at Beijing and also commanded the famous mounted Horse Marines that guarded the American legation. Without returning to the United States, Puller next began a tour of sea duty with the Marine detachment in the cruiser USS *Augusta*. He did serve stateside from June 1936 until May 1939, when he deployed again to Asia to serve once more, briefly, in the USS *Augusta* before joining the 4th Marines in Shanghai, China. He served as a battalion executive officer and commanding officer with that unit until returning home in August 1941.

Puller next took command of the 1st Battalion, 7th Marines at Camp Lejeune and was still in command of that unit when it landed at Guadalcanal. On the night of October 23–24, 1942, Puller and his battalion defended a mile-long front against a regiment of battle-hardened Japanese troops. In pouring jungle rain, and as the enemy repeatedly attacked his unit, Puller moved up and down the line to encourage his Marines. The enemy was repulsed with some 1,400 killed while Puller's Marines incurred just 70 casualties. For this achievement, Puller was awarded his third Navy Cross.

Two weeks after that action, Puller was wounded in action and received his one and only Purple Heart. It happened about 2 PM on November 8, 1942, when Puller's men had just left the beach at the mouth of the Metapona River and were moving upstream. As Burke Davis wrote in *Marine!*, "Puller was 300 to 400 yards behind the point of his column (of Marines). For the first time in a combat career spanning twenty-three years, his luck ran out under enemy fire. He was blown from his feet by a spray of flying metal; shell fragments had torn his legs and lower body and he was bleeding freely. . . . (As Puller) struggled unsteadily to his feet . . . an enemy sniper shot him twice through the flesh of his arm with small caliber bullets. He sank back to the ground."[11] Although the doctors advised Puller to go to Australia for medical care for his seven wounds, he refused, and spent eight days in a field hospital before returning to duty.[12]

In January 1943 then–Lieutenant Colonel Puller returned to the United States at the request of General Marshall, and spent the next three months giving speeches to military audiences about Guadalcanal. Puller returned to the Pacific theater in March, and subsequently served as the executive officer of the 7th Marines.

Puller received a fourth Navy Cross for his leadership at Cape Gloucester in January 1944. When an attack by two U.S. Marine battalions stalled after their commanders were wounded, Puller took over the units and moved through heavy machine-gun and mortar fire to reorganize them for attack. He subsequently led them in capturing a strongly fortified Japanese position.

In February 1944 Puller, who had been promoted to full colonel, took command of the 1st Marines and led that regiment for the remainder of the island-hopping campaign. He saw some of his hardest fighting on Peleliu in September and October 1944 before returning to the United States after the Japanese surrendered in August 1945. Puller than served with the Infantry Training Regiment at Camp Lejeune.

Shortly after the start of the Korean War in June 1950, Puller reestablished and took command of the 1st Marine Regiment at Camp Pendleton. He landed with them in the amphibious assault at Inchon in September 1950 and led his men in vicious house-to-house fighting against the North Koreans in Seoul. He received a Silver Star for gallantry in action during this period.

In December 1950 Puller was with the 1st Marines as part of the UN forces' advance into North Korea. When the Chinese cut off and surrounded the Marines at Chosin Reservoir, Puller was in the thick of the fighting. Despite being overwhelmed by the enemy, Puller's Marines held onto the village of Koto-ri, broke the Chinese assault, and ensured that the 5th Marine Regiment and 7th Marine Regiment could fight their way to Hungnam and safety. Puller was the last Marine to leave Koto-ri, and his heroism saved a division and resulted in the award of an unprecedented fifth Navy Cross.

As the citation for that decoration explains,

Fighting continuously in sub-zero weather against a vastly outnumbering hostile force, Colonel Puller drove off repeated and fanatical enemy attacks upon his Regimental defense sector and supply points. Although the area was frequently covered by grazing machine gun fire and intense artillery and mortar fire, he coolly moved among his troops to insure their correct tactical employment, reinforced the lines as the situation demanded and successfully defended his perimeter, keeping open the main supply routes for the movement of the Division.

During the attack from Koto-ri to Hungman, he expertly utilized his Regiment as the Division rear guard, repelling two fierce enemy assaults which severely threatened the security of the unit, and personally supervised the care and prompt evacuation of all casualties.

By his unflagging determination, he served to inspire his men to heroic efforts in defense of their positions and assured the safety of much valuable equipment which would otherwise have been lost to the enemy. His skilled leadership, superb courage and valiant devotion to duty in the face of overwhelming odds reflect the highest credit upon Colonel Puller and the United States Naval Service.[13]

Puller also received a Distinguished Service Cross—the Army's equivalent to the Navy Cross—for his heroism at Chosin Reservoir.

After being promoted to brigadier general in January 1951, Puller was named assistant commander of the 1st Marine Division. He received his second star in September 1953 and took command of the 2nd Marine Division in July 1954. After a mild stroke, however, Puller was forced to accept that his thirty-seven years of Marine Corps service were over. He was promoted to lieutenant general and placed on the temporary disability retirement list on November 1, 1955. Puller died in October 1971 after a long illness. He remains one of the most famous Marines in history, and no one has equaled his unprecedented five awards of the Navy Cross.

Lewis Burwell "Lew" Puller Jr. was slightly wounded in September 1968 when shrapnel from a booby trap wounded his hand. He was wounded a second time when he stepped on an enemy booby trap on October 11, 1968, and was critically injured.

Born August 18, 1945, Puller entered the Marine Corps after graduating from the College of William and Mary in 1967. After completing training at Quantico, he deployed to Vietnam. In September 1968, after another Marine set off a booby trap, Puller "took a piece of shrapnel in the hand" and received his first Purple Heart.[14]

A few weeks later, then–First Lieutenant Puller was leading his platoon on a patrol when he stepped on a "booby-trapped howitzer round" and was severely injured.[15] Puller later wrote that while his first Purple Heart had been "cheap, the second award could hardly have been paid for more dearly."[16] He also received a Silver Star for gallantry in action.

The prognosis following Puller's second injury was grim, as he had lost both of his legs and parts of both hands. But those who knew him insisted that Puller's iron will and stubborn refusal to die would ensure his survival. After a lengthy period of hospitalization, Puller did leave the hospital and returned to William and Mary to earn a law degree. He subsequently spent many years as a Defense Department attorney in the Pentagon.

Puller was active in veteran's affairs and spoke frequently about his Vietnam experiences. His inspiring and critically acclaimed autobiography, *Fortunate Son: The Healing of a Vietnam Vet*, won the Pulitzer Prize for biography in 1992. That book tells how he overcame his physical disabilities and achieved a measure of serenity.

In his later years, however, Puller suffered from depression and alcoholism. He took his own life on May 11, 1994, when he was forty-eight years old. Puller is interred at Arlington National Cemetery.

Joseph K. Taussig, Father, Navy: Purple Heart—June 20, 1900
Joseph K. Taussig Jr., Son, Navy: Purple Heart—December 7, 1941

Joseph Knefler Taussig and Joseph Knefler Taussig Jr. appear to have been the first father and son to both receive Purple Hearts.

The elder Taussig was born in Dresden, Germany, in August 1877 and entered the U.S. Naval Academy when he was eighteen years old. While still a midshipman, he served in the battleship USS *New York* and was present at the naval Battle of Santiago off Cuba in 1898. After graduating from Annapolis in 1899, he was assigned to the cruiser USS *Newark* and took part in the Boxer Rebellion. Navy records show that Taussig was "wounded in action on June 20, 1900, in action against Chinese troops."

According to the official Navy Website, Taussig served "two years as a naval cadet" before being commissioned as an ensign in January 1901 and embarking on "a series of promotions and distinctions that would underscore his illustrious service to the Navy."[17] Over the next fifteen years Taussig served in battleships, cruisers, and destroyers. He made history when in July 1916, he took the first group of American destroyers across the Atlantic to participate in World War I. For his successful command of Division 8, Destroyer Force, Taussig was awarded a Navy Distinguished Service Medal.

After the war Taussig served in a variety of assignments, including holding command of a battleship division. He initially retired from the Navy as a vice admiral in 1941 but was recalled to active duty during World War II. The elder Taussig died in October 1947.

★ ★ ★

Joseph Taussig Jr. was every bit as remarkable as his father. Born in May 1920, he too graduated from the Naval Academy. On December 7, 1941, twenty-year-old Ensign Taussig was officer of the deck on the battleship USS *Nevada* in Pearl Harbor. When Japanese aircraft attacked Battleship Row, Taussig sounded the alert and then manned an antiaircraft gun.

In the battle that followed, Taussig received a severe injury to his left leg and high praise for his bravery. In a December 2008 newspaper article, *Nevada* boatswain's mate Robert "Bob" Norman remembered rescuing Taussig. When Norman began to pick up the young officer to carry him below, Taussig ordered Norman to leave him be. "I'm sorry sir," replied Norman. "But this is one order I'm going to have to disobey."[18] Taussig later received a Navy Cross for his heroism, as well as a Purple Heart for his leg wound. Norman was awarded a Silver Star for his bravery in saving the young ensign's life.

Taussig's injuries were so bad that he spent the remainder of World War II in the hospital. Unfortunately, his left leg never healed, and it was amputated in April 1946. When he was medically retired in 1954, Taussig was thirty-four years old and the youngest captain in the Navy.

He then began a second career in both the private and public sectors. In the mid-1980s, as the special assistant for safety and survivability for the Secretary of the Navy, Taussig introduced new technology and procedures to help sailors fight shipboard fires. His ideas resulted in a significant savings in lives and money from fire damages. Taussig died in Annapolis in December 1999 at the age of seventy-nine.

HUSBANDS AND WIVES

Given the relatively few numbers of women serving in the U.S. Armed Forces until the 1980s, awards of Purple Hearts to women have been rare. The number of female recipients of the Purple Heart has increased steadily over the past twenty years, however, and, with some of these women married to male military personnel, Purple Hearts to husbands and wives now join those to brothers and fathers and sons in the Purple Hearts to Families category.

While there apparently have been awards of the Purple Heart to married couples in the past, the most recent of these awards have been made to couples who were wounded in Iraq.

Clayton E. Erickson, Husband, Army: Purple Heart—August 4, 2004
Heidi Erickson, Wife, Army: Purple Heart—August 14–15, 2004

Sgt. Clayton "Eric" Erickson was wounded when a vehicle carrying explosives drove into his convoy on August 4, 2004. He suffered "a blast concussion to his right ear" and bleeding in his eardrum. Less than a dozen days later, his wife, Sgt. Heidi Erickson, was wounded in action when a tanker truck exploded as her convoy passed it. She was "showered with glass fragments" that cut her face.[19]

Residents of Central City, Nebraska, the Ericksons were mobilized in fall 2003 with different reserve units and deployed to Iraq in early 2004. Heidi Erickson served in Iraq as a gun truck driver; Eric Erickson served as a heavy equipment truck driver. The Ericksons were awarded their Purple Hearts during a special ceremony in Central City in 2006.

David Romero, Husband, Army: Purple Heart, April 2004
Nancy Romero, Wife, Army: Purple Heart, March 12, 2004

On March 12, 2004, Spc. Nancy Romero, a member of 418th Transportation Company, 118th Transportation Battalion, a part of the 13th Corps Support Command, was in a convoy to deliver heavy construction equipment. In a 2004 interview Romero explained that she "knew something was up" when the convoy entered Al Hillah, Iraq. She said,

> It was very strange. . . . There were no children in the street. . . . The Iraqis stared at us as our convoy drove past. . . . We saw a mountain of dust up in front of us. . . . When we started to pass the dust, the IED went off . . . . I heard the explosion, there was glass everywhere. . . . I was very upset.

Sgt. David Romero and Spc. Nancy Romero were both wounded in action in Iraq in 2004, and both were awarded the Purple Heart. (U.S. Army)

. . . I was thinking, "Why me? Why us?" I was feeling anger and a mix of emotions. . . . Then I had an adrenaline rush and we had to pull security.[20]

Two soldiers were killed in the blast. Romero received minor injuries, including cuts on her hands and arms and ringing in her ears.

A month later, Nancy's husband, Sgt. David Romero was wounded when an IED blew out the windows off the truck he was driving. At the time David Romero was a member of the 96th Transportation Company, also a unit in the 13th Corps Support Command. On the day he was wounded, Romero had "volunteered to go on a mission in order to provide other soldiers with some downtime."

When Romero's convoy was "about an hour outside Camp Caldwell, Iraq," they "got ambushed" when an explosion "hit us from behind." As David Romero remembered, "I felt hot and cold and saw glass all over the place. . . . Then I saw blood. . . . The truck rocked back and forth. . . . I had to avoid hitting the Humvee in front of me. . . . It took me a while to get my truck to stop. . . . Everything seemed like it was happening in slow motion. . . . I grabbed my M16A1 rifle and jumped out (of my truck). . . . I thought, 'If I am going to die, I'm going to die fighting.' "[21]

Like his wife, David Romero received only minor injuries. On October 7, 2004, the Romeros became the first husband and wife soldiers in thirty years to receive their Purple Hearts in the same awards formation.[22]

Celebrities: Artists and Entertainers, Politicians, Athletes, and Other Public Figures

More than one million Purple Hearts have been awarded since the Army revived General Washington's Badge of Military Merit as a full-sized military decoration in 1932. Among this multitude of recipients are individuals who later had careers in movies, television, theater, publishing, athletics, politics, and other aspects of public life.

Not every celebrity who received the Purple Heart is listed in this chapter, if for no other reason than identifying an individual as a "celebrity" is very subjective. Additionally, some high-profile personalities have claimed to have received the Purple Heart when there is no proof that the decoration was awarded to them. For example, actor Brian M. Dennehy, who has starred in a variety of television series and is perhaps best known for portraying an overzealous sheriff in Sylvester Stallone's 1982 film *First Blood*, once claimed to have been wounded in Vietnam while serving there as a Marine. But Dennehy is not included in this chapter because his Marine Corps records indicate that he was never in Vietnam and never received the Purple Heart.[1] Consequently, unless official military records confirm the award of a Purple Heart, celebrities claiming the award are not profiled.

The celebrities profiled in this chapter are in alphabetical order by type of celebrity:

Artists and Entertainers
- James Arness
- Neville Brand
- Art Carney
- Charles Durning
- James Garner
- Lee Marvin
- Audie Murphy
- Peter Ortiz

Politicians
- Maurice Britt
- Robert Dole
- William Donovan
- Charles Hagel
- Alexander Haig
- Daniel Inouye
- John Kennedy
- John McCain
- Colin Powell
- Eric Shinseki
- James Stockdale
- Strom Thurmond
- James Webb

Athletes
- Henry "Hank" Bauer
- Ralph Houk
- Robert Shepard
- Warren Spahn

Other Public Figures
- David Hackworth
- Jessica Lynch
- Douglas MacArthur
- Oliver North
- Charles "Chuck" Yeager

ARTISTS AND ENTERTAINERS

Celebrities in arts and entertainment, including actors and technical advisors to the movie industry, authors, and journalists, have received the Purple Heart—some more than one.

James K. Arness (née Aurness): Purple Heart—February 1, 1944

James Arness, who was wounded by German machine-gun fire during World War II, is best known for portraying U.S. Marshal Matt Dillon in the long-running television series *Gunsmoke*.

Born on May 26, 1923, in Minneapolis, Arness was a college student when the United States declared war on Germany, Italy, and Japan in December 1941. He dreamed of flying for the Navy but was rejected because, at six foot seven inches, he was too tall to fit any cockpits. Eager to serve, however, Arness wrote his local draft board asking to be inducted as soon as possible. As a result, he was drafted into the Army in February 1943, completed basic training at Camp Wheeler, Georgia, and joined the 7th Infantry Regiment, 3rd Infantry Division. According to Arness' autobiography, his height, which had kept him from flying, resulted in him being chosen to be the first soldier off the landing craft in order to test the water depth when his division waded ashore at Anzio. While the January 1944 landings were essentially unopposed, German opposition soon stiffened. On February 1, 1944, while on a night patrol in a sector east of the beach, then-Private Arness was badly wounded in his right leg by enemy machine-gun fire. He spent more than a year in the hospital.[2] Arness was subsequently awarded both a Purple Heart and a Bronze Star Medal.

Arness returned to Minneapolis in 1945, where he worked as a radio announcer for a short time before moving to Hollywood to start an acting career. He had supporting roles in *The Farmer's Daughter*, a 1947 romantic-comedy starring Joseph Cotten and Loretta Young, who won an Oscar as Best Actress for her role, and *Them!*, the 1954 science-fiction classic in which Arness and others battle ants that have mutated into giant monsters.

While he would continue to make movies, Arness achieved lasting fame on the CBS television series *Gunsmoke*, which aired from 1955 to 1975 and is considered one of the best television shows of all time. Arness played the lawman who keeps the peace in the frontier town of Dodge City, Kansas, along with Milburn Stone as Doc Adams, Ken Curtis as Festus Haggen, and Amanda Blake as "Miss Kitty" Russell.

James Arness, best known for portraying U.S. Marshal Matt Dillon in the television series *Gunsmoke*, was wounded by German machine-gun fire during World War II. (James Arness)

Gunsmoke was a top-ten-rated show for thirteen of its twenty seasons. Since five *Gunsmoke* television movies were produced and broadcast in the 1980s and 1990s, it is the only prime time television series to span five consecutive decades.

Just as his height had affected his military career, it remained a challenge for those filming Arness in movies and television. In *Gunsmoke*'s medium-close shots, the other actors often stood on elevated platforms so that their faces would be in the camera frame with Arness'.[3]

Neville L. Brand: Purple Heart—April 7, 1945

Neville L. Brand, who was wounded in his right arm by an enemy bullet during World War II, is probably best known for playing Al Capone in four episodes of the television series *The Untouchables* during 1960 and 1961 and for his role as Bull Ransom, the sympathetic prison guard in 1962's *Birdman of Alcatraz*, which starred Burt Lancaster and Karl Malden.

Born on August 13, 1920, in Griswold, Iowa, Brand enlisted as a private in Company F of the 129th Infantry Regiment, Illinois Army National Guard on October 23, 1939. He completed infantry training at Camp Carson, Colorado, and deployed to Europe. He landed in France in July 1944 and was assigned to Company B of the 331st Infantry Regiment, 83rd Infantry "Thunderbolt" Division.

Then-Sergeant Brand took part in the Ardennes, Rhineland, and Central European campaigns and was an infantry platoon sergeant when he was struck in his upper right arm by a bullet near the Weser River in Germany on April 7, 1945. He was decorated with both a Purple Heart and a Silver Star for gallantry in action.[4]

Brand left active duty in October 1945 and, after acting briefly in several off-Broadway productions, moved to Hollywood. He had supporting roles in *D.O.A.* in 1950, *Stalag 17* in 1953, and *Love Me Tender* in 1956, in which he killed the character played by Elvis Presley. Brand was more active as a television actor, however, appearing in more than one hundred shows as a guest star or recurring character, including *Bonanza*, *Daniel Boone*, *Fantasy Island*, *McCloud*, and *The Twilight Zone*. He also starred in the NBC television series *Laredo* between 1965 and 1967, playing Texas Ranger Reese Bennett.

Brand died on April 16, 1992, in Sacramento, California, at the age of 71.

Art Carney: Purple Heart—August 15, 1944

Arthur William Matthew Carney, who was wounded by shrapnel in France during World War II, is best known for playing Edward "Ed" Lillywhite Norton opposite comedian Jackie Gleason's Ralph Kramden on the television series *The Honeymooners*.

Born in Mount Vernon, New York, on November 4, 1918, Carney went to Normandy in July 1944 as a replacement in the 28th Infantry Division. On August 15, 1944, Carney was near St. Lo, France, and was a member of a .30-caliber machine-gun squad when he was hit in the right leg by mortar shrapnel. After receiving medical treatment in the field, he was returned to Great Britain and the United States for hospitalization. He is alleged to have said, "I never fired a shot and maybe never wanted to. I really cost the government money."[5]

After the war Carney got his start in radio and had a few parts in movies. His first big break came in television on *The Morey Amsterdam Show*. He then moved to *The Jackie Gleason Show* and made his name as the loyal, friendly but dimwitted Ed Norton on *The Honeymooners*. His typical greeting, "Hey-Hey, Ralphie boy!" became a classic line, and his comic style meshed perfectly with Gleason's more bombastic approach. Most critics consider *The Honeymooners* to be one of the greatest television comedies of all time, and Carney was critical to its success. He would eventually receive five Emmys for his supporting role.

During the 1960s Carney appeared on the television series *Batman* between 1966 and 1968, and also in various movies and on the stage. He reached the pinnacle of his career with 1974's *Harry and Tonto*, in which he portrayed an elderly widower who is forced from his apartment in New York City and eventually travels across the country with his cat. His performance in the film earned him an Oscar for Best Actor.

Carney died on November 9, 2003, in Chester, Connecticut, at the age of 85.

Charles E. Durning: Purple Heart—June 15, 1944

Charles E. Durning, who received his Purple Heart when he was wounded by a German mine in Normandy during World War II, is perhaps best known for his acting in 1982's *The Best Little Whorehouse in Texas* and 1983's *To Be or Not to Be*, since he was nominated for Best Supporting Actor Oscars for both films.

Born February 28, 1923, in Highland Falls, New York, Durning was drafted into the Army on January 27, 1943. He was twenty-one years old when he arrived in Normandy shortly after the Allied invasion on June 6,

1944. On June 15, he was severely wounded by fragments from an exploding German S-mine near Les Mare des Mares, France. According to his official military records, Durning was injured in his "legs, hand, chest and head."[6] Medically evacuated from France, he was hospitalized in the 122nd General Hospital in England.

Some publications claim that Durning was a "seventeen-year old infantryman" who landed on Omaha Beach on June 6, 1944, and that he subsequently "was taken prisoner during the Battle of the Bulge." There also is a story that Durning is "one of a few survivors" of the infamous murder of U.S. prisoners of war at Malmedy. Finally, there is a claim that he finished the war with three Purple Hearts.[7]

Durning's official military records, however, contain no evidence that he was on Omaha Beach on D-day, taken prisoner, or at the Malmedy massacre. His official records only reflect the award of one Purple Heart and a Silver Star for gallantry in action, a Good Conduct Medal, an American Campaign Medal, a European–African–Middle Eastern Campaign Medal, and a World War II Victory Medal. These same records show that, having recovered from his wounds, then–Private First Class Durning was honorably discharged at Fort Dix, New Jersey, on January 30, 1946.

After the war Durning began an acting career on stage, in film, and on television. He has more than 180 movies to his credit, including Robert Redford's *The Sting* in 1973 and Al Pacino's *Dog Day Afternoon* in 1975. In 1979 Durning played Doc Hopper, the principal villain in *The Muppet Movie*, and he was a suitor to a cross-dressing Dustin Hoffman in the hit 1982 film *Tootsie*. While Durning won neither of the Oscars for which he was nominated, he did receive the Screen Actors Guild Lifetime Achievement Award in 2008.

James Garner (née Bumgarner): Purple Hearts—September 1950 and April 23, 1951

James Garner, who received two Purple Hearts for wounds received during the Korean War, is best known for playing professional gambler Bret Maverick in the television series *Maverick* from 1957 to 1961 and detective Jim Rockford in *The Rockford Files* from 1974 to 1980.

Born James Bumgarner on April 7, 1928, in Norman, Oklahoma, Garner was an outstanding high school athlete in football, basketball, and track, but he left school before graduating to join the U.S. Merchant Marine. After completing a tour as a seaman, he returned to Oklahoma, finished high

James Garner, who starred as Bret Maverick in *Maverick* and as Jim Rockford in *The Rockford Files*, was twice wounded during the Korean War and was awarded two Purple Hearts. (James Garner)

school, and joined the Oklahoma National Guard. When the Korean War started in June 1950, then–Army Reserve Private Bumgarner was drafted and, after completing basic training as an infantryman, was assigned to the 5th Regimental Combat Team, 24th Infantry Division and sent to Korea.

On his second day in country, Garner was wounded by enemy fire while on patrol. As James E. Wise Jr. and Paul W. Wilderson III wrote in *Stars in Khaki*, he was "hit in the hand and face with enemy shrapnel." Garner "went back to an aid station and started picking bits of metal from his face using a jeep mirror." An officer who saw this "ordered him to go inside the aid station and have his wound recorded" and treated.[8] For that wound, Garner received his first Purple Heart.

On April 23, 1951, Garner was wounded a second time when U.S. Navy F9F Panther jets firing 20-mm rockets mistakenly attacked Garner and his fellow soldiers. He was hit in the buttocks, he had phosphorous burns on his neck, and his rifle was shattered. Believing that his foxhole offered little safety, Garner "scurried out of his position and jumped off the side of a cliff." When he came to a stop one hundred feet down the hill, he discovered that a South Korean soldier who had also had jumped off the cliff about the same time was with him.

Climbing back up to the ridge line, Garner, with no weapon but still wearing his helmet, and the South Korean, armed with a rifle, found that they were alone. They saw no one along the ridge. Garner could not speak Korean and the ROK (Republic of Korean) soldier spoke no English, but both sensed they should move south along the ridge line in order to catch up with their units.

The two eventually reached the valley they had occupied the day before only to come across a group of soldiers who were neither Americans nor South Koreans. The large group of idle North Korean soldiers paid little attention to the two soldiers as they passed, probably thinking the Korean, who held the rifle behind Garner, was one of them and the American was his prisoner. Six hours later, still on the move, they heard the familiar sounds of Sherman tanks approaching. The ROK soldier immediately gave his rifle to Garner and took Garner's helmet and placed it on his head. He positioned himself ahead of Garner, giving the appearance to the American troops that he was Garner's prisoner and thus ensuring his own safety. Garner later commented on the ROK soldier's actions, "That guy really picked up on all of it better than I did."[9]

Garner did not receive the Purple Heart for the wounds he received in that friendly-fire incident until January 24, 1983, when Army Maj. Gen. Lyle J. Barker Jr. presented a Purple Heart with oak leaf cluster to Garner during an award ceremony in the offices of Lorimar Productions in Los Angeles. Said Garner at the ceremony, "After 32 years it's better to receive this now than posthumously.... It is indeed an honor and I tried to serve my country to the best of my ability."[10]

After leaving Korea Garner spent nine months in Japan working in an Army post office before being honorably discharged from the Army in June 1952. When he took off his uniform, he was wearing the Combat Infantryman Badge, Purple Heart, Korean Service Medal, United Nations Service Medal, and National Defense Service Medal.

Garner worked briefly with his father in the carpet business before beginning his acting career on the stage. He also had several roles in movies, including *Sayonara* in 1957, in which he played a supporting role as a Marine officer opposite Marlon Brando. Garner's big break came in television when, in 1957, he got the lead part of professional gambler Bret Maverick in the Warner Brothers western-comedy *Maverick*. By that time he had legally changed his surname to Garner, apparently after a studio publicity release used that name to identify him.

Through the late 1950s and 1960s Garner starred in a variety of films, including *Darby's Rangers* in 1958, *Up Periscope* in 1959, *Boys' Night Out* in 1962, *The Great Escape* in 1963, *The Americanization of Emily* in 1964, *Grand Prix* in 1966, and *Support Your Local Sheriff!* in 1969. He again became a household name in 1974, when he appeared as private investigator Jim Rockford in *The Rockford Files*. The show ran for six seasons, and Garner received an Emmy for Best Actor in 1977. Garner later starred in a series of *Rockford Files* television movies during the 1990s.

Although he had made his name in television, Garner was nominated for an Oscar for Best Actor in a Leading Role in 1985, when he played opposite Sally Field in *Murphy's Romance*. In 2000 he appeared in the movie *Space Cowboys* with Clint Eastwood, Tommy Lee Jones, and Donald Sutherland, and in 2004, Garner received a Screen Actors Guild nomination for Outstanding Performance by a Male Actor in a Supporting Role for his work in the movie version of Nicholas Sparks' novel *The Notebook*.

Lee Marvin: Purple Heart—June 18, 1944

Lee Marvin, who was wounded while fighting as a Marine on Saipan during World War II, was an actor who starred in a variety of films and television shows, including 1965's *Cat Ballou*, for which he won an Oscar for Best Actor, and 1967's *The Dirty Dozen*.

Born in New York City on February 19, 1924, Marvin enlisted in the Marine Corps on August 12, 1942. He did his recruit training at Parris Island and, in January 1944, shipped out to the Pacific with the 4th Marine Division.

On June 15, 1944, then–Private First Class Marvin waded ashore on Saipan. As he told author Donald Zec in 1980, the combat with the Japanese was ferocious. Marvin, who was with I Company of the 3rd Battalion, 24th Marines, remembered that on June 18, the day he was wounded, his company "had started out with 247 men and fifteen minutes later, there was six of us.... Anyway, it was my turn to get nailed.... There are two prominent parts in view to the enemy—your head and your ass. If you present one, you get killed. If you raise the other, you get shot in the ass. I got shot in the ass."[11]

Marvin was awarded his Purple Heart while in a Guadalcanal naval hospital, and he spent a total of thirteen months receiving medical treatment before being honorably discharged on July 24, 1945. The GI Bill paid for formal acting classes at the American Theater Wing in New York, and Marvin appeared in both on- and off-Broadway productions from 1948 to 1950.

After starting in movies and television in 1950, Marvin was often typecast as a tough guy. He appeared as a villain or an outlaw in *The Big Heat* in 1953, *The Wild One* in 1953, and *The Man Who Shot Liberty Valance* in 1962. While the role earned him no major individual awards, Lee is probably best known today for playing the battle-hardened Maj. John Reisman in the classic war film *The Dirty Dozen*. The story about Marvin selecting twelve soldiers who have been sentenced to death and leading them on a suicidal top-secret mission in France in early 1944 may have been far-fetched, but it was wildly popular with young male audiences.[12]

Marvin died on August 27, 1987, and is buried at Arlington National Cemetery.[13]

Audie L. Murphy: Purple Hearts—September 14–15, 1944; October 1944; and January 25, 1945

Audie Leon Murphy, who received three Purple Hearts in addition to a Medal of Honor, was one of the most decorated soldiers in U.S. history. He also was an actor and made more than forty films, including *Red Badge of Courage* in

1951 and 1955's *To Hell and Back*, the story of his own experiences in combat during World War II.

Born in Hunt County, near Kingston, Texas, on June 20, 1924, Murphy was the son of poor sharecroppers and had only five years of formal schooling. In early June 1941 he lied about his age (he was only 16 years old) and attempted to enlist in the Marine Corps but, standing just five foot five inches, was rejected as being too short.. Reluctantly, he joined the Army and, after completing basic training as an infantryman at Camp Wolters, Texas, shipped overseas to join the 15th Regiment, 3rd Infantry Division. Murphy first saw combat in Sicily in July 1943 as a part of Company B of the 1st Battalion, and he demonstrated that he was not only a good soldier but understood small-unit tactics. Murphy subsequently fought at Salerno and at Anzio and was part of the Allied force that captured Rome.

Murphy left Italy with the rest of the 3rd Infantry Division and landed in southern France as part of Operation Anvil-Dragoon. He received his first Purple Heart for wounds he suffered on September 14–15, 1944, while fighting near Vy-les-Lure, France. Murphy was "caught in (a) mortar barrage. . . . While he waited for the fire to clear, a shell exploded at his feet and knocked him unconscious. . . . A fragment of metal pierced his foot."[14]

Murphy, having received a battlefield commission as a second lieutenant, was wounded in action again, and received a second Purple Heart, in October 1944. At that time Murphy was leading his platoon through a forest. An enemy sniper shot and killed Murphy's radioman, and a second bullet ricocheted off a tree and struck Murphy in his right hip. The sniper then tried to kill Murphy, who was lying prone on the ground. "The German tried to finish him off with a shot through the helmet," Wise and Wilderson wrote in *Stars in Khaki*. "But Murphy was not in his helmet and before the German could get off another round, Murphy swung around and fired with his carbine pistol-fashion, dropping the enemy soldier with a well-placed bullet through the German's head."[15]

After spending three months in the hospital recovering from the hip wound, Murphy rejoined Company B on January 23, 1945. Two days later he was wounded a third time, being hit by fragments from a German mortar round that killed two others nearby. This resulted in a third award of the Purple Heart.

Murphy earned lasting fame as a soldier on January 27, 1945, near the village of Holtzwihr. After the more-senior officer went down with a wound, Murphy assumed command of his company as it came under fierce attack. As the citation for Murphy's Medal of Honor explains:

2nd Lt. Murphy commanded Company B, which was attacked by 6 tanks and waves of infantry. 2nd Lt. Murphy ordered his men to withdraw to prepared positions in a woods, while he remained forward at his command post and continued to give fire directions to the artillery by telephone. Behind him, to his right, 1 of our tank destroyers received a direct hit and began to burn. Its crew withdrew to the woods. 2nd Lt. Murphy continued to direct artillery fire which killed large numbers of the advancing enemy infantry. With the enemy tanks abreast of his position, 2nd Lt. Murphy climbed on the burning tank destroyer, which was in danger of blowing up at any moment, and employed its .50 caliber machinegun against the enemy. He was alone and exposed to German fire from 3 sides, but his deadly fire killed dozens of Germans and caused their infantry attack to waver. The enemy tanks, losing infantry support, began to fall back. For an hour the Germans tried every available weapon to eliminate 2nd Lt. Murphy, but he continued to hold his position and wiped out a squad which was trying to creep up unnoticed on his right flank. Germans reached as close as 10 yards, only to be mowed down by his fire. He received a leg wound, but ignored it and continued the single-handed fight until his ammunition was exhausted. He then made his way to his company, refused medical attention, and organized the company in a counterattack which forced the Germans to withdraw. His directing of artillery fire wiped out many of the enemy; he killed or wounded about 50. 2nd Lt. Murphy's indomitable courage and his refusal to give an inch of ground saved his company from possible encirclement and destruction, and enabled it to hold the woods which had been the enemy's objective.[16]

Although the citation for his Medal of Honor indicates that Murphy had received a leg wound, which would have merited the award of a fourth Purple Heart, this apparently was not true. Rather, "by some miracle, Murphy had not been hit by the murderous enemy fire, but his old hip wounds had opened and he was bleeding profusely."[17]

When the fighting ended in Europe in May 1945, Murphy was still a month shy of his twenty-first birthday. Yet this young soldier was the Army's most-decorated soldier. In addition to a Medal of Honor and three Purple Hearts, he also had been awarded a Distinguished Service Cross, two Silver Stars, the Legion of Merit, and two Bronze Star Medals.

Murphy returned to the United States as a hero. His face graced the July 16, 1945, cover of *Life* magazine, and, after visiting Hollywood at the invitation of actor James Cagney, Murphy began appearing in movies. For the next twenty years Murphy had parts in more than forty movies. His first role was in 1948's *Beyond Glory*. Many critics consider his best performance to have been in *Red Badge of Courage* in 1951, but his portrayal of himself in *To Hell and Back* in 1955 also received high marks.

After retiring from acting, Murphy began a less-than-successful career as a businessman. He also spoke publicly about the psychological effects that combat had had on him, admitting to suffering what psychologists now recognize as PTSD and to sleeping with a pistol under his pillow. Murphy was killed when the private plane in which he was a passenger crashed near Roanoke, Virginia, on May 28, 1971. He was forty-six years old at the time of his death.

Murphy is buried at Arlington National Cemetery, and a special walkway has been built to his government-issued headstone. The stone marker records that he was an Army major—Murphy had joined the Army Reserve in 1950 and reached this rank—but it is too small to list all his awards and decorations.[18]

Peter J. Ortiz: Purple Heart—March 1943[19]

Peter Julien "Pete" Ortiz, who received the Purple Heart while fighting as a Marine officer attached to the Office of Strategic Services (OSS), also had a distinguished career in Hollywood as an actor and technical advisor.

Born in New York City on July 5, 1913, to a French father and an American mother, Ortiz grew up in France. He attended both high school and college there and spoke fluent French. He joined the French Foreign Legion in 1932, when he was nineteen years old, and was decorated for heroism in combat while serving as a legionnaire.

Ortiz left the Legion at the end of his five-year commitment in 1937 after attaining the position of acting lieutenant in command of an armored car squadron. He then moved to Hollywood and worked for a year at 20th Century Fox Film Corporation as a technical adviser on movies "with Foreign Legion details."[20] But when fighting began in Europe in 1939, Ortiz returned to France and reenlisted as a legionnaire. In June 1940 Ortiz was wounded in action and captured by the Germans. He spent fifteen months as a prisoner of war in Germany, Poland, and Austria before escaping to Portugal in September 1941.

After returning to the United States, Ortiz enlisted in the Marine Corps in June 1942. He arrived at boot camp at Parris Island wearing his French decorations and medals, which caught the attention of Marine Corps head-quarters.[21] Unsurprisingly, given his background and proven abilities, Ortiz was destined for greater responsibility.

On July 14, 1942, Col. Louis R. Jones, who was then serving as chief of staff at Parris Island, wrote to the commandant of the Marine Corps that Ortiz should be given a commission. Noted Jones:

> Private Ortiz had made an extremely favorable impression upon the under-signed. His knowledge of military matters is far beyond that of the normal recruit instructor. Ortiz is a very well set up man and makes an excellent appearance. The undersigned is glad to recommend Ortiz for a commission in the Marine Corps Reserve and is of the opinion that he would be a decided addition to the Reserve Officer list. In my opinion he has the mental, moral, professional, and physical qualifications for the office for which he has made application.[22]

The result was that Ortiz was offered a commission as a reserve second lieutenant. He took his oath on August 16, 1942, with date of rank July 24, 1942, and then completed training at the Parachute School at Camp Lejeune.

The Corps then offered Ortiz to the Army. He was assigned to the OSS, deployed to Tunisia, and led Arab tribesmen on reconnaissance missions. Ortiz received his first Purple Heart after being wounded in mid-March 1943. According to a March 24, 1943, letter from OSS Director William J. Donovan to the commandant of the Marine Corps, then-Captain Ortiz was "on reconnaissance . . . when he was severely wounded in the right hand while engaged in a personal encounter with a German patrol. He dispersed the patrol with grenades and . . . is making good recovery in a hospital at Algiers. The Purple Heart is awarded to him."[23]

In July 1943 Ortiz was attached to U.S. Naval Command, OSS, in London. On January 8, 1944, he parachuted into occupied France. His citation for his first Navy Cross explains that Ortiz's mission was to "reorganize existing Maquis (French Resistance) groups and organize additional groups in the region of Rhone." Ortiz "by his tact, resourcefulness and leadership . . . effected the acceptance of the mission by the local resistance leaders . . . and organized parachute operations for the delivery of arms, ammunition and equipment."[24]

The Gestapo learned that Ortiz was operating with the French Resistance, chiefly because he insisted on wearing his Marine Corps captain's uniform—and not civilian clothing. As Robert E. Mattingly wrote in *Herringbone Cloak—GI Dagger:*

It might be reasonable to suppose that the team remained hidden in the high country, but this was not the case. Ortiz in particular was fond of going straight into the German-occupied towns. On one occasion, he strolled into a cafe dressed in a long cape. Several Germans were drinking and cursing the Maquis. One mentioned the fate which would befall the "filthy American swine" (Ortiz) when he was caught. This proved a great mistake. Captain Ortiz threw back the cape revealing his Marine uniform. In each hand he held a .45 automatic. When the shooting stopped, there were fewer Nazis to plan his capture and Ortiz was gone into the night.[25]

Although there are various tellings of this episode, it appears to be true to the extent that there was a gunfight in a cafe, and the Germans lost.

Despite the increased danger of being captured—and, more than likely, executed—by the enemy, Ortiz also "took a heavy responsibility and ran great risks in looking after four R.A.F. (Royal Air Force) officers who had been brought down in his neighborhood." He "voluntarily accompanied these men to the Spanish border" and then returned to his duties. The British would later award Ortiz the Order of the British Empire "for his gallant and brave work."[26]

Ortiz returned to England in May 1944 but was back in France on August 1, 1944, when he parachuted behind German lines into the Savoie Department of France. While "valiantly" continuing "his work in coordinating and leading resistance groups" in that area, Ortiz and his team "were attacked and surrounded during a special mission designed to immobilize enemy reinforcements stationed that area." On August 16, 1944, near Haute Savoie, Ortiz again showed extraordinary heroism when, "in an effort to spare villagers severe reprisals by the Gestapo," he surrendered. Ortiz was imprisoned and, although "subject to numerous interrogations, he divulged nothing, and the story of this intrepid Marine Major and his team (became) a brilliant legend in that section of France where acts of bravery were considered commonplace."[27]

Ortiz spent the remainder of the war at various prison camps in France and Germany and was not liberated until April 27, 1945.

Then-Major Ortiz left active duty in December 1945 and settled in La Jolla, California. He then resumed his Hollywood career, working primarily with director John Ford. He had small acting roles in *The Outcast* (1954), *The Wings of Eagles* (1957), *Rio Grande* (1950), and *Retreat Hell!* (1952), in which he played a Marine officer at the Chosin Reservoir battle of 1950. Additionally, Ortiz's own wartime service aiding the French Resistance and rescuing the downed RAF pilots provided the basic story for two other films: 1947's *13 Rue Madeleine*, which starred James Cagney, and 1952's *Operation Secret*, which starred Cornell Wilde.

Ortiz died in Prescott, Arizona, on May 16, 1988. He is buried at Arlington National Cemetery.[28]

Ernest T. Pyle: Purple Heart—April 18, 1945

See chapter 7, "Civilians: World War II to the War on Terrorism."

POLITICIANS

Maurice Britt: Purple Hearts—September 1943; November 10, 1943; and January 24, 1944

Maurice "Footsie" Britt was wounded twice in combat during World War II; once by shrapnel from a mortar shell in September 1943, and again in November 1943, when he was hit by shrapnel from German grenades. Britt received his third Purple Heart in January 1944, when the blast from an armor piercing shell tore off his right arm at the elbow and broke his leg. Britt's war record—which included awards of the Medal of Honor, Distinguished Service Cross, and Silver Star—helped him when he entered state politics, and he became the first Republican elected lieutenant governor in Arkansas since Reconstruction when he won that office in 1966.

Born in Carlisle, Arkansas, Britt was a college football All-American and played professionally with the Detroit Lions. At the end of the 1942 football season, Britt reported for duty as an Army second lieutenant and joined Company L of the 30th Infantry Regiment, 3rd Infantry Division.

Britt served as a platoon leader in North Africa in 1942 and in Sicily in 1943. On September 19, 1943, he landed with his unit at Salerno, Italy and assumed command of Company L after its commander was wounded. On September 22 Britt received the Silver Star when he single-handedly knocked out a German machine-gun emplacement that was holding up the advance. He "also earned his first Purple Heart, when later during the advance, a mortar shell landed nearby and his arm caught a piece of shrapnel."[29]

On November 10, 1943, Britt was wounded a second time in savage fighting for the German-held hill of Monte Rotundo, which Britt's regiment had been ordered to seize. During the firefight Britt threw between ten and twelve grenades at the Germans and fired seventy-five rounds from his carbine, changing clips five times before exhausting his ammunition. But he was also badly injured; "his face, chest and hands were covered from wounds caused by three German 'potato masher' grenades." Britt also had been shot "and was bleeding through his uniform in four different places."[30] For his extraordinary heroism at Monte Rotundo, Britt would later be awarded a Medal of Honor. Then-Captain Britt received his third Purple Heart shortly after he and the 30th Infantry Regiment landed at Anzio. On January 24, 1944, a German tank fired an armor-piercing shell, and the blast tore off the lower part of Britt's right arm. He would later receive a Distinguished Service Cross for his gallantry in combat during that time.

After being medically evacuated to the United States, Britt left active duty and returned to the University of Arkansas before starting an aluminum products manufacturing firm. As Wolfgang Saxon wrote in the *New York Times*, Britt subsequently entered state politics as a Republican and "paved the way for a new generation of Arkansas politicians, including Democrats in a new mold, like Bill Clinton." Britt served two terms as lieutenant governor and was "known for his robust and jolly campaign style."[31] He later spent fourteen years heading the Arkansas Small Business Administration.

Britt died on November 26, 1995, at the age of 76.

Robert J. Dole: Purple Heart—April 1944

Robert Joseph "Bob" Dole, who was twice wounded in action while serving as an infantry officer in the 10th Mountain Division in Italy during World War II, is best known for his years as a Republican U.S. Senator representing Kansas from 1968 to 1996. He also was the Republican Party's candidate for U.S. president in 1996.

Born in Russell, Kansas, on July 22, 1923, Dole graduated from high school in 1941 and enrolled at the University of Kansas that fall. According to Dole's official Website, he joined the Army Enlisted Reserve Corps in 1942 and, after interrupting his studies for active duty, earned a commission as an infantry second lieutenant. In April 1945 Dole was fighting in northern Italy when one of the soldiers in his platoon was shot. Dole "crawled out of his foxhole to help him, but it was too late . . . and Dole was hit by machine gun fire in the upper right back and his right arm was so badly damaged that it was unrecognizable."[32]

While a medic gave Dole a shot of morphine and—using Dole's blood—marked his forehead with an "M" to alert other medical personnel not to administer more morphine, Dole was not expected to survive. After nine long hours, however, the young officer was taken to the 15th Evacuation Hospital. It took three years and nine months for Dole to recover. Although he took part in extensive physical therapy during his recuperation to strengthen his injured right arm, he was no longer able to write with his right hand and, consequently, had to learn how to write with his left hand. During his hospitalization at Percy Jones Army Hospital in Battle Creek, Michigan, he met another badly wounded soldier who also would go on to have a successful career in politics: Hawaiian-native Daniel Inouye.

After being discharged from the hospital, Dole returned to Kansas, where he completed college. He was elected to the Kansas House of Representatives in 1950 and subsequently finished law school in 1952. He practiced law in his hometown of Russell before being elected to the U.S. House of Representatives in 1960. Dole was elected to the Senate in 1968 and served until 1996, when he resigned to campaign for U.S. president as the Republican Party's nominee.

Dole was awarded the Presidential Medal of Freedom in January 1997 and today practices law in Washington, D.C. His wife, Elizabeth H. Dole, was a Republican U.S. senator from North Carolina between 2002 and 2008.[33]

William J. Donovan: Purple Heart—October 14–15, 1918

William Joseph "Wild Bill" Donovan, who was wounded in combat in France during World War I and who received a Medal of Honor for his extraordinary heroism in combat, is best remembered as the founder of the OSS, the predecessor of the Central Intelligence Agency. He also served as U.S. ambassador to Thailand in 1953.

Born on New Year's Day 1883 in Buffalo, New York, Donovan graduated from Columbia University in 1905 and completed law school there in 1908. He then became a successful Wall Street lawyer. When the United States entered World War I in April 1917, however, the thirty-four-year-old Donovan, who had previously soldiered in the New York State Militia, left civilian life for duty with the Army in France.

Then–Lieutenant Colonel Donovan was with the 16th Infantry, 42nd Division when, on October 14–15, 1918, he "personally led the assaulting wave" of U.S. soldiers "in an attack upon a very strongly organized position." As the citation for his Medal of Honor explains, "When our troops were suffering heavy casualties he encouraged all near him by his example, moving among his men in exposed positions, reorganizing decimated platoons, and accompanying them forward in attacks. When he was wounded in the leg by machine-gun bullets, he refused to be evacuated and continued with his unit until it withdrew to a less exposed position."[34]

Brig. Gen. William J. "Wild Bill" Donovan, best remembered as the founder of the Office of Strategic Services—the predecessor of the Central Intelligence Agency—was wounded in France in October 1918. (National Archives and Records Administration)

Alexander M. Haig Jr.: Purple Heart—March 31–April 2, 1967

Alexander Meigs Haig Jr. was wounded in action in Vietnam while commanding the 1st Battalion, 26th Infantry. Although he retired from the Army as a four-star general, he is perhaps better known for his service as White House chief of staff and secretary of state.

Born in Pennsylvania on December 2, 1924, Haig grew up in the Philadelphia suburb of Bala Cynwyd. After attending the University of Notre Dame for one year, nineteen-year-old Haig entered the U.S. Military Academy. He did not excel as a cadet, graduating 214th in the 310-member class of 1947. But anyone who thought Haig would be a mediocre officer was soon mistaken. Then-Lieutenant Haig first served in Japan on General MacArthur's staff and subsequently deployed to Korea at the outbreak of hostilities on the peninsula. He proved to be an outstanding officer, as evidenced by his service as aide-de-camp to the X Corps commander Lt. Gen. Edward M. Almond and by his receipt of two Silver Stars for gallantry in action and a Bronze Star Medal with Combat *V* for valor.

After completing studies at the Army War College in 1966, then–Lieutenant Colonel Haig deployed to Vietnam, where he first served as operations officer (G-3) for the 1st Infantry Division before taking command of the 1st Battalion, 26th Infantry. Between March 31, 1967, and April 2, 1967, Haig again proved that he was an outstanding combat commander. As George J. Church wrote in a *Time* magazine cover story on Haig in 1981, "He led his battalion to victory in the battle of Ap Gu, one of the major engagements in the biggest American offensive of the time. It was a classic Vietnam operation; Haig's troops were helicoptered into an area thought to be infested with Viet Cong guerrillas, drew an enemy attack and held their ground in bloody hand-to-hand fighting, while Haig called in heavy artillery and air strikes."[35]

Haig later received a Distinguished Service Cross—second only to the Medal of Honor in the hierarchy of U.S. military awards and decorations—for his heroism at Ap Gu. The citation for that award explains that after two of his battalion's companies were pinned down by a much larger Viet Cong force, Haig "landed amid a hail of fire, personally took charge of the units, called for artillery and air fire support and succeeded in soundly defeating the insurgent force." The next day, the enemy resumed the attack with "a series of human wave assaults." Yet Haig continually "braved intense hostile fire to survey the battlefield" and "inspire his men to fight with previously unimagined power."[36] He was wounded during the Battle of Ap Gu and subsequently received a Purple Heart. By the end of his one-year tour in Vietnam, Haig had also received two Legions of Merit, three Distinguished Flying Crosses, and twenty-four Air Medals.

In 1969 Haig went to the White House, where he served as military assistant to Henry Kissinger, who was President Richard M. Nixon's presidential assistant for national security affairs. Haig was promoted the following year to deputy assistant to the president for national security affairs and remained in this high-profile position until January 1973, when he was appointed vice chief of staff of the Army.

Five months later, however, in May 1973, then-General Haig retired from the Army in order to become White House chief of staff under Nixon. For the next fourteen months, as the Watergate scandal grew in intensity, Haig "in effect held the White House together while Nixon battled to stave off impeachment," and he "is widely credited with having persuaded Nixon . . . to resign."[37] Further, no one disputes that Haig played a significant role in ensuring that there was a smooth transfer of power from President Nixon to President Ford.[38] Although Haig briefly continued as White House chief of staff under President Gerald Ford, he left Washington in 1974 to take up duties in Europe as NATO commander.

After retiring again in June 1979, Haig spent a year as president of United Technologies Corporation. In January 1981, however, President Reagan selected Haig to be his secretary of state and, after a stormy confirmation hearing, Haig was confirmed by a Senate vote of 93–6.

Haig's tenure at the State Department was not without trouble, however. "He was almost constantly fighting," *Time* reported in 1984, and he resigned abruptly in July 1982. Most observers concluded that he had lost Reagan's confidence, and his conduct in claiming he was "in charge" on March 30, 1981, when the president was shot in an assassination attempt, did not help his stature among his colleagues.[39] Haig died on February 20, 2010.

Charles T. Hagel: Purple Hearts—1967–1968

Charles Timothy "Chuck" Hagel, who was twice wounded while serving as an infantryman in Vietnam from 1967 to 1968, is best known as a Republican U.S. senator from Nebraska.

Born in North Platte, Nebraska, in October 1946, Hagel completed high school and, interested in a broadcasting career, then attended the Brown Institute of Radio and Television in Mendota Heights, Minnesota, from which he graduated in 1966. Hagel next served as an infantry sergeant in Vietnam from 1967 to 1968, and was twice wounded in combat. In addition to a Purple Heart with oak leaf cluster, Hagel also received an Army Commendation Medal, Vietnamese Cross of Gallantry, and Combat Infantryman Badge.

After being honorably discharged from the Army, Hagel returned to Omaha, where he was a newscaster and talk show host from 1969 to 1971. He also completed his studies at the University of Nebraska and got his first taste of politics when he was hired as an administrative assistant to U.S. Rep. John Y. McCollister (R-Neb.). Hagel later served as a deputy administrator in the U.S. Department of Veterans Affairs from 1981 to 1982.

Hagel's big break on the national stage came in 1996, when he ran success-fully for the U.S. Senate, defeating Ben Nelson, who was then the sitting governor of Nebraska. Hagel was reelected in 2002 with more than 83 percent of the vote, which stands as the largest ever margin of victory in any statewide race in Nebraska. Hagel left office in January 2009. Having said during his first campaign for senator that he would only serve two terms, he was not a candidate for reelection in 2008.[40]

Daniel K. Inouye: Purple Heart—April 21, 1945

Daniel Ken Inouye was wounded in action while serving with the Army in Italy in 1944. He is best known as a politician and long-serving U.S. senator from Hawaii.

Born in Honolulu on September 7, 1924, Inouye grew up in Hawaii, and, in the aftermath of the Japanese attack on the islands, he used his first aid training to assist the wounded. According to his official U.S. Senate biography, Inouye enlisted in the Army in March 1943 after his 18th birthday and, after completing basic training as an infantryman, deployed to Italy with the 442nd "Go-For-Broke" Regimental Combat Team. Inouye then "slogged through nearly three bloody months of the Rome–Arno campaign with the U.S. Fifth Army and established himself as an outstanding patrol leader."[41]

He moved with his unit from Italy to France in late 1944 and saw more hard combat before returning to Italy in March 1945. By that time, Inouye had received a battlefield commission as a second lieutenant and been awarded a Bronze Star Medal.

On April 21, 1945, while leading his platoon against the enemy at San Terenzo, Inouye was badly wounded when he was hit in the stomach by a bullet that exited from his back and barely missed his spine. Despite this devastating injury he continued his attack and was shot in his right arm as he was about to hurl a grenade. Undeterred, Inouye threw the grenade with his left hand. He then continued to fire his machine gun until he and his fellow soldiers had overrun the enemy. For his extraordinary heroism that day, Inouye received a Distinguished Service Cross, the Army's second highest award for combat heroism.

After twenty months in Army hospitals, Inouye returned to Hawaii and left active duty as a captain. He then enrolled at the University of Hawaii and, after graduation, returned to the mainland and earned a degree from the George Washington University School of Law in Washington, D.C. Inouye entered politics in 1954 and was elected to Hawaii's Territorial House of Representatives. He became Hawaii's first congressman in 1959 and was reelected to the U.S. House for a full term in 1960. He entered the U.S. Senate in 1962 and is today one of the nation's most senior senators.[42]

In June 2000 Inouye's Distinguished Service Cross—along with twenty other such medals that had been awarded to Asian Americans in World War II—was upgraded to a Medal of Honor.[43]

John F. Kennedy: Purple Heart—August 2, 1943

John Fitzgerald "Jack" Kennedy was wounded in action while serving as a Navy motor torpedo boat commander during World War II. He is best known, however, as a politician who served as the 35th U.S. president from 1961 to 1963.

Born on May 29, 1917, Kennedy joined the Navy prior to the Japanese attack on Pearl Harbor and, after receiving motor torpedo boat training, deployed to the Pacific. On August 2, 1943, then–Lieutenant (junior grade) Kennedy was in command of *PT-109* and was participating in a nighttime patrol near New Georgia in the Solomon Islands. After the Japanese destroyer *Amagiri* collided with Kennedy's boat—cutting it in half and sinking it—two sailors were lost, and two more were badly wounded. Kennedy, however, "unhesitatingly braved the difficulties and hazards of darkness to direct rescue operations, swimming many hours to secure aid and food after he had succeeded in getting his crew ashore" to a nearby island.[44] Six days later Kennedy and the remaining crewmembers were rescued. For his heroism, Kennedy was awarded a Navy and Marine Corps Medal, the highest award for noncombat valor, and a Purple Heart for the injuries he received in the collision.

After the war Kennedy's brush with death was popularized in magazines and newspapers, and his status as a war hero helped smooth his entry into politics in Massachusetts. Kennedy was elected to the U.S. House of Representatives in 1947, and to the U.S. Senate in 1953. He then defeated sitting vice president and Republican candidate Richard Nixon for the presidency in 1960.

Kennedy's presidency was eventful—encompassing the Bay of Pigs invasion in 1961, the construction of the Berlin Wall in 1961, and the Cuban

John F. Kennedy is the only U.S. president to have been awarded the Purple Heart. (Naval Historical Center)

Missile Crisis in 1962—but short-lived. He was assassinated in Dallas on November 22, 1963. Despite the passage of time, Kennedy remains one of the most popular presidents.

John McCain: Purple Heart—October 26, 1967

John Sidney McCain III was wounded when his airplane was shot down over North Vietnam. He is best known as a politician and has served in the U.S. Senate since 1986. He also was the Republican candidate for president in 2008.

Born on August 29, 1936, McCain graduated from the U.S. Naval Academy in 1958 and began a career as a naval aviator. According to his official Senate biography, McCain was on his twenty-third bombing mission over North Vietnam on October 26, 1967, when "a missile struck his plane and forced him to eject, knocking him unconscious and breaking both his arms and his leg."[45] He later received a Purple Heart for these injuries.

He was taken as a POW and eventually confined in Hanoi, where he was denied medical treatment and was repeatedly tortured by the North Vietnamese. For his heroism while imprisoned, McCain would later be awarded a Silver Star and Legion of Merit.

After being released from captivity in 1973, McCain remained in the Navy and last served as naval liaison to the U.S. Senate before retiring from active duty in 1981. He was elected to the House of Representatives from Arizona in 1982 and, after two terms there, was elected to the U.S. Senate. He sought the Republican nomination for president three times, reaching the top of the ticket in 2008.

Colin L. Powell: Purple Heart—July 23, 1963

Colin Luther Powell received his Purple Heart for wounds he received in Vietnam in 1963. He subsequently had a distinguished career in the Army, which culminated in his service as chairman of the Joint Chiefs of Staff. After retiring from active duty, Powell embarked on a political career and was U.S. secretary of state from 2001 to 2005.

Born on April 5, 1937, in Harlem, Powell graduated from the City College of New York in 1958. Having also been enrolled in the ROTC program, Powell was commissioned as an infantry second lieutenant.

On Christmas Day 1962, a twenty-five-year-old Powell arrived in South Vietnam and, after a few days of indoctrination in Saigon, headed north to "serve as an advisor to the four hundred-man 2nd Battalion, 3rd Infantry Regiment, 1st Division," a South Vietnamese Army unit "posted in the tropical forest along the Laotian border at a place called A Shau."[46] Powell saw

Gen. Colin L. Powell was awarded the Purple Heart as the result of wounds received in Vietnam in 1963. After retiring as a four-star general, Powell became America's top statesman as U.S. secretary of state. (U.S. Army)

considerable combat as an advisor but was not wounded in a firefight. Rather, he was awarded his Purple Heart for injuries received when he "stepped into a punji trap" on July 23, 1963. The Viet Cong routinely set up such booby traps along well-traveled trails, and the sharp punji sticks in these traps were poisoned by dipping them in dung. In Powell's case, a punji pierced his boot and went into his foot, causing an infection that required his evacuation to a hospital for treatment.[47]

Then-Major Powell returned to Vietnam in July 1968 and initially was assigned as the executive officer of the 3rd Battalion, 1st Infantry, 11th Infantry Brigade, which was part of the 23rd Infantry "American" Division. He subsequently became that division's G-3 and was serving in that position on November 16, 1968, when the UH-1H helicopter in which he was traveling crashed. Powell broke his ankle and had some lacerations, but he was in good enough shape to rescue several survivors, including Maj. Gen. Charles M. Gettys, the division commander.[48] Powell later received a Soldier's Medal for his noncombat heroism that day.[49]

Powell subsequently held a series of prestigious assignments in Washington, D.C., including a White House Fellowship in 1972–1973 and membership on the National Security Council staff during the Carter administration. He commanded a battalion in Korea, a brigade at Fort Campbell, and a corps in Germany.

In 1987 then–Lieutenant General Powell was appointed as President Reagan's national security advisor. Powell received his fourth star in 1989, becoming one of only a few soldiers to reach that rank without commanding a division. After briefly commanding Army Forces Command in Atlanta, he returned to Washington to assume duties as chairman of the Joint Chiefs of Staff. The successful Allied defense of Saudi Arabia and Kuwait during Operation Desert Shield and Operation Desert Storm in 1990 and 1991 occurred during his tenure.

Although Powell retired from active duty in 1993, his service to the nation was not at an end. President George W. Bush selected him to be U.S. secretary of state, and Powell served as America's chief diplomat from January 2001 to January 2005.

Eric K. Shinseki: Purple Hearts—September 1966 and 1970
Eric Ken Shinseki was twice wounded in Vietnam and retired as a four-star general and Army chief of staff. In 2008 he began a political career as the secretary of veterans affairs.

Born in Honolulu on November 28, 1942, Shinseki graduated from the U.S. Military Academy in 1965. After completing the Artillery Officer Basic Course, then-Lieutenant Shinseki deployed to Vietnam and joined the 2nd Battalion, 9th Field Artillery, 25th Infantry Division as a forward observer. He was wounded in action and was awarded his first Purple Heart.

Shinseki then served two years in Hawaii as assistant secretary and, later, secretary to the General Staff, U.S. Army Hawaii. After completing the Armor Officer Advanced Course, then-Captain Shinseki returned to South Vietnam in 1969 to take command of Troop A, 3rd Squadron, 5th Cavalry Regiment. He received a second Purple Heart during this tour of duty after he stepped on a land mine and lost part of his foot.

Shinseki subsequently served in a variety of increasingly important assignments, including command of a battalion (3rd Squadron, 7th Cavalry, Schweinfurt, Germany), brigade (2nd Brigade, 3rd Infantry Division, Kitzingen, Germany), and division (1st Cavalry Division, Fort Hood). In July 1996 then–Lieutenant General Shinseki became the Army's deputy chief of staff for operations. A year later, he received his fourth star and a new assignment as commanding general of U.S. Army Europe and the Seventh Army. Shinseki subsequently served as vice chief of staff of the Army before becoming the 34th chief of staff of the Army in June 1998.

As chief of staff Shinseki pushed the Army to modernize by developing the wheeled-vehicle Stryker Force Brigade Combat Teams. He retired from active duty in June 2003 and remains the only officer of Japanese American or Asian American ancestry to serve as the most senior officer in the Army.[50]

In 2008 President Barak H. Obama named Shinseki to be the seventh secretary of veterans affairs.

James B. Stockdale: Purple Hearts—September 9, 1965, and September 1969

Medal of Honor recipient and POW in North Vietnam for seven years, James Bond Stockdale was also the Reform Party's candidate for U.S. vice president in 1992.

Born December 23, 1923, in Abington, Illinois, Stockdale graduated from the U.S. Naval Academy in 1947 and attended naval flight school at Pensacola. He was an outstanding pilot and, according to the "official site for Admiral James Stockdale" he "was the first to amass more than one thousand hours in the F-8U Crusader, the Navy's hottest fighter."[51]

On August 6, 1964, flying off the carrier USS *Oriskany,* Stockdale led the first U.S. air raid of the Vietnam War on North Vietnamese oil refineries. Slightly more than a year later, on September 9, 1965, then-Captain Stockdale, commanding officer of VF-51 and of Carrier Air Group 16, departed the *Oriskany* in an A-4 Skyhawk for what would be his final mission of the war.

Stockdale was hit by enemy antiaircraft fire, and he ejected from his aircraft. He broke a bone in his back and badly dislocated his knee, and these combat injuries would later result in the award of his first Purple Heart.

Captured by the North Vietnamese, Stockdale was taken to Hoa Lo prison in Hanoi—the infamous "Hanoi Hilton"—and, for the next seven years, Stockdale was the highest ranking naval officer in captivity. Given his high rank, his captors were anxious to use him for propaganda purposes. Stockdale, however, had other ideas. At great personal risk, he led his fellow prisoners in resisting enemy attempts to use them for propaganda purposes. Stockdale suffered repeated torture, was denied food and medical treatment, and was kept in solitary confinement for more than four years. He would later receive his second Purple Heart—a gold star in lieu of a second award—in recognition of the wounds inflicted upon him by prison guards in Hanoi. He also received four Silver Stars and three Distinguished Flying Crosses for his service.

At one point, when the North Vietnamese sought to take photographs of him, Stockdale mutilated himself. He later said that he was prepared to kill himself rather than submit. As his Medal of Honor citation explains, Stockdale "deliberately inflicted a near mortal wound to his person in order to convince his captors of his willingness to give up his life rather than capitulate." He cut his own wrists and was bleeding to death in his prison cell when discovered by the North Vietnamese. The enemy, finally convinced that Stockdale would not be broken, stopped brutalizing him and, and according to his Medal of Honor citation, also "abated their employment of excessive harassment and torture of all (other) prisoners of war."[52] After returning to the United States in March 1973, Stockdale resumed his naval career. Widely admired and respected for his intellectual abilities and his extraordinary courage, Stockdale served as the president of the Naval War College. He made major changes to the curriculum, including requiring students to study the 2,500-year-old conflict between Athens and Sparta because then–Vice Admiral Stockdale believed that the Peloponnesian War had lessons to teach Americans about the war in Vietnam.

Stockdale retired from active duty in 1978 and began an academic career that included fifteen years at the Hoover Institute on War, Revolution and

Peace. In 1992, at the request of his friend H. Ross Perot, Stockdale agreed to run for vice president on the Reform Party ticket.

In 1990 Stockdale published *In Love and War: The Story of a Family's Ordeal and Sacrifice During the Vietnam Years*, which he coauthored with his wife, Sybil. In his later years he suffered from Alzheimer's disease, and he died on July 5, 2005, at the age of eighty-one. He is buried at the U.S. Naval Academy.

J. Strom Thurmond: Purple Heart—1944

James Strom Thurmond was wounded in France during World War II. He is best known as a one-time presidential candidate and as the first U.S. senator to reach one hundred years of age while in office.

Born in Edgefield, South Carolina, in December 1902, Strom Thurmond graduated from Clemson Agricultural College of South Carolina, which is today's Clemson University, in 1923. After studying law with his father, he was admitted to the bar in South Carolina in 1930 and subsequently served as the Edgefield county attorney for much of the next decade.

Thurmond had joined the Army Reserve in 1924 and, when the United States entered World War II, he was called to active duty. Thurmond participated in the Normandy invasion, landing by glider with the 82nd Airborne Division and becoming wounded in action. He finished the war as a lieutenant colonel, but remained active in the Army Reserve after leaving active duty and retired from military service as a major general. In addition to a Purple Heart, Thurmond's military awards and decorations include two Legions of Merit, a Bronze Star with Combat *V*, a Belgian Order of the Crown, and a French Croix de Guerre.

In 1946 Thurmond ran as the Democratic Party candidate for governor of South Carolina. He was elected but soon broke with his party over President Truman's civil rights initiatives and, in 1948, ran for president as a Dixiecrat. Thurmond carried only three states but made a name for himself in southern politics.

Elected to the U.S. Senate in 1954 as a write-in candidate, Thurmond remained in Congress for the next forty-nine years. When he left the Senate in January 2003 at age one hundred, Thurmond was the first serving U.S. senator to reach the century mark. Thurmond died in South Carolina in June 2003.[53]

James H. Webb Jr.: Purple Hearts—July 10, 1969

James Henry "Jim" Webb Jr. was twice wounded while serving as a Marine officer in Vietnam, and he received a Navy Cross for extraordinary heroism.

He subsequently began a career in politics and was elected to the U.S. Senate in 2006.

Born in February 1946 Webb "grew up on the move, attending more than a dozen different schools across the U.S. and in England." His father was a career Air Force officer, and the younger Webb, too, wanted to try military service—but in the sea services. After attending the University of Southern California for one year, Webb entered the U.S. Naval Academy in 1964.

When he graduated in 1968 Webb chose to join the Marine Corps and finished first in his class of 243 at The Basic School in Quantico. He subsequently served with the 1st Battalion, 5th Marine Regiment in Vietnam, where he was a rifle platoon and company commander.[54]

On July 10, 1969, then–First Lieutenant Webb was wounded in action and received a Purple Heart. His extraordinary heroism that day also resulted in his being awarded a Navy Cross. According to the citation for that award, Webb and his platoon were on a company-sized search and destroy mission when they

discovered a well-camouflaged bunker complex that appeared to be unoccupied. Deploying his men into defensive positions, Webb was advancing to the first bunker when three enemy soldiers armed with hand grenades jumped out. Reacting instantly, he grabbed the closest man and, brandishing his .45 caliber at the other, apprehended all three of the soldiers. Accompanied by one of his men, Webb then approached the second bunker and called for the enemy to surrender. When the hostile soldiers failed to answer him and threw a grenade that detonated dangerously close to him, Webb detonated a claymore mine in the bunker aperture, accounting for two enemy casualties and disclosing the entrance to a tunnel. Despite the smoke and debris from the explosion and the possibility of enemy soldiers hiding in the tunnel, he then conducted a thorough search that yielded several items of equipment and numerous documents containing valuable intelligence data. Continuing the assault, he approached a third bunker and was preparing to fire into it when the enemy threw another grenade. Observing the grenade land dangerously close to his companion, Webb simultaneously fired his weapon at the enemy, pushed the Marine away from the grenade, and shielded him from the explosion with his own body. Although sustaining painful fragmentation wounds from the explosion, he managed to throw a grenade into the aperture and completely destroy the remaining bunker.[55]

Webb left the Marine Corps in 1972, entered Georgetown University Law Center, and graduated in 1975. He then began a career in government, serving first in the U.S. Congress as counsel to the House Committee on Veterans Affairs from 1977 to 1981. In 1987 Webb became the first Naval Academy graduate in history to serve in the military and then become secretary of the Navy. He resigned from that position in 1988 after refusing to agree to sign off on reductions in the Navy's force structure.

In 2006 Webb was the Democratic candidate for a U.S. Senate seat from Virginia, and he won election in a hard-fought contest. Webb is also an accomplished author, having penned both nonfiction and fiction books, including the highly acclaimed 1978 Vietnam War novel *Fields of Fire*.

ATHLETES

Henry A. Bauer: Purple Hearts—July–August 1944 and March–June 1945

Henry Albert "Hank" Bauer was wounded twice while serving as a Marine during World War II. He is best known as an all-star outfielder who played in nine World Series with the New York Yankees and, as a manager, led the Baltimore Orioles to a stunning World Series victory in 1966.

Born in July 1922 in East St. Louis, Bauer "was the youngest of nine children of an Austrian immigrant who had lost a leg working in an aluminum mill."[56] He was a talented athlete and played high school baseball. After graduating from high school, Bauer, standing six feet tall and weighing 202 lbs. became a pipefitter and repaired furnaces. His brother, who was a player in the Chicago White Sox farm system, arranged for a tryout for Hank in 1941, and Hank won a spot on the Oshkosh team in the Class D Wisconsin State League.

After the Japanese attack on Pearl Harbor, Bauer enlisted in the Marine Corps. He completed basic training and shipped out to the Pacific, where he spent the next thirty-two months in a Marine rifle platoon. He received his first Purple Heart when he was wounded by shrapnel in his back during fighting on Guam between March 1944 and July 1944. Bauer was wounded a second time during the Battle of Okinawa between March 1945 and June 1945, when he was hit in the thigh by shrapnel. By the end of the war Bauer also had been awarded two Bronze Star Medals.

He went back to pipefitting when he returned from the Pacific, but a scout for the Yankees remembered him and signed him to a farm team. Two years later Bauer, then twenty-six years old, was called up to New York.

Bauer was on the American League All-Star team three times from 1952 to 1954, but he is best remembered for playing in the World Series. In 1951, when the Yankees beat the New York Giants four games to two, Bauer "almost singlehandedly won the sixth and deciding game, hitting a bases-loaded triple and making a diving catch of a line drive for the game's final out with the tying run on base."[57] Bauer again showed his value to the Yankees in the 1958 Series when he hit four home runs. His power hitting helped the Yankees beat the Milwaukee Braves, four games to three.

But Bauer is remembered for more than his playing. The Orioles team he managed in 1966 improbably swept the Los Angeles Dodgers to win the World Series. Future Hall of Famers Frank Robinson, Brooks Robinson, and Jim Palmer played for the Orioles that year, while Sandy Koufax and Don Drysdale were on the Dodgers' roster.

Bauer died on February 9, 2007, in Shawnee Mission, Kansas, at the age of eighty-four.

Ralph G. Houk: Purple Heart—December 1944–January 1945

Ralph G. Houk was wounded in action in Germany while serving with the 9th Armored Division in World War II. He is better known for playing catcher for the New York Yankees from 1947 to 1954 and for serving as a general manager for the Yankees, Detroit Tigers, and Red Sox.

Born in Lawrence, Kansas, in August 1919, Houk was an outstanding high school athlete who played football and baseball. He also was a track sprinter. Although he had several college scholarship offers, Houk signed with the Yankees in 1939. He enlisted in the Army on February 22, 1942, and, after completing Armor Officer Candidate School, was commissioned as a second lieutenant.

In July 1944 Houk sailed to England with Company I of the 89th Cavalry Reconnaissance Squadron (Mechanized), 9th Armored Division. He deployed to Normandy in October but did not see combat until the Battle of the Bulge in December 1944 and January 1945. During that period, he received a Purple Heart for a shrapnel wound to his calf. Houk was still with the 9th Armored on March 7, 1945, when the division captured the Ludendorff Bridge at Remagen. After crossing the Rhine that day, Houk became one of the first American soldiers to set foot on German soil.

Houk left active duty as a major and joined the Yankees as a catcher in 1947. He spent the next seven seasons as the backup for Yogi Berra. In 1961,

Houk replaced Casey Stengel as general manager for New York and remained in that job until 1966. From 1974 to 1978 Houk served as general manager for the Tigers, and he then managed the Red Sox from 1981 to 1984.[58]

Robert E. Shepard: Purple Heart—May 21, 1944

Robert Earl "Bert" Shepard was wounded while flying his 34th mission over Germany when his airplane was hit by antiaircraft fire and his right leg was badly damaged. After World War II Shepard became an "instant celebrity" and "an inspirational figure to the country" as a pitcher for the original Washington Nationals.

Born in Dana, Indiana, on June 28, 1920, Bert Shepard grew up in Clinton, Indiana, and worked in the Civilian Conservation Corps during high school. He was an outstanding baseball player and played semiprofessional baseball "in the low minor leagues" in the late 1930s. After being drafted into the Army in 1942, Shepard volunteered for flight training, even though he "had never been near an airplane." But he earned his wings and sailed to England, where he began flying P-38 Lightning fighters.

On May 21, 1944, Shepard's aircraft was struck by antiaircraft fire, and he "felt a sledge-hammer-like blow to his ankle." Shepard also was hit in the chin by a bullet and lost consciousness before his airplane crashed at an estimated speed of 380 miles per hour. Taken prisoner by the Germans, Shepard received medical treatment that resulted in the amputation of his right leg below the knee. He also had part of a bone over his right eye removed.

Shepard returned to the United States in February 1945 and was given an artificial leg at Walter Reed Army Medical Center. According to an article written by Matt Schudel in 2008, "when Secretary of War Robert Patterson asked Shepard what he wanted to do in life, Mr. Shepard said he wanted to play professional baseball."[59]

Shepard telephoned Clark Griffith, the owner of the Washington Nationals, and Shepard got a tryout. He subsequently made the team as a left-handed pitcher and first baseman. Shepard pitched in several exhibition games before being named to the team's active roster in July 1945.

When World War II ended and more able-bodied players returned to the United States, Shepard was sent down to the minor leagues. But he continued to play, and records show that he struck out Stan Musial and Yogi Berra and got a hit off Bob Feller. In 1949 Shepard became a player-manager with a team in Waterbury, Connecticut. He continued playing professional baseball until 1955.

Shepard subsequently became an outstanding golfer and won the National Amputee Golf Championship in 1968 and 1971. He died June 16, 2008, at the age of eighty-seven.

Warren E. Spahn: Purple Heart—1944

Warren Edward Spahn enlisted in the Army in 1942 and received a Purple Heart for wounds received in combat in Europe in 1944. He is best known as a left-handed Major League Baseball pitcher and 1957 Cy Young Award winner.

Born in Buffalo in April 1921, Spahn made his first professional baseball appearance with the Boston Braves in April 1942. He joined the Army at the end of the 1942 season and saw combat in France and Germany and also took part in the Battle of the Bulge. Then–Staff Sergeant Spahn also made history with the 276th Engineer Combat Battalion at the Ludendorff Bridge at Remagen and was one of the first Americans to cross the Rhine.[60]

OTHER PUBLIC FIGURES

David H. Hackworth: Purple Hearts—February 6, 1951; May 31, 1951; September 27, 1951; November 4, 1951; February 12, 1969; March 21, 1969; March 25, 1969; and May 11, 1969

David Haskell Hackworth was a controversial magazine columnist for *Newsweek* magazine and the author of books on military topics, including *About Face: The Odyssey of an American Warrior* (1989), *Brave Men* (1993), *Hazardous Duty* (1997), *The Price of Honor* (1999) and *Steel My Soldiers' Hearts* (2002).

Hackworth was awarded a record eight Purple Hearts—four for wounds received in combat in Korea in 1951 and four for wounds received in combat in Vietnam in 1969. Only World War II soldier Robert T. Frederick has received as many Purple Hearts.

Born November 11, 1930, in Santa Monica, California, Hackworth lied about his age and enlisted in the Army for three years on May 21, 1946, when he was still fifteen years old. After completing basic training as an infantryman, he served with the 351st Infantry in Trieste as a medium tank crewman.

After reenlisting in May 1949 then–Private First Class Hackworth deployed the following year to Korea as a member of Company G of the 27th Infantry. He was promoted to sergeant and was awarded his first Purple Heart after

Col. David H. Hackworth received eight Purple Hearts—four in Korea and four in Vietnam. In this October 1966 photograph, Army Chief of Staff Gen. Harold K. Johnson decorates Hackworth with a Distinguished Service Cross, two Silver Stars, a Legion of Merit, a Bronze Star Medal, an Air Medal, and an Army Commendation Medal. (National Archives and Records Administration)

receiving a gunshot wound to his head on February 6, 1951. He also received his first of ten Silver Stars for gallantry in action on that date. According to the official citation for the award, Hackworth's task force came under heavy enemy small-arms and mortar fire. Ignoring his own safety, Hackworth "mounted a tank and directed a heavy volume of effective machine gun fire at hostile emplacements.... He continued his mission until he was severely wounded."[61]

After receiving a battlefield commission, Lieutenant Hackworth was wounded three more times. On May 31, 1951, he suffered a shrapnel wound to his back, and on September 27, 1951, he took shrapnel to his hands. On November 4, 1951, shrapnel or a bullet hit Hackworth's left arm. He also was awarded two more Silver Stars before his tour of duty in Korea ended.

After returning to the United States, Hackworth served in a variety of locations, including Fort Benning; Fort MacArthur, California; Fort Campbell; Germany; and Vietnam. In 1969 then-Colonel Hackworth returned to Vietnam as the commander of the 4th Battalion, 39th Infantry. Between February and May of that year he was wounded on four separate occasions and received fourth (February 12), fifth (March 21), sixth (March 25) and seventh (May 11) oak leaf clusters to his Purple Heart.

During that tour in Vietnam, Hackworth also was awarded six more Silver Stars, giving him his record number of ten. He also received a second award of the Distinguished Service Cross. His first Distinguished Service Cross was awarded to him during a previous Vietnam tour.

Although under investigation for a variety of criminal offenses, Hackworth avoided trial by court-martial and retired as a colonel in 1971. He moved to Australia, where he was a successful businessman and restaurant owner. He returned to the United States in the mid-1980s and embarked on a highly successful career in journalism. He remained a controversial figure, and his weekly newspaper column "Defending America" routinely criticized Pentagon officials for alleged shortcomings involving the military. Hackworth died of cancer in Mexico in May 2005. He was seventy-four years old at the time of his death.

Jessica D. Lynch: Purple Heart—March 23, 2003

Jessica Dawn Lynch was wounded in action when the convoy in which she was riding was ambushed by the Iraqis. She was taken prisoner, and her subsequent rescue by U.S. special operations personnel was front-page news and made her a celebrity.

Born in Palestine, West Virginia, in April 1983, Lynch enlisted in the Army after high school and was trained as a unit supply specialist at the Quartermaster School at Fort Lee, Virginia. On March 23, 2003, then–Private First Class Lynch was a supply clerk with the 507th Maintenance Company and was traveling in a convoy near Nasiriyah, Iraq. When the driver of the Humvee in which she was a passenger made a wrong turn into enemy-held territory, they were attacked by Iraqi soldiers. Eleven U.S. soldiers were killed, and five others, including Lynch, were captured.

Lynch was eventually taken by the Iraqi troops to a hospital in Nasiriya for treatment. After several informants, including an Iraqi physician at the facility, told U.S. officials about her location, she was rescued in a daring April 1, 2003, rescue that received worldwide news coverage. Initial reports were that Lynch's first words to her rescuers were "I am a soldier, too" and that she had fought until being wounded and captured.

Lynch was medically discharged from the Army in August 2003, and she then returned home to West Virginia. Lynch testified before Congress in April 2007 that she had never fired her M-16 rifle because it had malfunctioned and that she had been unconscious after the ambush that caused her Humvee to crash. She denied being a hero and criticized the Pentagon for portraying her as one. Lynch later wrote a book with Pulitzer Prize–winning journalist Rick Bragg detailing her experiences.[62]

Douglas MacArthur: Purple Hearts—March 11, 1918, and October 14, 1918

Douglas MacArthur was twice wounded by gas while fighting in France during World War I.[63]

Born in Little Rock, Arkansas, on January 26, 1880, MacArthur spent most of his youth at various Army installations because his father, Arthur MacArthur, was a career officer. In 1899 the younger MacArthur arrived at the U.S. Military Academy, where he demonstrated a brilliant intellect and graduated first in his class in 1903. Commissioned as a second lieutenant of engineers, MacArthur served in the Philippines before returning to Washington, D.C., where he was an aide to President Theodore Roosevelt.

In 1914 then-Captain MacArthur participated in the landings at Veracruz, Mexico, before returning to a posting with the War Department. During World War I then-Colonel MacArthur deployed to France, where he served first as chief of staff for the 42nd Division. After receiving a promotion to brigadier general, MacArthur took command of the 84th Infantry Brigade and fought in the St. Mihiel offensive and Meuse–Argonne offensive. He later commanded the 42nd Division in the Sedan offensive in 1918.

As William Manchester wrote in his biography of MacArthur, MacArthur refused to carry a gas mask when he was at the front even though "he severely disciplined subordinates who followed his example."[64] As a result of this irresponsible behavior, the thirty-eight-year-old MacArthur was seriously injured—the poison vapor threatened his sight and he had to wear a blindfold for eight days—on March 11, 1918. Seven months later, on October 14, 1918, then–Brigadier General MacArthur again "encountered mustard and tear gas" and once more paid the penalty for refusing to carry a mask.[65]

MacArthur received Purple Heart No. 1, which was engraved "Douglas MacArthur" on the reverse. A July 16, 1932, letter from the adjutant general to the quartermaster general directed that MacArthur's Purple Heart be issued with one oak leaf cluster "on account of wounds received in action on March 11, 1918, while serving as colonel, General Staff, 42d Division, and October 14, 1918, while serving as brigadier general, 84th Infantry Brigade."[66] MacArthur also received Silver Star Medal No. 1 with six oak leaf clusters reflecting that

·

Gen. Douglas MacArthur was twice wounded by gas while fighting in France during World War I. MacArthur was awarded Purple Heart No. 1 in 1932. (National Archives and Records Administration)

he had been awarded a record seven Silver Stars.

After World War I MacArthur served with the Army of Occupation in Germany before returning to the United States to assume duties as super-intendent at West Point. After leaving that assignment in 1922, MacArthur successively commanded the District of Manila, Fourth and III Corps Areas, and the IX Corps Area. In 1930 he was promoted to four-star rank and became Army chief of staff. During his tenure the Army developed plans for industrial mobilization and manpower procurement in the event of war. It also established an air headquarters and administered the Civilian Conservation Corps.

In 1935 MacArthur reverted to two-star rank and became military advisor to the government of the Philippines. Although he retired from active duty in December 1937, MacArthur continued to serve as an advisor in Manila. In July 1941 he was recalled to active duty, promoted to lieutenant general, and named commander, U.S. Army Forces Far East.

When the Japanese struck on December 8, 1941, MacArthur and his staff withdrew to the Bataan peninsula. Despite making a valiant stand, U.S. forces in the Philippines were doomed, and MacArthur was ordered to escape. After a perilous journey through Japanese-held waters, MacArthur reached Australia, where he received a Medal of Honor for his heroic defense of the Philippines and where MacArthur famously declared that he would return one day to liberate the islands from the Japanese.

During World War II MacArthur proved time and again that he was a brilliant strategist, and he enjoyed phenomenal success in coordinating massive land, sea, and air forces to achieve victory at relatively little cost. He arrived in Japan in 1945 and remained there, directing the reconstruction of the nation and its government for six years. With near-dictatorial powers, he remade the Japanese political landscape. Japanese militarism was eliminated, and in its place, MacArthur put a liberal constitution that granted freedom of speech, a free press, and rights for women.

When the North Koreans invaded South Korea in June 1950, MacArthur was made supreme commander of all UN forces. Initially, the war went badly, but, eventually, U.S. Eighth Army commander Gen. Walton Walker managed to consolidate a defensive perimeter around the port of Pusan. MacArthur then used a brilliant amphibious landing at Inchon to surprise the North Koreans and smash their lines. Almost all historians consider this surprise strike to be the pinnacle of MacArthur's career.

MacArthur and the UN forces pursued the North Koreans northward, and victory seemed inevitable. But in late November 1950, as they approached the Yalu River, which marks the border between North Korea and China, 300,000 Chinese struck back.

The Americans and their allies retreated. MacArthur managed to stabilize the situation on the ground and then proposed to President Truman that the U.S. bomb Chinese installations in Manchuria and use nuclear weapons to win the war, if necessary. Truman, however, did not want the war to escalate, and he relayed this decision to MacArthur personally during a meeting on Wake Island in December 1950. When MacArthur refused to accept Truman's decision and began to publicly criticize the president, Truman relieved him from command in April 1951.

Although MacArthur returned to the United States and a hero's welcome, his reputation had been damaged, and he remains a controversial historical figure. MacArthur died in Washington, D.C., in April 1964.

Oliver North: Purple Hearts—December 1968–August 1969

Oliver Laurence North was wounded twice while serving as an infantry platoon commander in Vietnam from December 1968 to August 1969. Today, he is best known for his involvement in the so-called Iran–Contra affair and his work as a syndicated newspaper columnist and television commentator on Fox News Channel.

Born in San Antonio, Texas, in October 1943, North graduated from Ockawamick Central High School in Philmont, New York, in June 1961. He joined the Marine Corps Reserve in December and earned a regents diploma from the College at Brockport, State University of New York in June 1963. North subsequently entered the U.S. Naval Academy and, upon graduating in June 1968, was commissioned as a second lieutenant in the Marine Corps.

After completing the Basic School at Quantico in November 1968, North deployed to Vietnam, where he joined K Company, 3rd Battalion, 3rd Marine Division. North saw considerable combat and, in addition to his Purple Hearts, was decorated with a Silver Star for gallantry under fire on May 25, 1969, when he led a series of assaults against the North Vietnamese. A the citation for his award explains, K Company was participating in Operation Virginia Ridge near the demilitarized zone when the lead platoon "came under a heavy volume of machine gun and automatic weapons fire, supported by rocket propelled grenades, directional mines and mortars. In the initial burst of fire, the platoon commander and point squad leader were seriously wounded. Realizing the need for immediate action, 2nd Lt. North rapidly maneuvered his second platoon through the lines of the beleaguered unit and personally initiated an aggressive assault against the North Vietnamese Army emplacement."

North's attack so stunned the enemy that they withdrew to another hill, and this allowed the Marines to treat and evacuate their casualties. But North was not yet finished, and, after "regrouping his forces, he fearlessly led an attack on the enemy's new position, killing one soldier as his men closed with the enemy."

The North Vietnamese withdrew again to a previously prepared entrenchment on the ridgeline. North, however, reorganized his men and, with complete disregard for his own safety and "oblivious to the intense machine gun fire impacting around him," led his men in yet another assault against the North Vietnamese.[67]

As the battle continued, and as Marine casualties increased and ammunition began to run short, North halted the attack. He then repeatedly exposed

himself to heavy fire from the enemy while he directed the resupply of his platoon and the evacuation of the wounded Marines. After calling in fixed-wing air strikes on the North Vietnamese positions, North initiated a fourth assault, which pushed the remainder of the enemy off the ridgeline and permitted the Marines to seize their objective.

In August 1969 North transferred from K Company to the division headquarters. He was promoted to first lieutenant on September 5 and spent the remainder of his tour in Vietnam in a G-3 operations billet. After returning from Vietnam in late November 1969, North served in a variety of assignments, including instructor and company commander at The Basic School, officer in charge of the 3rd Marine Division schools detachment on Okinawa, and manpower analyst at Marine Corps headquarters in Washington, D.C.

In 1981 then-Major North was assigned to the White House with the National Security Council. While serving as deputy director for political–military affairs, North became involved in an illegal plan to transfer moneys obtained from the secret sale of weapons to Iran to the Contra rebel group fighting the Sandinista government in Nicaragua. After these clandestine sales and money transfers became public knowledge, North was dismissed from his National Security Council position. Summoned to testify before Congress, North admitted that he had lied under oath about his activities but insisted that he had acted in good faith and in the best interests of the United States.

In May 1989 North was found guilty in U.S. District Court of aiding and abetting in the obstruction of a congressional inquiry and destruction of documents by his assistant Fawn Hall. He received a three-year suspended sentence of imprisonment and was fined $150,000. In 1990, however, North's convictions were reversed on appeal on the basis that his trial might have been impermissibly affected by his testimony before Congress, which had been given under a grant of immunity. All charges against North were dismissed in 1991.

North retired from active duty in 1990. Although he made an unsuccessful bid for the U.S. Senate in 1994, North subsequently began a successful career as the host of a nationally syndicated radio program called the *Oliver North Radio Show*. Today, he appears regularly as a commentator on the Fox News Channel and is the host of the television series *War Stories With Oliver North*. He has also published a number of best-selling books.[68]

Maj. Gen. Charles E. "Chuck" Yeager is best known as the first man to fly faster than the speed of sound. He was also a successful fighter pilot during World War II and was awarded a Purple Heart for injuries received in March 1944. (U.S. Air Force)

Charles Yeager: Purple Heart—March 5, 1944

Charles Elwood "Chuck" Yeager, who was wounded in action when he was shot down over France during World War II, is best known as the first man to fly faster than the speed of sound.

Considered to be the most famous test pilot in American aviation history, Yeager was born in Myra, West Virginia, on February 13, 1923. He enlisted in the Army Air Corps after graduating from high school and served as a crew chief for six months before starting pilot training at Luke Field, Arizona, in July 1942. After earning his wings in March 1943, Yeager deployed to Europe as an enlisted pilot, where he eventually joined the 363rd Fighter Squadron as a P-51 Mustang pilot.

His first brush with disaster came on March 5, 1944, when twenty-one-year-old Yeager was shot down over France by a German FW 190, only one day after having downed an enemy fighter himself. As he wrote in *Yeager: An Autobiography*, he "was barely able to unfasten his safety belt and crawl over the seat" before his burning P-51 Mustang "began to snap and roll, heading for the ground.[69] Wounded and on the run after only eight combat missions, Yeager was befriended by a French woodcutter and, with the aid of the French Resistance, managed to evade capture and cross the Pyrenees into neutral Spain.

Yeager returned to England in May 1944 and, having successfully escaped from enemy occupied territory, was not supposed to fly combat missions again. But after the Allied invasion of Normandy on June 6, 1944, Yeager convinced his superiors that he should be allowed to fly in combat. He was commissioned as a second lieutenant in July 1944 and eventually flew another fifty-six missions before World War II ended.

After the war then-Captain Yeager began a new career as a flight instructor and test pilot. From August 1945 until June 1951, Yeager was a performance and experimental flight test pilot at Wright Field, Ohio, and at Edwards Air Force Base in California. Tasked with testing the rocket-powered X-1, he became the first person to fly faster than sound on October 14, 1947. Until that day, some questioned whether an aircraft could break the sound barrier, and whether a human could survive the experience. Yeager made history when he proved it could be done, and he received the prestigious MacKay Trophy and Collier Trophy for his achievement.

During the 1950s Yeager served in a variety of assignments, including command of an F-86H Sabre squadron in Germany and France. In July 1966 then-Colonel Yeager took command of 405th Fighter Wing, based at

Clark Air Force Base in the Philippines, and logged more than four hundred hours of combat time over Vietnam, principally in the B-57 Canberra, a light bomber and reconnaissance plane.

Yeager was promoted to brigadier general in June 1969 and then served as vice commander of the Seventeenth Air Force in Ramstein, Germany. In 1971 he became the U.S. defense representative to Pakistan, and spent two years advising the Pakistan Air Force. Yeager returned to the United States in 1973 and retired in 1975. When he left active duty Yeager had flown more than 10,000 hours in more than three hundred different types and models of aircraft. In 1985 Ronald Reagan awarded Yeager the Presidential Medal of Freedom, and in 2005, President George W. Bush promoted Yeager to major general on the retired list.[70]

Conclusion

Because more than one million individuals have been awarded the Purple Heart since 1932, a book about the recipients of this decoration is necessarily limited to examining the details of a relatively small number of those men and women.

In some cases, particularly with early awards to sailors and Marines, little is known about the recipients except their names and the date they were wounded or killed in action. On the other hand, much more information is available about recipients who became film stars or politicians. In any event, those who have read *For Military Merit* should now know the following facts about Purple Heart recipients:

- The most Purple Hearts—about 750,000—have been awarded to soldiers, and the fewest—less than 1,150—have been awarded to Coast Guard personnel.
- Some World War I and World War II recipients of the Purple Heart received the decoration for meritorious service or achievement rather than for combat-related injuries; the Purple Heart did not become a wounds-only medal until 1942.
- Today, men and women in uniform may be awarded the Purple Heart if they are wounded or killed while fighting against an enemy of the United States or against a hostile foreign force, while serving on a peacekeeping force, or as a result of an act of international terrorism.
- At least fourteen Civil War Army veterans are known to have been awarded the Purple Heart—a remarkable fact when one considers that these soldiers had to be alive to apply for the Purple Heart when it was revived in 1932.

- The rarest Purple Hearts are those awarded to soldiers who were wounded in action while fighting in the Indian Wars; only two are known.
- Purple Heart No. 1 was awarded to Douglas MacArthur, undoubtedly because the decoration was revived while he was serving as Army chief of staff.
- The record for the most Purple Hearts to a single individual is jointly held by Robert T. Frederick and David Hackworth, who each received eight. But Frederick gets the nod over Hackworth because Frederick was awarded all his Purple Hearts during World War II, while Hackworth received four Purple Hearts during the Korean War and four during the Vietnam War.
- The top Marine Corps recipient is James L. Day, who received six Purple Hearts for wounds received in action in World War II, Korea, and Vietnam. Day also was awarded a Medal of Honor for his extraordinary combat heroism.
- No one knows who holds the record number of Purple Hearts in the Navy, Air Force, or Coast Guard, but it is likely to be fewer than the Army and Marine Corps records given the nature of combat experienced by sailors, airmen, and Coast Guardsmen.
- The first female recipient was Beatrice M. MacDonald, an Army nurse who was wounded on the night of August 17, 1917. She received a Purple Heart from the War Department in January 1936.
- The only female recipient of the Purple Heart to reach flag rank to date is Brig. Gen. Rhonda Cornum, who was badly wounded when the helicopter in which she was a passenger was shot down over Iraq in 1991.
- About one hundred Purple Hearts were awarded to civilians serving alongside uniformed personnel as civil service employees, war correspondents, Red Cross employees, and the like. The first such awards were made during World War II, and the practice continued until the late 1990s, when Congress enacted legislation restricting the decoration to military personnel.
- The most famous civilian recipient of the Purple Heart was probably Ernest Pyle, who was beloved by millions of Americans for his World War II reporting from the front lines. Pyle was killed by Japanese machine-gun fire in April 1945 and was awarded a posthumous Purple Heart by the Army in April 1983.

- Probably the most well-known film and television stars to have been awarded the Purple Heart are James Arness, who gained fame in the Western *Gunsmoke*, and James Garner, whose most successful television series were *Maverick* and *The Rockford Files*.
- The only American president to have been awarded the Purple Heart was John F. Kennedy, who was seriously wounded when a Japanese warship cut his patrol boat in half.
- Purple Hearts run in families, with more than a few awards going to fathers and sons and husbands and wives. The sad record for the most Purple Hearts to members of a single family undoubtedly belongs to the Sullivan brothers, all five of whom lost their lives at sea during World War II.

The Purple Heart is highly prized by all who have received it. While this is certainly because it is a beautiful medal with an unusual heart-shaped design, it is mostly because the Purple Heart is unique as the only individual American military decoration that does not depend on any person's favor for its award. After all, if a soldier, sailor, airman, Marine, or Coast Guardsman satisfies the criteria, he or she receives a Purple Heart. No other award—from the top-ranking Medal of Honor to the very junior medals for commendation or achievement—is like it.

Notes

Chapter 1: A Short History of the Purple Heart: Background, Design, and Award Criteria

1. Albert F. Gleim, *Purple Heart Reference Materials* (Arlington, VA: Planchet Press, 1988), 1–2.
2. Col. John W. Wright, Army War College, letter to Capt. George M. Chandler, Office of the Quartermaster General, U.S. War Department, April 18, 1925, author's files.
3. J. C. Fitzpatrick, assistant chief of the Manuscripts Division of the Library of Congress, letter to Capt. George M. Chandler, Office of the Quartermaster General, War Department, April 21, 1925, author's files.
4. Carleton S. Gifford, letter to President Calvin Coolidge, November 18, 1925, authors files.
5. Lt. Col. E. S. Hartshorn, memo to assistant chief of staff (G-1), subj: Order of Military Merit, December 3, 1925, author's files.
6. Fred L. Borch and Charles P. McDowell, *Sea Service Medals: Military Awards of the Navy, Marine Corps, and Coast Guard* (Annapolis, MD: Naval Institute Press, 2009), 98–99.
7. Gen. Douglas MacArthur, letter to Charles Moore, April 8, 1931, National Archives and Records Administration Record Group 66, Commission of Fine Arts, Entry 4 (files pertaining to Badge of Military Merit and Purple Heart; hereinafter NARA RG 66).
8. Charles Moore, letter to Gen. Douglas MacArthur, April 18, 1931, NARA RG 66, reprinted in Frederic L. Borch and F. C. Brown, *The Purple Heart: A History of America's Oldest Military Decoration* (Tempe, AZ: Borch and Westlake Publishing, 1994), 39.
9. *General Orders No. 3*, War Department (Washington, DC, February 22, 1932).
10. *Personnel: Award and Supply of Decorations*, Army Regulation 600-45 (Washington, DC, August 8, 1932), paras. 11(a)–11(b).
11. *Purple Heart—Changes*, War Department Circular No. 6 (Washington, DC, February 22, 1932), para. 16.

12. Leopold Strauss, Adjutant General's Office 201 award card (St. Louis, MO: National Archives and Records Administration National Personnel Records Center [hereinafter AGO 201 award card]); Obituary of Leopold Strauss, *New York Times*, October 5, 1952; Charles E. Laird, Citation for Meritorious Services, *General Orders No. 1*, 164th Infantry Brigade (Camp Dix, NJ, May 14, 1919).

13. Gen. Douglas MacArthur, radio message to the War Department, June 27, 1938, MacArthur Archives, Record Group 1, Box 2, Folio 1, Norfolk, VA.

14. War Department Circular 125 (Washington, DC, April 28, 1942).

15. Executive Order no. 9277, *Award of the Purple Heart to Persons Serving with the Navy, Marine Corps or Coast Guard of the United States*, December 3, 1942.

16. Executive Order no. 11,016, *Authorizing Award of the Purple Heart*, April 25, 1962.

17. Executive Order no. 12,464, *Award of the Purple Heart*, February 23, 1984.

18. Public Law 103-160, *U.S. Code* 57 (1993), Sec. 1129.

19. Award of Purple Heart to Members Killed or Wounded in Action by Friendly Fire, Public Law 103-160, *U.S. Code* 57 (1993), Sec. 1141.

20. *National Defense Authorization Act for Fiscal Year 1996*, Public Law 104-106, *U.S. Code* 1129 (1996), Sec. 521,

21. "How Much Abuse for a Medal?" *Army Times*, May 24, 1999, 2.

22. Michael L. Dominguez, Office of the Undersecretary of Defense, memo to the secretaries of the military departments, subj: Posthumous Award of the Purple Heart Medal to Prisoners of War Who Died While in Captivity as a Prisoner of War, October 1, 2008; U.S. Department of Defense, "DoD Revises Purple Heart Eligibility Criteria to Allow Award to POWs Who Die in Captivity," press release, October 6, 2008.

23. William H. McMichael, "Pentagon: No Purple Heart for PTSD," *Army Times*, January 19, 2009, 21.

24. See, for example, *Military Awards*, Army Regulation 600-8-22, Department of the Army (Washington, DC, December 11, 2006), para. 2-28.

Chapter 2: Soldiers: Revolutionary War to Afghanistan and Iraq

1. Borch and McDowell, *Sea Service Medals*, 95–96.

2. Ibid. 95.

3. Ibid. 93–94.

4. *Personnel*, Army Regulation 600-45, para. 11(a).

5. Grand Army of the Republic, *Journal of the 74th National Encampment* (Springfield, IL, September 8–13, 1940).

6. Ballinger attended the 75th Gettysburg Reunion in 1938, and his photograph appears on page 136 of the fourth volume of the *Report of the Pennsylvania Commission: The*

Seventy-Fifth Anniversary of the Battle of Gettysburg, which was compiled by Paul Roy and published in 1939. Ballinger's Purple Heart award is recorded on an AGO 201 award card.

7.   War Department Adjutant General's Office, letter to William R. Bell directing "that Purple Heart, engraved with name of recipient, be issued to Mr. William R. Bell, General Delivery, Creston, Iowa," August 26, 1932.

8.   AGO 201 award card for Henry N. Comey. For more on Comey, see Lynman R. Comey, ed., *A Legacy of Valor: The Memoirs and Letters of Captain Henry Newton Comey, 2nd Massachusetts Infantry* (Nashville, TN: University of Tennessee Press, 2004).

9.   "Crandall Civil War Vet Will Visit Reunion," American-News Dakota News Service, June 28, 1938; American Civil War Research Database, http://www.civilwardata.com (accessed January 29, 2009).

10. AGO 201 award card for Ludwick D. Davis.

11. AGO 201 award card for Andrew C. Gibbs.

12. "*Life* Visits a 100-Year-Old Veteran," *Life*, June 19, 1944, 118–21.

13. AGO 201 award card for Charles W. McKibben.

14. AGO 201 award card for Thomas F. Palmer.

15. AGO 201 award card for Oran J. Randlett; Oran J. Randlett, Application for Medal, War Department Form No. 0714, June 19, 1937, author's files.

16. AGO 201 award card for George N. Smith; Theo F. Rodenbaugh and William L. Haskin, *Army of the United States: Historical Sketches of Staff and Line with Portraits of Generals-in-Chief* (New York: Maynard, Merrill & Co., 1896), 651.

17. AGO 201 award card for William H. Thomas. Thomas' amazing life is examined in John D. Smith, *American Judas: William Hannibal Thomas and the American Negro* (Athens, GA: University of Georgia Press, 1999).

18. AGO 201 award card for Frank Williams.

19. Borch and Brown, *The Purple Heart*, 91.

20. Merrill E. Gates, *Men of Mark in America* (Washington, DC: Men of Mark Publishing, 1905), 172; Glenn M. Stein, "General David L. Brainard, U.S. Army: Last Survivor of the United States' Lady Franklin Bay Expedition (1881–84)," Part 1, *Polar Times* 3 (July 2008); Stein "General David L. Brainard," Part 2, *Polar Times* (January 2009); "David Legg Brainard, Colonel, United States Army," Arlington National Cemetery Website, http://www.arlingtoncemetery.net/dlbraina.htm (accessed August 25, 2009).

21. AGO 201 award card for Hans Villumsen.

22. AGO 201 award card for Joseph Wehr.

23. For more on the Philippine Insurrection, see Brian McAllister Linn, *The U.S. Army and Counterinsurgency in the Philippine War, 1899–1902* (Chapel Hill, NC: University of North Carolina Press, 2000).

24. AGO 201 award card for Charles B. Allen.

25. Todd Wheatley, "The State of Washington's Medal for Philippine Service," *Medal Collector* (June 1991): 9; Borch and Brown, *The Purple Heart*, 120–21.

26. AGO 201 award card for Alvin F. Plottner.

27. *General Orders No. 59*, War Department (Washington, DC, 1919).

28. Louise Arnold-Friend, "Calvin Pearl Titus," *Reference Guide to U.S. Military History, 1865–1919* (New York: Facts on File, 1993), 216–17; Maj. Gen. John A. Klein, Adjutant General, Department of the Army, letter to Lt. Col. (ret.) Calvin P. Titus, subj: Letter Orders—Purple Heart, February 17, 1955, author's files; "The Great Day at West Point," *Army & Navy Journal*, June 14, 1902, 1031.

29. Stephen Carr, "The Case of the Non-Posthumous Posthumous Award," *Medal of Honor Roundtable*, 1970.

30. Max Boot, *The Savage Wars of Peace* (New York: Basic Books, 2002), 196.

31. *General Orders 96*, War Department (Washington, DC, October 26, 1918), para. III; AGO 201 award card for James B. Ord, No. 45192 (1934); West Point Association of Graduates, "Ord Graduation No. 5378," *Register of Graduates* (West Point, NY: WPAOG, 1992).

32. Herbert Molloy Mason Jr., *The Great Pursuit* (New York: Konecky & Konecky, 1970), 20.

33. *General Orders 96*, War Department (Washington, DC, October 26, 1918), para. IV.

34. War Department Bureau of Public Relations, Radio Branch, "Army Decorations to Nation's Heroes," educational release, January 27, 1942, 3.

35. William D. Alexander, Report of Separation (Department of Defense Form 214) [hereinafter DD Form 214], October 31, 1952; "Colonel (then Captain) William Alexander, O-4632, Artillery, France, 27 July 1918," Purple Heart Certificate, May 11, 1960.

36. *General Orders No. 1*, "Charles E. Laird, Citation for Meritorious Services," 164th Infantry Brigade (Camp Dix, NJ, May 14, 1919).

37. AGO 201 award cards for Beatrice M. MacDonald; *General Orders No. 17*, War Department (Washington, DC, August 12, 1926), para. IV.

38. AGO 201 award card for Joseph Sink.

39. AGO 201 award card for Leopold Strauss; Obituary of Leopold Strauss, *New York Times*, October 5, 1952.

40. Borch and Brown, *The Purple Heart*, 125–29.

41. Thomas Taylor, *The Simple Sounds of Freedom: The True Story of the Only Soldier to Fight for Both America and the Soviet Union* (New York: Random House, 2002), 56.

42. Joe Holley, "Paratrooper Joe Beyrle Dies," *Washington Post*, December 15, 2004.

43. World War II Recreation Society, "T/Sgt Llewellyn Chilson," 179th Infantry Regiment Thunderbirds, http://www.45thdivision.org/Veterans/Chilson.htm (accessed August 25, 2009).

44. Fred L. Borch and Robert F. Dorr, "Above, Beyond and Forgotten," *World War II*, April 2006, 26–33.

45. *General Orders No. 31*, First U.S. Army (Fort Jay, NY, July 1, 1944), para. III; Cole C. Kingseed, *From Omaha Beach to Dawson's Ridge: The Combat Journal of Captain Joe Dawson* (Annapolis, MD: Naval Institute Press, 2005).

46. Obituary of Annie G. Fox, *San Francisco Examiner*, January 25, 1987; Dorothea Buckingham, "First Lt. Annie G. Fox, Army Nurse Corps," Women of World War II Hawaii, http://www.womenofworldwariihawaii.com/2008/12/first-lt-annie-g-fox-army-nurse-corps.html (accessed June 12, 2009).

47. Anne Hicks, *The Last Fighting General: The Biography of Robert Tyron Frederick* (Atglen, PA: Schiffer Publishing, 2008), 136.

48. Robert Frederick, "Wounds Received as a Result of Action with Enemy Forces," DD Form 214, September 16, 1957, para. 29; Hicks, *Last Fighting General*, 145.

49. Russell P. Reeder Jr., *Born at Reveille: Memoirs of an American Soldier* (Quechee, VT: Vermont Heritage Press, 1994), 284.

50. Robert Asahina, *Just Americans: How Japanese Americans Won a War at Home and Abroad* (New York: Gotham Books, 2006), 181.

51. Ibid., 191, 197.

52. "Profile of a LOV Member: S. Donald Singlestad, DSC," *General Orders*, January–February 2009, 8–9.

53. Charles Alvin Wirt, "Wounds Received as a Result of Action with Enemy Forces," DD Form 214, October 31, 1963, para. 27; "Charles Alvin Wirt, No. 13335, Class of January 1943," *Assembly*, October 1989, 171.

54. *General Orders No. 122*, 1st Infantry Division (Field Headquarters, Germany, July 10, 1945).

55. *General Orders No. 150*, 1st Infantry Division (Field Headquarters, Germany, August 10, 1945).

56. *General Orders No. 137*, Third U.S. Army (Cheshire, England, June 11, 1945).

57. Fred L. Borch and Robert F. Dorr, "Blair's Bravery Inspired His Soldiers in Korea," *Army Times*, June 25, 2007, 43; Margaret Menge, "Colonel Russell Blair Dies at 92," *Cornwall (New York) Local*, April 25, 2008.

58. Borch and Dorr, "Blair's Bravery."

59. Larry Smith, *Beyond Glory* (New York: W. W. Norton, 2003), 143–57.

60. Adam Bernstein, "Daring Soldier Was Awarded Medal of Honor," *Washington Post*, November 18, 2009.

61. *General Orders No. 17*, 3rd Infantry Division (Fort McCoy, WI, January 24, 1951); *General Orders No. 320*, 3rd Infantry Division (Fort McCoy, WI, July 11, 1951); Fred L. Borch and Robert F. Dorr, "Decorated Chaplain Was Spiritual Leader, Lifesaver," *Army Times*, December 19, 2007, 38.

62. Military Awards Branch, U.S. Army Human Resources Command, "Statistics by Conflict, Operation or Incident," U.S. Army Human Resources Command, https://www.hrc.army.mil/site/active/tagd/awards/STATS/historical.htm (accessed March 10, 2009).

63. *General Orders 5903*, U.S. Army, Vietnam (Cam Ranh, Vietnam, December 30, 1968).

64. Robert C. Knight, letter to the author, March 25, 2009, author's files.

65. H. Norman Schwarzkopf, *It Doesn't Take a Hero*, with Peter Petre (New York: Bantam Books, 1992), 97–125.

66. Ibid., 128–30.

67. Ibid., 170.

68. Ibid., 170–72.

69. *General Orders No. 1621*, U.S. Army, Vietnam (Cam Ranh, Vietnam, April 11, 1967).

70. Madeline Sapienza, *Peacetime Awards of the Purple Heart in the Post-Vietnam Period* (Washington, DC: Center of Military History, 1987), 5.

71. Ibid., 9.

72. Nancy Montgomery, "Baader-Meinhof Gang Attacked U.S. Troops, Bases in 1970s–1980s," *Stars and Stripes*, August 5, 2005, European edition.

73. Sapienza, *Peacetime Awards of the Purple Heart*, 10.

74. Ibid., 6–7.

75. Ibid., 8.

76. Ibid.

77. Ibid.

78. Ibid.

79. U.S. Army Operations Support Directorate, electronic message, subj: Clarification of Purple Heart Criteria, December 31, 1990.

80. Rhonda Cornum, *She Went to War: The Rhonda Cornum Story*, as told to Peter Copeland (Novato, CA: Presidio Press, 1992), 11.

81. "A Woman's Burden," *Time*, March 28, 2003.

82. Ibid.

83. Erick Trickey, "Rhonda Cornum," *Encyclopedia of World Biography*, http://www.notablebiographies.com/newsmakers2/2006-A-Ec/Cornum-Rhonda.html (accessed November 29, 2009); "Notable Books 1992," *New York Times*, December 6, 1992.

84. Andrew Leyden, "Casualties of Operation Desert Storm," *Gulf War Debriefing Book*, http://www.leyden.com/gulfwar/casualties.html (accessed November 29, 2009).

85. For the story of the events of October 3–4, 1993, see Mark Bowden, *Black Hawk Down: A Study of Modern Warfare* (New York: Atlantic Monthly Press, 1999).

86. "Pentagon to Grant Medals in Copter Incident," *Washington Post*, April 5, 1995; Clint Claybrook, "Soldiers Killed by Friendly Fire to Get Medals," *Columbus (Ga.) Ledger-Enquirer*, April 5, 1995.

87. For an account of the attack, see Robin Wright, "Saudi Attack Is Blamed on Repression: 5 Americans Killed in the Explosion," *Honolulu Advertiser*, November 14, 1995. For a list of the sixty men and women awarded the Purple Heart, see "60 bomb victims get Purple Heart," *Army Times*, December 25, 1995.

88. Ian Fisher, "G. I. Hurt in Bosnia Is Said to Be in Good Condition," *New York Times*, January 1, 1996; Phillip P. Pan, "Rockville Man Is First American Injured in Bosnian Peace Mission," *Washington Post*, December 31, 1995.

89. David Josar, "After Stepping on Landmine in Kosovo, Soldier Stayed Calm, Treated His Wound," *Stars and Stripes*, June 28, 2001, 1.

90. "Soldiers Awarded Purple Hearts," *Soldiers*, September 1999, 14; "Purple Heart for 2 in Kosovo," *Army Times*, August 2, 1999.

91. Ibid.

92. "How much Abuse for a Medal?" *Army Times*, May 24, 1999.

93. "Wounded Soldier Honored with Purple Heart," *Talon (Task Force Eagle)*, February 9, 1996, 5.

94. For the authoritative history of the 9/11 attack on the Pentagon, see Alfred Goldberg and others, *Pentagon 9/11* (Washington, DC: Department of Defense, 2007).

95. "Awards: Decorations Follow Attack," *Army Times*, November 5, 2001.

96. Gina Cavallaro, "Honoring Courage," *Army Times*, November 5, 2001.

97. Brian Birdwell, Ginger Kolbaba, and Mel Birdwell, *Refined by Fire: A Family's Triumph of Love and Faith: A Soldier's Story of 9-11* (New York and Carol Stream, IL: Tyndale House, 2004).

98. Soldier Programs and Services Division, U.S. Army Human Resources Command, "Wartime Award Statistics, Operation Enduring Freedom, December 5, 2001 to March 31, 2009," U.S. Army Human Resources Command, https://www.hrc.army. mil/site/active/tagd/awards/STATS/OEF_Statistics.htm (accessed August 6, 2009).

99. Heike Hasenauer, "Focus on People," *Soldiers*, May 2003, 33–34.

100. "60262 Laura Margaret Walker USA, usma2003-C3," West-Point.org, http://www. west-point.org/users/usma2003/60262 (accessed November 29, 2009).

101. Carlos H. Conde, "An American Soldier Is Killed by a Bomb in the Philippines," *Washington Post*, October 3, 2002.

102. Soldier Programs and Services Division, U.S. Army Human Resources Command, "Wartime Award Statistics, Operation Iraqi Freedom, March 15, 2003 to April 30, 2009," U.S. Army Human Resources Command, https://www.hrc.army.mil/site/ active/tagd/awards/index.htm#.html (accessed August 6, 2009).

103. "Family of Staff Sergeant to Receive His DSC," *Army Times*, November 5, 2008; Jennie Burrett, "2-14 Infantry Soldiers Honor Fallen Comrades," *The (Fort Drum, NY) Mountaineer*, December 6, 2007, 14.

104. Public and Intergovernmental Affairs, U.S. Department of Veterans Affairs, "VA Official Biography: The Honorable L. Tammy Duckworth," Department of Veterans Affairs, http://www1.va.gov/opa/bios/biography.asp?id=90 (accessed November 29, 2009).

105. Michele Tan, "Amputee Soldier Helps Anchor Parachute Team," *Army Times*, May 11, 2009.

106. Mark Berman, "Soldier, 22, Killed in Mortar Attack," *Washington Post*, June 9, 2009.

107. Ibid.

Chapter 3: Sailors: Spanish–American War to Afghanistan and Iraq

1. "Spectacular Purple Heart Group for the Battle of Manila Bay to Seaman William Sneath, U.S. Navy," Lot 272, *FJP Auctions Catalogue 141*, August 10, 2005.

2. Charles P. McDowell, ed., *Index to Recipients of the Navy Cross*, Planchet Research Group Publication PR-16a. (Orange, VA: Foxfall Press, 2002), 33.

3. "John McCloy, Lieutenant Commander, United States Navy," Arlington National Cemetery Website, http://www.arlingtoncemetery.net/jmccloy.htm (accessed March 16, 2009).

4. U.S. Senate, Committee on Veterans Affairs, *Medal of Honor Recipients, 1863–1978* (Washington, DC: Government Printing Office, 1979), 415.

5. "John McCloy," http://www.arlingtoncemetery.net/jmccloy.htm.

6. "John McCloy Won Two Honor Medals; Retired Naval Hero Dies in Jersey—Cited for Deeds in China, at Vera Cruz Served on U.S.S. *Newark* in North Sea Patrol," *New York Times*, May 26, 1945.

7. "James Patrick Lannon, Rear Admiral, United States Navy," Arlington National Cemetery Website, http://www.arlingtoncemetery.net/jplannon.htm (accessed March 18, 2009).

8. U.S. Navy Naval Historical Center, "Casualties: U.S. Navy and Marine Corps Personnel Killed and Wounded in Wars, Conflicts, Terrorist Acts, and Other Hostile Incidents," Frequently Asked Questions, http://www.history.navy.mil/faqs/faq56-1.htm (accessed July 20, 2009).

9. "Micszlav Rutyna, Ens., USNR," award card, U.S. Navy Board of Decorations and Medals, May 6, 1944, author's files.

10. For more on the USS *Panay*, see H. Darby Perry, *The Panay Incident* (New York: Macmillan Publishing, 1969); Nick T. Sparks et al., The USS *Panay* Memorial Website, http://www.usspanay.org (accessed March 11, 2009).

11. Perry, *Panay Incident*, 44.

12. Jordan Vause, *U-Boat Ace: The Story of Wolfgang Luth* (Annapolis, MD: Naval Institute Press, 2001), 100. See, generally, Andrew Williams, *The Battle of the Atlantic: Hitler's Gray Wolves of the Sea and the Allies' Desperate Struggle to Defeat Them* (New York: Basic Books, 2003).

13. Louis T. Bobe award card, U.S. Navy Board of Decorations and Medals, January 22, 1945, author's files.

14. U.S. Navy, "Casualties," http://www.history.navy.mil/faqs/faq56-1.htm (accessed December 16, 2009);

15. U.S. Senate, *Medal of Honor Recipients*, 593–94. M. C. Griffin, memorandum to Office of the Quartermaster General, Department of the Army, subj: Estimate of number of Purple Hearts awarded by Department of the Navy, September 8, 1958, author's files.

16. U.S. Senate, *Medal of Honor Recipients*, 700.

17. Bert V. Webb award card (USN 201746), U.S. Navy Board of Decorations and Medals, September 13, 1944.

18. Albert H. Wilson Jr. award card (USN 70314), U.S. Navy Board of Decorations and Medals, June 5, 1944, author's files.

19. U.S. Navy, "Casualties," http://www.history.navy.mil/faqs/faq56-1.htm (accessed December 16, 2009); M. C. Griffin, memorandum, Estimate of number of Purple Hearts, September 8, 1958, authors files.

20. Lt. (j.g.) Billy E. Cochran citation (temporary), Bronze Star Medal with Combat Distinguishing Device, U.S. Navy, April 1951, author's files.

21. W. V. Harlin, director, Personnel Affairs Division, Bureau of Naval Personnel, Department of the Navy, letter to Mr. and Mrs. George L. Cochran, March 1, 1955, author's files.

22. Defense Prisoner of War/Missing Personnel Office, "U.S. Personnel with the Last Name Beginning with 'C'," PMKOR Database Reports (Personnel Missing—Korea), http://www.dtic.mil/dpmo/pmkor/HTML/pmkor_html_c.htm (accessed December 16, 2009).

23. "Donald Mason, U.S.N.," Navy Cross Recipients, Legion of Valor, http://www.legion-ofvalor.com/citation_parse.php?uid=1045699138 (accessed December 16, 2009); Fred L. Borch and Robert F. Dorr, "Mason's Care Under Fire Earned Navy Cross in '52," *Navy Times*, June 18, 2007, 45.

24. U.S. Navy, "Casualties," http://www.history.navy.mil/faqs/faq56-1.htm (accessed December 16, 2009)

25. Bobbi Hovis, *Station Hospital Saigon: A Navy Nurse in Vietnam, 1963–1964* (Annapolis, MD: Naval Institute Press, 1992).

26. For more on Flynn in China, see Fred L. Borch and Robert F. Dorr, "Interview: I Survived 2,030 Days of Solitary in Mao's China," *Vietnam*, February 2009, 54–58.

27. James M. Ennes Jr., *Assault on the Liberty: The True Story of the Israeli Attack on an American Intelligence Ship* (New York: Random House, 1979); U.S. Senate, *Medal of Honor Recipients*, 889.

28. "William Loren McGonagle, Captain, United States Navy," Arlington National Cemetery Website, http://www.arlingtoncemetery.net/wlmcgon.htm (accessed July 18, 2009); Jame M. Ennes Jr., USS *Liberty* Memorial, http://www.ussliberty.org (accessed July 18, 2009).

29. Sapienza, *Peacetime Awards of the Purple Heart*, 15.

30. Lloyd M. Bucher, "The Pueblo Incident: Commander Bucher Replies," *Naval History* (Winter 1989): 44–50; Tony Perry, "Lloyd Bucher, Captain of North Korea-seized *Pueblo*, Dies at 76," *Los Angeles Times*, January 30, 2004.

31. For more on the USS *Pueblo*, see Mitchell B. Lerner, *The Pueblo Incident: A Spy Ship and the Failure of American Foreign Policy* (Lawrence, KS: University Press of Kansas, 2009).

32. "Guatemala: Caught in the Crossfire," *Time*, January 26, 1968, 23.

33. Sapienza, *Peacetime Awards of the Purple Heart*, 15.

34. Ibid. 16.

35. Ibid.

36. Maj. C. J. N. Sproule, Royal Canadian Dragoons, letter to chief of naval technical training, Naval Air Station Memphis, subj: Wounding of Lt. Robert E. Nelson— Eyewitness Account, January 7, 1985, author's files.

37. Sapienza, *Peacetime Awards of the Purple Heart*, 16–17.

38. "U.S. Navy Officer, Driver, Killed by Turkish Terrorists," *Los Angeles Times*, April 16, 1980; "Navy Officer Assassinated in Turkey," *Evening Independent* (St. Petersburg, FL), April 16, 1980.

39. Sapienza, *Peacetime Awards of the Purple Heart*, 17.

40. Ibid. 18.

41. David Van Biema, "Lt. Cmdr. Albert Schaufelberger, the First U.S. Military Casualty in El Salvador, Comes Home," *People*, June 13, 1983, 43.

42. James Willwerth, "Death at the University," *Time*, June 6, 1983.

43. Secretary of the Navy, letter, SER 512, June 3, 1983, author's files.

44. R. A. Gormly, commanding officer SEAL Team SIX, personal award recommendation to the secretary of the Navy for the Silver Star Medal for Donald Kim Erskine, OPNAV Form 1650/3, January 11, 1984, author's files.

45. Adriana Ierodiaconou, "U.S. Attaché Killed in Athens," *Washington Post*, November 16, 1983.

46. Kevin Costelloe, "Sailor's Suffering at Hands of Hijackers Recalled," *Columbus (Ohio) Dispatch*, October 9, 1988.

47. For more on the attack on the USS *Stark*, see Harold L. Wise, *Inside the Danger Zone: The U.S. Military in the Persian Gulf 1987–1988* (Annapolis, MD: Naval Institute Press, 2007).

48. U.S. Navy, "Casualties," http://www.history.navy.mil/faqs/faq56-1.htm (accessed December 16, 2009).

49. Deborah Schmidt, "Navy Medic Awarded First Purple Heart in Desert Storm," *Navy Times*, February 4, 1991; "Desert Storm's First Purple Heart," *Navy Medicine*, January–February 1991, 11.

50. For arguments in favor of Speicher's survival and captivity, see Amy W. Yarsinske, *No One Left Behind: The Lt. Comdr. Michael Scott Speicher Story* (New York: Dutton, 2002). Despite such claims, members of the U.S. intelligence community concluded that he was deceased in October 2008. The Department of Defense reversed that conclusion once more with the March 10, 2009, immediate release titled "Navy Changes Speicher's Status to Missing in Action." With the recovery of Speicher's remains in July 2009, the evidence is now overwhelming that he was killed when his plane was shot down over Anbar Province, Iraq. For the most up-to-date account, see Greg Jaffe, "After 18 Years, Remains of Pilot Shot Down in Iraq Found," *Washington Post*, August 3, 2009.

51. Robert F. Dorr, "POWs in Iraq Survived Thanks to Training, Courage, Faith," *Naval Aviation News*, September–October 1991, 24–25.

52. Hospitalman Jarin Connell, personal award recommendation for the Purple Heart, OPNAV Form 1650/3, July 31, 1995, author's files.

53. Senior U.S. Military Observer—Cambodia, letter to commander, U.S. Military Observer Group—Washington, subj: Recommendation for Award, Lt. Steven J. Corley, U.S. Navy, September 15, 1993, author's files.

54. Joseph Gunder, "Five Sides of Terror: Pentagon Sailors of 9/11," *All Hands*, July 2002, 41.

55. Del Quentin Wilber, "Navy Veteran on Trial for Fraud in Disputed Sept. 11 Compensation," *Washington Post*, March 11, 2009; Del Quentin Wilber, "Mistrial in Case of Pentagon Worker Accused of Fraud," *Washington Post*, April 16, 2009.

56. "Patrick Dunn, Commander, United States Navy," Arlington National Cemetery Website, http://www.arlingtoncemetery.net/pdunn.htm (accessed July 18, 2009).

57. Bryant Jordan, "Five Lives: One Defining Moment," *Army Times*, September 9, 2002.

58. Andrew Scutro, "Hero SEAL Breaks His Silence," *Navy Times*, July 27, 2009.

59. See Marcus Luttrell, *Lone Survivor* (New York: Little, Brown and Company, 2007). Luttrell's book received the Colby Award in 2009, which the Tawani Foundation sponsors for a first work of fiction or nonfiction that makes a significant contribution to the public's "understanding of military history, intelligence operations, or international affairs."

60.   William H. McMichael, "Deadly Duty: Suicide Boat Explosion Killed Three," *Navy Times*, May 10, 2004, 5.

Chapter 4: Airmen: World War I to Afghanistan and Iraq

1.   George Churchill Kenney and Horace Moss Guilbert, *History of the 91st Aero Squadron* (Coblenz, Germany: Gebruder Breuer, 1919), 7.

2.   I. C. B. Dear and M. R. D. Foot, eds., *Oxford Companion to the Second World War* (New York: Oxford University Press), 1194–97.

3.   Robert F. Dorr and Fred L. Borch, "Gunner Earned Silver Star on Ploesti Mission," *Air Force Times*, July 21, 2008.

4.   George Kenney's Purple Heart was announced in *General Orders 34*, South West Pacific Area General Headquarters (Brisbane, Australia, September 15, 1942).

5.   Robert F. Dorr and Fred L. Borch, "P-38 Pilot Earned Second Highest Award," *Military Trader*, January 2008, 7–10.

6.   *General Orders 59*, Eighth Air Force (High Wycombe, England, February 16, 1944).

7.   Mike O'Shea, "Heroes: G. I. Beginnings," *On Patrol*, April 2009, 46.

8.   Anne Leland and Mari-Jana Oboroceanu, *American War and Military Operations Casualties: Lists and Statistics* (Washington, DC: Congressional Research Service, 2009), 3.

9.   Boston Publishing Co., eds., *Above and Beyond: A History of the Medal of Honor from the Civil War to Vietnam* (Boston: Boston Publishing Co., 1985), 268.

10.   Ibid. 269.

11.   "Air Force to Honor Spy Mission Crew Lost in 1952," *Washington Post*, October 20, 1995.

12.   Fred L. Borch and Jeffrey B. Floyd, *The Air Force Cross: A History of Extraordinary Heroism* (Tempe, AZ: Borch & Westlake Publishing, 2004), 5.

13.   Leland and Oboroceanu, *American War and Military Operations Casualties*, 3.

14.   Stuart I. Rochester and Frederick Kiley, *Honor Bound* (Annapolis, MD: Naval Institute Press, 1999), 175.

15.   Jeremiah Denton Jr., *When Hell Was in Session* (New York: Reader's Digest Press, 1976), 104.

16.   Borch and Floyd, *Air Force Cross*, 22.

17.   Ibid., 26–27; Fred L. Borch and Robert F. Dorr, "Helo Pilot's Heroism in Laos Earned Him Air Force Cross," *Air Force Times*, October 23, 2006.

18.   Rochester and Kiley, *Honor Bound*, 311.

19.   Borch and Floyd, *Air Force Cross*, 32.

20.   George E. Day, *Return With Honor* (Mesa, AZ: Champlin Museum Press, 1989), 257.

21.   Col. John C. Giraudo, commander, 355th Tactical Fighter Wing, APO San Francisco 96273, letter to Mrs. Elizabeth L. Mercer (wife), January 23, 1968, author's files; Report of casualty for Pollard Hugh Mercer Jr., DD Form 1300, January 26, 1968, author's files.

22.   Borch and Floyd, *Air Force Cross*, 113.

23.   Michael C. Leonard, "Former POW Talks About Confinement," *Capitol Flyer* (Andrews Air Force Base, MD), March 22, 1991.

24.   Borch and Floyd, *Air Force Cross*, 115–17.

25.   Ibid., 121–22.

26.   Ginger Schreitmueller, "Enlisted Air Force Cross Recipient Retires," *Air Force News*, July 24, 2001.

27.   For more on the 1994 shootdown, see Scott A. Snook, *Friendly Fire: The Accidental Shootdown of U.S. Black Hawks over Northern Iraq* (Princeton, NJ: Princeton University Press, 2000).

28.   "Operation Deny Flight," GlobalSecurity.org, http://www.globalsecurity.org/military/ops/deny_flight.htm (accessed August 10, 2009).

29.   For more on John Chapman and Jason Cunningham, see Michael Hirsch, *None Braver: U.S. Air Force Pararescuemen in the War on Terrorism* (New York: New American Library, 2003), and Sean D. Naylor, "An Act of Courage," *Army Times*, April 29, 2002.

30.   "Airman Killed in Afghanistan," *Air Force Times*, March 30, 2009.

31.   "Bronze Star With Valor," *Air Force Times*, March 16, 2009.

32.   Bruce Rolfson, "2 Killed in IED Blast Shared Love of Job," *Air Force Times*, June 8, 2009.

33.   Bruce Rolfsen, "A Flat-Out Hero," *Air Force Times*, March 16, 2009.

34.   "Intel Officer Killed," *Air Force Times*, June 1, 2009.

35.   Angela Shepherd, "1st SOLRS Airman Receives Purple Heart," *Air Force Print News Today*, http://www2.hurlburt.af.mil/news/story_print.asp?id=123106007 (accessed August 10, 2009).

36.   Ibid.

37.   Chance Babin, "Rescue Wing Airmen Injured in Iraq, Receives Purple Heart," Air Force Reserve Command, http://www.afrc.af.mil/news/story.asp?id=123069884 (accessed August 10, 2009).

Chapter 5: Marines: Spanish–American War to Afghanistan and Iraq

1.   *Personnel: Award and Supply of Decorations*, Army Regulation 600-45 (Washington, DC, August 8, 1932), para. 11(a); AGO 201 award card for James D. Bourke.

2. Trevor K. Plante, "U.S. Marines in the Boxer Rebellion," *Prologue* 31 (Winter 1999): 284–89; "Lieutenant General John T. Myers, USMC (Deceased)," United States Marine Corps History Division, http://www.tecom.usmc.mil/HD/Whos_Who/ Myers_JT.htm (accessed July 18, 2009).

3. Ibid.

4. Lt. Cdr. Kersting, director, Medals and Awards Division, Bureau of Naval Personnel, memorandum, February 1, 1950, author's files.

5. Commanding officer, Marine Corps Schools Detachment, Quantico, Virginia, letter to the major general commandant, Headquarters, U.S. Marine Corps, subj: Recommendation for appointment of Cpl. Wilburt S. Brown, USMC, as second lieutenant, January 28, 1924, author's files.

6. Wilburt Brown citation for the Silver Star Medal, 1st Marine Division, Serial 2271, DLA-298-lhl/03960.

7. Wilburt S. Brown, *Amphibious Campaign for West Florida and Louisiana, 1814–1815: A Critical Review of Strategy and Tactics at New Orleans*. (Tuscaloosa, AL: University of Alabama Press, 1969).

8. For more on Robert Denig, see George B. Clark, *United States Marine Corps Generals in World War II* (Jefferson, NC: McFarland & Co., 2007).

9. George Barnett, major general commandant, letter to chief of the Bureau of Navigation, subj: Recommendation for award in case of Gunnery Sergeant Robert G. Robinson, March 26, 1919, author's files.

10. "First Lieutenant Robert G. Robinson, USMCR (Deceased)," United States Marine Corps History Division, http://www.tecom.usmc.mil/HD/Whos_Who/Robinson_ RG.htm (accessed May 11, 2009).

11. Secretary of State P. C. Knox, letter to President William Howard Taft, August 12, 1912, *Papers Relating to the Foreign Relations of the United States* (Washington, DC: U.S. Department of State, 1912), 1,032.

12. For more on Marines in Nicaragua, see Bernard C. Nalty, *Marines in Nicaragua, 1910– 1933* (Washington, DC: Marine Corps Historical Branch, 1968).

13. Harry Hutchcroft's Purple Heart was advertised for sale in 1990; see, George B. Harris, "List No. 29," *Military and Historical Americana* (New York: Alfred, 1990), 34.

14. Leland and Oboroceanu, *American War and Military Operations Casualties*, 3.

15. Stanley Sirmans, "Submariner Purple Hearts," *Submarine Review*, July 1998, 69.

16. "Gunnery Sergeant John Basilone, USMC (Deceased)," United States Marine Corps History Division, http://www.tecom.usmc.mil/HD/Whos_Who/Basilone_J.htm (accessed July 19, 2009).

17. "Brigadier General Evans Fordyce Carlson, USMCR (Deceased)," United States Marine Corps History Division, http://www.tecom.usmc.mil/HD/Whos_Who/ Carlson_EF.htm (accessed July 19, 2009).

18.   Ibid.

19.   Ibid.

20.   For more on his career, see Ray Davis, *The Story of Ray Davis General of Marines* (Durham, NC: Research Triangle Publishing, 1995).

21.   Doug Sterner, telephone conversation with the author, March 3, 2009.

22.   "James L. Day; Received Medal of Honor 53 Years Late," *Los Angeles Times*, October 31, 1998.

23.   "Major General James Lewis Day, USMC (Deceased)," United States Marine Corps History Division, http://www.tecom.usmc.mil/HD/Whos_Who/Day_JL.htm (accessed July 20, 2009).

24.   Adm. C. W. Nimitz, commander in chief, U.S. Pacific Fleet, Citation for the Navy Cross (Temporary) for Cpl. Emil Elias, U.S. Marine Corps, 1944, author's files.

25.   Alexander Bielakowski, *African American Troops in World War II* (New York: Osprey Publishing, 2007), 49.

26.   U.S. Navy, "Casualties," http://www.history.navy.mil/faqs/faq56-1.htm (accessed July 20, 2009).

27.   "Awards of the Silver Star for Conspicuous Gallantry in China, 1947: Jereb, Jacob P.," Home of Heroes Awards & Citations Database, http://www.homeofheroes.com/valor/02_awards/silverstar/3_China/china_1947.html (accessed December 17, 2009).

28.   "Awards of the Silver Star for Conspicuous Gallantry in China, 1947: Perkey, Alfred E.," Home of Heroes Awards & Citations Database, http://www.homeofheroes.com/valor/02_awards/silverstar/3_China/china_1947.html (accessed December 17, 2009).

29.   "Awards of the Silver Star for Conspicuous Gallantry in China, 1947: Stankiewicz, Peter R. Jr.," Home of Heroes Awards & Citations Database, http://www.homeofheroes.com/valor/02_awards/silverstar/3_China/china_1947.html (accessed December 17, 2009).

30.   M. C. Griffin, memorandum, Estimate of number of Purple Hearts awarded, author's files.

31.   Wesley L. Fox, *Marine Rifleman: Forty-three Years in the Corps* (Washington, DC: Brassey's, 2002), 70–71.

32.   Fox, *Marine Rifleman*, 3.

33.   Ibid., 253.

34.   U.S. Senate, *Medal of Honor Recipients*, 842.

35.   Donald N. Hamblen and Bruce H. Norton, *One Tough Marine* (New York: Ballentine Books, 1993), 129–33.

36.   Hamblen and Norton, *One Tough Marine*, 254–315; see, also, Bruce H. Norton, "Donald Hamblen: One Tough Marine and Purple Heart Recipient," *Vietnam*, June 1996.

37. U.S. Senate, *Medal of Honor Recipients*, 855–56.

38. "3 Marines Hurt at Gitmo to Get Citation Here; Marines Get Purple Heart," *Philadelphia Inquirer*, January 17, 1963.

39. Leland and Oboroceanu, *American War and Military Operations Casualties*, 3.

40. Fred L. Borch and Robert F. Dorr, "Honoring Junior NCOs' Combat Achievements," *Marine Corps Times*, December 31, 2007.

41. For more on Ripley's heroism on Easter Sunday 1972, see John G. Miller, *The Bridge at Dong Ha* (Annapolis, MD: Naval Institute Press, 1989).

42. R. Goldich and J. Schaefer, *U.S. Military Operations, 1965–1994 (Not Including Vietnam): Data on Casualties, Decorations and Personnel Involved* (Washington, DC: Congressional Research Service, 1994), 17–18.

43. Sapienza, *Peacetime Awards of the Purple Heart*, 23.

44. R. Goldich and J. Schaefer, *U.S. Military Operations*, 19. For recent scholarship on the seizure and recapture of the SS *Mayaguez*, see George M. Watson Jr., "The *Mayaguez* Rescue," *Air Force Magazine*, July 2009, 68–72, and Ralph Wetterhahn, *The Last Battle: The* Mayaguez *Incident and the End of the Vietnam War* (New York: DeCapo Press, 2001).

45. Leland and Oboroceanu, *American War and Military Operations Casualties*, 5.

46. Ronald H. Spector, *U.S. Marines in Grenada 1983* (Washington, DC: U.S. Marine Corps, 1987), 10–11.

47. Sapienza, *Peacetime Awards of the Purple Heart*, 24.

48. Frank Langfitt, "Dying Marine Receives a 'Long Overdue' Honor," *Baltimore Sun*, June 14, 1996.

49. T. Bush, "31 *Roberts* Crewmen Receive Awards for Gallantry," *Navy Times*, May 23, 1988.

50. Thomas Donnelly, Margaret Roth, and Caleb Baker, *Operation Just Cause* (New York: Lexington Books, 1991), xi.

51. Robin L. Higgins, *Patriot Dreams: The Murder of Col. Rich Higgins* (Central Point, OR: Hellgate Publishing, 2000).

52. Leland and Oboroceanu, *American War and Military Operations Casualties*, 3.

53. Edwin H. Simmons, *The United States Marines: A History*, 4th ed. (Annapolis, MD: Naval Institute Press, 2003), 322.

54. Amy Waldman, "Bombings in East Africa: The American Dead, Their Quiet Lives," *New York Times*, August 10, 1998.

55. "Marine Recognized for Bombing Rescue," *Augusta (Ga.) Chronicle*, January 10, 1999.

56. Gidget Fuentes, "Lance Cpl. Gets Navy Cross for Afghan Heroism," *Marine Corps Times*, April 6, 2009; "Eagan Marine Awarded Navy Cross for Valor," *Star Tribune*, March 27, 2009.

57. James E. Wise Jr. and Scott Baron, *The Navy Cross* (Annapolis, MD: Naval Institute Press, 2007), 59–66.

58. Ibid., 55.

59. Mike Dougherty, "Wounded in Haiti, Marine Receives Purple Heart," *Henderson Hall News*, March 26, 2004.

Chapter 6: Coast Guardsmen: World War I to Afghanistan and Iraq

1. Angela Moore, "Honor Long Overdue Recalls Crewmen's Sacrifice During WWI," *St. Petersburg (FL) Times*, January 25, 2001.

2. Ibid.

3. Malcolm E. Willoughby, *The U.S. Coast Guard in World War II* (Annapolis, MD: Naval Institute Press, 1957), 8.

4. "Coast Guard History Frequently Asked Questions: In What Wars and Conflicts Did Personnel From the Coast Guard (or Its Predecessors) Serve and What Were the Coast Guard's Casualties in Each?" United States Coast Guard, http://www.uscg.mil/History/faqs/wars.asp (accessed May 20, 2009).

5. U.S. Coast Guard Public Relations Division, *Book of Valor: A Fact Book on Medals and Decorations*, United States Coast Guard, http://www.uscg.mil/history/awards/Book_of_Valor_WWII.asp (accessed May 20, 2009).

6. Willoughby, *Coast Guard in World War II*, 311; Dean S. Veremakis and Jeffrey B. Floyd, *World War II U.S. Coast Guard Awards and Decorations* (n.p.: Orders and Medals Society of America Monograph, 2008), 28.

7. Willoughby, *Coast Guard in World War II*, 311; Veremakis and Floyd, *World War II U.S. Coast Guard*, 43.

8. Willoughby, *Coast Guard in World War II*, 311; Veremakis and Floyd, *World War II U.S. Coast Guard*, 44.

9. Willoughby, *Coast Guard in World War II*, 311; Veremakis and Floyd, *World War II U.S. Coast Guard*, 78.

10. Edward F. Murphy, *Heroes of World War II* (Novato, CA: Presidio Press, 1990), 37.

11. Willoughby, *Coast Guard in World War II*, 263.

12. U.S. Coast Guard Oral History Program, "Interviewee: Raymond O'Malley," United States Coast Guard, http://www.uscg.mil/history/WEBORALHISTORY/R_OMalley_Oral_History.asp (accessed May 20, 2009).

13. Veremakis and Floyd, *World War II U.S. Coast Guard*, 100–101.

14. Willoughby, *Coast Guard in World War II*, 311; Veremakis and Floyd, *World War II U.S. Coast Guard*, 111.

15. "Coast Guard History Frequently Asked Questions," http://www.uscg.mil/History/ faqs/wars.asp (accessed May 20, 2009).

16. *Point Welcome*, 1962," United States Coast Guard, http://www.uscg.mil/history/ WEBCUTTERS/Point_Welcome.asp (accessed December 17, 2009).

17. "Silver Star Jack C. Rittichier, USCG," *Foundation*, Spring 1991, 30; *Special Order G-299*, Pacific Air Forces (Hickam Air Force Base, HI, December 17, 1968); "Coast Guard History Famous Coast Guardsmen: Lieutenant Jack C. Rittichier," United States Coast Guard, http://www.uscg.mil/history/people/RittichierJackDecorations. asp (accessed May 20, 2009).

18. Robert Yered's Silver Star was awarded in *General Orders No. 4309*, U.S. Army, Vietnam (Cam Ranh, Vietnam, September 11, 1968).

19. Michael Laris, "Family Bids Farewell," *Washington Post*, May 8, 2004; Judy Silverstein, "A Coast Guard Hero Is Laid to Rest," *Coast Guard Reservist* 51 (5): 14–17; "DC3 Bruckenthal: A Hero in Today's World," *The Cutter* 20 (Spring 2006): 6–11.

Chapter 7: Civilians: World War II to the War on Terrorism

1. Secretary of War Henry L. Simpson, letter to President Franklin D. Roosevelt, May 31, 1943, author's files; Fred L. Borch, "The Story of Purple Hearts Awarded to Civilians: An Unusual History from Beginning to End," *Journal of the Orders and Medals Society of America* 53 (July–August 2002): 4.

2. *General Orders No. 66*, Fifth Army (Field Headquarters, April 25, 1944), para. I.

3. Ibid.

4. M. L. Stein, *Under Fire: The Story of American War Correspondents* (New York: Julian Messner, 1968), 95.

5. "Recognition," *Time*, November 29, 1943; *General Orders 137*, North African Theater of Operations (1943).

6. "Reward of Patience," *Time*, June 12, 1950.

7. Raymond Clapper award card, U.S. Navy Board of Decorations and Medals, January 26, 1945, author's files.

8. Joe J. Custer award card, U.S. Navy Board of Decorations and Medals, January 19, 1945, author's files.

9. Elizabeth W. King, "Heroes of Wartime Science and Mercy," *National Geographic Magazine*, December 1943, 719.

10. "Indiana Popular History: Ernie Pyle," Indiana Historical Society, http://www.india-nahistory.org/pop_hist/people/pyle.html (accessed December 18, 2009).

11. Thomas M. Pryor, "*The Story of G. I. Joe*," movie review, *New York Times*, October 6, 1945.

12.   "Recognition," *Time.*

13.   Phil Mayer, "Firefighters' Deeds During Attack on Pearl Recalled," *Honolulu Star-Bulletin,* October 4, 1984.

14.   Ibid.

15.   Juan Lujan award card, U.S. Navy Board of Decorations and Medals, March 14, 1946, author's files.

16.   Antonio P. Manibusan award card, U.S. Navy Board of Decorations and Medals, September 9, 1946, author's files.

17.   Jon Herskovitz, "Japanese WWII Soldier Who Hid for Decades Dies," *New York Times,* September 23, 1997.

18.   Joaquin Cepeda Rabon award card, U.S. Navy Board of Decorations and Medals, February 24, 1947, author's files.

19.   V. S. Sablan award card, U.S. Navy Board of Decorations and Medals, March 14, 1947, author's files.

20.   *General Orders No. 6,* U.S. Army Forces Central Pacific Area (Fort Shafter, HI, January 7, 1944).

21.   Dan Van der Vat, *Pearl Harbor: An Illustrated History* (New York: Basic Books, 2001), 142; Stan Cohen, *East Wind Rain* (Missoula, MT: Pictorial Histories Publishing, 1981), 166.

22.   Secretary of the Navy, letter, SER 5356, April 19, 1968.

23.   *General Orders No. 1548,* U.S. Army, Vietnam (Cam Ranh, Vietnam May 30, 1970).

24.   Secretary of the Navy, memo to chief of naval operations, subj: Recommendation for Purple Heart Medal for Edward C. Gaumer, SER NDBDM/2455, December 13, 1993.

25.   Bradley Graham, "Bomb Kills 23 Americans at Saudi Base," *Washington Post,* June 26, 1996.

26.   John Pulley, "Khobar Towers Survivor Awarded Purple Heart," *Army Times,* October 28, 1996.

Chapter 8: Families: Brothers, Fathers and Sons, and Husbands and Wives

1.   John R. Satterfield, *We Band of Brothers: The Sullivans and World War II* (Parkersburg, IA: Mid-Prairie Books, 1995).

2.   *General Orders No. 6,* North African Theater of Operations (Algiers, Algeria, 1944), sec. I.

3.   For more on Mark Clark, see Martin Blumenson, *Mark Clark: The Last of the Great World War II Commanders* (New York: Congdon & Weed, 1984).

4. *General Orders No. 70*, Eighth U.S. Army (Seoul, Korea, February 5, 1952), sec. 1.

5. *General Orders No. 80*, North African Theater of Operations (Algiers, Algeria, August 19, 1943), para. IV.

6. Brian M. Sobel, *The Fighting Pattons* (Westport, CT: Praeger, 1977), 103.

7. Ibid., 156.

8. *General Orders No. 5468*, U.S. Army, Vietnam (Cam Ranh, Vietnam, November 27, 1968).

9. *General Orders No. 839*, U.S. Army, Vietnam (Cam Ranh, Vietnam, March 9, 1969).

10. Dennis Ryan, "George S. Patton Buried in Arlington Cemetery," *Pentagram*, September 3, 2004.

11. Burke Davis, *Marine!* (Boston: Little Brown, 1962), 166.

12. Davis, *Marine!*, 168–69, 205.

13. "Lieutenant Lewis B. 'Chesty' Puller, USMC (Deceased)," United States Marine Corps History Division, http://www.tecom.usmc.mil/HD/Whos_Who/Puller_LB.htm (December 18, 2009).

14. Lewis B. Puller Jr., *Fortunate Son: The Healing of a Vietnam Vet* (New York: Grove Weidenfeld, 1991), 125–26, 128.

15. Ibid., 156.

16. Ibid., 160.

17. U.S. Navy Naval Historical Center, "Joseph K. Taussig," *Dictionary of American Naval Fighting Ships*, http://www.history.navy.mil/danfs/j4/joseph_k_taussig.htm (accessed May 18, 2009).

18. Manny Gamallo, "Pearl Harbor Survivor Recounts Action on Ship," *Tulsa World*, December 7, 2008.

19. Hillary A. Luton, "Army Reserve Couple Receive Purple Hearts," *Army Reserve Magazine*, December 26, 2006.

20. Maria L. Yost, "Husband and Wife Receive Purple Heart Medals," *Fort Hood Sentinel*, Nov. 10, 2004.

21. Ibid.

22. Ibid.

Chapter 9: Celebrities: Artists and Entertainers, Politicians, Athletes, and Other Public Figures

1. B. G. Burkett and Glenna Whitley, *Stolen Valor* (Dallas, TX: Verity Press, 1998), 81, 164, 339.

2. James Arness and James E. Wise Jr., *James Arness: An Autobiography* (Jefferson, NC: McFarland & Co., 2001). See also, James E. Wise Jr. and Paul W. Wilderson III, *Stars in Khaki* (Annapolis, MD: Naval Institute Press, 2000), 184.

3.   For more on Arness, see the "official Website for James Arness" at http://www.james-arness.com (accessed March 8, 2009). Acting runs in the family: Arness' brother is the actor Peter Graves (née Aurness), who is known for starring in the CBS television series *Mission: Impossible* from 1966 to 1973 and the films *Airplane!* in 1980 and *Airplane II: The Sequel* in 1982.

4.   Wise and Wilderson, *Stars in Khaki*, 13; Robert E. Witter, "Neville Brand: Setting the Record Straight," CombatFan.com, http://www.jodavidsmeyer.com/combat/military/neville_brand.html (accessed March 10, 2009).

5.   For more on Art Carney, see Jim Bishop, *The Golden Ham: A Candid Biography of Jackie Gleason* (New York: Simon and Schuster, 1956), and Maurice Zolotow, "The All-out Art of Art Carney," *Reader's Digest*, October 1989.

6.   Charles E. Durning, Report of Physical Examination of Enlisted Personnel Prior to Discharge, Release from Active Duty or Retirement, War Department Adjutant General's Office Form 38, January 29, 1946, author's files.

7.   "Biography for Charles Durning," IMDb: The Internet Movie Database, http://www.imdb.com/name/nm0001164/bio (accessed December 15, 2009); "SAG to Honor Durning With Lifetime Award," *USA Today*, September 24, 2007.

8.   Wise and Wilderson, *Stars in Khaki*, 46.

9.   Ibid., 46–47.

10. "Garner Decorated 32 Years After Fact," *Washington Post*, January 25, 1983.

11. Donald Zec, *Marvin: The Story of Lee Marvin* (New York: St. Martin's Press, 1980), 36–40.

12. Robert Johnson Jr., "Lee Marvin," *Leatherneck*, July 1986, 33.

13. "Lee Marvin, Private First Class, United States Marine Corps, Movie Actor," Arlington National Cemetery Website, http://www.arlingtoncemetery.net/lmarvin.htm (accessed March 11, 2009).

14. Wise and Wilderson, *Stars in Khaki*, 61.

15. Ibid., 62–63.

16. *General Orders No. 65*, War Department (Washington, DC, August 16, 1945).

17. Wise and Wilderson, *Stars in Khaki*, 66.

18. For more on Audie Murphy, see http://www.audiemurphy.com (accessed March 11, 2009) and "Audie Leon Murphy, Major, United States Army," Arlington National Cemetery Website, http://www.arlingtoncemetery.net/audielmu.htm (accessed March 11, 2009).

19. Although some publications state that Peter Ortiz received two Purple Hearts, his Marine Corps records reflect the award of only a single Purple Heart.

20. Peter Julien Ortiz, U.S. Marine Corps Report of Separation, September 21, 1945, para. 31, author's files.

21. Ortiz's official Marine Corps records reflect that he was awarded the following deco-
     rations and medals as a Legionnaire: Citation a L'Ordre de la Brigade (January 23,
     1936), Medal Coloniale (December 18, 1935), and Citation a L'Ordre du Regiment
     (September 22, 1934).

22. "Peter Julien Ortiz, Colonel, United States Marine Corps," Arlington National
     Cemetery Website, http://www.arlingtoncemetery.net/pjortiz.htm (accessed April 24,
     2008).

23. William J. Donovan, letter to Lt. Gen. Thomas Holcomb, commandant, U.S. Marine
     Corps, March 24, 1943, author's files.

24. Peter J. Ortiz, Citation for the Navy Cross, signed Harold R. Stark, commander,
     U.S. Naval Forces in Europe, SER 002027, author's files. Admiral Stark personally
     presented this decoration to Major Ortiz in London on July 6, 1944.

25. Robert E. Mattingly, *Herringbone Cloak—GI Dagger*, draft manuscript (Washington,
     DC: Marine Corps History Division).

26. Ortiz was made an honorary member of the Most Excellent Order of the British
     Empire in 1946.

27. Peter J. Ortiz, Citation for the Navy Cross (Gold Star in lieu of Second Award),
     Commander, 12th Fleet, SER 14928.

28. For more on Ortiz, see Steven J. Legge, "U.S. Marine Colonel Peter Ortiz Served
     Covertly with the Resistance in France," *World War II*, July 1998; Harry W. Edwards,
     A Different War: Marines in Europe and North Africa, Marines in World War II
     Commemorative Series (Washington, DC: Marine Corps Historical Center, 1994);
     and "Peter Julien Ortiz," http://www.arlingtoncemetery.net/pjortiz.htm (accessed
     April 24, 2008); Alfonso A. Narvaez, "Col. Peter J. Ortiz, 75, Legendary Marine
     Officer," *New York Times*, May 21, 1988.

29. Jack Mason, "My Favorite Lion, Maurice Britt," *Army*, May 2008, 73.

30. Ibid., 74.

31. Wolfgang Saxon, "Maurice Britt, 76; Helped Shift Arkansas Politics," *New York Times*,
     November 29, 1995.

32. BobDole.org, http://www.bobdole.org/bio (accessed March 11, 2009).

33. For an autobiography, see Robert Dole, *One Soldier's Story: A Memoir* (New York:
     Harper Collins, 2005).

34. U.S. Senate, *Medal of Honor Recipients*, 439.

35. George J. Church, "The Vicar Takes Charge," *Time*, March 16, 1981, 13.

36. *General Orders No. 2318*, U.S. Army, Vietnam (Cam Ranh, Vietnam, May 22, 1967);
     Bernard W. Rogers, *Cedar Falls Junction City: A Turning Point*, Vietnam Studies
     (Washington, DC: Department of the Army, 1989), 141–48.

37. Church, "Vicar Takes Charge," 14.

38. For details on Haig's involvement in this transfer of power, see Bob Woodward, *Shadow: Five Presidents and the Legacy of Watergate* (New York: Simon & Schuster, 1999).

39. "Alexander Haig," *Time*, April 2, 1984, 7–11.

40. For a biography of Hagel, see Charlyne Berens, *Chuck Hagel: Moving Forward* (Lincoln, NE: University of Nebraska Press, 2006).

41. "The Honorable Senator Daniel K. Inouye," United States Senator for Hawaii Daniel Inouye, http://inouye.senate.gov/Who_is_Dan/upload/Dan-Inouye-Biography.pdf (accessed March 20, 2009).

42. Ibid.

43. Rudi Williams, "21 Asian American World War II Vets to Get Medal of Honor," Armed Forces Press Service, http://www.defenselink.mil/news/newsarticle. aspx?id=45192 (accessed March 20, 2009).

44. John F. Kennedy, Citation for the Navy and Marine Corps Medal, August 1943, reprinted in Fred L. Borch, " 'For Heroism Not Involving Actual Conflict with an Enemy': A History of the Navy and Marine Corps Medal," *Journal of the Orders and Medals Society of America* 52 (July–August 2001): 13–14; Memorandum, B. R. Weitt and J. C. McClure, memorandum to Commander, Motor Torpedo Boat Flotilla One, subj: Sinking of *PT 109* and Subsequent Rescue of Survivors, author's file.

45. U.S. Senator John McCain, Arizona, http://mccain.senate.gov/ (accessed March 23, 2009).

46. Colin Powell, *My American Journey*, with Joseph Persico (New York: Random House, 1995), 80.

47. Powell, *American Journey*, 98.

48. Ibid., 137–39.

49. Ibid., 144. Powell's award of the Soldier's Medal was announced in *General Orders No. 9285*, Americal Division (Chu Lai, Vietnam, December 3, 1968).

50. Public and Intergovernmental Affairs, U.S. Department of Veterans Affairs, "VA Official Biography: The Honorable Eric K. Shinseki," Department of Veterans Affairs, http://www1.va.gov/opa/bios/biography.asp?id=76 (accessed December 19, 2009).

51. "Biography: An American Hero," Admiral Stockdale, http://www.admiralstockdale.us (accessed March 8, 2009).

52. U.S. Senate, *Medal of Honor Recipients*, 928–29.

53. For more biographical details on Thurmond, see Nadine Cohodas, *Strom Thurmond and the Politics of Southern Change* (New York: Simon and Schuster, 1993).

54. "About Jim Webb," James Webb Enterprises, http://www.jameswebb.com/about/about.htm (accessed March 29, 2009).

55. Paul Drew Stevens, ed., *The Navy Cross Vietnam* (Forest Ranch, CA: Sharp & Dunnigan, 1987), 338–39.

56. "Hank Bauer, 84, World Series Star, Dies," *New York Times*, February 10, 2007.

57. Ibid.

58. Gary Bedingfield, "Ralph Houck," Baseball in Wartime, http://www.baseballinwartime.co.uk/player_biographies/houk_ralph.htm (March 12, 2009).

59. Matt Schudel, "Bert Shepard: Amputation Didn't Stop MLB Pitcher, *Washington Post*, June 22, 2008.

60. Gary Bedingfield, "Warren Spahn," Baseball in Wartime, http://www.baseballinwartime.com/player_biographies/spahn_warren.htm (accessed December 18, 2009).

61. *General Orders 208*, 25th Infantry Division (Nagoya, Japan, April 13, 1951).

62. Rick Bragg, *I Am a Soldier Too: The Jessica Lynch Story* (New York: Knopf, 2003). For more on Lynch, see "Private First Class Mom," *People*, February 19, 2007, 66–67.

63. Stanley Weintraub, *15 Stars: Eisenhower, MacArthur, Marshall: Three Generals Who Saved the American Century* (New York: Free Press, 2007).

64. William Manchester, *American Caesar* (New York: Dell Publishing Co., 1978), 103.

65. Ibid., 119.

66. War Department Adjutant General's Office, Douglas MacArthur letter to the Quartermaster General, subj: Purple Heart and Oak Leaf Cluster, AG 201, July 16, 1932.

67. Oliver L. North Citation for the Silver Star Medal, 1969, author's files.

68. For more on Oliver North, see http://www.olivernorth.com (accessed March 25, 2009).

69. Charles E. Yeager, *Yeager: An Autobiography*, with Leo Janos (New York, Bantam, 1995), 26.

70. For more on Chuck Yeager, see "the official website of an aviation legend!" http://www.chuckyeager.com (accessed March 13, 2009).

Selected Bibliography

GOVERNMENT DOCUMENTS, REGULATIONS, AND REPORTS

U.S. Air Force. *Air Force Awards and Decorations Program.* Air Force Instruction 36-2803. Washington, DC, June 15, 2001.

U.S. Army. *Military Awards.* Army Regulation 600-8-22. Washington, DC, December 11, 2006.

————. *Wear and Appearance of Army Uniforms and Insignia.* Army Regulation 670-1. Washington, DC: February 3, 2005.

U.S. Coast Guard. *Roll of Honor, April 6, 1917–November 30, 1918: Supplement to the Report of the Secretary of the Navy.* Washington, DC: Government Printing Office, 1919.

————. *Medals and Awards Manual.* Coast Guard Commandant Instruction M1650.25D. Washington, DC, May 5, 2008.

U.S. Congress. Senate. Committee on Veterans Affairs. *Medal of Honor Recipients 1863-1978.* Washington, DC: Government Printing Office, 1979.

U.S. Department of Defense. *Military Awards Program.* Department of Defense Instruction 1348.33. Washington, DC, July 1, 2004.

U.S. Navy. *Navy and Marine Corps Awards Manual.* Secretary of the Navy Instruction 1650.1H. Washington, DC, September 27, 2006.

U.S. War Department. *Personnel: Award and Supply of Decorations for Individuals.* Army Regulation 600-45. Washington, DC, August 8, 1932.

SECONDARY SOURCES

Books and Monographs

Blakeney, Jane. *Heroes, U.S. Marine Corps, 1861–1955.* Washington, DC: Privately published, 1957.

Borch, Fred L., and Frank C. Brown. *The Purple Heart: A History of America's Oldest Military Decoration.* Tempe, AZ: Borch and Westlake Publishing, 1994.

Borch, Fred L, and Charles P. McDowell. *Sea Service Medals.* Annapolis, MD: Naval Institute Press, 2009.

Congressional Medal of Honor Society. *Above and Beyond: A History of the Medal of Honor from the Civil War to Vietnam.* Boston: Boston Publishing Co., 1985.

Edwards, Harry W. *A Different War: Marines in Europe and North Africa.* Marines in World War II Commemorative Series. Washington, DC: Marine Corps Historical Center, 1994.

Emerson, William K. *United States Army Badges 1921–2006.* N.p.: Orders and Medals Society of America Monograph, 2006.

Goldich, Robert L., and John C. Schaefer. *U.S. Military Operations, 1965–1994 (Not Including Vietnam): Data on Casualties, Decorations, and Personnel Involved.* Washington, DC: Congressional Research Service, 1994.

Grosvenor, Gilbert. *Insignia and Decorations of the U.S. Armed Forces.* Washington, DC: National Geographic Society, 1943.

————. *Insignia and Decorations of the U.S. Armed Forces.* Washington, DC: National Geographic Society, 1944.

Hicks, Anne. *The Last Fighting General: The Biography of Robert Tyron Frederick.* Atglen, PA: Schiffer Publishing, 2006.

Kingseed, Cole C. *From Omaha Beach to Dawson's Ridge: The Combat Journal of Captain Joe Dawson.* Annapolis, MD: Naval Institute Press, 2005.

Leland, Anne, and Mari-Jana Oboroceanu. *American War and Military Operations Casualties: Lists and Statistics.* Washington, DC: Congressional Research Service, 2009.

Lerner, Mitchell B. *The Pueblo Incident: A Spy Ship and the Failure of American Foreign Policy.* Lawrence, KS: University Press of Kansas, 2009.

Manchester, William. *American Caesar.* New York: Dell Publishing Co., 1978.

Miller, John G. *The Bridge at Dong Ha.* Annapolis, MD: Naval Institute Press, 1989.

Murphy, Audie. *To Hell and Back.* New York: Holt, 1949.

Murphy, Edward F. *Vietnam Medal of Honor Heroes.* New York: Ballantine Books, 1987.

————. *Heroes of World War II.* Novato, CA: Presidio Press, 1990.

————. *Korean War Heroes.* Novato, CA: Presidio Press, 1992.

Nalty, Bernard C. *Marines in Nicaragua (1910–1933).* Washington, DC: Marine Corps Historical Branch, 1968.

Price, Scott T. *The U.S. Coast Guard at Normandy.* Washington, DC: U.S. Coast Guard Historian's Office, 1994.

Puller, Lewis B., Jr. *Fortunate Son: The Healing of a Vietnam Vet.* New York: Grove Press, 1991.

Reeder, Russell P. *Born at Reveille.* Quechee, VT: Vermont Heritage Press, 1999.

Rochester, Stuart I., and Frederick T. Kiley. *Honor Bound: American Prisoners of War in Southeast Asia (1961–1973).* Annapolis, MD: Naval Institute Press, 1999.

Saluzzi, Joseph A. *Red Blood—Purple Hearts: the Marines in the Korean War: Compiled from Official Citations, Action Reports, and Personal Interviews.* Brooklyn, NY: Eagle Productions, 1993.

Sapienza, Madeline, ed. *Peacetime Awards of the Purple Heart in the Post-Vietnam Period.* Washington, DC: Staff Support Branch, U.S. Army Center of Military History, 1987.

Smith, Larry. *Beyond Glory: Medal of Honor Heroes in Their Own Words.* New York: W. W. Norton, 2003.

Stockdale, James B., and Sybil Stockdale. *In Love and War: The Story of a Family's Ordeal and Sacrifice During the Vietnam Years.* Annapolis, MD: Naval Institute Press, 1990.

Strandberg, John E., and Roger James Bender. *The Call of Duty: Military Awards and Decorations of the United States of America.* San Jose, CA: R. J. Bender Publishing, 2004.

Taylor, Thomas. *The Simple Sounds of Freedom: The True Story of the Only Soldier to Fight for Both America and the Soviet Union.* New York: Random House, 2002.

The Legacy of the Purple Heart. 4th rev. ed. Paducah, Ky.: Turner Publishing Company, 2001.

Weintraub, Stanley. *15 Stars: Eisenhower, MacArthur, Marshall: Three Generals Who Saved the American Century.* New York: Free Press, 2007.

Willoughby, Malcolm F. *The U.S. Coast Guard in World War II.* Annapolis, MD: Naval Institute Press, 1989.

Wise, James E., Jr., and Scott Baron. *The Navy Cross.* Annapolis, MD: Naval Institute Press, 2007.

———. *The Silver Star.* Annapolis, MD: Naval Institute Press, 2008.

Wise, James E., Jr., and Paul W. Wilderson III. *Stars in Khaki.* Annapolis, MD: Naval Institute Press, 2000.

Yeager, Charles. *Yeager: An Autobiography.* New York: Bantam Books, 1995.

Articles

Borch, Fred L. " 'For Wounds Received . . .'" *Military History,* September 2006, 44–49.

———. "Purple Hearts for Meritorious Achievement or Service: Army and Army Air Forces Awards During World War II." *Journal of the Orders and Medals Society of America* 51 (November–December 2000): 3–15.

———. "Purple Hearts to Foreign Combat Wounded: Myth or Reality?" *Journal of the Orders and Medals Society of America* 60 (September–October 2009): 3–13.

―――. "The Story of Purple Hearts Awarded to Civilians: An Unusual History From Beginning to End." *Journal of the Orders and Medals Society of America* 53 (July–August 2002): 3–16.

―――. "Wounded in Action: The Curious History of Combat Injuries Qualifying for the Purple Heart." *Journal of the Orders and Medals Society of America* 57 (March–April 2006): 2–18.

Borch, Fred L., and Robert F. Dorr. "Above, Beyond and Forgotten." *World War II*, April 2006, 26–33.

Fegan, J. C. "The Purple Heart Badge and the Order of Military Merit." *Marine Corps Gazette*, August 1932, 39–44.

Legge, Steven J. "U.S. Marine Colonel Peter Ortiz Served Covertly with the Resistance in France." *World War II*, July 1998, 22–25.

Mason, Jack. "My Favorite Lion, Maurice Britt." *Army*, May 2008, 71–76.

Montgomery, Nancy. "Baader-Meinhof Gang Attacked U.S. Troops, Bases in 1970s–1980s." *Stars and Stripes*, August 5, 2005, European edition, 1.

"Recognition." *Time*, November 29, 1943.

"Reward of Patience." *Time*, June 12, 1950.

Saxon, Wolfgang. "Maurice Britt, 76; Helped Shift Arkansas Politics." *New York Times*, November 29, 1995.

Sirmans, Stan. "The Navy's World War II Purple Hearts." *Journal of the Orders and Medals Society of America* 42 (May 1991): 29–36.

Weaver, Barry C. "Classification of World War II Named Purple Hearts Awarded to Navy and Marine Corps Personnel." *Journal of the Orders and Medals Society of America* 40 (November 1989): 15–25.

Websites

Arlington National Cemetery Website. "Peter Julien Ortiz: Colonel, United States Marine Corps." http://www.arlingtoncemetery.net/pjortiz.htm.

"The Sullivan Brothers: World War II Casualties of the USS *Juneau*." http://www.arlington-cemetery.net/sullivan-brothers.htm.

Bedingfield, Gary. "Baseball in Wartime." http://www.baseballinwartime.co.uk.

PBS. "The Gulf War—War Story: Rhonda Cornum." *Frontline*. http://www.pbs.org/wgbh/pages/frontline/gulf/war/5.html.

Spark, Nick T., et al. "The Story of the *Panay* Incident." The USS *Panay* Memorial Web site. http://www.usspanay.org.

U.S. Army Human Resources Command, Military Awards Branch, Soldier Programs and Services Division. "Historical Perspective on Numbers of Individual Awards and Decorations." U.S. Army. https://www.hrc.army.mil/site/active/tagd/awards/STATS/historical.htm.

Index

About the Author

Fred L. Borch served twenty-five years active duty as an Army lawyer and retired in 2005. A professionally trained historian (MA, University of Virginia), he now serves as the Regimental Historian and Archivist for the U.S. Army Judge Advocate General's Corps. He is the author and coauthor of many books and articles on military medals. The Naval Institute Press published his books, *Sea Service Medals: Military Awards and Decorations of the Navy, Marine Corps and Coast Guard* (coauthored with Charles P. McDowell), in 2009 and *Kimmel, Short and Pearl Harbor* (coauthored with USS *Arizona* Memorial historian Daniel Martinez), in 2005.

The **Naval Institute Press** is the book-publishing arm of the U.S. Naval Institute, a private, nonprofit, membership society for sea service professionals and others who share an interest in naval and maritime affairs. Established in 1873 at the U.S. Naval Academy in Annapolis, Maryland, where its offices remain today, the Naval Institute has members worldwide.

Members of the Naval Institute support the education programs of the society and receive the influential monthly magazine *Proceedings* or the colorful bimonthly magazine *Naval History* and discounts on fine nautical prints and on ship and aircraft photos. They also have access to the transcripts of the Institute's Oral History Program and get discounted admission to any of the Institute-sponsored seminars offered around the country.

The Naval Institute's book-publishing program, begun in 1898 with basic guides to naval practices, has broadened its scope to include books of more general interest. Now the Naval Institute Press publishes about seventy titles each year, ranging from how-to books on boating and navigation to battle histories, biographies, ship and aircraft guides, and novels. Institute members receive significant discounts on the Press's more than eight hundred books in print.

Full-time students are eligible for special half-price membership rates. Life memberships are also available.

For a free catalog describing Naval Institute Press books currently available, and for further information about joining the U.S. Naval Institute, please write to:

Member Services
U.S. Naval Institute
291 Wood Road
Annapolis, MD 21402-5034
Telephone: (800) 233-8764
Fax: (410) 571-1703
Web address: www.usni.org